Hands-On Game Development with WebAssembly

Learn WebAssembly C++ programming by building a retro space game

Rick Battagline

BIRMINGHAM - MUMBAI

Hands-On Game Development with WebAssembly

Acquisition Editor: Ashitosh Gupta
Content Development Editor: Smit Carvalho
Technical Editor: Ralph Rosario, Jane D'souza
Copy Editor: Safis Editing
Project Coordinator: Kinjal Bari
Proofreader: Safis Editing
Indexer: Tejal Daruwale Soni
Graphics: Alishon Mendonsa
Production Coordinator: Jayalaxmi Raja

First published: May 2019

Production reference: 1300519

Published by Packt Publishing Ltd.
Livery Place
35 Livery Street
Birmingham
B3 2PB, UK.

ISBN 978-1-83864-465-9

www.packtpub.com

To Kate, Luke, Lilly, and Cora – you are my world.

– Rick Battagline

`mapt.io`

Mapt is an online digital library that gives you full access to over 5,000 books and videos, as well as industry leading tools to help you plan your personal development and advance your career. For more information, please visit our website.

Why subscribe?

- Spend less time learning and more time coding with practical eBooks and Videos from over 4,000 industry professionals

- Improve your learning with Skill Plans built especially for you

- Get a free eBook or video every month

- Mapt is fully searchable

- Copy and paste, print, and bookmark content

Packt.com

Did you know that Packt offers eBook versions of every book published, with PDF and ePub files available? You can upgrade to the eBook version at `www.packt.com` and as a print book customer, you are entitled to a discount on the eBook copy. Get in touch with us at `customercare@packtpub.com` for more details.

At `www.packt.com`, you can also read a collection of free technical articles, sign up for a range of free newsletters, and receive exclusive discounts and offers on Packt books and eBooks.

Contributors

About the author

Rick Battagline is a game developer who has been working with web- and browser-based technologies since 1997. He wrote his first computer game in 1996 and, in 2006, he founded BattleLine Games LLC., an independent game studio where he works to this day. That same year, his game, Epoch Star, was nominated for an award at the Slamdance Guerrilla Games Competition, and was listed in Game Informer Magazine issue 156 as one of "The top ten games you've never heard of."

Since then, Rick has written hundreds of games for platforms including the web, Windows PC, iOS, Android, Wii U, and Nintendo Entertainment System emulators. He has developed games in web technologies including WebAssembly, HTML5, WebGL, JavaScript, TypeScript, Flash, and PHP.

I want to thank Prasad Annadata and Steve Tack for their tremendous contributions to this book. Without your help, I would have never finished this. Special thanks to my editors, Ashitosh Gupta, Ralph Rosario, and Smit Carvalho, for all of their hard work. I would also like to thank my father, Richard, and my brother, John, who are there for me when I need them.

Finally, I want to thank my wife, Kate, and my children, Luke, Lilly, and Cora. You mean everything to me.

About the reviewers

Prasad Annadata is a senior technologist with experience ranging from mainframes to cloud computing. His foray into game development started when he adopted classic minesweeper game to Unix. Recruited right out of college into a major consulting firm his career spawned consulting and major financial institutions. Prasad Annadata has been an author of several peer-reviewed papers on privacy and security, a professional technology reviewer for a chapter on Cyber Law in the book Chitty on Contracts: Hong Kong and a sole inventor of a B2B technology patent.

He has a bachelors and masters degrees in Computer Science and currently serves as an SVP in a major financial institution and his interests include cloud computing and cloud security.

> *I wish to thank the author, Rick Battagline, for thinking of me when it came to providing a technical review of this book. Also, I thank Packt Publishing for the opportunity.*

Steve Tack is a software developer with 28 years of experience. Since the 1980s, he's enjoyed making computers do fun things, from programming simple games in BASIC on a Sinclair ZX81 to creating real-time 3D graphics on modern hardware.

Packt is searching for authors like you

If you're interested in becoming an author for Packt, please visit `authors.packtpub.com` and apply today. We have worked with thousands of developers and tech professionals, just like you, to help them share their insight with the global tech community. You can make a general application, apply for a specific hot topic that we are recruiting an author for, or submit your own idea.

Table of Contents

Preface

WebAssembly is a technology that will change the web as we know it within the next few years. WebAssembly promises a world where web-based applications run at near-native speeds. It is a world where you can write an application for the web in any language you like, and compile it for native platforms as well as the web. It is early days for WebAssembly, but this technology is already taking off like a rocket. If you are interested in where the web is going, as much as where it is today, read on!

I wrote this book to reflect the way I like to learn new skills. I will walk you through the development of a game using WebAssembly and all of its related technologies. I am a long-time game and web developer, and I have always enjoyed learning new programming languages by writing games. In this book, we will be covering a lot of ground on a lot of topics using both web and game development tools that go hand in hand with WebAssembly. We will learn how to write games that target WebAssembly utilizing a plethora of programming languages and tools, including Emscripten, C/C++, WebGL, OpenGL, JavaScript, HTML5, and CSS. As a long-time owner of an independent game development studio that specializes in the development of web-based games, I have found that it is essential to have a broad understanding of web- and game-based technologies and I have stuffed this book full of them. You will be learning a sample platter of skills with a focus on getting your apps up and running with WebAssembly. If you want to learn how to develop games with WebAssembly, or if you would like to create web-based applications that are lightning fast, this book is for you.

Who this book is for

This book is not an introduction to programming. It is intended for people who know how to code in at least one programming language. It would be helpful, but is not strictly necessary, to have at least a rudimentary understanding of some web-based technologies, such as HTML. This book contains instructions on how to install the required tools on Windows or Ubuntu Linux, and, out of the two, I would recommend using Ubuntu, as its installation process is much simpler.

What this book covers

Chapter 1, *Introduction to WebAssembly and Emscripten*, introduces WebAssembly, why the web needs it, and why it is so much faster than JavaScript. We will introduce Emscripten, why we need it for WebAssembly development, and how to install it. We will also discuss technologies related to WebAssembly, such as asm.js, LLVM, and WebAssembly Text.

Chapter 2, *HTML5 and WebAssembly*, discusses how WebAssembly modules integrate with HTML using the JavaScript "glue code". We will learn how to create our own Emscripten HTML shell file, and we will learn how to make calls to and from our WebAssembly module, which we will write in C. Finally, we will learn how to compile and run an HTML page that interacts with our WebAssembly module, and we will learn how to build a simple HTML5 Canvas app with Emscripten.

Chapter 3, *Introduction to WebGL*, introduces WebGL and the new canvas contexts that support it. We will learn about shaders, what they are, and how WebGL uses them to render geometry to the canvas. We will learn how to use WebGL and JavaScript to draw a sprite to the canvas. And finally, we will write an app that integrates WebAssembly, JavaScript, and WebGL that displays a sprite and moves it across the canvas.

Chapter 4, *Sprite Animations in WebAssembly with SDL*, teaches you about the SDL library and how we use it to simplify calls to WebGL from WebAssembly. We will learn how to use SDL to render, animate, and move sprites on the HTML5 canvas.

Chapter 5, *Keyboard Input*, looks at how to take input from the keyboard from JavaScript and make calls to the WebAssembly module. We will also learn how to accept keyboard input using SDL inside our WebAssembly module, and use the input to move a sprite around the HTML5 canvas.

Chapter 6, *Game Objects and the Game Loop*, explores some basic game design. We will learn about the game loop, and how a game loop in WebAssembly is different than in other games. We will also learn about game objects and how to create an object pool from within our game. We will end the chapter by coding the beginning of our game, with two spaceships that move about the canvas and shoot projectiles at each other.

Chapter 7, *Collision Detection*, introduces collision detection into our game. We will explore the types of 2D collision detection, implement a basic collision detection system, and learn a little about the trigonometry that makes it work. We will modify our game so that projectiles destroy the spaceships when they collide.

Chapter 8, *Basic Particle System*, introduces particle systems and discusses how they can visually improve our game. We will talk about the virtual filesystem, and we learn how to add files to it through a web page. We will briefly introduce SVG and Vector graphics, and how to use them for data visualization. We will further discuss trigonometry and how we will be using it in our particle systems. We will build a new HTML5 WebAssembly app that will help us to configure and test particle systems that we will later add to our game.

Chapter 9, *Improved Particle Systems*, goes into improving our particle system configuration tool by adding particle scaling, rotation, animation, and color transitions. We will modify the tool to allow the particle systems to loop, and add a burst effect. We will then update our game to support particle systems and add in particle system effects for our engine exhaust and explosions.

Chapter 10, *AI and Steering Behaviors*, introduces the concept of AI and game AI and discusses the difference between them. We will discuss the AI concepts of finite state machines, autonomous agents, and steering behaviors, and we will implement these behaviors in an enemy AI that will avoid obstacles and combat the player.

Chapter 11, *Designing a 2D Camera*, brings in the concept of 2D camera design. We will begin by adding a render manager to our game and creating a camera that locks on to the player's spaceship, following it around an expanded gameplay area. We will then add the advanced 2D camera features of projected focus and camera attractors.

Chapter 12, *Sound FX*, covers the use of SDL Audio in our game. We will discuss where we can get our sound effects online, and how to include those sounds in our WebAssembly module. We will then add sound effects to our game.

Chapter 13, *Game Physics*, introduces the concept of physics in computer games. We will be adding elastic collisions between our game objects. We will add Newton's third law to the physics of our game in the form of recoil when the spaceships launch projectiles. We will add a gravitational field to our star that will attract the spaceships.

Chapter 14, *UI and Mouse Input*, discusses adding a user interface to be managed and rendered within our WebAssembly module. We will gather requirements and translate them into new screens for our game. We will add a new button object and learn how we can manage mouse input from within our WebAssembly module using SDL.

Chapter 15, *Shaders and 2D lighting*, dives into how to create a new app that mixes OpenGL and SDL. We will create a new shader that loads and renders multiple textures to a quad. We will learn about normal maps, and how we can use normal maps to approximate the Phong lighting model in 2D, using OpenGL in our WebAssembly module.

Chapter 16, *Debugging and Optimization,* introduces the basic methods for debugging and optimizing WebAssembly modules. We will start with debug macros and stack traces from WebAssembly. We will introduce the concepts of source maps and how web browsers use them to debug WebAssembly modules. We will learn about optimizing WebAssembly code using optimization flags. We will discuss using a profiler to optimize our WebAssembly code.

To get the most out of this book

You must understand the basics of computer programming.

It is helpful to have a basic understanding of web technologies such as HTML and CSS.

Download the example code files

You can download the code bundle for this book from here: https://github.com/PacktPublishing/Hands-On-Game-Development-with-WebAssembly.

We also have other code bundles from our rich catalog of books and videos available at https://github.com/PacktPublishing/. Check them out!

Download the color images

We also provide a PDF file that has color images of the screenshots/diagrams used in this book. You can download it here: https://www.packtpub.com/sites/default/files/downloads/9781838644659_ColorImages.pdf.

Conventions used

You can download the example code files for this book from your account at www.packt.com. If you purchased this book elsewhere, you can visit www.packt.com/support and register to have the files emailed directly to you.

You can download the code files by following these steps:

1. Log in or register at www.packt.com.
2. Select the **SUPPORT** tab.

3. Click on **Code Downloads & Errata**.
4. Enter the name of the book in the **Search** box and follow the onscreen instructions.

Once the file is downloaded, please make sure that you unzip or extract the folder using the latest version of:

- WinRAR/7-Zip for Windows
- Zipeg/iZip/UnRarX for Mac
- 7-Zip/PeaZip for Linux

The code bundle for the book is also hosted on GitHub at **https://github.com/PacktPublishing/Hands-On-Game-Development-with-WebAssembly**. In case there's an update to the code, it will be updated on the existing GitHub repository.

We also have other code bundles from our rich catalog of books and videos available at https://github.com/PacktPublishing/. Check them out!

Conventions used

There are a number of text conventions used throughout this book.

CodeInText: Indicates code words in text, database table names, folder names, filenames, file extensions, pathnames, dummy URLs, user input, and Twitter handles. Here is an example: "We are going to copy the basic_particle_shell.html file to a new shell file that we will call advanced_particle_shell.html."

A block of code is set as follows:

```
<label class="ccontainer"><span class="label">loop:</span>
<input type="checkbox" id="loop" checked="checked">
<span class="checkmark"></span>
</label>
<br/>
```

When we wish to draw your attention to a particular part of a code block, the relevant lines or items are set in bold:

```
<label class="ccontainer"><span class="label">loop:</span>
<input type="checkbox" id="loop" checked="checked">
<span class="checkmark"></span>
</label>
<br/>
```

Any command-line input or output is written as follows:

```
emrun --list_browsers
```

Bold: Indicates a new term, an important word, or words that you see on screen. For example, words in menus or dialog boxes appear in the text like this. Here is an example: "Select **System info** from the **Administration** panel."

Warnings or important notes appear like this.

Tips and tricks appear like this.

Get in touch

Feedback from our readers is always welcome.

General feedback: If you have questions about any aspect of this book, mention the book title in the subject of your message and email us at customercare@packtpub.com.

Errata: Although we have taken every care to ensure the accuracy of our content, mistakes do happen. If you have found a mistake in this book, we would be grateful if you would report this to us. Please visit www.packt.com/submit-errata, selecting your book, clicking on the Errata Submission Form link, and entering the details.

Piracy: If you come across any illegal copies of our works in any form on the internet, we would be grateful if you would provide us with the location address or website name. Please contact us at copyright@packt.com with a link to the material.

If you are interested in becoming an author: If there is a topic that you have expertise in, and you are interested in either writing or contributing to a book, please visit authors.packtpub.com.

Reviews

Please leave a review. Once you have read and used this book, why not leave a review on the site that you purchased it from? Potential readers can then see and use your unbiased opinion to make purchase decisions, we at Packt can understand what you think about our products, and our authors can see your feedback on their book. Thank you!

For more information about Packt, please visit `packt.com`.

Introduction to WebAssembly and Emscripten

1

Welcome to the exciting new world of WebAssembly! These are early days for WebAssembly, but the technology is currently taking off like a rocket, and by reading this book, you are in a position to get in on the ground floor. If you are interested in game development on the web, or you are interested in learning as much about this new technology as you can to position yourself for when it does reach maturity, you are in the right place. Even though WebAssembly is in its infancy, all major browser vendors have adopted it. These are early days and use cases are limited, but lucky for us, game development is one of them. So, if you want to be early to the party for the next generation of application development on the web, read on, adventurer!

In this chapter, I will introduce you to WebAssembly, Emscripten, and some of the underlying technologies around WebAssembly. I will teach you the basics of the Emscripten toolchain, and how you can use Emscripten to compile C++ code into WebAssembly. We will discuss what LLVM is and how it fits into the Emscripten toolchain. We will talk about WebAssembly's **Minimum Viable Product (MVP)**, the best use cases for WebAssembly in its current MVP form, and what will soon be coming to WebAssembly. I will introduce **WebAssembly text (.wat)**, how we can use it to understand the design of WebAssembly bytecode, and how it differs from other machine bytecodes. We will also briefly discuss **asm.js**, and its historical significance in the design of WebAssembly. Finally, I will show you how to install and run Emscripten on Windows and Linux.

In this chapter, we will cover the following topics:

- What is WebAssembly?
- Why do we need WebAssembly?
- Why is WebAssembly faster than JavaScript?
- Will WebAssembly replace JavaScript?
- What is asm.js?
- A brief introduction to LLVM
- A brief introduction to WebAssembly text
- What is Emscripten and how do we use it?

What is WebAssembly?

WebAssembly is not a high-level programming language like JavaScript, but a compiled binary format that all major browsers are currently able to execute. WebAssembly is a kind of machine bytecode that was not designed to run directly on any real machine hardware, but runs in the JavaScript engine built into every browser. In some ways, it is similar to the old **Java Virtual Machine** (**JVM**); for example, it is a platform-independent compiled bytecode. One major problem with JavaScript bytecode is its requirement for a plugin to be downloaded and installed in the browser for the bytecode to run. Not only is **WebAssembly** designed to be run directly in a browser without a plugin, but it is also intended to produce a compact binary format that executes efficiently inside a web browser. The MVP version of the specification leverages existing work by the browser makers designing their JavaScript **just-in-time** (**JIT**) compiler. WebAssembly is currently a young technology and many improvements are planned. However, developers using the current version of WebAssembly have already seen performance improvements over JavaScript of 10–800%.

 An MVP is the smallest set of features that can be given to a product to allow it to appeal to early adopters. Because the current version is an MVP, the feature set is small. For more information, see this excellent article discussing the "post-MVP future" of WebAssembly: `https://hacks.mozilla.org/2018/10/webassemblys-post-mvp-future/`.

Why do we need WebAssembly?

JavaScript has been around for a long time. It has evolved from a little scripting language that allowed bells and whistles to be added to a web page, to a sprawling JIT compiled language with a massive ecosystem that can be used to write fully fledged applications. Today, JavaScript is doing a lot of things that were probably never imagined when it was created by Netscape in 1995. JavaScript is an interpreted language, meaning that it must be parsed, compiled, and optimized on the fly. JavaScript is also a dynamically typed language, which creates headaches for an optimizer.

 Franziska Hinkelmann, a member of the Chrome V8 team, gave a great talk at the *Web Rebels 2017* conference where she discusses all the performance improvements made to JavaScript over the past 20 years, as well as the difficulties they had in squeezing every bit of performance imaginable out of the JavaScript V8 engine: `https://youtu.be/ihANrJ1Po0w`.

WebAssembly solves a lot of the problems created by JavaScript and its long history in the browser. Because the JavaScript engine is already in bytecode format, it does not need to run a parser, which removes a significant bottleneck in the execution of our application. This design also allows the JavaScript engine to know what data types it is dealing with at all times. The bytecode makes optimization a lot easier. The format allows multiple threads in the browsers to work on compiling and optimizing different parts of the code at the same time.

 For a detailed explanation of what is happening when the Chrome V8 engine is parsing code, please refer to this video from the *JSConf EU 2017*, in which Marja Hölttä (who works on the Chrome V8 tool) goes into more detail than you ever imagined you wanted to learn about parsing JavaScript: `https://www.youtube.com/watch?v=Fg7niTmNNLgt=123s`.

WebAssembly is not a high-level programming language, but a binary file with opcodes for a virtual machine. Currently, it is considered to be in an MVP stage of development. The technology is still in its infancy, but even now it offers notable performance and file size benefits for many use cases, such as game development. Because of the current limitations of WebAssembly, we have only two choices for languages to use for its development—C/C++ or Rust. The long-term plan for WebAssembly is to support a wide selection of programming languages for its development. If I wanted to write at the lowest level of abstraction, I could write everything in **Web Assembly Text (WAT)**, but WAT was developed as a language to support debugging and testing and was not intended to be used by developers for writing applications.

Why is WebAssembly faster than JavaScript?

As I have mentioned, WebAssembly is 10–800% faster than JavaScript, depending on the application. To understand why, I need to talk a little about what a JavaScript engine does when it runs JavaScript code versus what it has to do when it runs WebAssembly. I am going to talk specifically about V8 (the Chrome JavaScript engine), although, to my knowledge, the same general process exists within SpiderMonkey (Firefox) and the Chakra (IE & Edge) JavaScript engines.

The first thing the JavaScript engine does is parse your source code into an **Abstract Syntax Tree (AST)**. The source is broken into branches and leaves based on the logic within your application. At this point, an interpreter starts processing the language that you are currently executing. For many years, JavaScript was just an interpreted language, so, if you ran the same code in your JavaScript 100 times, the JavaScript engine had to take that code and convert it to machine code 100 times. As you can imagine, this is wildly inefficient.

The Chrome browser introduced the first JavaScript JIT compiler in 2008. A JIT compiler contrasts with an **Ahead-of-Time (AOT)** compiler in that it compiles your code as it is running that code. A profiler sits and watches the JavaScript execution looking for code that repeatedly executes. Whenever it sees code executed a few times, it marks that code as "warm" for JIT compilation. The compiler then compiles a bytecode representation of that JavaScript "stub" code. This bytecode is typically an **Intermediate Representation (IR)**, one step removed from the machine-specific assembly language. Decoding the stub will be significantly faster than running the same lines of code through our interpreter the next time.

Here are the steps needed to run JavaScript code:

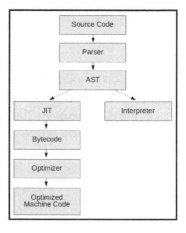

Figure 1.1: Steps required by a modern JavaScript engine

While all of this is going on, there is an **optimizing compiler** that is watching the profiler for "hot" code branches. The optimizing compiler then takes these code branches and optimizes the bytecode that was created by the JIT into highly optimized machine code. At this point, the JavaScript engine has created some super fast running code, but there is a catch (or maybe a few).

The JavaScript engine must make some assumptions about the data types to have an optimized machine code. The problem is, JavaScript is a dynamically typed language. Dynamic typing makes it easier for a programmer to learn how to program JavaScript, but it is a terrible choice for code optimizers. The example I often see is what happens when JavaScript sees the expression c = a + b (although we could use this example for almost any expression).

Just about any machine code that performs this operation does it in three steps:

1. Load the a value into a register.

2. Add the b value into a register.
3. Then store the register into c.

The following pseudo code was taken from section 12.8.3 of the *ECMAScript® 2018 Language Specification* and describes the code that must run whenever the addition operator (+) is used within JavaScript:

```
1. Let lref be the result of evaluating AdditiveExpression.
2. Let lval be ? GetValue(lref).
3. Let rref be the result of evaluating MultiplicativeExpression.
4. Let rval be ? GetValue(rref).
5. Let lprim be ? ToPrimitive(lval).
6. Let rprim be ? ToPrimitive(rval).
7. If Type(lprim) is String or Type(rprim) is String, then
   a. Let lstr be ? ToString(lprim).
   b. Let rstr be ? ToString(rprim).
   c. Return the string-concatenation of lstr and rstr.
8. Let lnum be ? ToNumber(lprim).
9. Let rnum be ? ToNumber(rprim).
10.Return the result of applying the addition operation to lnum and
   rnum.
```

You can find the *ECMAScript® 2018 Language Specification* on the web at https://www.ecma-international.org/ecma-262/9.0/index.html.

This pseudo code is not the entirety of what we must evaluate. Several of these steps are calling high-level functions, not running machine code commands. GetValue for example, has 11 steps of its own that are, in turn, calling other steps. All of this could end up resulting in hundreds of machine opcodes. The vast majority of what is happening here is type checking. In JavaScript, when you execute a + b, each one of those variables could be any one of the following types:

- Integer
- Float
- String
- Object
- Any combination of these

To make matters worse, objects in JavaScript are also highly dynamic. For example, maybe you have defined a function called Point and created two objects with that function using the new operator:

```
function Point( x, y ) {
    this.x = x;
    this.y = y;
}

var p1 = new Point(1, 100);
var p2 = new Point( 10, 20 );
```

Now we have two points that share the same class. Say we added this line:

```
p2.z = 50;
```

This would mean that these two points would then no longer share the same class. Effectively, p2 has become a brand new class, and this has consequences for where that object exists in memory and available optimizations. JavaScript was designed to be a highly flexible language, but this fact creates a lot of corner cases, and corner cases make optimization difficult.

Another problem with optimization created by the dynamic nature of JavaScript is that no optimization is definitive. All optimizations around typing have to use resources continually checking to see whether their typing assumptions are still valid. Also, the optimizer has to keep the non-optimized code just in case those assumptions turn out to be false. The optimizer may determine that assumptions made initially turn out not to have been correct assumptions. That results in a "bailout" where the optimizer will throw away its optimized code and deoptimize, causing performance inconsistencies.

Finally, JavaScript is a language with **Garbage Collection (GC)**, which allows the authors of the JavaScript code to take on less of the burden of memory management while writing their code. Although this is a convenience for the developer, it just pushes the work of memory management on to the machine at run time. GC has become much more efficient in JavaScript over the years, but it is still work that the JavaScript engine must do when running JavaScript that it does not need to do when running WebAssembly.

Executing a WebAssembly module removes many of the steps required to run JavaScript code. WebAssembly eliminates parsing because the AOT compiler completes that function. An interpreter is unnecessary. Our JIT compiler is doing a near one-to-one translation from bytecode to machine code, which is extremely fast. JavaScript requires the majority of its optimizations because of dynamic typing that does not exist in WebAssembly. Hardware agnostic optimizations can be done in the AOT compiler before the WebAssembly compiles. The JIT optimizer need only perform hardware-specific optimizations that the WebAssembly AOT compiler cannot.

Here are the steps performed by the JavaScript engine to run a WebAssembly binary:

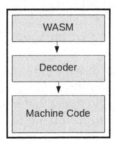

Figure 1.2: The steps required to execute WebAssembly

The last thing that I would like to mention is not a feature of the current MVP, but a potential future enabled by WebAssembly. All the code that makes modern JavaScript fast takes up memory. Keeping old copies of the nonoptimized code for bailout takes up memory. Parsers, interpreters, and garbage collectors all take up memory. On my desktop, Chrome frequently takes up about 1 GB of memory. By running a few tests on my website using `https://www.classicsolitaire.com`, I can see that with the JavaScript engine turned on, the Chrome browser takes up about 654 MB of memory.

Here is a Task Manager screenshot:

Figure 1.3: Chrome Task Manager process screenshot with JavaScript

With JavaScript turned off, the Chrome browser takes up about 295MB.

Here is a Task Manager screenshot:

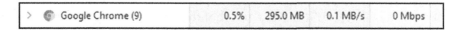

Figure 1.4: Chrome Task Manager process screenshot without JavaScript

Because this is one of my websites, I know there are only a few hundred kilobytes of JavaScript code on that website. It's a little shocking to me that running that tiny amount of JavaScript code can increase my browser footprint by about 350 MB. Currently, WebAssembly runs on top of the existing JavaScript engines and still requires quite a bit of JavaScript glue code to make everything work, but in the long run, WebAssembly will not only allow us to speed up execution on the web but will also let us do it with a much smaller memory footprint.

Will WebAssembly replace JavaScript?

The short answer to this question is not anytime soon. At present, WebAssembly is still in its MVP stage. At this stage, the number of use cases is limited to applications where WebAssembly has limited back and forth with the JavaScript and the **Document Object Model (DOM)**. WebAssembly is not currently able to directly interact with the DOM, and Emscripten uses JavaScript "glue code" to make that interaction work. That interaction will probably change soon, possibly by the time you are reading this, but in the next few years, WebAssembly will need additional features to increase the number of possible use cases.

WebAssembly is not a "feature complete" platform. Currently, it cannot be used with any languages that require GC. That will change and, eventually, almost all strongly typed languages will target WebAssembly. In addition, WebAssembly will soon become tightly integrated with JavaScript, allowing frameworks such as React, Vue, and Angular to begin replacing significant amounts of their JavaScript code with WebAssembly without impacting the **application programming interface (API)**. The React team is currently working on this to improve the performance of React.

In the long run, it is possible that JavaScript may compile into WebAssembly. For technical reasons, this is a very long way off. Not only does JavaScript require a GC (not currently supported), but because of its dynamic nature, JavaScript also requires a runtime profiler to optimize. Therefore, JavaScript would produce very poorly optimized code, or significant modifications would be needed to support strict typing. It is more likely that a language, such as TypeScript, will add features that allow it to compile into WebAssembly.

The *AssemblyScript* project in development on GitHub is working on a TypeScript-to-WebAssembly compiler. This project creates JavaScript and uses Binaryen to compile that JavaScript into WebAssembly. How AssemblyScript handles the problem of garbage collection is unclear. For more information, refer to `https://github.com/AssemblyScript/assemblyscript`.

JavaScript is currently ubiquitous on the web; there are a tremendous number of libraries and frameworks developed in JavaScript. Even if there were an army of developers eager to rewrite the entire web in C++ or Rust, WebAssembly is not yet ready to replace these JavaScript libraries and frameworks. The browser makers have put immense efforts into making JavaScript run (relatively) fast, so JavaScript will probably remain as the standard scripting language for the web. The web will always need a scripting language, and countless developers have already put in the work to make JavaScript that scripting language, so it seems unlikely that JavaScript will ever go away.

There is, however, a need for a compiled format for the web that WebAssembly is likely to fulfill. Compiled code may be a niche on the web at the moment, but it is a standard just about everywhere else. As WebAssembly approaches feature-complete status, it will offer more choices and better performance than JavaScript, and businesses, frameworks, and libraries will gradually migrate toward it.

What is asm.js?

One early attempt to achieve native-like speed in the web browser using JavaScript was asm.js. Although that goal was reached and asm.js was adopted by all the major browser vendors, it never achieved widespread adoption by developers. The beauty of asm.js is that it still runs in most browsers, even in those that do not optimize for it. The idea behind asm.js was that typed arrays could be used in JavaScript to fake a C++ memory heap. The browser simulates pointers and memory allocation in C++, as well as types. A well-designed JavaScript engine can avoid dynamic type checking. Using asm.js, browser makers could get around many of the optimization problems created by the dynamic nature of JavaScript, by just pretending that this version of JavaScript is not dynamically typed. Emscripten, designed as a C++-to-JavaScript compiler, quickly adopted asm.js as the subset of JavaScript that it would compile to because of its improved performance in most browsers. The performance improvements driven by asm.js lead the way to WebAssembly. The same engine modifications used to make asm.js perform well could be used to bootstrap the WebAssembly MVP. Only the addition of a bytecode-to-bytecode compiler was required to take the WebAssembly bytecode and directly convert it into the IR bytecode used by the browser.

At the time of writing, Emscripten does not compile directly from LLVM to WebAssembly. Instead, it compiles to asm.js and uses a tool called Binaryen to convert the asm.js output from Emscripten into WebAssembly.

A brief introduction to LLVM

Emscripten is the tool we will be using to compile C++ into WebAssembly. Before I discuss Emscripten, I need to explain a technology called LLVM and its relationship to Emscripten.

First, take a moment to think of airlines (stay with me here). Airlines want to get passengers from one airport to another airport. But it's challenging to offer a direct flight from every single airport to every other airport on Earth. That would mean that airlines would have to provide a vast number of direct flights, such as Akron, Ohio to Mumbai, India. Let's travel back in time to the 1990s—that was the state of the compiler world. If you wanted to compile from C++ to ARM, you needed a compiler capable of compiling C++ to ARM. If you needed to compile from Pascal to x86, you needed a compiler that could compile from Pascal to x86. These are like having only direct flights between any two cities: a compiler for every combination of language and hardware. The result is either that you have to limit the number of languages you write compilers for, limit the number of platforms you can support with that language, or more likely, both.

In 2003, a student at the University of Illinois named Chris Lattner wondered, "What if we created a hub-and-spoke model for programming languages?" His idea led to LLVM, which originally stood for "Low-Level Virtual Machine." The idea was that, instead of compiling your source code for any possible distribution, you compile it for LLVM. There are then compilers between the intermediate language and your final output language. In theory, this means that if you develop a new target platform on the right side of the following diagram, you get all languages on the left side right away:

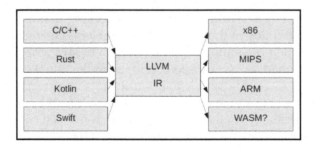

Figure 1.5: LLVM as a hub between programming languages and the hardware

To learn more about LLVM, visit the LLVM project home page at `https://llvm.org` or read the *LLVM Cookbook, Mayur Padney, and Suyog Sarda, Packt Publishing*: `https://www.packtpub.com/application-development/llvm-cookbook`.

A brief introduction to WebAssembly text

WebAssembly binary is not a language, but a build target similar to building for ARM or x86. The bytecode, however, is structured differently than other hardware-specific build targets. The designers of the WebAssembly bytecode had the web in mind. The aim was to create a bytecode that was compact and streamable. Another goal was that the user should be able to do a "view/source" on the WebAssembly binary to see what is going on. WebAssembly text is a companion code to the WebAssembly binary that allows the user to view the bytecode instructions in a human-readable form, similar to the way an assembly language would let you see what opcodes execute in a machine-readable form.

WebAssembly text may initially look unfamiliar to someone used to writing assembly for hardware such as ARM, x86, or 6502 (if you're old school). You write WebAssembly text in S-expressions, which has a parentheses-heavy tree structure. Some of the operations are also strikingly high level for an assembly language, such as if/else and loop opcodes. That makes a lot more sense if you remember that WebAssembly was not designed to run directly on computer hardware, but to download and translate into machine code quickly.

Another thing that will seem a little alien at first when you are dealing with WebAssembly text is the lack of registers. WebAssembly is designed to be a virtual *stack machine*, which is an alternative to a *register machine*, such as x86 and ARM, with which you might be familiar. A stack machine has the advantage of producing significantly smaller bytecode than a register machine, which is one good reason to choose a stack machine for WebAssembly. Instead of using a series of registers to store and manipulate numbers, every opcode in a stack machine pushes values on or off a stack (and sometimes does both). For example, a call to `i32.add` in WebAssembly pulls two 32-bit integers off the stack, adds them together, then pushes their value back on to the stack. The computer hardware can make the best use of whichever registers are available to perform this operation.

Emscripten

Now that we know what LLVM is, we can discuss Emscripten. Emscripten was developed to compile LLVM IR into JavaScript, but has recently been updated to compile LLVM into WebAssembly. The idea is that, when you get the LLVM compiler working, you can have the benefit of all the languages that compile to LLVM IR. In practice, the WebAssembly specification is still in its early days and does not support common language features such as GC. Therefore, only non-GC languages such as C/C++ and Rust are currently supported. WebAssembly is still in the early MVP phase of its development, but the addition of GC and other common language features are coming soon. When that happens, there should be an explosion of programming languages that will compile to WebAssembly.

When Emscripten was released in 2012, it was intended to be an LLVM-to-JavaScript compiler. In 2013, support was added for asm.js, which is a faster, easily optimized subset of the JavaScript language. In 2015, Emscripten began to add support for LLVM-to-WebAssembly compiling. Emscripten also provides a **Software Development Kit (SDK)** for both C++ and JavaScript that provides glue code to give users better tools for interaction between JavaScript and WebAssembly than those currently offered by the WebAssembly MVP alone. Emscripten also integrates with a C/C++-to-LLVM compiler called Clang, so that you can compile your C++ into WebAssembly. In addition, Emscripten will generate the HTML and JavaScript glue code you need to get your project started.

 Emscripten is a very dynamic project and changes to the toolchain happen frequently. To stay up to date with the latest changes in Emscripten, visit the project home page at https://emscripten.org.

Installing Emscripten on Windows

I am going to keep this section brief because these instructions are subject to change. You can supplement these instructions with the official Emscripten download and install instructions found on the Emscripten website: https://emscripten.org/docs/getting_started/downloads.html.

We will need to download and build Emscripten from the emsdk source files on GitHub. First, we will walk through what to do on Windows.

Python 2.7.12 or higher is a prerequisite. If you do not have a version of Python higher than 2.7.12 installed, you will need to get the windows installer from python.org and install that first: https://www.python.org/downloads/windows/.

If you have installed Python and you are still getting errors telling you that Python is not found, you may need to add Python to your Windows PATH variable. For more information, refer to this tutorial: `https://www.pythoncentral.io/add-python-to-path-python-is-not-recognized-as-an-internal-or-external-command/`.

If you have Git installed already, cloning the repository is relatively simple:

1. Run the following command to clone the repository:

   `git clone https://github.com/emscripten-core/emsdk.git`

2. Wherever you run this command, it will create an `emsdk` directory. Enter that directory using the following:

   `cd emsdk`

You may not have Git installed, in which case, the following steps will bring you up to speed:

1. Go to the following URL in a web browser: `https://github.com/emscripten-core/emsdk`.
2. You will see a green button on the right-hand side that says **Clone or download**. Download the ZIP file:

3. Unzip the downloaded file to the `c:\emsdk` directory.

4. Open up a Windows Command Prompt by typing `cmd` into the start menu and pressing *Enter*.

5. From there, you can change to the `c:\emsdk\emsdk-master` directory by typing the following:

```
cd \emsdk\emsdk-master
```

At this point, it does not matter whether you had Git installed or not. Let's move forward:

1. Install `emsdk` from the source code running the following command:

```
emsdk install latest
```

2. Then activate the latest `emsdk`:

```
emsdk activate latest
```

3. Finally, set up our path and environment variables:

```
emsdk_env.bat
```

 This last step will need to be rerun from your install directory every time you open a new command-line window. Unfortunately, it does not permanently set the Windows environment variables. Hopefully, that will change in the future.

Installing Emscripten on Ubuntu

If you are installing on Ubuntu, you should be able to use the `apt-get` package manager and git for the complete install. Let's move forward:

1. Python is required, so if you do not have Python installed, be sure to run the following:

```
sudo apt-get install python
```

2. If you do not already have Git installed, run the following:

```
sudo apt-get install git
```

3. Now you will need to clone the Git repository for emsdk:

```
git clone https://github.com/emscripten-core/emsdk.git
```

4. Change your directory to move into the emsdk directory:

```
cd emsdk
```

5. From here, you need to install the latest version of the SDK tools, activate it, and set your environment variables:

```
./emsdk install latest
./emsdk activate latest
source ./emsdk_env.sh
```

6. To make sure everything was installed correctly, run the following command:

```
emcc --version
```

Using Emscripten

We run Emscripten from the command line; therefore, you can use any text editor you choose to write your C/C++ code. Personally, I am partial to Visual Studio Code, which you can download here: https://code.visualstudio.com/download.

One beautiful thing about Visual Studio Code is that it has a built-in command-line terminal, which lets you compile your code without switching windows. It also has an excellent C/C++ extension that you can install. Just search for C/C++ from the extensions menu and install the Microsoft C/C++ Intellisense extension.

Whatever you choose for your text editor or integrated development environment, you need a simple piece of C code to test out the emcc compiler.

1. Create a new text file and name it hello.c.
2. Type the following code into hello.c:

```
#include <emscripten.h>
#include <stdlib.h>
#include <stdio.h>

int main() {
    printf("hello wasm\n");
}
```

3. Now I can compile the `hello.c` file into WebAssembly and generate a `hello.html` file:

```
emcc hello.c --emrun -o hello.html
```

4. The `--emrun` flag is necessary if you want to run the HTML page from `emrun`. This flag adds code that will capture `stdout`, `stderr`, and exit in the C code and `emrun` will not work without it:

```
emrun --browser firefox hello.html
```

Running `emrun` with the `--browser` flag will pick the browser where you would like to run the script. The behavior of `emrun` seems to be different between browsers. Chrome will close the window when the C program exits. That can be annoying because we are just trying to display a simple print message. If you have Firefox, I would suggest running `emrun` using the `--browser` flag.

 I do not want to imply that Chrome cannot run WebAssembly. Chrome does have different behavior when a WebAssembly module exits. Because I was trying to keep our WebAssembly module as simple as possible, it exits when the main function completes. That is what is causing problems in Chrome. These problems will go away later when we learn about game loops.

To find out what browsers are available to you, run the following:

```
emrun --list_browsers
```

`emrun` should open an Emscripten-templated HTML file in a browser.

Make sure you have a browser capable of running WebAssembly. The following versions of the major browsers should work with WebAssembly:

- Edge 16
- Firefox 52
- Chrome 57
- Safari 11
- Opera 44

If you are familiar with setting up your own web server, you may want to consider using it rather than emrun. After using emrun for the first few chapters of this book, I returned to using my Node.js web server. I found it easier to have a Node-based web server up and running at all times, rather than restarting the emrun web server every time I wanted to test my code. If you know how to set up an alternative web server (such as one for Node, Apache, and IIS), you may use whatever web server you prefer. Although IIS requires some additional configuration to handle WebAssembly MIME types.

Additional installation resources

Creating an installation guide for Emscripten is going to be somewhat problematic. The WebAssembly technology changes frequently and the installation process for Emscripten may be different by the time you read this. I would recommend consulting the download and install instructions on the Emscripten website if you have any problems: `https:// emscripten.org/docs/getting_started/downloads.html`.

You may also want to consult the Emscripten page on GitHub: `https://github.com/ emscripten-core/emsdk`.

Google Groups has an Emscripten discussion forum where you may ask questions if you are having installation problems: `https://groups.google.com/forum/?nomobile= true#!forum/emscripten-discuss`.

You can also contact me on Twitter (`@battagline`), and I will do my best to help you: `https://twitter.com/battagline`.

Summary

In this chapter, we learned what WebAssembly is and why it will be the future of application development on the web. We learned why we need WebAssembly, even though we already have a robust language like JavaScript. We learned why WebAssembly is so much faster than JavaScript, and how it has the potential to increase its performance lead. We have also discussed the possibility of WebAssembly replacing JavaScript as the de facto standard for application development on the web.

We have discussed the practical side of creating a WebAssembly module as it is done today using Emscripten and LLVM. We have talked about WebAssembly text and how it is structured. We have also discussed using Emscripten to compile our first WebAssembly module, as well as using it to create the HTML and JavaScript glue code to run that module.

In the next chapter, we will go into further detail on how to use Emscripten to create our WebAssembly module, as well as the HTML/CSS and JavaScript used to drive it.

HTML5 and WebAssembly
2

In this chapter, we will show you how the C code we write to target WebAssembly comes together with HTML5, JavaScript, and CSS to create a web page. We will teach you how to create a new HTML shell file to be used by Emscripten in the creation of our WebAssembly app. We will discuss the `Module` object and how Emscripten uses it as an interface between our JavaScript and the WebAssembly module. We will show you how to call WebAssembly functions written in C from within JavaScript on our HTML page. We will also show you how to call JavaScript functions from our C code. We will discuss how to use CSS to improve the look of our web page. We will introduce you to the HTML5 Canvas element and show how it is possible to display images to the canvas from within JavaScript. We will briefly discuss moving those images around the canvas from our WebAssembly module. This chapter will give you an understanding of how everything works together and lays the foundation for other features we are developing for our WebAssembly applications.

Beginning with this chapter and continuing through the remainder of the book, you will need image and font files from the GitHub project to compile the examples. For this chapter, you will need the /Chapter02/spaceship.png image file from the project directory. Please download the project from the following URL: https://github. com/PacktPublishing/Hands-On-Game-Development-with-WebAssembly.

I highly recommend working along as you read each section of this chapter. You may use your favorite code editor and the command line to follow along. Even though we have provided links to download the code directly, it cannot be emphasized enough how much you will learn by actually following edits suggested in this chapter. You are going to make mistakes and learn a lot from them. If you decide to work along, another suggestion is the following: do not proceed to the next section unless your edit/steps in the current section are successful. If you need help, contact me on twitter (@battagline).

In this chapter, we will cover the following topics:

- The Emscripten minimal shell file
- Creating a new HTML shell and C file
- Defining our CSS
- HTML5 and game development
- Adding a canvas to the Emscripten template

The Emscripten minimal shell file

The first build we created with Emscripten used a default HTML shell file. If you have a website, this is probably not the way you would prefer your web page to look. You would probably prefer to design your look and feel using CSS and HTML5 specific to your design or business needs. For instance, the templates I use for my websites typically include advertisements to the left and right of the game's canvas. That is how traffic to these sites is monetized. You may choose to add a logo for your website above your game's canvas. There is also a text area where Emscripten logs output from `printf` or other standard IO calls. You may choose to remove this `textarea` element altogether, or you may keep it, but keep it hidden because it is useful for debugging later.

To build the HTML file based on a new shell file that is not the default Emscripten shell, we must use the `--shell-file` parameter, passing it the new HTML template file we would like to use, instead of Emscripten's default. The new `emcc` command will look like this:

```
emcc hello.c --shell-file new_shell.html --emrun -o hello2.html
```

Do not execute this command just yet. We do not currently have a `new_shell.html` file in our project directory, so running the command before that file exists will result in an error message. We need to create the `new_shell.html` file and use it as the HTML shell instead of Emscripten's default HTML shell. This shell file must follow a specific format. To construct it, we have to start with Emscripten's minimum HTML shell file, which you can find at GitHub here:

https://github.com/emscripten-core/emscripten/blob/master/src/shell_minimal.html

We will be writing our own HTML shell, using the `shell_minimal.html` file as a starting point. Much of what is in the minimal shell is not required, so we will make some significant edits to it. We will remove much of the code to suit our purpose. When you open `shell_minimal.html` in your text editor, you will see that it starts with a standard HTML header and a `style` tag:

```
<style>
  .emscripten { padding-right: 0; margin-left: auto; margin-right: auto;
              display: block; }
  textarea.emscripten { font-family: monospace; width: 80%; }
  div.emscripten { text-align: center; }
  div.emscripten_border { border: 1px solid black; }
  /* the canvas *must not* have any border or padding, or mouse coords
     will be wrong */
  canvas.emscripten { border: 0px none; background-color: black; }
  .spinner {
            height: 50px;
            width: 50px;
            margin: 0px auto;
            -webkit-animation: rotation .8s linear infinite;
            -moz-animation: rotation .8s linear infinite;
            -o-animation: rotation .8s linear infinite;
            animation: rotation 0.8s linear infinite;
            border-left: 10px solid rgb(0,150,240);
            border-right: 10px solid rgb(0,150,240);
            border-bottom: 10px solid rgb(0,150,240);
            border-top: 10px solid rgb(100,0,200);
            border-radius: 100%;
            background-color: rgb(200,100,250);
        }
  @-webkit-keyframes rotation {
        from {-webkit-transform: rotate(0deg);}
        to {-webkit-transform: rotate(360deg);}
  }
  @-moz-keyframes rotation {
        from {-moz-transform: rotate(0deg);}
        to {-moz-transform: rotate(360deg);}
  }
  @-o-keyframes rotation {
        from {-o-transform: rotate(0deg);}
        to {-o-transform: rotate(360deg);}
  }
  @keyframes rotation {
        from {transform: rotate(0deg);}
        to {transform: rotate(360deg);}
  }
</style>
```

This code is based on the version of `shell_minimal.html` available at the time of writing. No changes to this file are anticipated. However, WebAssembly is evolving quickly. Unfortunately, we cannot say with complete certainty that this file will remain unchanged by the time you read this. As mentioned earlier, if you run into problems, please feel free to contact me on Twitter (`@battagline`).

We remove this style tag so you can style your code any way you like. It is necessary if you like their spinner loading image and want to keep it, but it is preferable to yank all of this out and replace it with CSS loaded externally from a CSS file with the link tag, as follows:

```
<link href="shell.css" rel="stylesheet" type="text/css">
```

Scroll down a little further, and you will see the loading indicators they use. We are going to replace that with our own eventually, but for now, we are testing all of this locally, and our files are all tiny, so we would remove this code as well:

```
<figure style="overflow:visible;" id="spinner">
    <div class="spinner"></div>
    <center style="margin-top:0.5em"><strong>emscripten</strong></center>
</figure>
<div class="emscripten" id="status">Downloading...</div>
    <div class="emscripten">
        <progress value="0" max="100" id="progress" hidden=1></progress>
    </div>
```

After that, there is an HTML5 `canvas` element and some other tags related to it. We will eventually need to add a `canvas` element back in, but for now, we will not be using the `canvas`, so that part of the code is not necessary either:

```
<div class="emscripten">
    <input type="checkbox" id="resize">Resize canvas
    <input type="checkbox" id="pointerLock" checked>Lock/hide mouse
     pointer     
    <input type="button" value="Fullscreen" onclick=
    "Module.requestFullscreen(document.getElementById
    ('pointerLock').checked,
            document.getElementById('resize').checked)">
  </div>
```

After the `canvas`, there is a `textarea` element. That is also not necessary, but it would be good to use it as the location where any `printf` commands executed from my C code are printed. The shell has surrounded it with two `<hr/>` tags, used for formatting, so we can remove those as well:

```
<hr/>
<textarea class="emscripten" id="output" rows="8"></textarea>
<hr/>
```

The next thing we have is our JavaScript. That starts with three variables that represent HTML elements that we removed earlier, so we are going to need to remove all of those JavaScript variables as well:

```
var statusElement = document.getElementById('status');
var progressElement = document.getElementById('progress');
var spinnerElement = document.getElementById('spinner');
```

The `Module` object inside JavaScript is the interface that the Emscripten-generated JavaScript *glue* code uses to interact with our WebAssembly module. It is the most crucial part of a shell HTML file, and it is essential to understand what it is doing. The `Module` object begins with two arrays, `preRun`, and `postRun`. These are arrays of functions that will run before and after the module is loaded, respectively.

```
var Module = {
  preRun: [],
  postRun: [],
```

For demonstration purposes, we could add functions to these arrays like this:

```
preRun: [function() {console.log("pre run 1")},
          function() {console.log("pre run 2")}],
postRun: [function() {console.log("post run 1")},
          function() {console.log("post run 2")}],
```

This would produce the following output from our hello WASM app that we created in `Chapter1`, *Introduction to WebAssembly and Emscripten*:

```
pre run 2
pre run 1
status: Running...
Hello wasm
post run 2
post run 1
```

Notice that the `preRun` and `postRun` functions run in the reverse order in which they are placed in the array. We could use the `postRun` array to call a function that would initialize our WebAssembly wrappers, but, for demonstration purposes, we will instead call a JavaScript function from within our C `main()` function.

The next two functions inside the `Module` object are the `print` and `printErr` functions. The `print` function is used to print out the output of the `printf` calls to both the console and to the `textarea` that we have named `output`. You can change this `output` to print out to any HTML tag, but, if your output is raw HTML, there are several commented-out text replace calls that must run. Here is what the `print` function looks like:

```
print: (function() {
    var element = document.getElementById('output');
    if (element) element.value = ''; // clear browser cache
    return function(text) {
        if (arguments.length > 1) text =
        Array.prototype.slice.call(arguments).join(' ');
        // These replacements are necessary if you render to raw HTML
        //text = text.replace(/&/g, "&amp;");
        //text = text.replace(/</g, "&lt;");
        //text = text.replace(/>/g, "&gt;");
        //text = text.replace('\n', '<br>', 'g');
        console.log(text);
        if (element) {
            element.value += text + "\n";
            element.scrollTop = element.scrollHeight; // focus on
            bottom
        }
    };
})(),
```

The `printErr` function is run by the glue code when an error or warning occurs in either our WebAssembly module or the glue code itself. The output of `printErr` is only the console, although, in principle, if you wanted to add code that would write to an HTML element, you could do that as well. Here is the `printErr` code:

```
printErr: function(text) {
    if (arguments.length > 1) text =
    Array.prototype.slice.call(arguments).join(' ');
    if (0) { // XXX disabled for safety typeof dump == 'function') {
      dump(text + '\n'); // fast, straight to the real console
    } else {
        console.error(text);
    }
},
```

After the `print` functions, there is a `canvas` function. This function is set up to alert the user to a lost WebGL context. We do not need that code right now, because we have removed the HTML Canvas. When we add the `canvas` element back in, we will need to restore this function. It also makes sense to update it to handle a lost context event, instead of just alerting the user.

```
canvas: (function() {
    var canvas = document.getElementById('canvas');
    // As a default initial behavior, pop up an alert when webgl
       context is lost. To make your
    // application robust, you may want to override this behavior
       before shipping!
    // See http://www.khronos.org/registry/webgl/specs/latest/1.0/#5.15.2
    canvas.addEventListener("webglcontextlost", function(e) {
        alert('WebGL context lost. You will need to reload the page.');
        e.preventDefault(); }, false);
    return canvas;
})(),
```

 There are several different situations when your web page could lose its WebGL context. The context is your portal into the GPU, and your app's access to the GPU is managed by both the browser and the operating system. Let's take a trip to *The Land of Metaphor*, where we imagine the GPU is a bus, the web browser is the bus driver, and the apps using their context are a bunch of rowdy middle school kids. If the bus driver (browser) feels that the kids (apps) are getting too rowdy, he can stop the bus (GPU), throw all the kids off the bus (make the apps lose their context), and let them come back one at a time if they promise to behave.

After that, the minimal shell has some code that keeps track of the module's status and dependencies. In this code, we can remove references to the `spinnerElement`, `progressElement`, and `statusElement`. Later, if we choose, we can replace these with elements to keep track of the state of loaded modules, but, for the moment, they are not needed. Here is the status and run dependency monitoring code in the minimal shell:

```
setStatus: function(text) {
    if (!Module.setStatus.last) Module.setStatus.last = { time:
        Date.now(), text: '' };
    if (text === Module.setStatus.last.text) return;
    var m = text.match(/([^(]+)\((\d+(\.\d+)?)\/(\d+)\)/);
    var now = Date.now();

    // if this is a progress update, skip it if too soon
    if (m && now - Module.setStatus.last.time < 30) return;
```

```
        Module.setStatus.last.time = now;
        Module.setStatus.last.text = text;
        if (m) {
            text = m[1];
        }
        console.log("status: " + text);
    },
    totalDependencies: 0,
    monitorRunDependencies: function(left) {
      this.totalDependencies = Math.max(this.totalDependencies, left);
        Module.setStatus(left ? 'Preparing... (' + (this.totalDependencies-
                        left) + '/' + this.totalDependencies + ')' : 'All
                        downloads complete.');
    }
    };
    Module.setStatus('Downloading...');
```

The final piece of JavaScript code inside the minimal shell file determines what JavaScript will do in the event of a browser error:

```
window.onerror = function() {
    Module.setStatus('Exception thrown, see JavaScript console');
    Module.setStatus = function(text) {
        if (text) Module.printErr('[post-exception status] ' + text);
    };
```

After our JavaScript, there is one more important line:

```
{{{ SCRIPT }}}
```

This tag tells Emscripten to place the link to the JavaScript glue code here. Here is an example of what gets compiled into the final HTML file:

```
<script async type="text/javascript" src="shell-min.js"></script>
```

shell-min.js is the JavaScript glue code that is built by Emscripten. In the next section, we will learn how to create our own HTML shell file.

Creating a new HTML shell and C file

In this section, we are going to create a new `shell.c` file that exposes several functions called from our JavaScript. We will also use `EM_ASM` to call the `InitWrappers` function that we will define inside the new HTML shell file that we will be creating. This function will create wrappers inside JavaScript that can call functions defined in the WebAssembly module. Before creating the new HTML shell file, we need to create the C code that will be called by the JavaScript wrappers inside the HTML shell:

1. Create the new `shell.c` file as follows:

```
#include <emscripten.h>
#include <stdlib.h>
#include <stdio.h>

int main() {
    printf("Hello World\n");
    EM_ASM( InitWrappers() );
    printf("Initialization Complete\n");
}

void test() {
    printf("button test\n");
}

void int_test( int num ) {
    printf("int test=%d\n", num);
}

void float_test( float num ) {
    printf("float test=%f\n", num);
}

void string_test( char* str ) {
    printf("string test=%s\n", str);
}
```

The `main` function runs when the WebAssembly module is loaded. At this point, the `Module` object can use `cwrap` to create a JavaScript version of that function that we can tie to `onclick` events on the HTML elements. Inside the `main` function, the `EM_ASM( InitWrappers() );` code calls an `InitWrappers()` function that is defined inside JavaScript in the HTML shell file. The DOM uses events to call the next four functions.

Another way we could have initialized the wrappers is by calling the `InitWrappers()` function from the `Module` object `postRun: []` array.

We will tie a call to the `test()` function to a button click in the DOM. The `int_test` function will be passed as a value from an input field in the DOM and will print a message to the console and `textarea` element that includes that integer, by using a `printf` statement. The `float_test` function will be passed a number as a floating point, printed to the console and `textarea` element. The `string_test` function will print out a string that is passed in from JavaScript.

Now, we are going to add the following code to an HTML shell file and call it `new_shell.html`. The code is based on the *Emscripten minimal shell file* created by the Emscripten team and explained in the previous section. We will present the entire HTML page divided into four parts.

To begin with, there is the beginning of the HTML file and the `head` element:

```
<!doctype html>
<html lang="en-us">
<head>
    <meta charset="utf-8">
    <meta http-equiv="Content-Type" content="text/html; charset=utf-8">
    <title>New Emscripten Shell</title>
    <link href="shell.css" rel="stylesheet" type="text/css">
</head>
```

Next, is the beginning of the `body` tag. After that, we have several HTML `input` elements as well as the `textarea` element:

```
<body>
    <div class="input_box"> </div>
    <div class="input_box">
        <button id="click_me" class="em_button">Click Me!</button>
    </div>
    <div class="input_box">
        <input type="number" id="int_num" max="9999" min="0" step="1"
         value="1" class="em_input">
        <button id="int_button" class="em_button">Int Click!</button>
    </div>
    <div class="input_box">
        <input type="number" id="float_num" max="99" min="0"
          step="0.01" value="0.0" class="em_input">
        <button id="float_button" class="em_button">Float Click!</button>
    </div>
```

```html
<div class="input_box"> </div>
<textarea class="em_textarea" id="output" rows="8"></textarea>
<div id="string_box">
    <button id="string_button" class="em_button">String Click!</button>
    <input id="string_input">
</div>
```

After our HTML, we have the beginning of our `script` tag, and some JavaScript code we have added to the default shell file:

```html
<script type='text/javascript'>
    function InitWrappers() {
        var test = Module.cwrap('test', 'undefined');
        var int_test = Module.cwrap('int_test', 'undefined', ['int']);
        var float_test = Module.cwrap('float_test', 'undefined',
                                        ['float']);
        var string_test = Module.cwrap('string_test', 'undefined',
                                        ['string']);
        document.getElementById("int_button").onclick = function() {

        if( int_test != null ) {
            int_test(document.getElementById('int_num').value);
        }
    }

    document.getElementById("string_button").onclick = function() {
        if( string_test != null ) {
            string_test(document.getElementById('string_input').value);
        }
    }

    document.getElementById("float_button").onclick = function() {
        if( float_test != null ) {
            float_test(document.getElementById('float_num').value);
        }
    }

    document.getElementById("click_me").onclick = function() {
        if( test != null ) {
            test();
        }
    }
}

function runbefore() {
    console.log("before module load");
}
```

```
function runafter() {
    console.log("after module load");
}
```

Next, we have the `Module` object that we brought in from the default shell file. After the `Module` object, we have the end to the `script` tag, the `{{{ SCRIPT }}}` tag, which is replaced by Emscripten when compiled, and the ending tags in our file:

```
var Module = {
    preRun: [runbefore],
    postRun: [runafter],
    print: (function() {
        var element = document.getElementById('output');
        if (element) element.value = ''; // clear browser cache
            return function(text) {
                if (arguments.length > 1) text =
                    Array.prototype.slice.call(arguments).join(' ');
                /*
                // The printf statement in C is currently writing to a
                    textarea. If we want to write
                // to an HTML tag, we would need to run these lines of
                    codes to make our text HTML safe
                text = text.replace(/&/g, "&amp;");
                text = text.replace(/</g, "&lt;");
                text = text.replace(/>/g, "&gt;");
                text = text.replace('\n', '<br>', 'g');
                */
                console.log(text);
                if (element) {
                    element.value += text + "\n";
                    element.scrollTop = element.scrollHeight;
                     // focus on bottom
                }
            };
    })(),
    printErr: function(text) {
        if (arguments.length > 1) text =
            Array.prototype.slice.call(arguments).join(' ');
        if (0) { // XXX disabled for safety typeof dump ==
                'function') {
            dump(text + '\n'); // fast, straight to the real
console
        } else {
            console.error(text);
        }
    },
    setStatus: function(text) {
        if (!Module.setStatus.last) Module.setStatus.last = { time:
```

```
            Date.now(), text: '' };
        if (text === Module.setStatus.last.text) return;
        var m = text.match(/([^(]+)\((\d+(\.\d+)?)\/(\d+)\)/);
        var now = Date.now();

        // if this is a progress update, skip it if too soon
        if (m && now - Module.setStatus.last.time < 30) return;
        Module.setStatus.last.time = now;
        Module.setStatus.last.text = text;

        if (m) {
            text = m[1];
        }
        console.log("status: " + text);
    },
    totalDependencies: 0,
    monitorRunDependencies: function(left) {
        this.totalDependencies = Math.max(this.totalDependencies,
                                          left);
        Module.setStatus(left ? 'Preparing... (' +
        (this.totalDependencies-left) + '/' +
        this.totalDependencies + ')' : 'All downloads complete.');
    }
};
Module.setStatus('Downloading...');
window.onerror = function() {
Module.setStatus('Exception thrown, see JavaScript console');
Module.setStatus = function(text) {
    if (text) Module.printErr('[post-exception status] ' + text);
};
};
</script>
{{{ SCRIPT }}}
</body>
</html>
```

These previous four sections all make up a single shell file called `new_shell.html`. You can create this code by typing out the last four parts into a file you name `new_shell.html`, or you can download the file from our GitHub page at https://github.com/PacktPublishing/Hands-On-Game-Development-with-WebAssembly/blob/master/Chapter02/new_shell.html.

Now that we have seen the entire `new_shell.html` file in large chunks, we can spend a little time breaking down the essential parts and going over it at a granular level. You will notice that we removed all of the CSS style code and have created a new `shell.css` file included with the following line:

```
<link href="shell.css" rel="stylesheet" type="text/css">
```

Next, we have reworked the HTML code inside this file to create elements that will interact with the WebAssembly module. First, we are going to add a button that will call the `test()` function inside the WebAssembly module:

```
<div class="input_box">
    <button id="click_me" class="em_button">Click Me!</button>
</div>
```

We will style the button and its included `div` element inside the `shell.css` file that we have created. We will need to define the function that will be called by the `onclick` event of this `button` element inside the JavaScript code we will write later. We will do something similar for the two input/button pairs we will define in the HTML, as demonstrated in the following code block:

```
<div class="input_box">
    <input type="number" id="int_num" max="9999" min="0" step="1"
     value="1" class="em_input">
    <button id="int_button" class="em_button">Int Click!</button>
</div>
<div class="input_box">
    <input type="number" id="float_num" max="99" min="0" step="0.01"
     value="0.0" class="em_input">
    <button id="float_button" class="em_button">Float Click!</button>
</div>
```

Like we did with the first `button` element, we will tie these next two buttons to functions that will make calls into the WebAssembly module. These function calls will also pass the values defined in the `input` elements into the WebAssembly functions. We have left the `textarea` element as an output for the `printf` calls that happen within the WebAssembly module. We have styled it differently in the CSS file, but we will leave the functionality unchanged:

```
<textarea class="em_textarea" id="output" rows="8"></textarea>
<div id="string_box">
    <button id="string_button" class="em_button">String Click!</button>
    <input id="string_input">
</div>
```

Underneath the `textarea` element, we have added one more `button` and a `string input` element. This button will call the `string_test` function inside the WebAssembly module, passing it the value inside the `string_input` element as a C `char*` parameter.

Now that we have defined all of the elements we need in the HTML, we will go through and add some JavaScript code to tie the JavaScript and WebAssembly module together. The first thing we need to do is define the `InitWrappers` function. `InitWrappers` will be called from within the `main` function in the C code:

```
function InitWrappers() {
    var test = Module.cwrap('test', 'undefined');
    var int_test = Module.cwrap('int_test', 'undefined', ['int']);
    var float_test = Module.cwrap('float_test', 'undefined',
                                  ['float']);
    var string_test = Module.cwrap('string_test', 'undefined',
                                   ['string']);
    document.getElementById("int_button").onclick = function() {
        if( int_test != null ) {
            int_test(document.getElementById('int_num').value);
        }
    }

    document.getElementById("string_button").onclick = function() {
        if( string_test != null ) {
            string_test(document.getElementById('string_input').value);
        }
    }

    document.getElementById("float_button").onclick = function() {
        if( float_test != null ) {
            float_test(document.getElementById('float_num').value);
        }
    }

    document.getElementById("click_me").onclick = function() {
        if( test != null ) {
            test();
        }
    }
}
```

This function uses `Module.cwrap` to create JavaScript function wrappers around the exported functions inside the WebAssembly module. The first parameter we pass to `cwrap` is the name of the C function we are wrapping. All of these JavaScript functions will return `undefined`. JavaScript does not have a `void` type like C, so when we declare the `return` type in JavaScript, we need to use the `undefined` type instead. If the function were to return an `int` or a `float`, we would need to put the `'number'` value here. The final parameter passed into `cwrap` is an array of strings that represent the C type of the parameters passed into the WebAssembly module.

After we have defined the JavaScript wrappers around the functions, we need to call them from the buttons. The first one of these calls is to the WebAssembly `int_test` function. Here is how we set the `onclick` event for the `int_button`:

```
document.getElementById("int_button").onclick = function() {
    if( int_test != null ) {
        int_test(document.getElementById('int_num').value);
    }
}
```

The first thing we will do is check to see whether `int_test` is defined. If so, we call the `int_test` wrapper we explained earlier, passing it the value from the `int_num` input. We then do something similar for all of the other buttons.

The next thing we do is create a `runbefore` and `runafter` function that we place in the `preRun` and `postRun` arrays on the `Module` object:

```
function runbefore() {
    console.log("before module load");
}
function runafter() {
    console.log("after module load");
}
var Module = {
    preRun: [runbefore],
    postRun: [runafter],
```

That will cause "before module load" to be printed to the console before the module is loaded, and "after module load" is printed after the module is loaded. These functions are not required; they are designed to show how you might run code before and after a WebAssembly module is loaded. If you do not want to call the `InitWrappers` function from the `main` function in the WebAssembly module, you could instead put that function inside the `postRun` array.

The remainder of the JavaScript code is similar to what you would find inside the `shell_minimal.html` file created by Emscripten. We have removed code that is superfluous for this demonstration, such as code related to the `spinnerElement`, `progressElement`, and `statusElement`, as well as code having to do with the HTML5 `canvas`. It is not that there is anything wrong with leaving that code in JavaScript, but it is not truly necessary for our demonstration, so we have removed it to reduce this shell to the minimum required.

Defining the CSS

Now that we have some basic HTML, we need to create a new `shell.css` file. Without any CSS styling, our page looks pretty terrible.

A page without styling will be similar to the one shown as follows:

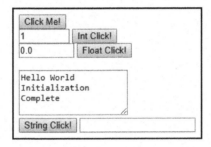

Figure 2.1: The Hello WebAssembly app without a CSS style

Luckily for us, a little bit of CSS goes a long way to make our web page look presentable. Here is what the new `shell.css` file we are creating looks like:

```
body {
    margin-top: 20px;
}

.input_box {
    width: 20%;
    display: inline-block;
}
.em_button {
    width: 45%;
    height: 40px;
    background-color: orangered;
    color: white;
```

```
        border: 2px solid white;
        font-size: 20px;
        border-radius: 8px;
        transition-duration: 0.5s;
    }

    .em_button:hover {
        background-color: orange;
        color: white;
        border: 2px solid white;
    }

    .em_input {
        width: 45%;
        height: 20px;
        font-size: 20px;
        background-color: darkslategray;
        color: white;
        padding: 6px;
    }

    #output {
        background-color: darkslategray;
        color: white;
        font-size: 16px;
        padding: 10px;
        padding-right: 0;
        margin-left: auto;
        margin-right: auto;
        display: block;
        width: 60%;
    }

    #string_box {
        padding-top: 10px;
        margin-left: auto;
        margin-right: auto;
        display: block;
        width: 60%;
    }

    #string_input {
        font-size: 20px;
        background-color: darkslategray;
        color: white;
        padding: 6px;
        margin-left: 5px;
        width: 45%;
```

```
    float: right;
}
```

Let me quickly walk through what we need to do to style this page. This book is not a book on CSS, but it does not hurt to cover the topic in a cursory fashion.

1. The first thing we will do is put a little 20-pixel margin on the page body to put a little bit of space between the browser toolbar and the content on our page:

   ```
   body {
       margin-top: 20px;
   }
   ```

2. We have created five input boxes that take up 20% of the browser width each. The boxes on the left and the right have nothing in them, so that the content takes up 60% of the browser width. They are displayed as an inline-block, so that they line up horizontally across the screen. Here is the CSS that makes it happen:

   ```
   .input_box {
       width: 20%;
       display: inline-block;
   }
   ```

3. We then have a few classes to style our buttons using a class called em_button:

   ```
   .em_button {
       width: 45%;
       height: 40px;
       background-color: orangered;
       color: white;
       border: 0px;
       font-size: 20px;
       border-radius: 8px;
       transition-duration: 0.2s;
   }

   .em_button:hover {
       background-color: orange;
   }
   ```

We have set the button width to take up 45% of the containing element. We set the button height to 40 pixels. We have set the button's color to orangered, and the text color to white. We remove the border by setting its width to 0 pixels. We have set the font size to 20 pixels and given it an 8 pixel border-radius, which provides the button with a rounded look. The last line sets the amount of time it takes to transition to a new color when the user hovers over the button.

After we finish the definition of the em_button class, we define
the em_button:hover class, which changes the color of the button when the user hovers
over it.

 Some versions of Safari require the line -webkit-transition-
duration: 0.2s; inside the em_button class definition to have a
transition to the hover state. Without this line, the button would instantly
change from orangered to orange in some versions of Safari, rather than
transitioning over 200 milliseconds.

The next class we define is for the input elements:

```
.em_input {
    width: 45%;
    height: 20px;
    font-size: 20px;
    background-color: darkslategray;
    color: white;
    padding: 6px;
}
```

We have set its height, width, and font-size at the beginning. We set the background
color to a darkslategray with white text. We have added 6 pixels of padding so that
there is a small space between the font and the edge of the input element.

The # in front of the name of a CSS element styles an ID instead of a class. An ID defines a
specific element where a class (preceded by a . in CSS) can be assigned to multiple
elements in your HTML. The next bit of CSS styles the textarea that has the ID of output:

```
#output {
    background-color: darkslategray;
    color: white;
    font-size: 16px;
    padding: 10px;
    margin-left: auto;
    margin-right: auto;
    display: block;
    width: 60%;
}
```

The first two lines set the background and text color. We set the font size to 16 pixels and add 10 pixels of padding. The next two lines use the left and right margin to center the textarea:

```
margin-left: auto;
margin-right: auto;
```

Setting display: block; puts this element on a line by itself. Setting the width to 60% makes the element take up 60% of the containing element, which, in this case, is the browser's body tag.

Finally, we style the string_box and string_input elements:

```
#string_box {
    padding-top: 10px;
    margin-left: auto;
    margin-right: auto;
    display: block;
    width: 60%;
}

#string_input {
    font-size: 20px;
    background-color: darkslategray;
    color: white;
    padding: 6px;
    margin-left: 5px;
    width: 45%;
    float: right;
}
```

The string_box is the box that contains the string button and the string input elements. We pad the top of the box to add some space between the string_box and the textarea above it. margin-left: auto and margin-right: auto center the box. Then, we use display:block and width: 60% to have it take up 60% of the web browser.

For the string_input element, we set the font size and the colors and pad it by 6 pixels. We set a left margin of 5 pixels to put some space on the left between the element and its button. We set it to take up 45% of the width of the containing element, while the float: right style pushes the element to the right side of the containing element.

To build our app, we need to run `emcc`:

```
emcc shell.c -o shell-test.html --shell-file new_shell.html -s
NO_EXIT_RUNTIME=1 -s EXPORTED_FUNCTIONS="['_test', '_string_test',
'_int_test', '_float_test', '_main']" -s
EXTRA_EXPORTED_RUNTIME_METHODS="['cwrap', 'ccall']"
```

`EXPORTED_FUNCTIONS` is used to define all of the functions called from JavaScript. They are listed with a preceding _ character. `EXTRA_EXPORTED_RUNTIME_METHODS` is used to make the `cwrap` and `ccall` methods available to the JavaScript inside our shell file. We are not currently using `ccall`, which is an alternative to `cwrap`, which we may choose to use in the future.

It is important to remember that you must run WebAssembly apps using a web server, or with `emrun`. If you would like to run your WebAssembly app using `emrun`, you must compile it with the `--emrun` flag. The web browser requires a web server to stream the WebAssembly module. If you attempt to open an HTML page that uses WebAssembly in a browser directly from your hard drive, that WebAssembly module will not load.

Now that we have added some CSS styling, we have a much nicer looking app:

Figure 2.2: The Hello WebAssembly app with a CSS style

In the next section, we will discuss HTML5 web game development.

HTML5 and game development

Most HTML rendering is done through the HTML **Document Object Model (DOM)**. The DOM is what is known as a *retained mode* graphical library. Retained mode graphics retain a tree known as a **scene graph**. This scene graph keeps track of all the graphical elements in our model and how to render them. The nice thing about retained mode graphics is that they are straightforward for a developer to manage. The graphical library does all the heavy lifting and keeps track of our objects for us as well as where they render. The downside is that a retained mode system takes up a lot more memory and provides a lot less control to the developer. When we write HTML5 games, we could take images rendered in the DOM using <IMG> HTML elements and move those elements around using JavaScript or CSS animations to manipulate the positions of those images within the DOM directly.

However, this would, in most circumstances, make the game painfully slow. Every time we move an object in our DOM, it forces our browser to recalculate the position of all other objects within our DOM. Because of this, manipulating objects from within our DOM to make web games is usually a non-starter.

Immediate mode versus retained mode

Immediate mode is frequently thought of as the opposite of retained mode, but, in practice, when we write code for an immediate mode system, we may build on top of an API that gives us some of the functionality of a retained mode library. Immediate mode forces the developer to do all or most of the heavy lifting done by a retained mode library. We, as developers, are forced to manage our scene graph, and understand what graphical objects we need to render and how and when those objects must render. In short, it is a lot more work, but if done well, the payoff is a game that will render much faster than what is possible to render using the DOM.

You might be asking yourself right now: *How do I go about using this Immediate Mode thingy?* Enter the HTML5 Canvas! In 2004, Apple Inc. developed the canvas element as an immediate mode display tag for Apple's proprietary browser technology. The canvas partitions off a section of our web page, which allows us to render to that area using immediate mode rendering. That will enable us to render to a part of the DOM (the canvas) without requiring the browser to recalculate the position of all the elements from within the DOM. That allows the browser to optimize the rendering of the canvas further, using the computer's **Graphical Processing Unit (GPU)**.

Adding a canvas to the Emscripten template

In an earlier part of this chapter, we discussed making calls to the Emscripten WebAssembly app from a shell template. Now that you know how to make the interaction work between JavaScript and WebAssembly, we can add a `canvas` element back into the template and start to manipulate that `canvas` using the WebAssembly module. We are going to create a new `.c` file that will call a JavaScript function passing it an `x` and `y` coordinate. The JavaScript function will manipulate a spaceship image, moving it around the `canvas`. We will also create a brand new shell file called `canvas_shell.html`.

As we did for the previous version of our shell, we will start by breaking this file down into four sections to discuss it at a high level. We will then discuss the essential parts of this file a piece at a time.

1. The beginning of the HTML file starts with the opening HTML tag and the `head` element:

```
<!doctype html>
<html lang="en-us">
<head>
    <meta charset="utf-8">
    <meta http-equiv="Content-Type" content="text/html;
charset=utf-8">
    <title>Canvas Shell</title>
    <link href="canvas.css" rel="stylesheet" type="text/css">
</head>
```

2. After that, we have the opening `body` tag, and we have removed many of the HTML elements that we had in the earlier version of this file:

```
<body>
    <canvas id="canvas" width="800" height="600"
oncontextmenu="event.preventDefault()"></canvas>
    <textarea class="em_textarea" id="output" rows="8"></textarea>
    <img src="spaceship.png" id="spaceship">
```

3. Next, there is the opening `script` tag, a few global JavaScript variables, and a few new functions that we added:

```
<script type='text/javascript'>
    var img = null;
    var canvas = null;
    var ctx = null;
    function ShipPosition( ship_x, ship_y ) {
        if( img == null ) {
```

```
                    return;
            }
        ctx.fillStyle = "black";
        ctx.fillRect(0, 0, 800, 600);
        ctx.save();
        ctx.translate(ship_x, ship_y);
        ctx.drawImage(img, 0, 0, img.width, img.height);
        ctx.restore();
    }
    function ModuleLoaded() {
        img = document.getElementById('spaceship');
        canvas = document.getElementById('canvas');
        ctx = canvas.getContext("2d");
    }
```

4. After the new JavaScript functions, we have the new definition of the `Module` object:

```
    var Module = {
        preRun: [],
        postRun: [ModuleLoaded],
        print: (function() {
            var element = document.getElementById('output');
            if (element) element.value = ''; // clear browser cache
            return function(text) {
                if (arguments.length > 1) text =
                Array.prototype.slice.call(arguments).join(' ');
                    // uncomment block below if you want to write
                       to an html element
                    /*
                    text = text.replace(/&/g, "&amp;");
                    text = text.replace(/</g, "&lt;");
                    text = text.replace(/>/g, "&gt;");
                    text = text.replace('\n', '<br>', 'g');
                    */
                    console.log(text);
                    if (element) {
                        element.value += text + "\n";
                        element.scrollTop = element.scrollHeight;
// focus on bottom
                    }
                };
            })(),
            printErr: function(text) {
                if (arguments.length > 1) text =
                    Array.prototype.slice.call(arguments).join(' ');
                console.error(text);
            },
```

```
        canvas: (function() {
            var canvas = document.getElementById('canvas');
            canvas.addEventListener("webglcontextlost",
            function(e) {
                alert('WebGL context lost. You will need to
                        reload the page.');
                e.preventDefault(); },
                false);
            return canvas;
        })(),
        setStatus: function(text) {
            if (!Module.setStatus.last) Module.setStatus.last =
            { time: Date.now(), text: '' };
            if (text === Module.setStatus.last.text) return;
            var m = text.match(/([^(]+)\((\d+
            (\.\d+)?)\/(\d+)\)/);
            var now = Date.now();

            // if this is a progress update, skip it if too
               soon
            if (m && now - Module.setStatus.last.time < 30)
return;
            Module.setStatus.last.time = now;
            Module.setStatus.last.text = text;
            if (m) {
                text = m[1];
            }
            console.log("status: " + text);
        },
        totalDependencies: 0,
        monitorRunDependencies: function(left) {
            this.totalDependencies =
            Math.max(this.totalDependencies, left);
            Module.setStatus(left ? 'Preparing... (' +
            (this.totalDependencies-left) +
                '/' + this.totalDependencies + ')' : 'All
                downloads complete.');
        }
    };
    Module.setStatus('Downloading...');
    window.onerror = function() {
        Module.setStatus('Exception thrown, see JavaScript
                            console');
        Module.setStatus = function(text) {
            if (text) Module.printErr('[post-exception status]
            ' + text);
        };
    };
```

The last few lines close out our tags and include the `{{{ SCRIPT }}}` Emscripten tag:

```
    </script>
{{{ SCRIPT }}}
</body>
</html>
```

Those previous four blocks of code define our new `canvas_shell.html` file. If you would like to download the file, you can find it on GitHub at the following address: `https://github.com/PacktPublishing/Hands-On-Game-Development-with-WebAssembly/blob/master/Chapter02/canvas.html`.

Now that we have looked at the code at a high level, we can look at the source in more detail. In the `head` section of the HTML, we are changing the `title` and the `name` of the CSS file that we are linking. Here is the change in the HTML `head`:

```
<title>Canvas Shell</title>
<link href="canvas.css" rel="stylesheet" type="text/css">
```

We do not need most of the elements that were in the previous `<body>` tag. We need a `canvas`, which we had removed from the `shell_minimal.html` file provided by Emscripten, but now we need to add it back in. We are keeping the `textarea` that was initially in the minimal shell, and we are adding a new `img` tag that has a spaceship image taken from a TypeScript canvas tutorial on the `embed.com` website at `https://www.embed.com/typescript-games/draw-image.html`. Here are the new HTML tags in the `body` element:

```
<canvas id="canvas" width="800" height="600"
oncontextmenu="event.preventDefault()"></canvas>
<textarea class="em_textarea" id="output" rows="8"></textarea>
<img src="spaceship.png" id="spaceship">
```

Finally, we need to change the JavaScript code. The first thing we are going to do is add three variables at the beginning to hold a reference to the `canvas` element, the canvas context, and the new spaceship `img` element:

```
var img = null;
var canvas = null;
var ctx = null;
```

The next thing we are adding to the JavaScript is a function that renders the spaceship image to the canvas at a given `x` and `y` coordinate:

```
function ShipPosition( ship_x, ship_y ) {
    if( img == null ) {
        return;
```

```
    }
    ctx.fillStyle = "black";
    ctx.fillRect(0, 0, 800, 600);
    ctx.save();
    ctx.translate(ship_x, ship_y);
    ctx.drawImage(img, 0, 0, img.width, img.height);
    ctx.restore();
}
```

This function first checks to see whether the `img` variable is a value other than `null`. That will let us know if the module has been loaded or not because the `img` variable starts set to null. The next thing we do is clear the canvas with the color black using the `ctx.fillStyle` = "black" line to set the context fill style to the color `black`, before calling `ctx.fillRect` to draw a rectangle that fills the entire canvas with a black rectangle. The next four lines save off the canvas context, translate the context position to the ship's x and y coordinate value, and then draw the ship image to the canvas. The last one of these four lines performs a context restore to set our translation back to (0,0) where it started.

After defining this function, the WebAssembly module can call it. We need to set up some initialization code to initialize those three variables when the module is loaded. Here is that code:

```
function ModuleLoaded() {
    img = document.getElementById('spaceship');
    canvas = document.getElementById('canvas');
    ctx = canvas.getContext("2d");
}
var Module = {
    preRun: [],
    postRun: [ModuleLoaded],
```

The `ModuleLoaded` function uses `getElementById` to set `img` and `canvas` to the spaceship and `canvas` HTML elements, respectively. We will then call `canvas.getContext("2d")` to get the 2D canvas context and set the `ctx` variable to that context. All of this gets called when the `Module` object finishes loading because we added the `ModuleLoaded` function to the `postRun` array.

We have also added back the `canvas` function that was on the `Module` object in the minimum shell file, which we had removed along with the canvas in an earlier tutorial. That code watches the canvas context and alerts the user if that context is lost. Eventually, we will want this code to fix the problem, but, for now, it is good to know when it happens. Here is that code:

```
canvas: (function() {
    var canvas = document.getElementById('canvas');
```

```
    // As a default initial behavior, pop up an alert when webgl
       context is lost. To make your
    // application robust, you may want to override this behavior
       before shipping!
    // See http://www.khronos.org/registry/webgl/specs/latest/1.0/#5.15.2
    canvas.addEventListener("webglcontextlost", function(e) {
        alert('WebGL context lost. You will need to reload the page.');
        e.preventDefault(); }, false);
    return canvas;
})(),
```

To go along with this new HTML shell file, we have created a new `canvas.c` file to compile into a WebAssembly module. Be aware that, in the long run, we will be doing a lot less in our JavaScript and a lot more inside our WebAssembly C/C++ code. Here is the new `canvas.c` file:

```
#include <emscripten.h>
#include <stdlib.h>
#include <stdio.h>

int ship_x = 0;
int ship_y = 0;

void MoveShip() {
    ship_x += 2;
    ship_y++;

    if( ship_x >= 800 ) {
        ship_x = -128;
    }

    if( ship_y >= 600 ) {
        ship_y = -128;
    }
    EM_ASM( ShipPosition($0, $1), ship_x, ship_y );
}

int main() {
    printf("Begin main\n");
    emscripten_set_main_loop(MoveShip, 0, 0);
    return 1;
}
```

To start, we create a `ship_x` and `ship_y` variable to track the ship's x and y coordinates. After that, we create a `MoveShip` function. This function increments the ship's x position by 2 and the ship's y position by 1 each time it is called. It also checks to see whether the ship's x coordinates have left the canvas on the right side, which moves it back to the left side if it has, and does something similar if the ship has moved off the canvas on the bottom. The last thing this function does is call our JavaScript `ShipPosition` function, passing it the ship's x and y coordinates. That final step is what will draw our spaceship to the new coordinates on the HTML5 canvas element.

In the new version of our `main` function, we have the following line:

```
emscripten_set_main_loop(MoveShip, 0, 0);
```

This line turns the function passed in as the first parameter into a game loop. We will go into more detail about how `emscripten_set_main_loop` works in a later chapter, but for the moment, know that this causes the `MoveShip` function to be called every time a new frame is rendered to our canvas.

Finally, we will create a new `canvas.css` file that keeps the code for the `body` and `#output` CSS and adds a new `#canvas` CSS class. Here are the contents of the `canvas.css` file:

```css
body {
    margin-top: 20px;
}

#output {
    background-color: darkslategray;
    color: white;
    font-size: 16px;
    padding: 10px;
    margin-left: auto;
    margin-right: auto;
    display: block;
    width: 60%;
}

#canvas {
    width: 800px;
    height: 600px;
    margin-left: auto;
    margin-right: auto;
    display: block;
}
```

After everything is complete, we will use `emcc` to compile the new `canvas.html` file as well as `canvas.wasm` and the `canvas.js` glue code. Here is what the call to `emcc` will look like:

```
emcc canvas.c -o canvas.html --shell-file canvas_shell.html
```

Immediately after `emcc`, we pass in the name of the `.c` file, `canvas.c`, which will be used to compile our WASM module. The `-o` flag tells our compiler that the next argument will be the output. Using an output file with a `.html` extension tells `emcc` to compile the WASM, JavaScript, and HTML files. The next flag passed in is `--shell-file`, which tells `emcc` that the argument to follow is the name of the HTML shell file, which will be used to create the HTML file of our final output.

 It is important to remember that you must run WebAssembly apps using a web server, or with `emrun`. If you would like to run your WebAssembly app using `emrun`, you must compile it with the `--emrun` flag. The web browser requires a web server to stream the WebAssembly module. If you attempt to open an HTML page that uses WebAssembly in a browser directly from your hard drive, that WebAssembly module will not load.

The following is a screenshot of `canvas.html`:

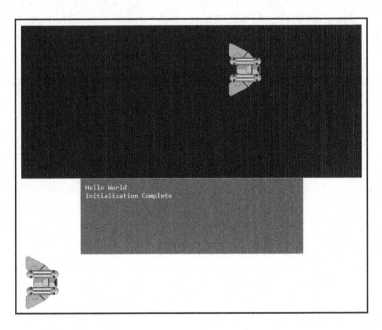

Figure 2.3: Our first WebAssembly HTML5 canvas app

Summary

In this chapter, we discussed the Emscripten minimal shell HTML file, what its various components are, and how they work. We also wrote about what parts of the file we can do without, if we are not using our shell to generate canvas code. You learned about the `Module` object, and how it is the interface that uses the JavaScript glue code to tie the JavaScript in our HTML and our WebAssembly together. We then created a new WebAssembly module that contained functions we exported to allow JavaScript to use `Module.cwrap` to create JavaScript functions we could then call from our DOM that executes our WebAssembly functions.

We created a brand new HTML shell file that used some of the `Module` code from the Emscripten minimal shell, but rewrote the HTML and CSS of the original shell almost entirely. We were then able to compile that new C code and HTML shell file into a working WebAssembly app that was able to call WebAssembly functions from JavaScript, as well as call JavaScript functions from WebAssembly.

We discussed the benefits of using the HTML5 canvas element, and the differences between immediate and retained mode graphics. We also explained why it makes sense for games and other graphics-intensive tasks to use immediate mode instead of retained mode.

We then created a shell file to make use of the HTML5 canvas element. We added JavaScript code to draw an image to the canvas and wrote C code that used WebAssembly to modify the position of that image on the canvas every frame creating the appearance of a moving spaceship on the HTML5 canvas.

In the next chapter, we will introduce you to WebGL, what it is, and how it improves graphics rendering on the web.

Introduction to WebGL

After Apple created the Canvas element, the Mozilla Foundation began working on a Canvas 3D prototype in 2006, and by 2007, there were implementations of this early version, which would eventually become WebGL. In 2009, a consortium called the Kronos Group began a WebGL Working Group. By 2011, this group had produced the 1.0 version of WebGL, which is based on the OpenGL ES 2.0 API.

As I stated earlier, WebGL was seen as a 3D rendering API that would be used with the HTML5 Canvas element. Its implementation eliminates some of the rendering bottlenecks of the traditional 2D canvas API and gives near-direct access to the computer's GPU. Because of this, it is typically faster to use WebGL to render 2D images to the HTML5 canvas than it is to use the original 2D canvas implementation. However, WebGL is significantly more complicated to use due to the added complexity of three-dimensional rendering. Because of this, several libraries are built on top of WebGL. This allows users to work with WebGL but use a simplified 2D API. If we were writing our game in traditional JavaScript, we might use a library such as Pixi.js or Cocos2d-x for 2D rendering on top of WebGL in order to simplify our code. Right now, WebAssembly uses an implementation of **Simple DirectMedia Layer (SDL)**, and is the library that's used by most developers to write games. This WebAssembly version of SDL is built on top of WebGL and provides high-end performance, but is much easier to use.

Using SDL does not prevent you from also using WebGL directly from within the C++ code compiled into WebAssembly. There are times where we may be interested in directly interacting with WebGL because the features we are interested in are not directly available from within SDL. One example of these use cases is creating custom shaders that allow for special 2D lighting effects.

 In this chapter, you will need an image file from the GitHub project to run the examples. The app requires the /Chapter03/spaceship.png image file from the project directory. Please download the project from the following URL: https://github.com/PacktPublishing/Hands-On-Game-Development-with-WebAssembly.

In this chapter, we will be covering the following topics:

- WebGL and canvas contexts
- An introduction to WebGL shaders
- WebGL and JavaScript

WebGL and canvas contexts

WebGL is a rendering context for drawing to the HTML5 element, and is an alternative to the 2D rendering context. Often, when someone mentions the canvas, they are referring to the 2D rendering context, which is accessed by calling getContext and passing in the string 2d. Both contexts are methods of rendering to the HTML5 canvas element. A context is a type of API for immediate mode rendering. Two different WebGL contexts can be requested, both of which provide access to different versions of the WebGL API. These contexts are *webgl* and *webgl2*. In the following examples, I will be using the *webgl* context and will be using the WebGL 1.0 API. There is also a rarely used context for rendering a bitmap to the canvas that we can access by passing in bitmaprenderer as a string value.

 I want to point out that the term canvas is sometimes used to refer to the 2D canvas context and sometimes used to refer to the immediate mode rendering HTML5 canvas element. When I refer to canvas in this book without mentioning the 2D context, I am referring to the HTML5 canvas element.

In the next section, I will introduce you to shaders and the GLSL shader language.

An introduction to WebGL shaders

When OpenGL or WebGL interact with a GPU, they pass in data to tell the GPU the geometry and textures it needs to render. At this point, the GPU needs to know how it must render those textures and the geometry associated with them into a single 2D image that will be displayed on your computer monitor. **OpenGL Shader Language (GLSL)** is a language that is used with both OpenGL and WebGL to instruct the GPU on how to render a 2D image.

 Technically, WebGL uses the GLSL ES shader language (sometimes referred to as ELSL), which is a subset of the GLSL language. GLSL ES is the shader language that's used with OpenGL ES, a mobile-friendly subset of OpenGL (the ES is for Embedded Systems). Because WebGL is based on OpenGL ES, it inherited the GLSL ES shader language. Note that whenever I refer to GLSL within the context of WebGL or WebAssembly, I am referring to GLSL ES.

The WebGL rendering pipeline requires us to write two types of shaders to render an image to the screen. These are the vertex shader, which renders the geometry on a per-vertex basis, and the fragment shader, which renders pixel candidates known as fragments. The GLSL looks a lot like the C language, so the code will look somewhat familiar if you work in C or C++.

This introduction to GLSL shaders will not go into a lot of detail. In a later chapter, I will discuss WebGL shaders more extensively. Right now, I only want to introduce the concept and show you a very simple 2D WebGL shader. I will go into a lot more detail in the chapter on 2D lighting. Here is an example of a simple vertex shader that is used to render quads for a 2D WebGL rendering engine:

```
precision mediump float;

attribute vec4 a_position;
attribute vec2 a_texcoord;

uniform vec4 u_translate;

varying vec2 v_texcoord;

void main() {
    gl_Position = u_translate + a_position;
    v_texcoord = a_texcoord;
}
```

This very simple shader takes in the position of a vertex and moves it based on a positional uniform value that's passed into the shader through WebGL. This shader will run on every single vertex in our geometry. In a 2D game, all geometry would be rendered as a quad (that is, a rectangle). Using WebGL in this way allows us to make better use of the computer's GPU. Let me briefly discuss what is going on in the code of this vertex shader.

 If you are new to game development, the concept of vertex and pixel shaders may feel a little foreign. They are not as mysterious as they may first seem. You may want to quickly read over the Wikipedia *Shader* article if you want a better understanding of what shaders are (`https://en.wikipedia.org/wiki/Shader`). If you are still feeling lost, feel free to ask me questions on Twitter (`@battagline`).

The first line of this shader sets the floating-point precision:

```
precision mediump float;
```

All floating-point operations on a computer are approximations for real fractions. We can approximate 1/3 with a low precision using 0.333 and with higher precision with 0.33333333. The precision line of the code indicates the precision of the floating-point values on the GPU. We can use one of three possible precisions: `highp`, `mediump`, or `lowp`. The higher the floating-point precision, the slower the GPU will execute the code, but the higher the accuracy of all the values of the computations. In general, I have kept this value at `mediump`, and that has worked well for me. If you have an application that demands performance over precision, you can change this to `lowp`. If you require high precision, be sure that you know the capabilities of the target GPUs. Not all GPUs support `highp`.

The attribute variables are values that are passed in with the vertex arrays into the pipeline. In our code, these values include the texture coordinates associated with the vertex, as well as the 2D translation matrix associated with the vertex:

```
attribute vec4 a_position;
attribute vec2 a_texcoord;
```

The uniform variable type is a type of variable that remains constant across all vertices and fragments. In this vertex shader, we are passing in one uniform vector, `u_translate`. Typically, you would not want to translate all your vertices by the same amount unless it is for a camera, but because we are only writing a WebGL program to draw a single sprite, using a `uniform` variable for `translate` will work fine:

```
uniform vec4 u_translate;
```

The `varying` variables (sometimes known as interpolators) are values that are passed from the vertex shader into the fragment shader, with each fragment in the fragment shader getting an interpolated version of that value. In this code, the only `varying` variable is the texture coordinate for the vertex:

```
varying vec2 v_texcoord;
```

In mathematics, an interpolated value is a calculated intermediate value. For example, if we interpolate the halfway point between 0.2 and 1.2, we would get a value of 0.7. That is, the starting value of 0.2, plus the average of (1.2 - 0.2) / 2 = 0.5. So, 0.2 + 0.5 = 0.7. Values passed from the vertex shader to the fragment shader using the `varying` keyword will be interpolated based on the position of the fragments relative to the vertex.

Finally, the code executed in the vertex shader is inside of the `main` function. This code takes the position of the vertex and multiplies it by the translation matrix to get the world coordinates of the vertex so that it can place them into `gl_Position`. It then sets the texture coordinate that's passed into the vertex shader directly into the varying variable so that it can pass it into the fragment shader:

```
void main() {
    gl_Position = u_translate + a_position;
    v_texcoord = a_texcoord;
}
```

After the vertex shader has been run, all the fragments that vertex shader generated are run through the fragment shader, which interpolates all of the varying variables for each fragment.

Here is a simple example of a fragment shader:

```
precision mediump float;

varying vec2 v_texcoord;

uniform sampler2D u_texture;

void main() {
    gl_FragColor = texture2D(u_texture, v_texcoord);
}
```

Just like in our vertex shader, we start by setting our floating-point precision to `mediump`. The fragments have a `uniform sample2D` texture that defines the texture map that's used to generate the 2D sprites in our game:

```
uniform sampler2D u_texture;
```

`uniform` is a little like a global variable that is passed into the pipeline and applies to either every vertex or every fragment in the shader that uses it. The code that's executed in the `main` function is also straightforward. It takes the interpolated texture coordinate from the `v_texcoord` varying variable and retrieves the color value from our sampled texture, and then uses that value to set the color of the `gl_FragColor` fragment:

```
void main() {
    gl_FragColor = texture2D(u_texture, v_texcoord);
}
```

Drawing a simple 2D image to the screen using WebGL directly inside of JavaScript requires a lot more code. In the next section, we will write out the simplest version of a 2D sprite rendering WebGL app I can think of, which happens to be a new version of the 2D canvas app we wrote in the previous chapter. I think it is worthwhile to see the differences between the two methods of rendering 2D images to the HTML canvas. Knowing more about WebGL will also help us understand what is going on behind the scenes when we eventually use the SDL API in WebAssembly. I am going to try and keep the demonstration and code as simple as I possibly can while creating the WebGL JavaScript app.

 As I mentioned previously, the point of this chapter is for you to get some hands-on experience with WebGL. For most of this book, we will not directly deal with WebGL, but rather use the simpler SDL API. If you are not interested in writing your own shaders, you can consider this chapter optional but beneficial information.

In the next section, we will learn how to draw to the canvas with WebGL.

WebGL and JavaScript

As we learned in the previous chapter, working with the 2D canvas was pretty straightforward. To draw an image, you just need to translate the context to the pixel coordinates where you want to draw the image, and call the `drawImage` context function by passing in the image, its width, and its height. You could make this even simpler and forget about the translation passing the x and y coordinates directly into the `drawImage` function if you prefer. With the 2D canvas, you are working with images, but with WebGL, you are always working with 3D geometry, even when you are coding a 2D game. With WebGL, you will need to render textures onto geometry. You need to work with vertex buffers and texture coordinates. The vertex shader we wrote earlier takes 3D coordinate data and texture coordinates and passes those values onto a fragment shader that will interpolate between the geometry, and use a texture sampling function to retrieve the proper texture data to render pixels to the canvas.

WebGL coordinate system versus 2D canvas

With WebGL, the center of the canvas element is the origin point (0,0). **Positive Y** is up, whereas **Positive X** is to the right. This is a bit more intuitive for someone who has never worked with 2D graphics, as it is similar to quadrants in coordinate geometry, which we learned about in grade school. With the 2D canvas, you are always working with pixels, and there are no negative numbers that appear on the canvas:

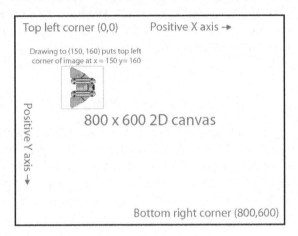

When you called `drawImage`, the X and Y coordinates were where the top left corner of the image would draw. WebGL is a bit different. Everything is using geometry, and both a vertex and a pixel shader are required. We convert the image into a texture and then stretch it over the geometry so that it's displayed. Here is what the WebGL coordinate system looks like:

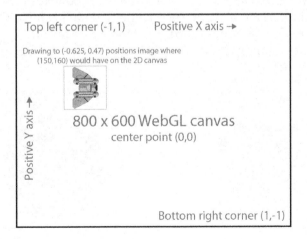

If you want to place an image at a specific pixel location on the canvas, you have to know the width and height of your canvas. The **center point** of your canvas is **(0,0)**, the **Top left corner** is **(-1, 1)**, and the **Bottom right corner** is **(1, -1)**. So, if you want to place an image at x=150, y=160 you need to use the following equation to find the WebGL x coordinate:

```
webgl_x = (pixel_x - canvas_width / 2) / (canvas_width / 2)
```

So, for a `pixel_x` position of 150, we have to subtract 400 from 150 to get -250. Then, we have to divide -250 by 400, and we would get -0.625. We have to do something similar to get the y coordinate for WebGL, but the sign of the axes are flipped, so instead of what we did for the `pixel_x` value, we need to do the following:

```
((canvas_height / 2) - pixel_y) / (canvas_height / 2)
```

By plugging in the values, we get ((600 / 2) - 160) / (600 / 2) or (300 - 160) / 300 = 0.47.

 I am skipping a lot of information about WebGL to simplify this explanation. WebGL is not a 2D space, even though I am treating it as a 2D space in this example. Because it is a 3D space, the size of the canvas in units is based on a view area known as clip space. Mozilla has an excellent article on clip space if you would like to learn more: `https://developer.mozilla.org/en-US/docs/Web/API/WebGL_API/WebGL_model_view_projection`.

Vertex and UV data

Before we look at a large chunk of scary WebGL JavaScript code, I want to briefly discuss data buffers and how we are going to pass the geometry and texture coordinate data into the shaders. We will be passing in 32-bit floating point data in a large buffer that will contain a combination of the X and Y coordinates for the vertex and UV texture coordinates for that same vertex. UV mapping is the method by which your GPU maps 2D texture coordinates onto 3D geometry:

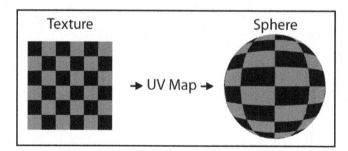

WebGL and OpenGL accomplish this by assigning a U and V coordinate to every vertex. A UV coordinate of (0,0) assigned to a vertex means that the vertex will be colored based on the color in the texture in the top left corner. A UV coordinate of (1,1) would imply that it would be painted based on what color is in the texture on the bottom right. As we interpolate between the points in our 3D object, we also interpolate between the different UV coordinates inside of the texture. Those UV coordinates can be sampled in our fragment shader using the `texture2D` built-in function by passing in the texture and the current UV coordinates.

Let's take a look at the vertex and texture data array that we are using inside of this WebGL app:

```
var vertex_texture_data = new Float32Array([
    //  X,       Y,       U,     V
      0.16,    0.213,   1.0,   1.0,
     -0.16,    0.213,   0.0,   1.0,
      0.16,   -0.213,   1.0,   0.0,
     -0.16,   -0.213,   0.0,   0.0,
     -0.16,    0.213,   0.0,   1.0,
      0.16,   -0.213,   1.0,   0.0
]);
```

This data has been typed out in rows and columns. Even though this is a linear array of data, the formatting allows you to see that we have four floating-point values that will be passed in for each vertex. There is a comment above the data showing what each column represents. The first two data values are the X and Y coordinates of the geometry. The second two values are the U and V coordinates that map the texture to the X and Y coordinates in the geometry. There are six rows here, even though we are rendering a rectangle. The reason we need six points instead of just four is that the geometry used by WebGL typically consists of triangles. Because of this, we will need to repeat two of the vertices.

You may be wondering, *why triangles?* Well, there was a time when computer graphics used geometry that was not decomposed into triangles. But a problem arises when you have a quad, and not all the points are coplanar (in the same plane). This is the same problem I have whenever I go to a bar that uses four-legged stools. I am pretty sure the existence of the four-legged stool is some sort of Illuminati plot to keep me off balance, but I digress. Because three points define a plane, a triangle is, by definition, always coplanar, just like a three-legged stool will never wobble.

2D canvas to WebGL

Let's begin by copying out canvas code from the `Chapter02` directory into the `Chapter03` directory. Next, we are going to rename the `canvas_shell.html` file to `webgl_shell.html`. We will rename `canvas.css` to `webgl.css`. Lastly, we will rename the `canvas.c` file `webgl.c`. We will also need to make sure that we copy over the `spaceship.png` file. We are not going to be changing the `webgl.css` file at all. We will make the most significant changes to the `webgl_shell.html` file. There is a lot of code that must be added to make the switch from 2D canvas to WebGL; almost all of it is additional JavaScript code. We will need to make some minor tweaks to `webgl.c` so that the ship's position in the `MoveShip` function reflects the WebGL coordinate system with its origin in the center of the canvas.

Before we begin, I would like to mention that this WebGL code is not meant to be production ready. The game we will be creating will not use WebGL in the way that I am demonstrating here. That is not the most efficient or scalable code. What we are writing will not be able to render more than one sprite at a time without significant changes. The reason I am walking you through what it takes to render 2D images using WebGL is to give you an idea of what is going on behind the scenes when you are using a library like SDL. If you do not care how things work behind the scenes, no one will fault you for skipping ahead. Personally, I always prefer knowing a little more.

Minor tweaks to the head tag

Inside of our `head` tag, we will want to change `title`, and because we renamed `canvas.css` to `webgl.css`, we will need to point our `link` tag to the new stylesheet name. Here are the only two tags that must change at the beginning of the HTML:

```
<title>WebGL Shell</title>
<link href="webgl.css" rel="stylesheet" type="text/css">
```

Later in the HTML, we will remove the `img` tag where the `src` is set to `"spaceship.png"`. It is not strictly necessary to do this. In the canvas version, we were using this tag to render an image to the canvas. In this WebGL version, we will load the image dynamically, so it is not necessary to keep it around, but if you forget to remove it, having it there will not harm the app in any way.

Major JavaScript changes

The `Module` code inside of the JavaScript portion of the `webgl_shell.html` file will remain the same, so you do not have to worry about modifying anything after the following line:

```
var Module = {
```

However, the top half of the code in the `script` tag is going to require some significant modifications. You may want to start fresh and delete the entire module.

WebGL global variables

The first thing we are going to do is create a lot of JavaScript global variables. If this code were meant for more than demonstration, using this many global variables is generally frowned upon and considered bad practice. But for what we are doing right now, it helps simplify things:

```
<script type='text/javascript'>
 var gl = null; // WebGLRenderingContext
 var program = null; // WebGLProgram
 var texture = null; // WebGLTexture
 var img = null; // HTMLImageElement
 var canvas = null;
 var image_width = 0;
 var image_height = 0;
 var vertex_texture_buffer = null; // WebGLBuffer
 var a_texcoord_location = null; // GLint
 var a_position_location = null; // GLint
 var u_translate_location = null; // WebGLUniformLocation
 var u_texture_location = null; // WebGLUniformLocation
```

The first variable, `gl`, is the new version of the rendering context. Typically, if you are using a 2D rendering context, you call it `ctx`, and if you are using a WebGL rendering context, you name it `gl`. The second line defines the program variable. When we compile the vertex and fragment shaders, we get a compiled version in the form of a `WebGLProgram` object stored inside of this `program` variable. The `texture` variable will hold a `WebGLTexture` that we will be loading from the `spaceship.png` image file. That is the image that we used in the previous chapter for the 2D canvas tutorial. The `img` variable will be used to load the `spaceship.png` image file that will be used to load the texture. The canvas variable will once again be a reference to our HTML canvas element and `image_width`, and `image_height` will hold the height and width of the `spaceship.png` image once it is loaded.

The `vertex_texture_buffer` attribute is a buffer that will be used to transfer vertex geometry and texture data to the GPU so that the shader we wrote in the previous section can use it. The `a_texcoord_location` and `a_position_location` variables will be used to hold references to the `a_texcoord` and `a_position` attribute variables in the vertex shader, and finally, `u_translate_location` and `u_texture_location` are used to reference the `u_translate` and `u_texture` uniform variables in the shader.

The return of vertex and texture data

Would you be upset if I told you we had some more variables to discuss? Well, the next one is a variable we discussed earlier, but I will mention it again because it is important. The `vertex_texture_data` array is an array that stores all of the vertex geometry and UV texture coordinate data that are used for rendering:

```
var vertex_texture_data = new Float32Array([
    // x,    y,      u,     v
     0.16,   0.213,  1.0,   1.0,
    -0.16,   0.213,  0.0,   1.0,
     0.16,  -0.213,  1.0,   0.0,
    -0.16,  -0.213,  0.0,   0.0,
    -0.16,   0.213,  0.0,   1.0,
     0.16,  -0.213,  1.0,   0.0
]);
```

One thing I did not mention earlier is why the x and y values range from -0.16 to 0.16 on the x-axis and -0.213 to 0.213 on the y-axis. Because we are rendering a single image, we do not need to scale the geometry to fit the image dynamically. The spaceship image we are using is 128 x 128 pixels. The canvas size we are using is 800 x 600 pixels. As we discussed earlier, no matter what size we use for the canvas, WebGL fits both axes into a range from -1 to +1. This makes the coordinate (0, 0) the center of the canvas element. It also means that the canvas width is always 2 and the canvas height is always 2, no matter how many pixels wide or high the canvas element is. So, if we want to figure out how wide we want our geometry to be to have it match the width of the image, we have to do some calculations. First, we need to figure out how many units of WebGL clip space width corresponds to one pixel. The WebGL clip space has a width of 2.0, and the actual canvas has a width of 800 pixels, so the width of a single pixel in WebGL space is 2.0 / 800 = 0.0025. We need to know how wide our image is in WebGL clip space, so we will multiply the 128 pixels by 0.0025 and get a WebGL clip space width of 0.32. Because we would like to have the x value at the center of our geometry to be 0, we have our x geometry range from -0.16 to +0.16.

Now that we have done the width, let's tackle the height. The height of the canvas is 600 pixels, but in WebGL clip space, the height of the canvas is always 2.0 (-1.0 Y to +1.0 Y). So, how many WebGL units are in a single pixel? 2.0 / 600 = 0.00333333…repeating. Obviously, this is an instance where floating-point precision is unable to match a real-world value. We are going to lop off some of those trailing 3s and hope that the precision is enough. Going back to figuring out the height of the image in WebGL clip space, it is 128-pixels high, so we need to multiply 128 by 0.0033333…repeating. The result is 0.4266666…repeating, which we will truncate to 0.426. So, our y geometry must go from `-0.213` to `+0.213`.

 I am doing my best to ignore the complexity of the WebGL clip space. This is a 3D volume and not a simple 2D drawing area like the 2D canvas context. For more information on this topic, please consult the Mozilla developer docs for clip space: `https://developer.mozilla.org/en-US/docs/Web/API/WebGL_API/WebGL_model_view_projection#Clip_space`.

As I said earlier, a lot of this will be managed for us by SDL when we work on our game, but in the future, you may wish to work with OpenGL in WebAssembly. The OpenGL ES 2.0 and OpenGL ES 3.0 libraries have been ported to WebAssembly, and those libraries more or less have direct analogs with WebGL. WebGL 1.0 is a modified version of OpenGL ES 2.0, which was a version of OpenGL that was designed to run on mobile hardware. WebGL 2.0 is a modified version of OpenGL ES 3.0. Understanding what WebGL is doing through calls to SDL can make us better game developers, even if SDL is doing a lot of the heavy lifting for us.

Buffer constants

I have chosen to use a single `Float32Array` to hold all of the vertex data for this application. That includes the X and Y coordinate data, as well as U and V texture coordinate data. Because of this, we are going to need to tell WebGL how to separate this data into different attributes when we load this data into the GPU's buffer. We will use the following constants to tell WebGL how the data in `Float32Array` is broken out:

```
const FLOAT32_BYTE_SIZE = 4; // size of a 32-bit float
const STRIDE = FLOAT32_BYTE_SIZE * 4; // there are 4 elements for every
vertex. x, y, u, v
const XY_OFFSET = FLOAT32_BYTE_SIZE * 0;
const UV_OFFSET = FLOAT32_BYTE_SIZE * 2;
```

The `FLOAT32_BYTE_SIZE` constant is the size of each variable in `Float32Array`. The `STRIDE` constant will be used to tell WebGL how many bytes are used for the data of a single vertex. The four columns we defined in the previous code represent *x*, *y*, *u*, and *v*. Since each one of those variables uses four bytes of data, we will multiply the number of variables by the number of bytes that are used by each variable to get the *stride*, or how many bytes are used by a single vertex. The `XY_OFFSET` constant is the starting location inside of each stride where we will find the *x* and *y* coordinate data. For consistency, I multiplied the floating-point byte size by the position, but since it is 0, we could have just used `const XY_OFFSET = 0`. Now, `UV_OFFSET` is the offset in bytes from the beginning of each stride where we will find the UV texture coordinate data. Since those are in positions 2 and 3, the offset is the number of bytes that's used for each variable, multiplied by 2.

Defining the shaders

I walked through everything that's being done by the shaders in the previous section. You may want to go through that section again as a refresher. The next part of the code defines the vertex shader code and the fragment shader code in multiline JavaScript strings. Here is the vertex shader code:

```
var vertex_shader_code = `
    precision mediump float;
    attribute vec4 a_position;
    attribute vec2 a_texcoord;
    varying vec2 v_texcoord;
    uniform vec4 u_translate;

    void main() {
        gl_Position = u_translate + a_position;
        v_texcoord = a_texcoord;
    }
`;
```

The fragment shader code is as follows:

```
var fragment_shader_code = `
    precision mediump float;
    varying vec2 v_texcoord;
    uniform sampler2D u_texture;

    void main() {
        gl_FragColor = texture2D(u_texture, v_texcoord);
    }
`;
```

Let's take a look at the attribute in the vertex shader code:

```
attribute vec4 a_position;
attribute vec2 a_texcoord;
```

Those two attributes will be passed in from the data in `Float32Array`. One of the neat tricks in WebGL is that if you are not using all four position variables (x,y,z,w), you can pass in the two you are using (x,y) and the GPU will know how to use appropriate values in the other two positions. These shaders will require passing in two attributes:

```
attribute vec4 a_position;
attribute vec2 a_texcoord;
```

Once again, we will be doing this using buffers and `Float32Array`. We will also need to pass in two `uniform` variables. The `u_translate` variable will be used by the vertex shader to translate the position of the sprite, and `u_texture` is a texture buffer that will be used by the fragment shader. These shaders are almost as simple as they get. Many tutorials start you out without a texture and just hardcode the color output of the fragment shader, like this:

```
gl_FragColor = vec4(1.0, 0.0, 0.0, 1.0);
```

Making this change would cause the fragment shader to always output a red color, so please don't make this change. The only things I can think of that could have made this tutorial simpler are not loading the texture and rendering a solid color, and not allowing the geometry to be moved.

The ModuleLoaded function

In the old 2D canvas code, we defined the `ShipPosition` JavaScript function before the `ModuleLoaded` function, but we have swapped these two functions for the WebGL demo. I felt it was better to explain the WebGL initialization before the rendering portion of the code. Here is the new version of the `ModuleLoaded` function in its entirety:

```
function ModuleLoaded() {
    canvas = document.getElementById('canvas');
    gl = canvas.getContext("webgl", { alpha: false }) ||
                        canvas.getContext("experimental-webgl", {
                        alpha: false });

    if (!gl) {
        console.log("No WebGL support!");
        return;
    }
```

```
gl.blendFunc( gl.SRC_ALPHA, gl.ONE_MINUS_SRC_ALPHA );
gl.enable( gl.BLEND );

var vertex_shader = gl.createShader(gl.VERTEX_SHADER);
gl.shaderSource( vertex_shader, vertex_shader_code );
gl.compileShader( vertex_shader );

if( !gl.getShaderParameter(vertex_shader, gl.COMPILE_STATUS) ) {
    console.log('Failed to compile vertex shader' +
                gl.getShaderInfoLog(vertex_shader));
    gl.deleteShader(vertex_shader);
    return;
}

var fragment_shader = gl.createShader(gl.FRAGMENT_SHADER);
gl.shaderSource( fragment_shader, fragment_shader_code );
gl.compileShader( fragment_shader );

if( !gl.getShaderParameter(fragment_shader, gl.COMPILE_STATUS) ) {
    console.log('Failed to compile fragment shader' +
                gl.getShaderInfoLog(fragment_shader));
    gl.deleteShader(fragment_shader);
    return;
}

program = gl.createProgram();

gl.attachShader(program, vertex_shader);
gl.attachShader(program, fragment_shader);
gl.linkProgram(program);

if( !gl.getProgramParameter(program, gl.LINK_STATUS) ) {
    console.log('Failed to link program');
    gl.deleteProgram(program);
    return;
}

gl.useProgram(program);

u_texture_location = gl.getUniformLocation(program, "u_texture");
u_translate_location = gl.getUniformLocation(program,
"u_translate");

a_position_location = gl.getAttribLocation(program, "a_position");
a_texcoord_location = gl.getAttribLocation(program, "a_texcoord");

vertex_texture_buffer = gl.createBuffer();
```

```
gl.bindBuffer(gl.ARRAY_BUFFER, vertex_texture_buffer);
gl.bufferData(gl.ARRAY_BUFFER, vertex_texture_data,
gl.STATIC_DRAW);

gl.enableVertexAttribArray(a_position_location);
gl.vertexAttribPointer(a_position_location, 2, gl.FLOAT, false,
STRIDE, XY_OFFSET);

gl.enableVertexAttribArray(a_texcoord_location);
gl.vertexAttribPointer(a_texcoord_location, 2, gl.FLOAT, false,
STRIDE, UV_OFFSET);

texture = gl.createTexture();

gl.bindTexture(gl.TEXTURE_2D, texture);
gl.texParameteri(gl.TEXTURE_2D, gl.TEXTURE_WRAP_S, gl.REPEAT);
gl.texParameteri(gl.TEXTURE_2D, gl.TEXTURE_WRAP_T, gl.REPEAT);

gl.texParameteri(gl.TEXTURE_2D, gl.TEXTURE_MAG_FILTER, gl.NEAREST);
gl.texParameteri(gl.TEXTURE_2D, gl.TEXTURE_MIN_FILTER, gl.NEAREST);

img = new Image();
img.addEventListener('load', function() {
    image_width = img.width;
    image_height = img.height;

    gl.bindTexture(gl.TEXTURE_2D, texture);
    gl.texImage2D(gl.TEXTURE_2D, 0, gl.RGBA, gl.RGBA,
    gl.UNSIGNED_BYTE, img );
});
img.src = "spaceship.png";

gl.viewport(0, 0, gl.canvas.width, gl.canvas.height);
}
```

The first few lines get the `canvas` element and use that to get a WebGL context. If the JavaScript fails to get the WebGL context, we alert the user, letting them know they have a browser that does not support WebGL:

```
canvas = document.getElementById('canvas');

gl = canvas.getContext("webgl", { alpha: false }) ||
                      canvas.getContext("experimental-webgl", {
                      alpha: false });
if (!gl) {
    console.log("No WebGL support!");
    return;
}
```

The two lines after that turn on alpha blending:

```
gl.blendFunc( gl.SRC_ALPHA, gl.ONE_MINUS_SRC_ALPHA );
gl.enable( gl.BLEND );
```

Compiling, loading, and linking the vertex and the fragment shader is a lot of challenging code. I am not sure why there is no function inside of the WebGL library that does all of this in one step. Almost everyone writing webgl for 2D to do this, and they either put it into a separate `.js` file, or they copy and paste it into their code for every project. For now, all you need to know about the following batch of code is that it is taking the vertex and fragment shader we wrote earlier and compiling it into the program variable. From that point on, we will be using the program variable to interact with the shaders. Here is the code:

```
var vertex_shader = gl.createShader(gl.VERTEX_SHADER);
gl.shaderSource( vertex_shader, vertex_shader_code );
gl.compileShader( vertex_shader );

if( !gl.getShaderParameter(vertex_shader, gl.COMPILE_STATUS) ) {
    console.log('Failed to compile vertex shader' +
    gl.getShaderInfoLog(vertex_shader));
    gl.deleteShader(vertex_shader);
    return;
}

var fragment_shader = gl.createShader(gl.FRAGMENT_SHADER);
gl.shaderSource( fragment_shader, fragment_shader_code );
gl.compileShader( fragment_shader );

if( !gl.getShaderParameter(fragment_shader, gl.COMPILE_STATUS) ) {
    console.log('Failed to compile fragment shader' +
    gl.getShaderInfoLog(fragment_shader));
    gl.deleteShader(fragment_shader);
    return;
}

program = gl.createProgram();
gl.attachShader(program, vertex_shader);
gl.attachShader(program, fragment_shader);
gl.linkProgram(program);

if( !gl.getProgramParameter(program, gl.LINK_STATUS) ) {
    console.log('Failed to link program');
    gl.deleteProgram(program);
    return;
}
gl.useProgram(program);
```

Now that we have the `WebGLProgram` object in our `program` variable, we can use that object to interact with our shaders.

1. The first thing we are going to do is grab references to the `uniform` variables in our shader programs:

   ```
   u_texture_location = gl.getUniformLocation(program, "u_texture");
   u_translate_location = gl.getUniformLocation(program,
   "u_translate");
   ```

2. After that, we will use the `program` object to get references to the attribute variables that are used by our vertex shader:

   ```
   a_position_location = gl.getAttribLocation(program, "a_position");
   a_texcoord_location = gl.getAttribLocation(program, "a_texcoord");
   ```

3. Now, it is time to start working with buffers. Do you remember when we created that `Float32Array` with all of our vertex data in it? It is time to use buffers to send that data to the GPU:

   ```
   vertex_texture_buffer = gl.createBuffer();

   gl.bindBuffer(gl.ARRAY_BUFFER, vertex_texture_buffer);
   gl.bufferData(gl.ARRAY_BUFFER, vertex_texture_data,
                 gl.STATIC_DRAW);

   gl.enableVertexAttribArray(a_position_location);
   gl.vertexAttribPointer(a_position_location, 2, gl.FLOAT, false,
                 STRIDE, XY_OFFSET);

   gl.enableVertexAttribArray(a_texcoord_location);
   gl.vertexAttribPointer(a_texcoord_location, 2, gl.FLOAT, false,
                 STRIDE, UV_OFFSET);
   ```

The first line creates a new buffer called `vertex_texture_buffer`. The line that starts with `gl.bindBuffer` binds `vertex_texture_buffer` to `ARRAY_BUFFER`, and then `bufferData` adds the data we had in `vertex_texture_data` to `ARRAY_BUFFER`. After that, we need to use the references to `a_position` and `a_texcoord` that we created earlier in the `a_position_location` and `a_texcoord_location` variables to tell WebGL where in this array buffer it will find the data for the `a_position` and `a_texcoord` attributes. The first thing it does is call `enableVertexAttribArray` to enable that attribute using the location variable we created. Next, `vertexAttribPointer` uses the `STRIDE` and `XY_OFFSET` or `UV_OFFSET` to tell WebGL where the attribute data is inside of the buffer data.

4. After that, we will create and bind a texture buffer:

```
texture = gl.createTexture();
gl.bindTexture(gl.TEXTURE_2D, texture);
```

5. Now that we have a bound texture buffer, we can configure that buffer for mirror wrapping and nearest neighbor interpolation when scaling:

```
gl.texParameteri(gl.TEXTURE_2D, gl.TEXTURE_WRAP_S, gl.REPEAT);
gl.texParameteri(gl.TEXTURE_2D, gl.TEXTURE_WRAP_T, gl.REPEAT);

gl.texParameteri(gl.TEXTURE_2D, gl.TEXTURE_MAG_FILTER, gl.NEAREST);
gl.texParameteri(gl.TEXTURE_2D, gl.TEXTURE_MIN_FILTER, gl.NEAREST);
```

We are using `gl.NEAREST` instead of `gl.LINEAR` because I would like the game to have an old-school pixelated look. In your game, you may prefer a different algorithm.

6. After configuring the texture buffer, we are going to download the `spaceship.png` image and load that image data into the texture buffer:

```
img = new Image();

img.addEventListener('load', function() {
    image_width = img.width;
    image_height = img.height;

    gl.bindTexture(gl.TEXTURE_2D, texture);
    gl.texImage2D(gl.TEXTURE_2D, 0, gl.RGBA, gl.RGBA,
                  gl.UNSIGNED_BYTE, img );
});

img.src = "spaceship.png";
```

7. The final thing we will do is set the viewport to go from (0,0) to the canvas width and height. The viewport tells WebGL how the space in the canvas element will relate to our WebGL clip space:

```
gl.viewport(0, 0, gl.canvas.width, gl.canvas.height);
```

The ShipPosition function

If this were production quality code, I would be doing a lot of the work that I am currently doing inside of the initialization routine in this rendering function. Moving sprites around independently on the canvas would require updates to our array buffers. I probably wouldn't define my geometry in the way I did, that is, calculating the sizes by hand. I am not currently making any changes to the array buffer or the texture buffer; I am trying to keep this code to the bare minimum necessary to render a sprite onto the canvas using WebGL. Here is what I have:

```
function ShipPosition( ship_x, ship_y ) {
    if( image_width == 0 ) {
        return;
    }

    gl.uniform4fv(u_translate_location, [ship_x, ship_y, 0.0, 0.0]);
    gl.drawArrays(gl.TRIANGLES, 0, 6);
}
```

1. The first few lines check to see whether the image download has completed. If not, we will exit out of this function:

   ```
   if( image_width == 0 ) {
       return;
   }
   ```

2. Next, we tell WebGL to load the uniform u_translate uniform variable with our spaceship's coordinates:

   ```
   gl.uniform4fv(u_translate_location, [ship_x, ship_y, 0.0, 0.0]);
   ```

3. Finally, we instruct WebGL to draw triangles with the six vertices in our array buffer:

   ```
   gl.drawArrays(gl.TRIANGLES, 0, 6);
   ```

The MoveShip function

We are going to need to jump back into the WebAssembly C module. The webgl.c file is a copied version of canvas.c where the only changes we need to make are inside of the MoveShip function. Here is the new version of MoveShip:

```
void MoveShip() {
    ship_x += 0.002;
```

```
        ship_y += 0.001;

        if( ship_x >= 1.16 ) {
            ship_x = -1.16;
        }

        if( ship_y >= 1.21 ) {
            ship_y = -1.21;
        }

        EM_ASM( ShipPosition($0, $1), ship_x, ship_y );
}
```

The changes are all conversions from pixel space into WebGL clip space. In the 2D canvas version, we were adding two pixels to the ship's x coordinate and one pixel to the ship's y coordinate every frame. But in WebGL, moving the x coordinate by two would be moving it by the entire width of the screen. So, instead, we have to modify these values into small units that would work with the WebGL coordinate system:

```
ship_x += 0.002;
ship_y += 0.001;
```

Adding 0.002 to the x coordinate moves the ship by 1/500th of the width of the canvas each frame. Moving the y coordinate by 0.001 moves the ship on the y-axis by 1/1,000th of the height of the screen each frame. You may notice that in the 2D canvas version of this app, the ship was moving to the right and down. That was because increasing the y coordinate in the 2D canvas coordinate system moves an image down the screen. In the WebGL coordinate system, the ship moves up. The only other thing we have to do is change the coordinates at which the ship wrapped its x and y coordinates to WebGL clip space:

```
if( ship_x >= 1.16 ) {
    ship_x = -1.16;
}

if( ship_y >= 1.21 ) {
    ship_y = -1.21;
}
```

Now that we have all of our source code, go ahead and run emcc to compile our new webgl.html file:

```
emcc webgl.c -o webgl.html --shell-file webgl_shell.html
```

Once you have `webgl.html` compiled, load it into a web browser. It should look like this:

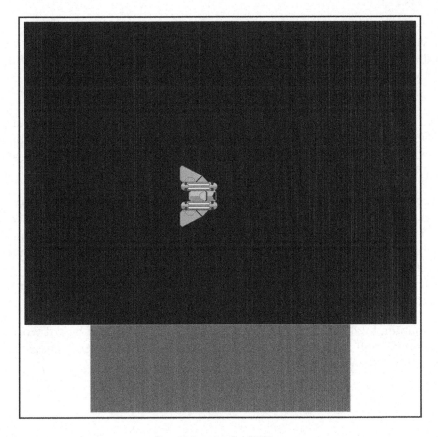

Figure 3.1: Screenshot of our WebGL app

It is important to remember that the app must be run from a web server, or using `emrun`. If you do not run the app from a web server, or use `emrun`, you will receive a variety of errors when the JavaScript glue code attempts to download the WASM and data files. You should also know that IIS requires additional configuration in order to set the proper MIME types for the `.wasm` and `.data` file extensions.

Now that we have all of this working in WebGL, in the next chapter, I will talk about how much easier all of this would have been if we just did it using SDL in the first place.

Summary

In this chapter, we have discussed WebGL and how it can improve performance in web games. I have introduced you to the concept of GLSL shaders and talked about vertex shaders and fragment shaders, what the differences between the two types of shaders are, and how they are used to render a combination of geometry and images to the HTML5 canvas.

We also recreated the moving spaceship that we created with the 2D canvas using WebGL. We have discussed how to use vertex geometry to render 2D images to a 3D canvas. We also talked about the differences between the pixel-based 2D canvas coordinate system and the 3D WebGL coordinate system.

WebGL is a broad topic to cover, so a single chapter can only give a very cursory introduction at best. WebGL is a 3D rendering space, and in this chapter, I went out of my way to ignore that and treat it like a 2D space. You could take what we have done here and build on it, but to improve the performance of our application, we will be using the WebAssembly SDL API for all of our interactions with WebGL in the future. If you would like to learn more about WebGL, Packt has a large selection of books devoted entirely to WebGL at https://search.packtpub.com/?query=webgl.

In the next chapter, I will teach you the basics of SDL, what it is, and how it works with WebAssembly. We will also learn how to render a sprite to the HTML5 canvas using SDL, animate it, and move it around the canvas.

4
Sprite Animations in WebAssembly with SDL

At the time of writing, **Simple DirectMedia Layer** (**SDL**) is the only 2D rendering library integrated into Emscripten for use in WebAssembly. But, even as more rendering libraries become available, SDL is a highly supported rendering library that has been ported to a large number of platforms and will remain both relevant and useful for WebAssembly and C++ development into the foreseeable future. Using SDL to render to WebGL saves us a tremendous amount of time, because we do not have to write the code to interface between our WebAssembly C++ code and WebGL ourselves. The large community also offers support and documentation. You can find more SDL resources online at libsdl.org.

 You will need to include several images in your build to make this project work. Make sure you include the /Chapter04/sprites/ and /Chapter04/font/ folders from the project's GitHub. If you haven't yet downloaded the GitHub project, you can get it online from: https://github.com/PacktPublishing/Hands-On-Game-Development-with-WebAssembly.

We will cover the following topics in this chapter:

- Using SDL in WebAssembly
- Rendering a sprite to the canvas
- Animating a sprite
- Moving the sprite

Using SDL in WebAssembly

At this point, I could roll my own system for interaction between the WebAssembly module and the JavaScript WebGL library. That would involve using a function table to call the JavaScript WebGL functions from within C++. Luckily for us, the Emscripten team has done most of this work. They have created a port of a popular 2D C++ graphics library that does this for us. SDL is a 2D graphics **Application Programming Interface (API)** built on top of OpenGL in most implementations. There is an Emscripten port that is used to help us render our 2D graphics on top of WebGL. If you would like to know what other libraries have been integrated into Emscripten, use the following emcc command:

```
emcc --show-ports
```

If you run this command, you will notice that several different SDL libraries are displayed. These include SDL2, SDL2_image, SDL2_gfx, SDL2_ttf, and SDL2_net. SDL was created with a modular design to allow the user to include only the parts of SDL that they need, allowing the core SDL library to remain small. This is very helpful if your goal is to create a web game where download size is limited.

The first thing we will do is get familiar with SDL by creating a simple "Hello World" application that writes some text to the HTML5 canvas element. To do this, we will need to include two of the Emscripten libraries listed when we ran the emcc --show-ports command. We will need to add the core SDL library to our Emscripten compiled with the USE_SDL=2, flag, and we will need to add the SDL TrueType font library by adding the USE_SDL_TTF=2 flag.

The .c source code that will display a message such as "HELLO SDL!" inside an HTML canvas is relatively simple:

```c
#include <SDL2/SDL.h>
#include <SDL2/SDL_ttf.h>
#include <emscripten.h>
#include <stdio.h>

#define MESSAGE "HELLO SDL!"
#define FONT_SIZE 16
#define FONT_FILE "font/Roboto-Black.ttf"

int main() {
    SDL_Window *window;
    SDL_Renderer *renderer;

    SDL_Rect dest = {.x = 160, .y = 100, .w = 0, .h = 0 };

    TTF_Font *font;
```

```
SDL_Texture* texture;

SDL_Init( SDL_INIT_VIDEO );
TTF_Init();

SDL_CreateWindowAndRenderer( 320, 200, 0, &window, &renderer );

SDL_SetRenderDrawColor( renderer, 0, 0, 0, 255 );
SDL_RenderClear( renderer );

font = TTF_OpenFont( FONT_FILE, FONT_SIZE );

SDL_Color font_color = {255, 255, 255, 255 }; // WHITE COLOR
SDL_Surface *temp_surface = TTF_RenderText_Blended( font,
                                                    MESSAGE,
                                                    font_color );

texture = SDL_CreateTextureFromSurface( renderer, temp_surface );

SDL_FreeSurface( temp_surface );
SDL_QueryTexture( texture,
                  NULL, NULL,
                  &dest.w, &dest.h ); // query the width and
                                         height

dest.x -= dest.w / 2;
dest.y -= dest.h / 2;

SDL_RenderCopy( renderer, texture, NULL, &dest );
SDL_RenderPresent( renderer );

return EXIT_SUCCESS;
}
```

Let me walk you through exactly what is going on here. The first four lines of code are the SDL header files, as well as the Emscripten header file:

```
#include <SDL2/SDL.h>
#include <SDL2/SDL_ttf.h>
#include <emscripten.h>
#include <stdio.h>
```

Following this, there are three preprocessor defines. If we wanted to change the message or font size quickly, we would modify these first two lines. The third define is a little less clear. We have something called FONT_FILE, which is a string that appears to be a filesystem location. That is a little bit weird, because WebAssembly does not have access to the local filesystem. To give the WebAssembly module access to the TrueType font file in the fonts directory, we will use the --preload-file flag when we compile the WASM file. This will generate a .data file from the contents of the font directory. The web browser loads this data file into the virtual filesystem, which is accessed by the WebAssembly module. That means that the C code that we are writing will have access to this file as if it were accessing it inside a local filesystem:

```
#define MESSAGE "HELLO SDL!"
#define FONT_SIZE 16
#define FONT_FILE "font/Roboto-Black.ttf"
```

Initializing SDL

Like in other targets for C/C++, the code begins execution from within the main function. We are going to start our main function by declaring some variables:

```
int main() {
    SDL_Window *window;
    SDL_Renderer *renderer;

    SDL_Rect dest = { .x = 160, .y = 100, .w = 0, .h = 0 };
    TTF_Font *font;

    SDL_Texture *texture;
```

The first two variables are the SDL_Window and SDL_Renderer objects. The window object would define the application window that we would be rendering into if we were writing code for a Windows, Mac, or Linux system. When we build for WebAssembly, there is a canvas in our HTML, but SDL still requires a window object pointer for initialization and cleanup. All calls to SDL use the renderer object to render images to the canvas.

The SDL_Rect dest variable is a rectangle that represents the destination where we will be rendering onto the canvas. We will render to the center of the 320x200 canvas, so we will start with an x and y value of 160 and 100. We do not yet know the width and height of the text we will render, so, at this point, we are going to set w and h to 0. We will reset this value later, so, in theory, we could set it to anything.

The `TTF_Font *font` variable is a pointer to the `SDL_TTF` library's `font` object. Later, we will use that object to load up a font from the virtual filesystem and render that font to the `SDL_Texture *texture` pointer variable. The `SDL_Texture` variables are used by SDL to render sprites to the canvas.

These next few lines are used to do some initialization work in SDL:

```
SDL_Init( SDL_INIT_VIDEO );
TTF_Init();

SDL_CreateWindowAndRenderer( 320, 200, 0, &window, &renderer );
```

The `SDL_Init` function is called with a single flag initializing only the video subsystem. As a side note, I am not aware of any use case for SDL that does not require the video subsystem to be initialized. Many developers use SDL as an OpenGL/WebGL graphics rendering system; so, unless you have designed a game that is audio only, you should always pass in the `SDL_INIT_VIDEO` flag. If you would like to initialize additional SDL subsystems, you would pass in the flags for those subsystems using a Boolean or | operator, as shown in the following code snippet:

```
SDL_Init( SDL_INIT_VIDEO | SDL_INIT_AUDIO | SDL_INIT_HAPTIC );
```

If we use the preceding line, SDL would have also initialized the audio and haptic subsystems, but we do not need them right now, so we will not be making that change.

The `TTF_Init();` function initializes our TrueType fonts, and `SDL_CreateWindowAndRenderer` returns a `window` and `renderer` object to us. We are passing `320` for the width of the canvas and `200` for the height. The third variable is the `window` flags. We pass `0` in for that parameter to indicate that we do not need any `window` flags. Because we are working with the SDL Emscripten port, we do not have control of the window, so these flags do not apply.

Clearing the SDL renderer

After the initialization is complete, we will need to clear out the renderer. We can clear our renderer with any color we choose. To do this, we will make a call to the `SDL_RenderDrawColor` function:

```
SDL_SetRenderDrawColor( renderer, 0, 0, 0, 255 );
SDL_RenderClear( renderer );
```

That sets the drawing color for the renderer to black with full opacity. `0, 0, 0` are the RGB color values, and `255` is the alpha opacity. These numbers all range from 0 to 255, where 255 is the full color on the color spectrum. We set this up so that when we call the `SDL_RenderClear` function in the next line, it will clear the renderer with the color black. If we wanted the color to clear red instead of black, we would have to modify the call in the following way:

```
SDL_SetRenderDrawColor( renderer, 255, 0, 0, 255 );
```

That is not what we want, so we will not make that change. I just wanted to point out that we could clear the renderer with any color we like.

Using the WebAssembly virtual filesystem

The next few lines will open up the TrueType font file in the virtual filesystem, and render it to `SDL_Texture`, which can be used to render to the canvas:

```
font = TTF_OpenFont( FONT_FILE, FONT_SIZE );
SDL_Color font_color = {255, 255, 255, 255 }; // WHITE COLOR
SDL_Surface *temp_surface = TTF_RenderText_Blended( font, MESSAGE,
                                                    font_color );
texture = SDL_CreateTextureFromSurface( renderer, temp_surface );
SDL_FreeSurface( temp_surface );
```

In the first line of the preceding code, we open the TrueType font by passing in the location of the file in the WebAssembly virtual filesystem, defined at the top of the program. We also need to specify the font's point size, which was defined as 16 at the top of the program as well. The next thing we do is create an `SDL_Color` variable that we will use for the font. This is a RGBA color, and we have all values set to 255 so that it is a fully opaque white color. After we have done this, we will need to render the text to a surface using the `TTF_RenderText_Blended` function. We pass the TrueType font we opened a few lines earlier, the `MESSAGE`, which was defined as `"HELLO SDL!"`, near the top of the program, and the font color, defined as white. Then, we will create a texture from our surface and free the surface memory we have just allocated. You should always free the memory from your surface pointers immediately after using them to create a texture, as once you have your textures the surfaces are no longer needed.

Rendering a texture to the HTML5 canvas

After we load a font from the virtual filesystem and then render that font to the texture, we need to take that texture and copy it to a location in our renderer object. After we have done that, we will need to take that renderer and present its contents to the HTML5 canvas element.

The following is the source code that renders the texture to the canvas:

```
SDL_QueryTexture( texture,
                  NULL, NULL,
                  &dest.w, &dest.h ); // query the width and height

dest.x -= dest.w / 2;
dest.y -= dest.h / 2;

SDL_RenderCopy( renderer, texture, NULL, &dest );
SDL_RenderPresent( renderer );
```

The call to the SDL_QueryTexture function is used to retrieve the width and height of the texture. We need to use these values in the destination rectangle so that we render our texture to the canvas without changing its dimensions. After that call, the program knows the width and height of the texture, so it can use those values to modify the x and y variables of the destination rectangle so that it can center our text on the canvas. Because the x and y values of the dest (destination) rectangle specify the top-left corner of that rectangle, we need to subtract half the width and half the height of the rectangle to make sure that it is centered. The SDL_RenderCopy function then renders this texture to our rendering buffer and SDL_RenderPresent moves that entire buffer to the HTML5 canvas.

At this point, all that is left to do in the code is return:

```
return EXIT_SUCCESS;
```

Returning with a value of EXIT_SUCCESS tells our JavaScript glue code that everything went well when running this module.

Cleaning up SDL

Something that you may notice is missing from this code, that would be in a Windows or Linux version of an SDL application, is code that does some SDL clean up at the end of the program. If we exited an application in Windows, for instance, and did not do our cleanup work, we would be exiting without clearing out some of the memory allocated by SDL. If this were not a WebAssembly module, the following lines would be included at the end of the function:

```
SDL_Delay(5000);
SDL_DestroyWindow(window);
SDL_Quit();
```

Because we have not spent the time to make a game loop, we would want to delay the cleanup and exiting of the program by five seconds using a call to `SDL_Delay(5000)`, 5000 being the number of milliseconds to wait before doing the cleanup. We want to reiterate that, because we are compiling to WebAssembly, we do not want to clean up our SDL. Doing so has different effects on different browsers.

When testing this code in Firefox, using the delay is unnecessary, because the web browser tab will stay open even after the WebAssembly module stops executing. However, the Chrome browser tab will display an error page as soon as SDL destroys the `window` object.

The `SDL_DestroyWindow` function would destroy the `window` object if this were a Windows environment. The `SDL_Quit` function terminates the SDL engine, and, finally, `return EXIT_SUCCESS;` exits successfully from the `main` function.

Compiling hello_sdl.html

Finally, we will compile and test our WebAssembly module using the Emscripten `emcc` compiler:

```
emcc hello_sdl.c --emrun --preload-file font -s USE_SDL=2 -s USE_SDL_TTF=2
-o hello_sdl.html
```

It is important to remember that you must run WebAssembly apps using a web server, or with `emrun`. If you would like to run your WebAssembly app using `emrun`, you must compile it with the `--emrun` flag. The web browser requires a web server to stream the WebAssembly module. If you attempt to open an HTML page that uses WebAssembly in a browser directly from your hard drive, that WebAssembly module will not load.

There are a few new flags we are using in this call to emcc, and we have temporarily left out the --shell-file new_shell.html flag that is used to generate a customized version of the template. If you would like to continue using emrun to test the app, you must include the --emrun flag, to run with the emrun command. If you are using a WebServer, such as Node.js, to serve the app, you may omit the --emrun flag from this point forward. If you like using emrun, continue to compile with that flag.

We have added the --preload-file font flag to allow us to create a virtual filesystem contained in the hello_sdl.data file. This file holds our TrueType font. The application uses the core SDL library and the additional SDL TrueType font module, so we have included the following flag, -s USE_SDL=2 -s USE_SDL_TTF=2, to allow calls to SDL and SDL_ttf. If everything went well in your compile, this is what the new hello_sdl.html file will look like when you bring it up in a browser:

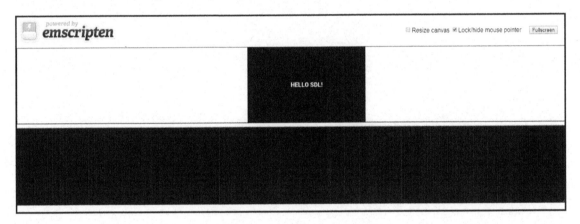

Figure 4.1: Hello SDL! app screenshot

In the next section, we will learn how to use SDL to render a sprite to the HTML5 canvas.

Render a sprite to the canvas

Now that we have learned how to render text to our HTML canvas element using SDL and Emscripten, we can take the next step and learn how to render sprites. The code used to render a sprite to the canvas is quite similar to the code that we used to render a TrueType font. We will still be using the virtual filesystem to generate a data file that contains the sprites we are using, but we will need a new SDL library to do this. We no longer need SDL2_ttf to load a TrueType font and render it to a texture. Instead, we need SDL2_image. We will show you how to change our call to emcc to include this new library a little later.

First, let's take a look at the new version of the SDL code that renders an image to our HTML canvas element instead of the text we rendered in the previous section:

```
#include <SDL2/SDL.h>
#include <SDL2/SDL_image.h>
#include <emscripten.h>
#include <stdio.h>
#define SPRITE_FILE "sprites/Franchise1.png"

int main() {
    SDL_Window *window;
    SDL_Renderer *renderer;
    SDL_Rect dest = {.x = 160, .y = 100, .w = 0, .h = 0 };
    SDL_Texture *texture;
    SDL_Init( SDL_INIT_VIDEO );
    SDL_CreateWindowAndRenderer( 320, 200, 0, &window, &renderer );
    SDL_SetRenderDrawColor( renderer, 0, 0, 0, 255 );
    SDL_RenderClear( renderer );
    SDL_Surface *temp_surface = IMG_Load( SPRITE_FILE );

    if( !temp_surface ) {
        printf("failed to load image: %s\n", IMG_GetError() );
        return 0;
    }

    texture = SDL_CreateTextureFromSurface( renderer, temp_surface );

    SDL_FreeSurface( temp_surface );

    SDL_QueryTexture( texture,
                      NULL, NULL,
                      &dest.w, &dest.h ); // query the width and
                      height

    dest.x -= dest.w / 2;
```

```
    dest.y -= dest.h / 2;

    SDL_RenderCopy( renderer, texture, NULL, &dest );
    SDL_RenderPresent( renderer );

SDL_Delay(5000);
SDL_DestroyWindow(window);
SDL_Quit();
    return 1;
}
```

This code is similar to the code we wrote in the last section, *HTML5 and WebAssembly*, for the *HELLO SDL!* application. Instead of using the SDL2_ttf module, we are using the SDL2_image module. Because of this, we will need to include the SDL2/SDL_image.h header file. We will also need to load a sprite file from the sprites directory, which we will add to the WebAssembly virtual filesystem:

```
SDL_Surface *temp_surface = IMG_Load( SPRITE_FILE );

if( !temp_surface ) {
    printf("failed to load image: %s\n", IMG_GetError() );
    return 0;
}
```

Below the call to IMG_Load, we add an error check that will let us know what went wrong if the file fails to load. Aside from that, the code is mostly the same. If we are successful, the canvas will display our 16x16 pixel image of the Starship Franchise:

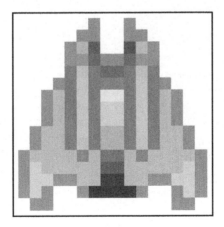

Figure 4.2: Franchise1.png

In the next section, we will learn how to use SDL to animate a sprite on our canvas.

Animating a sprite

In this section, we will learn how to make a quick and dirty little animation in our SDL application. That will not be the way we do animations in our final game, but it will give you an idea of how we could create animations from within SDL by swapping out textures over time. I am going to present the code to animate a sprite broken into two parts. The first part includes our preprocessor macros, global variables, and the show_animation function:

```
#include <SDL2/SDL.h>
#include <SDL2/SDL_image.h>

#include <emscripten.h>
#include <stdio.h>

#define SPRITE_FILE "sprites/Franchise1.png"
#define EXP_FILE "sprites/FranchiseExplosion%d.png"
#define FRAME_COUNT 7

int current_frame = 0;
Uint32 last_time;
Uint32 current_time;
Uint32 ms_per_frame = 100; // animate at 10 fps

SDL_Window *window;
SDL_Renderer *renderer;
SDL_Rect dest = {.x = 160, .y = 100, .w = 0, .h = 0 };
SDL_Texture *sprite_texture;
SDL_Texture *temp_texture;
SDL_Texture* anim[FRAME_COUNT];

void show_animation() {
    current_time = SDL_GetTicks();
    int ms = current_time - last_time;

    if( ms < ms_per_frame) {
        return;
    }

    if( current_frame >= FRAME_COUNT ) {
        SDL_RenderClear( renderer );
        return;
    }

    last_time = current_time;
    SDL_RenderClear( renderer );
```

```
    temp_texture = anim[current_frame++];

    SDL_QueryTexture( temp_texture,
                      NULL, NULL,
                      &dest.w, &dest.h ); // query the width and
                                                    height

    dest.x = 160 - dest.w / 2;
    dest.y = 100 - dest.h / 2;

    SDL_RenderCopy( renderer, temp_texture, NULL, &dest );
    SDL_RenderPresent( renderer );
}
```

After we define our `show_animation` function, we will need to define our module's `main` function:

```
int main() {
    char explosion_file_string[40];
    SDL_Init( SDL_INIT_VIDEO );
    SDL_CreateWindowAndRenderer( 320, 200, 0, &window, &renderer );

    SDL_SetRenderDrawColor( renderer, 0, 0, 0, 255 );
    SDL_RenderClear( renderer );

    SDL_Surface *temp_surface = IMG_Load( SPRITE_FILE );

    if( !temp_surface ) {
        printf("failed to load image: %s\n", IMG_GetError() );
        return 0;
    }

    sprite_texture = SDL_CreateTextureFromSurface( renderer,
    temp_surface );

    SDL_FreeSurface( temp_surface );

    for( int i = 1; i <= FRAME_COUNT; i++ ) {
        sprintf( explosion_file_string, EXP_FILE, i );
        SDL_Surface *temp_surface = IMG_Load( explosion_file_string );

        if( !temp_surface ) {
            printf("failed to load image: %s\n", IMG_GetError() );
            return 0;
        }

        temp_texture = SDL_CreateTextureFromSurface( renderer,
```

```
                    temp_surface );
            anim[i-1] = temp_texture;
            SDL_FreeSurface( temp_surface );
    }

    SDL_QueryTexture( sprite_texture,
                        NULL, NULL,
                        &dest.w, &dest.h ); // query the width and
                                                    height

    dest.x -= dest.w / 2;
    dest.y -= dest.h / 2;

    SDL_RenderCopy( renderer, sprite_texture, NULL, &dest );
    SDL_RenderPresent( renderer );

    last_time = SDL_GetTicks();
    emscripten_set_main_loop(show_animation, 0, 0);
    return 1;
}
```

There is a lot to unpack here. There are much more efficient ways to do this animation, but what we are doing here takes what we have already done and adds to it. In earlier versions of the code, we rendered a single frame to the canvas, then exited the WebAssembly module. That works well enough if your goal is to render something static to the canvas and never change it. If you are writing a game, however, you need to be able to animate your sprites and move them around the canvas. Here, we run into a problem that we do not have if we are compiling our C++ code for any target other than WebAssembly. Games typically run in a loop and are directly responsible for rendering to the screen. WebAssembly runs inside of the JavaScript engine in your web browser. The WebAssembly module itself cannot update our canvas. Emscripten uses the JavaScript glue code to update the HTML canvas indirectly from the SDL API. However, if the WebAssembly runs in a loop, and uses that loop to animate our sprite through SDL, the WebAssembly module never lets go of the thread it is in, and the JavaScript never has an opportunity to update the canvas. Because of this, we can not put the game loop inside the `main` function. Instead, we must create a different function, and use Emscripten to set up the JavaScript glue code to call that function every time the browser renders a frame. The function we will use to do that is as follows:

```
emscripten_set_main_loop(show_animation, 0, 0);
```

The first parameter we will pass to `emscripten_set_main_loop` is `show_animation`. This is the name of a function we defined near the top of the code. I will talk about the specifics of the `show_animation` function a little later. For now, it is enough to know that this is the function called every time the browser renders a new frame on the canvas.

The second parameter of `emscripten_set_main_loop` is **frames per second** (FPS). If you want to set the FPS of your game to a fixed rate, you can do so by passing the target frame rate into the function here. If you pass in 0, this tells `emscripten_set_main_loop` to run with the highest frame rate it can. As a general rule, you want your game to run with the highest frame rate possible, so passing in 0 is usually the best thing to do. If you pass in a value higher than what the computer is capable of rendering, it will merely render as fast as it is able anyway, so this value only puts a cap on your FPS.

The third parameter we pass in is `simulate_infinite_loop`. Passing in 0 is equivalent to passing a `false` value. If the value of this parameter is `true`, it forces the module to re-enter through the `main` function for every frame. I am not sure what the use case for this is. I would recommend keeping it at 0 and separating your game loop into another function as we have done here.

Before calling `emscripten_set_main_loop`, we will set up an array of SDL texture surface pointers:

```
for( int i = 1; i <= FRAME_COUNT; i++ ) {
  sprintf( explosion_file_string, EXP_FILE, i );
    SDL_Surface *temp_surface = IMG_Load( explosion_file_string );

    if( !temp_surface ) {
        printf("failed to load image: %s\n", IMG_GetError() );
        return 0;
    }

    temp_texture = SDL_CreateTextureFromSurface( renderer, temp_surface );
    anim[i-1] = temp_texture;
    SDL_FreeSurface( temp_surface );
}
```

This loop loads `FranchiseExplosion1.png` through `FranchiseExplosion7.png` into an array of SDL textures and stores them into a different array, called `anim`. That is the array we will loop through later in the `show_animation` function. There are more efficient ways to do this using sprite sheets, and by modifying the destination rectangle. We will discuss those techniques for rendering animated sprites in later chapters.

Near the top of the code, we defined the `show_animation` function, called every rendered frame:

```
void show_animation() {
    current_time = SDL_GetTicks();
    int ms = current_time - last_time;

    if( ms < ms_per_frame) {
```

```
        return;
    }

    if( current_frame >= FRAME_COUNT ) {
        SDL_RenderClear( renderer );
        return;
    }

    last_time = current_time;
    SDL_RenderClear( renderer );

    temp_texture = anim[current_frame++];

    SDL_QueryTexture( temp_texture,
                      NULL, NULL,
                      &dest.w, &dest.h ); // query the width and
                                          //                height

    dest.x = 160 - dest.w / 2;
    dest.y = 100 - dest.h / 2;

    SDL_RenderCopy( renderer, temp_texture, NULL, &dest );
    SDL_RenderPresent( renderer );
}
```

This function is designed to wait a certain number of milliseconds, then update the texture we are rendering. I have created a seven frame animation that blows up the Starship Franchise in a little pixelated explosion. The reason we need a short wait in this loop is that our refresh rate is probably 60+ FPS, and if we render a new frame of our animation every time show_animation is called, the entire animation would run in about 1/10 of a second. Classic arcade games frequently flipped through their animation sequences at a much slower rate than the games frame rate. Many classic **Nintendo Entertainment System (NES)** games used two-stage animations where the animation would alternate sprites every few hundred milliseconds, even though the NES ran with a frame rate of 60 FPS.

The core of this function is similar to the single texture render we created earlier. The primary difference is that we wait a fixed number of milliseconds before changing the frame of our animation by incrementing the current_frame variable. That takes us through all seven stages of our animation in a little less than a second.

Moving the sprite

Now that we have learned how to animate our sprite in a frame-by-frame animation, we will learn how to move a sprite around on our canvas. I want to keep our spaceship animated, but I would prefer it not run in an explosion loop. In our sprites folder, I have included a simple four-stage animation that causes our ship's engines to flicker. The source code is quite lengthy, so I will introduce it in three parts: a preprocessor and global variable section, the show_animation function, and the main function.

Here is the code that defines the preprocessor directives and the global variables at the beginning of our cpp file:

```
#include <SDL2/SDL.h>
#include <SDL2/SDL_image.h>

#include <emscripten.h>
#include <stdio.h>

#define SPRITE_FILE "sprites/Franchise1.png"
#define EXP_FILE "sprites/Franchise%d.png"

#define FRAME_COUNT 4

int current_frame = 0;
Uint32 last_time;
Uint32 current_time;
Uint32 ms_per_frame = 100; // animate at 10 fps

SDL_Window *window;

SDL_Renderer *renderer;
SDL_Rect dest = {.x = 160, .y = 100, .w = 0, .h = 0 };
SDL_Texture *sprite_texture;
SDL_Texture *temp_texture;
SDL_Texture* anim[FRAME_COUNT];
```

Following the preprocessor directives and global variables, our cpp file contains a show_animation function that defines our game loop. Here is the code for our show_animation function:

```
void show_animation() {
    current_time = SDL_GetTicks();
    int ms = current_time - last_time;

    if( ms >= ms_per_frame) {
        ++current_frame;
```

```
        last_time = current_time;
    }

    if( current_frame >= FRAME_COUNT ) {
        current_frame = 0;
    }

    SDL_RenderClear( renderer );
    temp_texture = anim[current_frame];

    dest.y--;

    if( dest.y < -16 ) {
        dest.y = 200;
    }

    SDL_RenderCopy( renderer, temp_texture, NULL, &dest );
    SDL_RenderPresent( renderer );
}
```

The final part of our cpp file defines the main function. That is the initialization code in our WebAssembly module:

```
int main() {
    char explosion_file_string[40];
    SDL_Init( SDL_INIT_VIDEO );
    SDL_CreateWindowAndRenderer( 320, 200, 0, &window, &renderer );
    SDL_SetRenderDrawColor( renderer, 0, 0, 0, 255 );
    SDL_RenderClear( renderer );
    SDL_Surface *temp_surface = IMG_Load( SPRITE_FILE );

    if( !temp_surface ) {
        printf("failed to load image: %s\n", IMG_GetError() );
        return 0;
    }

    sprite_texture = SDL_CreateTextureFromSurface( renderer,
    temp_surface );
    SDL_FreeSurface( temp_surface );

    for( int i = 1; i <= FRAME_COUNT; i++ ) {
        sprintf( explosion_file_string, EXP_FILE, i );
        SDL_Surface *temp_surface = IMG_Load( explosion_file_string );

        if( !temp_surface ) {
            printf("failed to load image: %s\n", IMG_GetError() );
            return 0;
        }
```

```
        temp_texture = SDL_CreateTextureFromSurface( renderer,
        temp_surface );

        anim[i-1] = temp_texture;
        SDL_FreeSurface( temp_surface );
    }

    SDL_QueryTexture( sprite_texture,
                    NULL, NULL,
                    &dest.w, &dest.h ); // query the width and
                                                height

    dest.x -= dest.w / 2;
    dest.y -= dest.h / 2;

    SDL_RenderCopy( renderer, sprite_texture, NULL, &dest );
    SDL_RenderPresent( renderer );

    last_time = SDL_GetTicks();
    emscripten_set_main_loop(show_animation, 0, 0);
    return 1;
}
```

This code is similar to our `sprite_animation` code. There are only a few modifications, and most of them are within the `show_animation` function:

```
void show_animation() {
    current_time = SDL_GetTicks();

    int ms = current_time - last_time;

    if( ms >= ms_per_frame) {
        ++current_frame;
        last_time = current_time;
    }

    if( current_frame >= FRAME_COUNT ) {
        current_frame = 0;
    }

    SDL_RenderClear( renderer );
    temp_texture = anim[current_frame];

    dest.y--;

    if( dest.y < -16 ) {
        dest.y = 200;
    }
```

```
    SDL_RenderCopy( renderer, temp_texture, NULL, &dest );
    SDL_RenderPresent( renderer );
}
```

We advance our frame whenever the value in ms, which tracks the milliseconds since the last frame change, exceeds ms_per_frame, which we set to a value of 100. Because the spaceship is moving, we still need to update our canvas every frame with the new spaceship position. We do this by modifying the dest.y value, which tells SDL where to render our spaceship on the y-axis. We subtract one from the dest.y variable every frame to move the spaceship up. We also perform a check to see whether this value has become smaller than -16. Because the sprite is 16-pixels high, this will happen when the sprite has moved entirely off the screen at the top. If this is the case, we need to move the sprite back down to the bottom of the game screen by setting the y value back to 200. In an actual game, to tie our movement directly to the frame rate like this would be a bad idea, but for this demonstration, it will be fine.

Compiling sprite.html

We can now compile our sprite WebAssembly app by using the emcc command. You will need the sprites folder from the Chapter02 folder on GitHub. After you have downloaded the sprites folder and placed it in your project's folder, you can compile the app with the following command:

```
emcc sprite_move.c --preload-file sprites -s USE_SDL=2 -s USE_SDL_IMAGE=2 -
s SDL2_IMAGE_FORMATS=["png"] -o sprite_move.html
```

It is important to remember that the app must be run from a web server, or using emrun. If you do not run the app from a web server, or use emrun, you will receive a variety of errors when the JavaScript glue code attempts to download the WASM and data files. You should also know that IIS requires additional configuration in order to set the proper MIME types for the .wasm and .data file extensions.

We are still using the --preload-file flag, however, this time we are passing in the sprites folder instead of the fonts folder. We will continue to use the -s USE_SDL=2 flag and will be adding the -s USE_SDL_IMAGE=2 flag, which will allow us to use images with SDL that are an alternative to the .bmp file format.

To tell `SDL_IMAGE` which file format to use, we pass in the `png` format using the following `-s SDL2_IMAGE_FORMATS=["png"]` flag:

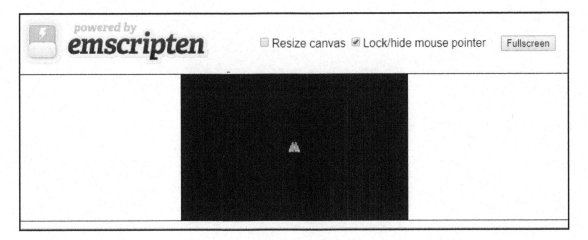

Figure 4.3: Screenshot of sprite_move.html

Summary

In this chapter, I have introduced you to SDL and its library of modules that are available for use within WebAssembly. We have learned about the WebAssembly virtual filesystem, and how Emscripten creates the `.data` files for access within the WebAssembly virtual filesystem. I have taught you how to use SDL to render images and fonts to the HTML canvas. Finally, we have learned how to use SDL to create a simple animation in our game.

In the next chapter, we will learn how to use keyboard input to move game objects on the canvas.

5
Keyboard Input

Now that we have sprites and animations, and can move these sprites around our canvas, we will need to add some interaction into our game. There are a few ways we can get keyboard input for our game. One way is through JavaScript, making calls to different functions in our WebAssembly module based on that input. The first section of our code will do just that. We will add some functions inside the WebAssembly module for us to wrap in JavaScript wrappers. We will also set up some JavaScript keyboard event handlers that we will use to make calls into our WebAssembly module whenever the keyboard events are triggered.

The other way we can get input into our WebAssembly module is to allow SDL to do all the heavy lifting for us. That involves adding C code into our WebAssembly module that captures the SDL_KEYDOWN and SDL_KEYUP events. The module will then look at the event keycode to determine what key triggered the event. There are costs and benefits to writing our code using either method. Generally speaking, having SDL managing our keyboard input costs us some of the flexibility of writing our keyboard input manager inside the JavaScript, while, at the same time, we gain the benefit of more straightforward code.

 You will need to include several images in your build to make this project work. Make sure you include the /Chapter05/sprites/ folder from the project's GitHub. If you haven't yet downloaded the GitHub project, you can get it online at: https://github.com/PacktPublishing/Hands-On-Game-Development-with-WebAssembly.

In this chapter, we will do the following:

- Learn how to use JavaScript keyboard events to make calls into our WebAssembly module
- Learn how to use SDL events to manage keyboard input from inside our WebAssembly module
- Demonstrate what we have learned by using keyboard input to move a spaceship sprite around the canvas

JavaScript keyboard input

The first thing we will do is learn how to listen for JavaScript keyboard events and make calls into our WebAssembly module based on those events. We will be reusing a lot of the code we wrote for Chapter 2, *HTML5 and WebAssembly*, so the first thing we should do is grab that code from the Chapter02 folder and copy it into our new Chapter05 folder. Copy the new_shell.html file from inside the Chapter02 directory to the Chapter05 directory, then rename that file jskey_shell.html. Next, copy shell.c from the Chapter02 directory to the Chapter05 directory and rename that file jskey.c. Finally, copy the shell.css file from the Chapter02 directory into the Chapter05 directory, but do not rename it. These three files will give us a starting point for writing the JavaScript keyboard input code.

First, let's take a look at the jskey.c file that we have just created from shell.c. We can get rid of most of the code inside this file right at the beginning. Delete all of the code after the end of the main function. That means you will be deleting all of the following code:

```
void test() {
    printf("button test\n");
}

void int_test( int num ) {
    printf("int test=%d\n", num);
}

void float_test( float num ) {
    printf("float test=%f\n", num);
}

void string_test( char* str ) {
    printf("string test=%s\n", str);
}
```

Next, we will modify the `main` function. We no longer want to use `EM_ASM` inside our `main` function to call our JavaScript wrapper initialization function, so delete the following two lines of code from the `main` function:

```
EM_ASM( InitWrappers() );
printf("Initialization Complete\n");
```

The only thing left in our `main` function is a single `printf` statement. We will change that line to let us know that the `main` function has run. You can change this code to say anything you like, or remove the `printf` statement entirely. The following code shows what we have for the `main` function:

```
int main() {
    printf("main has run\n");
}
```

Now that we have modified the `main` function, and removed all of the functions we no longer need, let's put in some functions called when a JavaScript `keyboard` event is triggered. We will add a function for a `keypress` event when the user presses one of the arrow keys on the keyboard. The following code will be called by those `keypress` events:

```
void press_up() {
    printf("PRESS UP\n");
}

void press_down() {
    printf("PRESS DOWN\n");
}

void press_left() {
    printf("PRESS LEFT\n");
}

void press_right() {
    printf("PRESS RIGHT\n");
}
```

We would also like to know when the user releases a key. So, to do this, we will add four `release` functions into the C module, as follows:

```
void release_up() {
    printf("RELEASE UP\n");
}

void release_down() {
    printf("RELEASE DOWN\n");
```

```
}

void release_left() {
    printf("RELEASE LEFT\n");
}

void release_right() {
    printf("RELEASE RIGHT\n");
}
```

Now that we have our new C file, we can change our shell file. Open up
jskey_shell.html. We do not need to change anything in the head tag, but inside the
body, we will want to remove a lot of the HTML elements that we will no longer be using.
Go ahead and delete all of the elements except the textarea element. We want to keep
our textarea element around so that we can see the output of the printf statements
inside our module. We need to delete the following HTML from the jskey_shell.html
before our textarea element:

```
<div class="input_box"> </div>
<div class="input_box">
    <button id="click_me" class="em_button">Click Me!</button>
</div>

<div class="input_box">
    <input type="number" id="int_num" max="9999" min="0" step="1"
     value="1" class="em_input">
    <button id="int_button" class="em_button">Int Click!</button>
</div>

<div class="input_box">
    <input type="number" id="float_num" max="99" min="0" step="0.01"
     value="0.0" class="em_input">
    <button id="float_button" class="em_button">Float Click!</button>
</div>

<div class="input_box"> </div>
```

Then, after the textarea element, we need to delete the following div and its contents:

```
<div id="string_box">
    <button id="string_button" class="em_button">String Click!</button>
    <input id="string_input">
</div>
```

After that, we have the `script` tag that contains all of our JavaScript code. We will need to add some global variables into that `script` tag. First, let's add some Boolean variables that will tell us if the player is pressing any of our arrow keys. Initialize all of these values to `false`, as per the following example:

```
var left_key_press = false;
var right_key_press = false;
var up_key_press = false;
var down_key_press = false;
```

Following our `key_press` flags, we will have all of the `wrapper` variables that will be used to hold the `wrapper` functions that call functions within our WebAssembly module. We will initialize all of these wrappers to `null`. Later, we will only call these functions if they are not `null`. The following code shows our wrappers:

```
var left_press_wrapper = null;
var left_release_wrapper = null;

var right_press_wrapper = null;
var right_release_wrapper = null;

var up_press_wrapper = null;
var up_release_wrapper = null;

var down_press_wrapper = null;
var down_release_wrapper = null;
```

Now that we have defined all of our global variables, we need to add functions triggered on the `key_press` and `key_release` events. The first of these functions is `keyPress`. The code we have for this function is as follows:

```
function keyPress() {
    event.preventDefault();
    if( event.repeat === true ) {
        return;
    }

    // PRESS UP ARROW
    if (event.keyCode === 38) {
        up_key_press = true;
        if( up_press_wrapper != null ) up_press_wrapper();
    }

    // PRESS LEFT ARROW
    if (event.keyCode === 37) {
        left_key_press = true;
        if( left_press_wrapper != null ) left_press_wrapper();
```

```
    }

    // PRESS RIGHT ARROW
    if (event.keyCode === 39) {
        right_key_press = true;
        if( right_press_wrapper != null ) right_press_wrapper();
    }

    // PRESS DOWN ARROW
    if (event.keyCode === 40) {
        down_key_press = true;
        if( down_press_wrapper != null ) down_press_wrapper();
    }
}
```

The first line of this function is `event.preventDefault();`. This line prevents the web browser from doing what it would normally do when the user presses the key in question. For instance, if you are playing a game, and you press the down arrow key to have your spaceship move down, you would not want the web page also to scroll down. Placing this `preventDefault` call at the beginning of the `keyPress` function will disable the default behavior for all key presses. In other projects, this may not be what you want. If you only wanted to disable the default behavior when pressing the down arrow key, you would place that call inside of the `if` block that manages the down arrow key press. The following block of code checks to see if the event is a repeat event:

```
if( event.repeat === true ) {
    return;
}
```

That would be true if you held down one of the keys. For example, if you held down the up arrow key, you would initially get one up arrow key press event, but, after a delay, you would start getting a repeat event for the up arrow key. You may have noticed that behavior inside a word processor if you have ever held down a single key, like the *F* key for instance. You would start with a single **f** that appears inside your word processor, but, after a second or so you would start to get **fffffffffffff**, and you would continue to see **f** repeated into your word processor for as long as you held down the *F* key. Generally speaking, this behavior may be helpful when you are using a word processor, but is detrimental when you are playing a game. The preceding `if` block causes us to exit the function when we are receiving repeat key events.

The next several `if` blocks in our function check the various JavaScript keycodes and make calls to our WebAssembly module based on those keycodes. Let's take a quick look at what happens when the player presses the up arrow key, as follows:

```
// PRESS UP ARROW
if (event.keyCode === 38) {
    up_key_press = true;
    if( up_press_wrapper != null ) up_press_wrapper();
}
```

The `if` statement is checking the event's keycode against the value 38, which is the keycode value for the up arrow. You can find a list of HTML5 keycodes at: `https://www.embed.com/typescript-games/html-keycodes.html`. If the triggering event was an up arrow key press, we set the `up_key_press` variable to `true`. If our `up_press_wrapper` is initialized, we call it, which in turn will call the `press_up` function inside our WebAssembly module. After the `if` block that checks against the up arrow keycode, we will need more `if` blocks to check against the other arrow keys, as shown in the following example:

```
        // PRESS LEFT ARROW
        if (event.keyCode === 37) {
            left_key_press = true;
            if( left_press_wrapper != null ) left_press_wrapper();
        }

        // PRESS RIGHT ARROW
        if (event.keyCode === 39) {
            right_key_press = true;
            if( right_press_wrapper != null ) right_press_wrapper();
        }

        // PRESS DOWN ARROW
        if (event.keyCode === 40) {
            down_key_press = true;
            if( down_press_wrapper != null ) down_press_wrapper();
        }
}
```

After the `keyUp` function, we need to create a very similar function: `keyRelease`. This function is pretty much the same as `keyUp`, except it will be calling the key release functions in the WebAssembly module. The following code shows what the `keyRelease()` function looks like:

```
function keyRelease() {
    event.preventDefault();

    // PRESS UP ARROW
```

```
        if (event.keyCode === 38) {
            up_key_press = false;
            if( up_release_wrapper != null ) up_release_wrapper();
        }

        // PRESS LEFT ARROW
        if (event.keyCode === 37) {
            left_key_press = false;
            if( left_release_wrapper != null ) left_release_wrapper();
        }

        // PRESS RIGHT ARROW
        if (event.keyCode === 39) {
            right_key_press = false;
            if( right_release_wrapper != null ) right_release_wrapper();
        }

        // PRESS DOWN ARROW
        if (event.keyCode === 40) {
            down_key_press = false;
            if( down_release_wrapper != null ) down_release_wrapper();
        }
    }
```

After we have defined these functions, we need to make them event listeners with the following two lines of JavaScript code:

```
document.addEventListener('keydown', keyPress);
document.addEventListener('keyup', keyRelease);
```

The next thing we need to do is modify our `InitWrappers` function to wrap the functions we created earlier. We do this using the `Module.cwrap` function. The new version of our `InitWrappers` function is as follows:

```
function InitWrappers() {
    left_press_wrapper = Module.cwrap('press_left', 'undefined');
    right_press_wrapper = Module.cwrap('press_right', 'undefined');
    up_press_wrapper = Module.cwrap('press_up', 'undefined');
    down_press_wrapper = Module.cwrap('press_down', 'undefined');

    left_release_wrapper = Module.cwrap('release_left', 'undefined');
    right_release_wrapper = Module.cwrap('release_right', 'undefined');
    up_release_wrapper = Module.cwrap('release_up', 'undefined');
    down_release_wrapper = Module.cwrap('release_down', 'undefined');
}
```

We have two functions that are no longer needed that we can remove. These are the `runbefore` and `runafter` functions. These functions were used in our shell in chapter 2, *HTML5 and WebAssembly,* to demonstrate the `preRun` and `postRun` module functionality. All they do is log a line out to the console, so please remove the following code from the `jskey_shell.html` file:

```
function runbefore() {
    console.log("before module load");
}

function runafter() {
    console.log("after module load");
}
```

Now that we have deleted these lines, we can remove the call to these functions from our module's `preRun` and `postRun` arrays. Because we had earlier removed the call to `EM_ASM( InitWrappers() );` inside our WebAssembly module's `main` function, we will need to run `InitWrappers` from the module's `postRun` array. The following code shows what the beginning of the `Module` object definition looks like after these changes:

```
preRun: [],
postRun: [InitWrappers],
```

Now we should build and test our new JavaScript keyboard handler. Run the following `emcc` command:

```
emcc jskey.c -o jskey.html  -s NO_EXIT_RUNTIME=1 --shell-file
jskey_shell.html -s EXPORTED_FUNCTIONS="['_main', '_press_up',
'_press_down', '_press_left', '_press_right', '_release_up',
'_release_down', '_release_left', '_release_right']" -s
EXTRA_EXPORTED_RUNTIME_METHODS="['cwrap', 'ccall']"
```

You will notice that we have used the `-s EXPORT_FUNCTIONS` flag to export all of our key press and key release functions. Because we are not using the default shell, we have used the `--shell-file jskey_shell.html` flag. The `-s NO_EXIT_RUNTIME=1` flag prevents the browser from exiting the WebAssembly module if there is no emscripten main loop. We also exported `cwrap` and `ccall` with `-s EXTRA_EXPORTED_RUNTIME_METHODS="['cwrap', 'ccall']"`.

The following is a screenshot of the app:

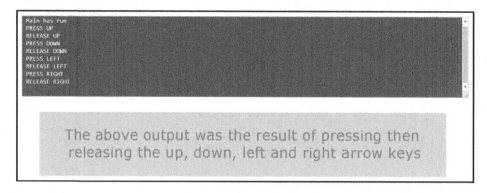

Figure 5.1: Screenshot of jskey.html

It is important to remember that the app must be run from a web server, or using emrun. If you do not run the app from a web server, or use emrun, you will receive a variety of errors when the JavaScript glue code attempts to download the WASM and data files. You should also know that IIS requires additional configuration in order to set the proper MIME types for the .wasm and .data file extensions.

In the next section, we will be using the SDL event handler and the default WebAssembly shell to capture and process keyboard events.

Adding SDL keyboard input to WebAssembly

SDL allows us to poll for keyboard input. Whenever the user presses a key, a call to SDL_PollEvent(&event) will return us an SDK_KEYDOWN SDL_Event. When a key is released, it will return an SDK_KEYUP event. We can look into the values in such a case to figure out which key has been pressed or released. We can use this information to set flags in our game to let us know when to move our spaceship, and in what direction. Later, we can add code that detects a space bar press that will fire our ship's weapons.

For now, we are going to go back to using the default Emscripten shell. For the rest of this section, we will be able to do everything from within the WebAssembly C code. I will walk you through creating a new keyboard.c file from scratch, which will handle keyboard events and print to the textarea in our default shell.

Start by creating a new `keyboard.c` file, and add the following `#include` directives at the top of the file:

```
#include <SDL2/SDL.h>
#include <emscripten.h>
#include <stdio.h>
#include <stdbool.h>
```

After that, we need to add our global `SDL` objects. The first two, `SDL_Window` and `SDL_Renderer`, should look familiar by now. The third one, `SDL_Event`, is new. We will be populating this event object using a call to `SDL_PollEvent` later in our code:

```
SDL_Window *window;
SDL_Renderer *renderer;
SDL_Event event;
```

Like the JavaScript version of this code, we will be using global variables to keep track of which arrow keys we are currently pressing. These will all be Boolean variables, as shown in the following code:

```
bool left_key_press = false;
bool right_key_press = false;
bool up_key_press = false;
bool down_key_press = false;
```

The first function we are going to define is `input_loop`, but before we can define that function, we need to declare two functions that `input_loop` will be calling, as follows:

```
void key_press();
void key_release();
```

This will allow us to define the `input_loop` function before actually defining what happens when `input_loop` calls those functions. The `input_loop` function will call `SDL_PollEvent` to get an event object. We can then look at the type of event, and, if it is an `SDL_KEYDOWN` or `SDL_KEYUP` event, we can call the appropriate function to handle those events, as follows:

```
void input_loop() {
    if( SDL_PollEvent( &event ) ){
        if( event.type == SDL_KEYDOWN ){
            key_press();
        }
        else if( event.type == SDL_KEYUP ) {
            key_release();
        }
```

```
        }
    }
```

The first of these functions that we will define will be the `key_press()` function. Inside this function, we will look at the keyboard event in a switch and compare the value to the different arrow key SDLK events. If the key had been previously up, it prints out a message that lets us know the key the user pressed. Then we should set the `keypress` flag to `true`. The following example shows the `key_press()` function in its entirety:

```
void key_press() {
    switch( event.key.keysym.sym ){
        case SDLK_LEFT:
            if( !left_key_press ) {
                printf("left arrow key press\n");
            }
            left_key_press = true;
            break;

        case SDLK_RIGHT:
            if( !right_key_press ) {
                printf("right arrow key press\n");
            }
            right_key_press = true;
            break;

        case SDLK_UP:
            if( !up_key_press ) {
                printf("up arrow key press\n");
            }
            up_key_press = true;
            break;

        case SDLK_DOWN:
            if( !down_key_press ) {
                printf("down arrow key press\n");
            }
            down_key_press = true;
            break;

        default:
            printf("unknown key press\n");
            break;
    }
}
```

The first line inside the `key_press` function is a switch
statement, `switch(event.key.keysym.sym)`. These are structures within structures.
Inside the `input_loop` function, we called `SDL_PollEvent`, passing a reference to
an `SDL_Event` structure. This structure contains event data for any possible event that may
be returned to us, as well as a type that tells us what kind of event this is. If the type
is `SDL_KEYDOWN` or `SDL_KEYUP`, that means the internal `key` structure, which is a structure
of type `SDL_KeyboardEvent`, is populated. If you would like to see the full definition of
the `SDL_Event` structure, you can find it on the SDL website, at: `https://wiki.libsdl.
org/SDL_Event`. Looking at the key variable inside of `SDL_Event`, you will notice it is a
structure of type `SDL_KeyboardEvent`. This structure has a lot of data in it that we will not
be using yet. It includes information such as timestamp, whether this key is a repeat press,
or whether this key is being pressed or released; but what we are looking at in our switch is
they `keysym` variable, which is a structure of type `SDL_Keysym`. For more information on
the `SDL_KeyboardEvent`, you can find its definition on the SDL website, at: `https://wiki.
libsdl.org/SDL_KeyboardEvent`. The `keysym` variable in
the `SDL_KeyboardEvent` structure is where you will find the `SDL_Keycode` in
the `sym` variable. This keycode is what we must look at to determine which key the player
pressed. That is why we have the switch statement built around `switch(
event.key.keysym.sym)`. A link to all of the possible values for the SDL keycodes is
available at: `https://wiki.libsdl.org/SDL_Keycode`.

All of the case statements inside our switch look pretty similar: if a given SDLK keycode is
pressed, we check to see if that key was pressed in the previous cycle, and we only print
out the value if it has not. Then we set the `keypress` flag to `true`. The following example
shows the code where we detect the press of the left arrow key:

```
case SDLK_LEFT:
    if( !left_key_press ) {
        printf("left arrow key press\n");
    }
    left_key_press = true;
    break;
```

Our application calls the `key_release` function when the event type is `SDL_KEYUP`. That
is very similar to the `key_down` function. The primary difference is that it is looking to see if
the user pressed the key, and only prints out a message when the state changes to
unpressed. The following example shows that function in its entirety:

```
void key_release() {
    switch( event.key.keysym.sym ){

        case SDLK_LEFT:
            if( left_key_press ) {
```

```
                                printf("left arrow key release\n");
                            }
                            left_key_press = false;
                            break;

                    case SDLK_RIGHT:
                            if( right_key_press ) {
                                printf("right arrow key release\n");
                            }
                            right_key_press = false;
                            break;

                    case SDLK_UP:
                            if( up_key_press ) {
                                printf("up arrow key release\n");
                            }
                            up_key_press = false;
                            break;

                    case SDLK_DOWN:
                            if( down_key_press ) {
                                printf("down arrow key release\n");
                            }
                            down_key_press = false;
                            break;

                    default:
                            printf("unknown key release\n");
                            break;
            }
    }
```

Our last function is a new version of the main function, called when our Module is loaded. We still need to use emscripten_set_main_loop to prevent our code from tying up the JavaScript engine. We have created an input_loop which we defined earlier. It uses SDL to poll for keyboard events. But, before that, we still need to do our SDL initialization. We are using the Emscripten default shell, so the call to SDL_CreateWindowAndRenderer will set the width and height of our canvas element. We will not be rendering to the canvas element inside our input_loop, but we still want to have it initialized here because, in the next section, we will be adapting this code to render a spaceship image to the canvas and to move it around with key presses. The following code shows what the new version of our main function will look like:

```
int main() {
    SDL_Init( SDL_INIT_VIDEO );
```

```
SDL_CreateWindowAndRenderer( 320, 200, 0, &window, &renderer );
SDL_SetRenderDrawColor( renderer, 0, 0, 0, 255 );

SDL_RenderClear( renderer );
SDL_RenderPresent( renderer );

emscripten_set_main_loop(input_loop, 0, 0);
return 1;
}
```

Now that we have all the code inside our keyboard.c file, we can compile our
keyboard.c file with the following emcc command:

```
emcc keyboard.c -o keyboard.html -s USE_SDL=2
```

When you run keyboard.html in the browser, you will notice that pressing the arrow
keys results in a message printed to the Emscripten default shell's textarea.

Consider the following screenshot:

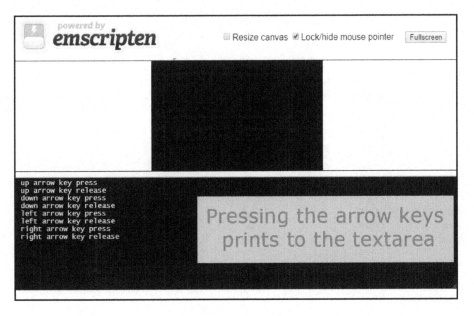

Figure 5.2: Screenshot of keyboard.html

In the next section, we will learn how to use this keyboard input to move a sprite around
our canvas.

Using keyboard input to move a sprite

Now that we know how to get keyboard input and use it in our WebAssembly module, let's figure out how we can take that keyboard input and use it to move our spaceship sprite around the HTML canvas. Let's begin by copying `sprite_move.c` from the `Chapter04` directory into the `Chapter05` directory. That will give us a good starting point. Now we can start modifying the code. We will need to add a single `#include` to the beginning of our `.c` file. Because we need Boolean variables, we must add `#include <stdbool.h>`. The new start of our `.c` file will now look as follows:

```
#include <SDL2/SDL.h>
#include <SDL2/SDL_image.h>
#include <emscripten.h>
#include <stdio.h>
#include <stdbool.h>
```

After that, all the `#define` directives will remain unchanged from what they were in the `sprite_move.c` file, as can be seen in the following code:

```
#define SPRITE_FILE "sprites/Franchise1.png"
#define ANIM_FILE "sprites/Franchise%d.png"
#define FRAME_COUNT 4
```

The `sprite_move.c` file had several global variables that we will continue to use in `keyboard_move.c`. Do not remove any of these variables; we will only be adding to them:

```
int current_frame = 0;

Uint32 last_time;
Uint32 current_time;
Uint32 ms_per_frame = 100; // animate at 10 fps

SDL_Window *window;
SDL_Renderer *renderer;
SDL_Rect dest = {.x = 160, .y = 100, .w = 0, .h = 0 };

SDL_Texture *sprite_texture;
SDL_Texture *temp_texture;
SDL_Texture* anim[FRAME_COUNT];
```

Now we need to bring in some variables from the `keyboard.c` file that we used in the previous section. We need the `SDL_Event` global variable so that we have something to pass into our call to `SDL_PollEvent`, and we need our Boolean key press flags, as follows:

```
SDL_Event event;

bool left_key_press = false;
bool right_key_press = false;
bool up_key_press = false;
bool down_key_press = false;
```

We then have the function declarations, which allow us to define the `key_press` and `key_release` functions after we have defined our `input_loop` function, as shown in the following example:

```
void key_press();
void key_release();
```

Next, we will bring in the `input_loop` function from our `keyboard.c` file. This is the function that we use to call `SDL_PollEvent`, and, based on the event type returned, either calls `key_press` or `key_release`. This function remains unchanged from the version we had in `keyboard.c`, as can be seen in the following example:

```
void input_loop() {
    if( SDL_PollEvent( &event ) ){
        if( event.type == SDL_KEYDOWN ){
            key_press();
        }
        else if( event.type == SDL_KEYUP ) {
            key_release();
        }
    }
}
```

The `key_press` and `key_release` functions follow the `input_loop` function and remain unchanged from the `keyboard.c` version. The primary purpose of these functions is to set the keypress flags. The `printf` statements are now unnecessary, but we will leave them there. This is not a good thing for performance because continuing to add lines to our `textarea` with every key press and release will eventually slow our game down, but, at this point, I feel it is better to leave these statements in for demonstration purposes:

```
void key_press() {
    switch( event.key.keysym.sym ){

        case SDLK_LEFT:
            if( !left_key_press ) {
```

```
                    printf("left arrow key press\n");
                }
                left_key_press = true;
                break;

            case SDLK_RIGHT:
                if( !right_key_press ) {
                    printf("right arrow key press\n");
                }
                right_key_press = true;
                break;

            case SDLK_UP:
                if( !up_key_press ) {
                    printf("up arrow key press\n");
                }
                up_key_press = true;
                break;

            case SDLK_DOWN:
                if( !down_key_press ) {
                    printf("down arrow key press\n");
                }
                down_key_press = true;
                break;

            default:
                printf("unknown key press\n");
                break;
        }
    }

void key_release() {
    switch( event.key.keysym.sym ){

        case SDLK_LEFT:
            if( left_key_press ) {
                printf("left arrow key release\n");
            }
            left_key_press = false;
            break;

        case SDLK_RIGHT:
            if( right_key_press ) {
                printf("right arrow key release\n");
            }
            right_key_press = false;
            break;
```

```
        case SDLK_UP:
            if( up_key_press ) {
                printf("up arrow key release\n");
            }
            up_key_press = false;
            break;

        case SDLK_DOWN:
            if( down_key_press ) {
                printf("down arrow key release\n");
            }
            down_key_press = false;
            break;

        default:
            printf("unknown key release\n");
            break;
    }
}
```

The next function in the keyboard_move.c file will be show_animation. This function will need to be changed significantly from the version that appears in sprite_move.c, to allow the player to control the spaceship and move it around the canvas. The following example shows you the new function in its entirety before we go through it a piece at a time:

```
void show_animation() {
    input_loop();

    current_time = SDL_GetTicks();
    int ms = current_time - last_time;

    if( ms >= ms_per_frame) {
        ++current_frame;
        last_time = current_time;
    }

    if( current_frame >= FRAME_COUNT ) {
        current_frame = 0;
    }

    SDL_RenderClear( renderer );
    temp_texture = anim[current_frame];

    if( up_key_press ) {
        dest.y--;
        if( dest.y < -16 ) {
```

```
                dest.y = 200;
            }
        }

        if( down_key_press ) {
            dest.y++;

            if( dest.y > 200 ) {
                dest.y = -16;
            }
        }

        if( left_key_press ) {
            dest.x--;

            if( dest.x < -16 ) {
                dest.x = 320;
            }
        }

        if( right_key_press ) {
            dest.x++;

            if( dest.x > 320 ) {
                dest.x = -16;
            }
        }

        SDL_RenderCopy( renderer, temp_texture, NULL, &dest );
        SDL_RenderPresent( renderer );
}
```

We added the very first line in `show_animation` to this new version of the function. The call to `input_loop` is used to set the key press flags every frame. After the call to `input_loop`, there is a chunk of the code that we have not changed from the `sprite_move.c` file, as shown in the following example:

```
current_time = SDL_GetTicks();
int ms = current_time - last_time;

if( ms >= ms_per_frame) {
    ++current_frame;
    last_time = current_time;
}

if( current_frame >= FRAME_COUNT ) {
    current_frame = 0;
```

```
}

SDL_RenderClear( renderer );
temp_texture = anim[current_frame];
```

This code calls `SDL_GetTicks()` to get the current time, and then subtracts the current time from the last time the current frame changed, to get the number of milliseconds it has been since we last had a frame change. If the number of milliseconds since the last frame change is greater than the number of milliseconds that we want to stay on any given frame, we need to advance the current frame. Once we have figured out whether or not we have advanced the current frame, we need to make sure that the current frame is not more than our frame count. If it is, we need to reset it to 0. After that, we need to clear out our renderer and set the texture we are using to the texture in our animation array that corresponds with the current frame.

In `sprite_move.c`, we moved the y coordinates of our spaceship up one pixel per frame with the following few lines of code:

```
dest.y--;

if( dest.y < -16 ) {
    dest.y = 200;
}
```

In the new keyboard app, we only want to change our y coordinate when the player presses the up arrow key. To do this, we must enclose the code that changes the y coordinate in an `if` block that checks the `up_key_press` flag. Here is the new version of that code:

```
if( up_key_press ) {
    dest.y--;

    if( dest.y < -16 ) {
        dest.y = 200;
    }
}
```

We also need to add code that moves the spaceship when the player presses the other arrow keys. The following code moves the spaceship down, left or right based on what keys the player is currently pressing:

```
if( down_key_press ) {
    dest.y++;

    if( dest.y > 200 ) {
        dest.y = -16;
```

```
        }
    }

    if( left_key_press ) {
        dest.x--;

        if( dest.x < -16 ) {
            dest.x = 320;
        }
    }

    if( right_key_press ) {
        dest.x++;

        if( dest.x > 320 ) {
            dest.x = -16;
        }
    }
```

Finally, we have to render the texture and present it, as follows:

```
SDL_RenderCopy( renderer, temp_texture, NULL, &dest );
SDL_RenderPresent( renderer );
```

The main function will not change from the version inside sprite_move.c because none of the initialization has changed. The following code shows the main function as it appears in keyboard_move.c:

```
int main() {
    char explosion_file_string[40];

    SDL_Init( SDL_INIT_VIDEO );
    SDL_CreateWindowAndRenderer( 320, 200, 0, &window, &renderer );
    SDL_SetRenderDrawColor( renderer, 0, 0, 0, 255 );
    SDL_RenderClear( renderer );

    SDL_Surface *temp_surface = IMG_Load( SPRITE_FILE );

    if( !temp_surface ) {
        printf("failed to load image: %s\n", IMG_GetError() );
        return 0;
    }

    sprite_texture = SDL_CreateTextureFromSurface( renderer, temp_surface
);

    SDL_FreeSurface( temp_surface );
```

```
for( int i = 1; i <= FRAME_COUNT; i++ ) {
    sprintf( explosion_file_string, ANIM_FILE, i );
    SDL_Surface *temp_surface = IMG_Load( explosion_file_string );

    if( !temp_surface ) {
        printf("failed to load image: %s\n", IMG_GetError() );
        return 0;
    }

    temp_texture = SDL_CreateTextureFromSurface( renderer, temp_surface
);
    anim[i-1] = temp_texture;
    SDL_FreeSurface( temp_surface );
}

SDL_QueryTexture( sprite_texture,
                  NULL, NULL,
                  &dest.w, &dest.h ); // query the width and height

dest.x -= dest.w / 2;
dest.y -= dest.h / 2;

SDL_RenderCopy( renderer, sprite_texture, NULL, &dest );
SDL_RenderPresent( renderer );

last_time = SDL_GetTicks();
emscripten_set_main_loop(show_animation, 0, 0);
return 1;
}
```

As I said earlier, this code is a combination of the last application we wrote in Chapter 4, *Sprite Animations in WebAssembly with SDL,* and the code we wrote in the section *Adding SDL keyboard input to WebAssembly* where we were taking input from the keyboard and logging our keys with the printf statement. We kept our input_loop function and added a call to it from the beginning of our show_animation function.

Inside show_animation, we no longer move the ship one pixel up every frame, but only move the ship up if we are pressing the up arrow key. Likewise, we move the ship left when the user presses the left arrow key, right when the right arrow key is pressed and down when the user presses the down arrow key.

Now that we have our new keyboard_move.c file, let's compile it and try out our new moving spaceship. Run the following emcc command to compile the code:

```
emcc keyboard_move.c -o keyboard_move.html --preload-file sprites -s
USE_SDL=2 -s USE_SDL_IMAGE=2 -s SDL2_IMAGE_FORMATS=["png"]
```

We need to add the `--preload-file sprites` flag to indicate that we want a virtual file system with the sprites folder included. We also need to add the `-s USE_SDL=2` and `-s USE_SDL_IMAGE=2 -s SDL2_IMAGE_FORMATS=["png"]` flags to allow us to load `.png` files from the virtual file system. Once you have compiled `keyboard_move.html`, load it into a browser and use the arrow keys to move the spaceship around the canvas. See the following screenshot:

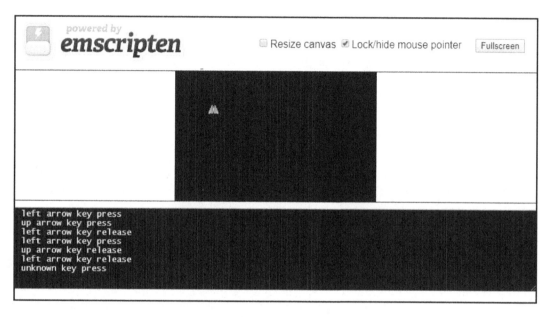

Figure 5.3: Screenshot of keyboard_move.html

Summary

In this chapter, we learned how to get keyboard input for use with WebAssembly. There are two primary methods. We could either take in keyboard input on the JavaScript side and communicate with WebAssembly through a wrapper made with `Module.cwrap`, or by calling WebAssembly functions directly with `Module.ccall`. The other way to accept keyboard input in WebAssembly is by using SDL keyboard input events. When we use this method, we can use the default Emscripten shell. This second method, using SDL events, will be our preferred method throughout the rest of this book.

In the next chapter, we will learn more about the game loop and how we will use it in our game, as well as games in general.

6
Game Objects and the Game Loop

In this chapter, we will begin to put the framework of a game into place. All games have **game objects** and a **game loop**. A game loop exists in every game ever written. Some tools, such as Unity, do their best to abstract away the game loop so that the developer does not necessarily need to know it is there, but even in these cases it still is. All games must take some control over the rendering capabilities of the operating system or hardware it is running on and draw images out to the screen while the game is running. All of the work of the game is done within a **big loop**. Game objects can be either an instance of classes in the case of **Object-Oriented Programming (OOP)** languages such as C++, or in the case of procedural languages such as C, they could be loose collections of variables or structures. In this chapter, we will be learning how to design a game loop and some early versions of our game objects from within C++ compiled into **WebAssembly**.

 You will need to include several images in your build to make this project work. Make sure you include the /Chapter06-game-object/sprites/ folder from the project's GitHub repository. If you haven't yet downloaded the GitHub project, you can get it online here: https://github.com/PacktPublishing/Hands-On-Game-Development-with-WebAssembly.

In this chapter, we will cover the following topics:

- Game loops
- Object pooling
- Player game object
- Enemy game object
- Projectiles

Understanding the game loop

A key concept in game design is the game loop. In any game, the code must run over and over again, performing a series of tasks such as input, AI, physics, and rendering. A game loop might look something like this:

```
while(loop_forever) {
    get_user_input();
    move_game_objects();
    collision_detection();
    render_game_objects();
    play_audio();
}
```

An SDL/C++ game targeting almost any platform except WebAssembly would have a while loop, probably located within the main function of the C++ code, that would exit only when the player exits the game. WebAssembly shares its runtime with the JavaScript engine inside your web browser. The JavaScript engine runs on a single thread, and Emscripten uses JavaScript **glue code** to take what you have done inside SDL within WebAssembly and render that to the HTML canvas element. Therefore, we need to use an Emscripten-specific piece of code for our game loop:

```
emscripten_set_main_loop(game_loop, 0, 0);
```

In the next few chapters, we will be adding some of these functions to our game:

- Game object management
- Collision detection between game objects
- Particle systems
- Enemy spaceship AI using a **finite state machine (FSM)**
- Game camera for tracking our player
- Play audio and sound effects
- Game physics
- User interface

These will be functions called from the game loop.

Writing a basic game loop

To some degree, we already have a simple game loop, although we did not create a function called `game_loop` explicitly. We are going to modify our code to have a more explicit game loop that will separate the `input`, `move`, and `render` functions. At this point, our `main` function becomes an initialization function that finishes by using Emscripten to set the game loop. The code for this new app is larger than earlier apps. Let's first walk through the code at a high level, introducing each section. Then we will walk through each of the individual sections of code in detail.

We begin the code with our `#include` and `#define` preprocessor macros:

```
#include <SDL2/SDL.h>
#include <SDL2/SDL_image.h>
#include <emscripten.h>
#include <stdio.h>
#include <stdbool.h>
#include <math.h>

#define SPRITE_FILE "sprites/Franchise.png"
#define PI 3.14159
#define TWO_PI 6.28318
#define MAX_VELOCITY 2.0
```

After the preprocessor macros, we have a few global time variables:

```
Uint32 last_time;
Uint32 last_frame_time;
Uint32 current_time;
```

We will then define several SDL-related global variables:

```
SDL_Window *window;
SDL_Renderer *renderer;
SDL_Rect dest = {.x = 160, .y = 100, .w = 16, .h = 16 };
SDL_Texture *sprite_texture;
SDL_Event event;
```

After our SDL global variables, we have a block of keyboard flags:

```
bool left_key_down = false;
bool right_key_down = false;
bool up_key_down = false;
bool down_key_down = false;
```

The last global variables track player data:

```
float player_x = 160.0;
float player_y = 100.0;
float player_rotation = PI;
float player_dx = 0.0;
float player_dy = 1.0;
float player_vx = 0.0;
float player_vy = 0.0;
float delta_time = 0.0;
```

Now that we have all of our global variables defined, we need two functions that rotate the player's spaceship left and right:

```
void rotate_left() {
    player_rotation -= delta_time;
    if( player_rotation < 0.0 ) {
        player_rotation += TWO_PI;
    }
    player_dx = sin(player_rotation);
    player_dy = -cos(player_rotation);
}

void rotate_right() {
    player_rotation += delta_time;
    if( player_rotation >= TWO_PI ) {
        player_rotation -= TWO_PI;
    }
    player_dx = sin(player_rotation);
    player_dy = -cos(player_rotation);
}
```

We then have three movement-related functions for our player's ship. We use them to accelerate and decelerate our spaceship, and to capp the velocity of our spaceship:

```
void accelerate() {
    player_vx += player_dx * delta_time;
    player_vy += player_dy * delta_time;
}

void decelerate() {
    player_vx -= (player_dx * delta_time) / 2.0;
    player_vy -= (player_dy * delta_time) / 2.0;
}

void cap_velocity() {
    float vel = sqrt( player_vx * player_vx + player_vy * player_vy );
    if( vel > MAX_VELOCITY ) {
```

```
        player_vx /= vel;
        player_vy /= vel;
        player_vx *= MAX_VELOCITY;
        player_vy *= MAX_VELOCITY;
    }
}
```

The move function performs the high-level movement of the game objects:

```
void move() {
    current_time = SDL_GetTicks();
    delta_time = (float)(current_time - last_time) / 1000.0;
    last_time = current_time;

    if( left_key_down ) {
        rotate_left();
    }
    if( right_key_down ) {
        rotate_right();
    }
    if( up_key_down ) {
        accelerate();
    }
    if( down_key_down ) {
        decelerate();
    }
    cap_velocity();

    player_x += player_vx;

    if( player_x > 320 ) {
        player_x = -16;
    }
    else if( player_x < -16 ) {
        player_x = 320;
    }

    player_y += player_vy;

    if( player_y > 200 ) {
        player_y = -16;
    }
    else if( player_y < -16 ) {
        player_y = 200;
    }
}
```

The input function determines the keyboard input states and sets our global keyboard flags:

```
void input() {
    if( SDL_PollEvent( &event ) ){
        switch( event.type ){
            case SDL_KEYDOWN:
                switch( event.key.keysym.sym ){
                    case SDLK_LEFT:
                        left_key_down = true;
                        break;
                    case SDLK_RIGHT:
                        right_key_down = true;
                        break;
                    case SDLK_UP:
                        up_key_down = true;
                        break;
                    case SDLK_DOWN:
                        down_key_down = true;
                        break;
                    default:
                        break;
                }
                break;
            case SDL_KEYUP:
                switch( event.key.keysym.sym ){
                    case SDLK_LEFT:
                        left_key_down = false;
                        break;
                    case SDLK_RIGHT:
                        right_key_down = false;
                        break;
                    case SDLK_UP:
                        up_key_down = false;
                        break;
                    case SDLK_DOWN:
                        down_key_down = false;
                        break;
                    default:
                        break;
                }
                break;

            default:
                break;
        }
    }
}
```

The `render` function draws the player's sprite to the canvas:

```
void render() {
    SDL_RenderClear( renderer );

    dest.x = player_x;
    dest.y = player_y;

    float degrees = (player_rotation / PI) * 180.0;
    SDL_RenderCopyEx( renderer, sprite_texture,
                        NULL, &dest,
    degrees, NULL, SDL_FLIP_NONE );

    SDL_RenderPresent( renderer );
}
```

The `game_loop` function runs all of our high-level game objects in each frame:

```
void game_loop() {
    input();
    move();
    render();
}
```

As always, the `main` function does all of our initialization:

```
int main() {
    char explosion_file_string[40];
    SDL_Init( SDL_INIT_VIDEO );
    SDL_CreateWindowAndRenderer( 320, 200, 0, &window, &renderer );
    SDL_SetRenderDrawColor( renderer, 0, 0, 0, 255 );
    SDL_RenderClear( renderer );
    SDL_Surface *temp_surface = IMG_Load( SPRITE_FILE );

    if( !temp_surface ) {
        printf("failed to load image: %s\n", IMG_GetError() );
        return 0;
    }

    sprite_texture = SDL_CreateTextureFromSurface( renderer,
                                                    temp_surface );
    SDL_FreeSurface( temp_surface );
    last_frame_time = last_time = SDL_GetTicks();

    emscripten_set_main_loop(game_loop, 0, 0);
    return 1;
}
```

You may have noticed that in the preceding code we have added a significant number of global variables to define player-specific values:

```
float player_x = 160.0;
float player_y = 100.0;
float player_rotation = PI;
float player_dx = 0.0;
float player_dy = 1.0;
float player_vx = 0.0;
float player_vy = 0.0;
```

In the *Game objects* section, we will begin to create game objects and move these values from global definitions into objects, but, for the time being, having them as global variables will work. We are adding the ability to move the player's ship around in a way that is similar to the classic arcade game *Asteroids*. In the final version of our game, we will have two spaceships fighting in a duel. To do this, we will need to keep track of the *x* and *y* coordinates of our ship and the ship's rotation; player_dx and player_dy make up a normalized direction vector for our spaceship.

The player_vx and player_vy variables are the player's current x and y velocities respectively.

Instead of having the left and right keys move the spaceship left or right while they are being held down, we are going to have those keys turn the spaceship to the left or the right. To do this, we will have our input function call the rotate_left and rotate_right functions:

```
void rotate_left() {
    player_rotation -= delta_time;
    if( player_rotation < 0.0 ) {
        player_rotation += TWO_PI;
    }
    player_dx = sin(player_rotation);
    player_dy = -cos(player_rotation);
}

void rotate_right() {
    player_rotation += delta_time;
    if( player_rotation >= TWO_PI ) {
        player_rotation -= TWO_PI;
    }
    player_dx = sin(player_rotation);
    player_dy = -cos(player_rotation);
}
```

If the player is turning left, we subtract the `delta_time` variable from the player rotation, which is the amount of time in seconds since the last frame rendered.

The `player_rotation` variable is the player's rotation in radians, where 180 degrees = π (3.14159…). That means that the player can turn 180 degrees by pressing and holding the left or right arrows for about three seconds. We also have to correct our rotation if the player's rotation goes below 0 or if the player's rotation goes above 2π (360 degrees). If you are not familiar with radians, it is an alternative to the system of measuring angles in which there are 360 degrees in a circle. Using radians, you think of how far you would have to walk around the circumference of a unit circle to get to that angle. A circle with a radius of 1 is called a **unit circle**.

The unit circle is on the left:

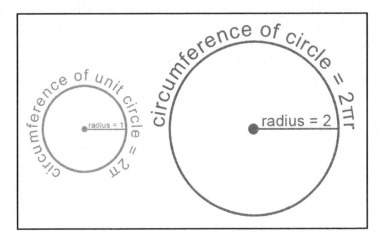

A unit circle and a circle with a radius of 2

The formula for the diameter of a circle is $2\pi r$ (in our code `2 * PI * radius`). So, 2π in radians is the same as saying 360 degrees. Most game engines and math libraries use radians instead of degrees, but for some reason SDL uses degrees when it rotates sprites, so we will need to change our rotation in radians back to degrees when we render our game objects (yuck!).

 Just to make sure everyone is following me, in our code the `PI` macro holds an approximate value for π that is defined as the ratio of a circle's diameter to its circumference. A typical approximation for π is 3.14, although we will approximate π as 3.14159 in our code.

We also need to accelerate or decelerate the spaceship if the player hits the up or down keys on the keyboard. To do this, we will create `accelerate` and `decelerate` functions that are called when the player holds down the up or down keys:

```
void accelerate() {
    player_vx += player_dx * delta_time;
    player_vy += player_dy * delta_time;
}

void decelerate() {
    player_vx -= (player_dx * delta_time) / 2.0;
    player_vy -= (player_dy * delta_time) / 2.0;
}
```

Both these functions take the `player_dx` and `player_dy` variables that were calculated using `sin` and `-cos` in our rotation functions and use those values to add to the player's x and y velocity stored in the `player_vx` and `player_vy` variables. We multiply the value by `delta_time`, which will set our acceleration to 1 pixel per second squared. Our decelerate function divides that value by 2, which sets our deceleration rate to 0.5 pixels per second squared.

After we define the `accelerate` and `decelerate` functions, we will need to create a function that will cap the x and y velocity of our spaceship to 2.0 pixels per second:

```
void cap_velocity() {
    float vel = sqrt( player_vx * player_vx + player_vy * player_vy );

    if( vel > MAX_VELOCITY ) {
        player_vx /= vel;
        player_vy /= vel;
        player_vx *= MAX_VELOCITY;
        player_vy *= MAX_VELOCITY;
    }
}
```

That is not the most efficient way to define this function, but it is the easiest to understand. The first line determines the magnitude of our velocity vector. If you do not know what that means, let me explain it a little better. We have a speed along the x axis. We also have a speed along the y axis. We want to cap the overall speed. If we capped the x and y velocities individually, we would be able to go faster by traveling diagonally. To calculate our total velocity, we need to use the Pythagorean theorem (do you remember high-school trigonometry?). If you don't remember, when you have a right triangle, to calculate its hypotenuse you take the square root of the sum of the square of the other two sides (remember $A^2 + B^2 = C^2$?):

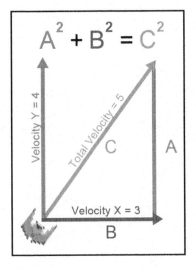

Using the Pythagorean theorem to determine the magnitude of the velocity using the x and y velocities

So, to calculate our velocity overall we need to square the x velocity, square the y velocity, add them together, and then take the square root. At this point, we check our velocity against the `MAX_VELOCITY` value, which we have defined as 2.0. If the current velocity is greater than this maximum velocity, we need to adjust our x and y velocities so that we are at a value of 2. We do this by dividing both the x and y velocities by the overall velocity, then multiplying by `MAX_VELOCITY`.

We will eventually need to write a move function that will move all of our game objects, but for the moment we will only be moving our player's spaceship:

```
void move() {
    current_time = SDL_GetTicks();
    delta_time = (float)(current_time - last_time) / 1000.0;
    last_time = current_time;

    if( left_key_down ) {
        rotate_left();
    }

    if( right_key_down ) {
        rotate_right();
    }

    if( up_key_down ) {
        accelerate();
    }
```

```
        if( down_key_down ) {
            decelerate();
        }

        cap_velocity();
        player_x += player_vx;

        if( player_x > 320 ) {
            player_x = -16;
        }
        else if( player_x < -16 ) {
            player_x = 320;
        }
        player_y += player_vy;

        if( player_y > 200 ) {
            player_y = -16;
        }
        else if( player_y < -16 ) {
            player_y = 200;
        }
    }
```

The first thing we need to do is get the current time for this frame, and then use that in combination with our previous frame time to calculate the `delta_time`.

The `delta_time` variable is the amount of time in seconds since the last frame time. We will need to tie much of the movement and animation to this value to get a consistent game speed that's independent of the frame rate on any given computer. After that, we need to rotate and accelerate or decelerate our spaceship based on the flags we set in our `input` function. We then cap our velocity and use the x and y values to modify the x and y coordinates of the player's spaceship.

There were a series of flags we used in the `move` function that told us whether we were currently holding down specific keys on the keyboard. To set those flags, we need an `input` function that uses `SDL_PollEvent` to find keyboard events and set the flags accordingly:

```
void input() {
    if( SDL_PollEvent( &event ) ){
        switch( event.type ){
            case SDL_KEYDOWN:
                switch( event.key.keysym.sym ){
                    case SDLK_LEFT:
                        left_key_down = true;
                        break;
                    case SDLK_RIGHT:
```

```
                                  right_key_down = true;
                                  break;
                         case SDLK_UP:
                                  up_key_down = true;
                                  break;
                         case SDLK_DOWN:
                                  down_key_down = true;
                                  break;
                         default:
                                  break;
                    }
                    break;
              case SDL_KEYUP:
                    switch( event.key.keysym.sym ){
                         case SDLK_LEFT:
                                  left_key_down = false;
                                  break;
                         case SDLK_RIGHT:
                                  right_key_down = false;
                                  break;
                         case SDLK_UP:
                                  up_key_down = false;
                                  break;
                         case SDLK_DOWN:
                                  down_key_down = false;
                                  break;
                         default:
                                  break;
                    }
                    break;
              default:
                    break;
         }
     }
}
```

This function includes a few `switch` statements that look for the arrow key presses and releases. If one of the arrow keys is pressed, we set the appropriate flag to `true`; if one is released, we set that flag to `false`.

Next, we define the `render` function. This function currently renders our spaceship sprite and will eventually render all of our sprites to the HTML canvas:

```
void render() {
    SDL_RenderClear( renderer );
    dest.x = player_x;
    dest.y = player_y;
```

```
        float degrees = (player_rotation / PI) * 180.0;
        SDL_RenderCopyEx( renderer, sprite_texture,
                            NULL, &dest,
                            degrees, NULL, SDL_FLIP_NONE );
        SDL_RenderPresent( renderer );
    }
```

This function clears the HTML canvas, sets the destination x and y values to `player_x` and `player_y`, calculates the player's rotation in degrees, and then renders that sprite to the canvas. We swapped out our previous call to `SDL_RenderCopy` with a call to `SDL_RenderCopyEx`. This new function allows us to pass in a value that rotates the sprite of our spaceship.

After we defined our `render` function, we have our new `game_loop` function:

```
void game_loop() {
    input();
    move();
    render();
}
```

This function will be called by `emscripten_set_main_loop` from within our `main` function. This function runs every frame that is rendered and is responsible for managing all the activities that go on within our game. It currently calls the `input`, `move`, and `render` functions that we defined earlier in our game code, and in the future it will call our AI code, sound effects, physics code, and more.

Compiling gameloop.html

Now that we have written our code, we can go ahead and compile our game loop app. Before you run this command, I want to reiterate that you need to have downloaded the project from GitHub (https://github.com/PacktPublishing/Hands-On-Game-Development-with-WebAssembly) because you will need the PNG files located in the /Chapter06-game-loop/sprites folder in order to build this project.

Once you have your folders set up properly, compile the app with the following command:

```
emcc game_loop.c -o gameloop.html  --preload-file sprites -s
NO_EXIT_RUNTIME=1 -s USE_SDL_IMAGE=2 -s SDL2_IMAGE_FORMATS=["png"] -s
EXTRA_EXPORTED_RUNTIME_METHODS="['cwrap', 'ccall']" -s USE_SDL=2
```

Serve the directory where you compiled it with a web server, or build and run it with emrun, and it should look like this when loaded into a web browser:

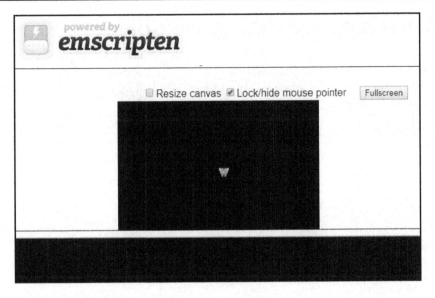

The screenshot gameloop.html

It is important to remember that you must run WebAssembly apps using a web server, or with `emrun`. If you would like to run your WebAssembly app using `emrun`, you must compile it with the `--emrun` flag. The web browser requires a web server to stream the WebAssembly module. If you attempt to open an HTML page that uses WebAssembly in a browser directly from your hard drive, that WebAssembly module will not load.

After the app has compiled, you should be able to move the spaceship around the canvas using the arrow keys. Now that we have a basic game loop, in the next section, we will be adding some game objects to our app, making it more of a game.

Game objects

Our approach so far has been entirely procedural and has been coded so that it could have been written in C and not C++. Developers have been writing games in C and even assembly language for a long time, so having an object-oriented approach to game design is not strictly necessary, but from a code management perspective OOP is a great way to design and write your games. Game objects can help us manage our allocated memory through object pooling. At this point, it will also make sense to begin breaking our program up into multiple files. My approach will be to have a single `.hpp` file that defines all of our game objects, and one `.cpp` file for each of our objects.

The player's spaceship game object

Up to this point, we have been keeping all of the values that track our player's ship in global variables. From an organizational perspective, this is less than ideal. The first game object we will create will be the player's ship object. We will start with a basic class and add more object-oriented features to our code later.

Here is the code for our new header file, game.hpp:

```
#ifndef __GAME_H__
#define __GAME_H__
#include <SDL2/SDL.h>
#include <SDL2/SDL_image.h>
#include <emscripten.h>
#include <stdio.h>
#include <stdbool.h>
#include <math.h>
#include <string>
#include <vector>

#define SPRITE_FILE "sprites/Franchise.png"
#define MAX_VELOCITY 2.0
#define PI 3.14159
#define TWO_PI 6.28318

extern Uint32 last_time;
extern Uint32 last_frame_time;
extern Uint32 current_time;
extern SDL_Window *window;
extern SDL_Renderer *renderer;
extern SDL_Rect dest;
extern SDL_Texture *sprite_texture;
extern SDL_Event event;
extern bool left_key_down;
extern bool right_key_down;
extern bool up_key_down;
extern bool down_key_down;
extern bool space_key_down;
extern float delta_time;
extern int diff_time;

class PlayerShip {
    public:
        float m_X;
        float m_Y;
        float m_Rotation;
        float m_DX;
```

```
        float m_DY;
        float m_VX;
        float m_VY;

        PlayerShip();
        void RotateLeft();
        void RotateRight();
        void Accelerate();
        void Decelerate();
        void CapVelocity();
        void Move();
        void Render();
    };

    extern PlayerShip player;
    #endif
```

All of our CPP files will include this `game.hpp` header file. The first few lines of this file are to make sure we do not include this file more than once. We are then defining all of the global variables we had defined in our older C files:

```
    extern Uint32 last_time;
    extern Uint32 last_frame_time;
    extern Uint32 current_time;
    extern SDL_Window *window;
    extern SDL_Renderer *renderer;
    extern SDL_Rect dest;
    extern SDL_Texture *sprite_texture;
    extern SDL_Event event;
    extern bool left_key_down;
    extern bool right_key_down;
    extern bool up_key_down;
    extern bool down_key_down;
    extern float delta_time;
```

In the header file, we are not allocating space on to the heap. The use of the `extern` keyword before our global variable definitions tells the compiler that we declared the global variable in one of the `.cpp` files. Right now, we still have a lot of global variables. We will be reducing the number of these globals as we make modifications to our code in this chapter.

If this were production code, it would make sense to move all of these values into classes, but, for now, we are only creating a `PlayerShip` object. We also have our class definition for `PlayerShip`. Developers usually create class definitions inside header files.

After we define all of our global variables, we will need our class definition.

Here is the definition of our `PlayerShip` class:

```
class PlayerShip {
    public:
        float m_X;
        float m_Y;
        float m_Rotation;
        float m_DX;
        float m_DY;
        float m_VX;
        float m_VY;

        PlayerShip();
        void RotateLeft();
        void RotateRight();
        void Accelerate();
        void Decelerate();
        void CapVelocity();
        void Move();
        void Render();
    };

    extern PlayerShip player;
```

In this book, we are going to declare all of our attributes `public`. That means our code can access them from anywhere, not just from inside this function. If you are working on a project with more than one developer, this is not usually considered to be a good practice. Preventing other classes from being able to directly modify some of our attributes such as m_DX and m_DY is a good idea if you do not want another developer to directly alter specific attributes that only functions in a class are meant to modify. For demonstration purposes, however, having everything in our class defined as `public` will simplify our design.

After we define our attributes, we have a series of functions that will be associated with this class once defined. The first function, `PlayerShip()`, has the same name as our class, which makes it the constructor, that is, the function that is called by default when our app creates an object of the `PlayerShip` type. If we wished, we could define a destructor function, which would run when the object was destroyed, by calling it `~PlayerShip()`. We do not currently need a destructor for that object so we will not define it here, which means we will rely on C++ to create a *default destructor* for this class.

All of the other functions we have defined in this class correspond to functions we created in previous C versions of our game. Moving all of these functions to a class allows us to organize our code better. Notice that after our class definition, we created another global variable that is a `PlayerShip` called `player`. The compiler shares this player object in all of the `.cpp` files that include our `game.hpp` file.

Object pooling

We have defined our first game object, which represents our player's spaceship, but all we can do is fly around the game screen. We need to allow our player to shoot a projectile. If we created a new projectile object every time a player shot a projectile, we would quickly fill up the WASM module's memory. What we need to do is create what is known as an **object pool**. Object pools are used to create objects with a fixed lifespan. Our projectiles only need to be alive long enough to either hit a target or travel a fixed distance before disappearing. If we create a set number of projectiles that is a little more than we need on the screen at one time, we can keep those objects in a pool in either an active or inactive state. When we need to launch a new projectile, we scan our object pool for an inactive one, then activate it and place it at the launch point. This way, we are not continually allocating and de-allocating memory to create our projectiles.

Let's go back to our `game.hpp` file and add a few class definitions right before the `#endif` macro:

```
class Projectile {
    public:
        const char* c_SpriteFile = "sprites/Projectile.png";
        const int c_Width = 8;
        const int c_Height = 8;
        SDL_Texture *m_SpriteTexture;
        bool m_Active;
        const float c_Velocity = 6.0;
        const float c_AliveTime = 2000;
        float m_TTL;
        float m_X;
        float m_Y;
        float m_VX;
        float m_VY;

        Projectile();
        void Move();
        void Render();
        void Launch(float x, float y, float dx, float dy);
};
```

```
class ProjectilePool {
    public:
        std::vector<Projectile*> m_ProjectileList;
        ProjectilePool();
        ~ProjectilePool();
        void MoveProjectiles();
        void RenderProjectiles();
        Projectile* GetFreeProjectile();
};

    extern ProjectilePool* projectile_pool;
```

So, we have defined all of our classes inside the game.hpp file. Right now, we have three classes: PlayerShip, Projectile, and ProjectilePool.

The PlayerShip class existed before, but we are adding some additional functionality to that class to allow us to fire projectiles. To allow for this new functionality, we are adding some new public attributes to our class definition:

```
public:
    const char* c_SpriteFile = "sprites/Franchise.png";
    const Uint32 c_MinLaunchTime = 300;
    const int c_Width = 16;
    const int c_Height = 16;
    Uint32 m_LastLaunchTime;
    SDL_Texture *m_SpriteTexture;
```

We moved a few of the values we had in #define macros directly into the class. The c_SpriteFile constant is the name of the PNG file we will load to render our player's spaceship sprite. The c_MinLaunchTime constant is the minimum amount of time in milliseconds between two launches of projectiles. We have also defined the width and height of our sprite with the c_Width and c_Height constants. This way, we can have different values for different object types. The m_LastLaunchTime attribute tracks the most recent projectile launch time in milliseconds. The sprite texture, which had previously been a global variable, will move into the attributes of the player's ship class.

After making our modifications to the PlayerShip class definition, we must add a class definition for two new classes. The first of these two classes is the Projectile class:

```
class Projectile {
    public:
        const char* c_SpriteFile = "sprites/Projectile.png";
        const int c_Width = 8;
        const int c_Height = 8;
        const float c_Velocity = 6.0;
        const float c_AliveTime = 2000;
```

```
        SDL_Texture *m_SpriteTexture;
        bool m_Active;
        float m_TTL;
        float m_X;
        float m_Y;
        float m_VX;
        float m_VY;

        Projectile();
        void Move();
        void Render();
        void Launch(float x, float y, float dx, float dy);
};
```

This class represents the projectile game objects that will be shot by the player, and later the enemy spaceship. We start with several constants that define where we place our sprite in the virtual filesystem, as well as the width and height:

```
class Projectile {
    public:
        const char* c_SpriteFile = "sprites/Projectile.png";
        const int c_Width = 8;
        const int c_Height = 8;
```

The next attribute is m_SpriteTexture, which is a pointer to the SDL texture used to render our projectiles. We need a variable to tell our object pool that this game object is active. We have called that attribute m_Active. Next, we have a constant that defines how fast our projectile will move in pixels per second, called c_Velocity, and a constant that indicates how long the projectile will stay alive in milliseconds before self-destructing, called c_AliveTime.

The m_TTL variable is a **time to live** variable that tracks how many milliseconds remain until this projectile will change its m_Active variable to false and recycle itself back into the **projectile pool**. The m_X, m_Y, m_VX, and m_VY variables are used to track the x and y position and the x and y velocity of our projectile.

We then declare four functions for our projectile class:

```
Projectile();
void Move();
void Render();
void Launch(float x, float y, float dx, float dy);
```

The `Projectile` function is our class constructor. If our projectile is currently active, `Move` and `Render` will be called once per frame. The `Move` function will manage the movement of an active projectile and `Render` will manage drawing the projectile sprite to our HTML canvas element. The `Launch` function will be called from our `PlayerShip` class to make our ship launch a projectile in the direction the ship is facing.

The final class definition we must add to our `game.hpp` file is the `ProjectilePool` class:

```
class ProjectilePool {
    public:
        std::vector<Projectile*> m_ProjectileList;
        ProjectilePool();
        ~ProjectilePool();
        void MoveProjectiles();
        void RenderProjectiles();
        Projectile* GetFreeProjectile();
};
```

This class manages a **pool** of 10 projectiles stored inside a vector attribute, `m_ProjectileList`. The functions for this class include a constructor and destructor, `MoveProjectiles`, `RenderProjectils`, and `GetFreeProjectile`.

The `MoveProjectiles()` function loops over our projectile list calling the `move` function on any active projectile. The `RenderProjectiles()` function loops over our projectile list and renders to canvas any active projectile, and `GetFreeProjectile` returns the first projectile in our pool that is not active.

Pooling the player's projectiles

Now that we have looked at the class definitions for our `Projectile` and `ProjectilePool` classes, we need to create a `projectile.cpp` file and a `projectile_pool.cpp` file to store the function code for those classes. Because this is in Chapter 6, *Game Objects and the Game Loop*, I would recommend creating a new folder named Chapter06 to hold these files. This code will do the work of pooling our projectiles, requesting an inactive projectile when we need one, and moving and rendering our active projectiles. First, let's look at the code we have in `projectile.cpp`:

```
#include "game.hpp"

Projectile::Projectile() {
    m_Active = false;
    m_X = 0.0;
    m_Y = 0.0;
```

```
    m_VX = 0.0;
    m_VY = 0.0;

    SDL_Surface *temp_surface = IMG_Load( c_SpriteFile );

    if( !temp_surface ) {
        printf("failed to load image: %s\n", IMG_GetError() );
        return;
    }

    m_SpriteTexture = SDL_CreateTextureFromSurface( renderer,
    temp_surface );

    if( !m_SpriteTexture ) {
        printf("failed to create texture: %s\n", IMG_GetError() );
        return;
    }

    SDL_FreeSurface( temp_surface );
}

void Projectile::Move() {
    m_X += m_VX;
    m_Y += m_VY;
    m_TTL -= diff_time;

    if( m_TTL <= 0 ) {
        m_Active = false;
        m_TTL = 0;
    }
}

void Projectile::Render() {
    dest.x = m_X;
    dest.y = m_Y;
    dest.w = c_Width;
    dest.h = c_Height;

    int return_val = SDL_RenderCopy( renderer, m_SpriteTexture,
                                     NULL, &dest );
    if( return_val != 0 ) {
        printf("SDL_Init failed: %s\n", SDL_GetError());
    }
}

void Projectile::Launch(float x, float y, float dx, float dy) {
    m_X = x;
    m_Y = y;
```

```
    m_VX = c_Velocity * dx;
    m_VY = c_Velocity * dy;
    m_TTL = c_AliveTime;
    m_Active = true;
}
```

That is the code that deals with moving, rendering, and launching a single projectile. The first function declared here is the constructor:

```
Projectile::Projectile() {
    m_Active = false;
    m_X = 0.0;
    m_Y = 0.0;
    m_VX = 0.0;
    m_VY = 0.0;

    SDL_Surface *temp_surface = IMG_Load( c_SpriteFile );

    if( !temp_surface ) {
        printf("failed to load image: %s\n", IMG_GetError() );
        return;
    }

    m_SpriteTexture = SDL_CreateTextureFromSurface( renderer,
    temp_surface );

    if( !m_SpriteTexture ) {
        printf("failed to create texture: %s\n", IMG_GetError() );
        return;
    }
    SDL_FreeSurface( temp_surface );
}
```

The primary concern of this constructor is to set the projectile to inactive and create an SDL texture that we will later use to render our sprite to the canvas element. After defining our constructor, we define our Move function:

```
void Projectile::Move() {
    m_X += m_VX;
    m_Y += m_VY;
    m_TTL -= diff_time;
    if( m_TTL <= 0 ) {
        m_Active = false;
        m_TTL = 0;
    }
}
```

This function changes the *x* and *y* position of our projectile based on the velocity, and reduces the time to live of our projectile, setting it to inactive and recycling it into the projectile pool if it's time to live is less than or equal to zero. The next function we define is our `Render` function:

```
void Projectile::Render() {
    dest.x = m_X;
    dest.y = m_Y;
    dest.w = c_Width;
    dest.h = c_Height;

    int return_val = SDL_RenderCopy( renderer, m_SpriteTexture,
                                     NULL, &dest );
    if( return_val != 0 ) {
        printf("SDL_Init failed: %s\n", SDL_GetError());
    }
}
```

This code is similar to the code we used to render our spaceship, so it should look pretty familiar to you. Our final projectile function is the `Launch` function:

```
void Projectile::Launch(float x, float y, float dx, float dy) {
    m_X = x;
    m_Y = y;
    m_VX = c_Velocity * dx;
    m_VY = c_Velocity * dy;
    m_TTL = c_AliveTime;
    m_Active = true;
}
```

This function is called from the `PlayerShip` class whenever the player presses the spacebar on the keyboard. The `PlayerShip` object will pass in the *x* and *y* coordinates of the player's ship, as well as the direction the ship is facing in the `dx` and `dy` parameters. These parameters are used to set the *x* and *y* coordinates for the projectile as well as the *x* and *y* velocity of the projectile. The game sets the time to live to the default alive time and then sets the object to active.

Now that we have fully defined our `Projectile` class, let's set the `ProjectilePool` class that will manage those projectiles. The following code will be in our `projectile_pool.cpp` file:

```
#include "game.hpp"

ProjectilePool::ProjectilePool() {
    for( int i = 0; i < 10; i++ ) {
        m_ProjectileList.push_back( new Projectile() );
```

```
    }
}

ProjectilePool::~ProjectilePool() {
    m_ProjectileList.clear();
}

void ProjectilePool::MoveProjectiles() {
    Projectile* projectile;
    std::vector<Projectile*>::iterator it;

    for( it = m_ProjectileList.begin(); it != m_ProjectileList.end(); it++
) {
        projectile = *it;
        if( projectile->m_Active ) {
            projectile->Move();
        }
    }
}

void ProjectilePool::RenderProjectiles() {
    Projectile* projectile;
    std::vector<Projectile*>::iterator it;

    for( it = m_ProjectileList.begin(); it != m_ProjectileList.end(); it++
) {
        projectile = *it;
        if( projectile->m_Active ) {
            projectile->Render();
         }
    }
}

Projectile* ProjectilePool::GetFreeProjectile() {
    Projectile* projectile;
    std::vector<Projectile*>::iterator it;
    for( it = m_ProjectileList.begin(); it != m_ProjectileList.end(); it++
) {
        projectile = *it;
        if( projectile->m_Active == false ) {
            return projectile;
        }
    }
    return NULL;
}
```

The first two functions are the constructor and destructor functions. These functions create and destroy the projectiles inside our list. The next function is the `MoveProjectiles` function, which loops through our `m_ProjectileList` looking for active projectiles and moving them. After that, we have a `RenderProjectiles` function, which is quite similar to our `MoveProjectiles` function. This function loops through our list calling the `Render` function on all active projectiles. The final function is the `GetFreeProjectile` function, which steps through `m_ProjectileList` looking for the first projectile that is not active in order to return it. Whenever we want to launch a projectile, we will need to call this function to find one that is not active.

Creating an enemy

So, now that we have a player ship that is shooting, we can work on adding an enemy ship. It will be similar to the `PlayerShip` class. Later, we will get into class inheritance so that we will not end up with a copied and pasted version of the same code, but for right now we will add a new class definition to our `game.hpp` file that is almost identical to our `PlayerShip` class:

```
enum FSM_STUB {
    SHOOT = 0,
    TURN_LEFT = 1,
    TURN_RIGHT = 2,
    ACCELERATE = 3,
    DECELERATE = 4
};

class EnemyShip {
    public:
        const char* c_SpriteFile = "sprites/BirdOfAnger.png";
        const Uint32 c_MinLaunchTime = 300;
        const int c_Width = 16;
        const int c_Height = 16;
        const int c_AIStateTime = 2000;

        Uint32 m_LastLaunchTime;
        SDL_Texture *m_SpriteTexture;

        FSM_STUB m_AIState;
        int m_AIStateTTL;

        float m_X;
        float m_Y;
        float m_Rotation;
```

```
            float m_DX;
            float m_DY;
            float m_VX;
            float m_VY;
            EnemyShip();
            void RotateLeft();
            void RotateRight();
            void Accelerate();
            void Decelerate();
            void CapVelocity();
            void Move();
            void Render();
            void AIStub();
    };
```

You will notice that before the EnemyShip class we defined an FSM_STUB enumeration. An enumeration is like a new data type that you can define inside your C or C++ code. We will be discussing **artificial intelligence** and **finite state machines** in another chapter, but right now we still want our enemy ship to do something, even if that something is not very intelligent. We created an FSM_STUB enumeration to define the things that our enemy ship can currently do. We have also created an AIStub inside our EnemyShip class that will act as a stand-in for future AI logic. The m_AIStateTTL integer attribute is a countdown timer to an AI state change. There is also a new constant called c_AIStateTime that has a value of 2000. That is the number of milliseconds our AI state will persist before it changes randomly.

We will create an enemy_ship.cpp file and add nine functions to it. The first function is our constructor, which is preceded by the #include of our game.hpp file:

```
#include "game.hpp"
EnemyShip::EnemyShip() {
 m_X = 60.0;
    m_Y = 50.0;
    m_Rotation = PI;
    m_DX = 0.0;
    m_DY = 1.0;
    m_VX = 0.0;
    m_VY = 0.0;
    m_LastLaunchTime = current_time;

    SDL_Surface *temp_surface = IMG_Load( c_SpriteFile );

    if( !temp_surface ) {
        printf("failed to load image: %s\n", IMG_GetError() );
        return;
    }
```

```
    else {
        printf("success creating enemy ship surface\n");
    }
    m_SpriteTexture = SDL_CreateTextureFromSurface( renderer,
    temp_surface );

    if( !m_SpriteTexture ) {
        printf("failed to create texture: %s\n", IMG_GetError() );
        return;
    }
    else {
        printf("success creating enemy ship texture\n");
    }
    SDL_FreeSurface( temp_surface );
}
```

After that, we have the functions `RotateLeft` and `RotateRight` which are used to turn the space ship:

```
void EnemyShip::RotateLeft() {
    m_Rotation -= delta_time;
    if( m_Rotation < 0.0 ) {
        m_Rotation += TWO_PI;
    }
    m_DX = sin(m_Rotation);
    m_DY = -cos(m_Rotation);
}
void EnemyShip::RotateRight() {
    m_Rotation += delta_time;

    if( m_Rotation >= TWO_PI ) {
        m_Rotation -= TWO_PI;
    }
    m_DX = sin(m_Rotation);
    m_DY = -cos(m_Rotation);
}
```

The functions `Accelerate`, `Decelerate` and `CapVelocity` are all used to modify the Enemy Ship's velocity.:

```
void EnemyShip::Accelerate() {
    m_VX += m_DX * delta_time;
    m_VY += m_DY * delta_time;
}

void EnemyShip::Decelerate() {
    m_VX -= (m_DX * delta_time) / 2.0;
    m_VY -= (m_DY * delta_time) / 2.0;
```

```
    }

    void EnemyShip::CapVelocity() {
        float vel = sqrt( m_VX * m_VX + m_VY * m_VY );

        if( vel > MAX_VELOCITY ) {
            m_VX /= vel;
            m_VY /= vel;

            m_VX *= MAX_VELOCITY;
            m_VY *= MAX_VELOCITY;
        }
    }
```

The next thing we add to the file is the Render function:

```
    void EnemyShip::Render() {
        dest.x = (int)m_X;
        dest.y = (int)m_Y;
        dest.w = c_Width;
        dest.h = c_Height;

        float degrees = (m_Rotation / PI) * 180.0;

        int return_code = SDL_RenderCopyEx( renderer, m_SpriteTexture,
                                            NULL, &dest,
                                            degrees, NULL, SDL_FLIP_NONE );

    if( return_code != 0 ) {
    printf("failed to render image: %s\n", IMG_GetError() );
    }
    }
```

Finally, we add the Move and AIStub functions:

```
    void EnemyShip::Move() {
        AIStub();

    if( m_AIState == TURN_LEFT ) {
        RotateLeft();
    }

    if( m_AIState == TURN_RIGHT ) {
        RotateRight();
    }

    if( m_AIState == ACCELERATE ) {
        Accelerate();
```

```
    }

    if( m_AIState == DECELERATE ) {
        Decelerate();
    }

    CapVelocity();
    m_X += m_VX;

    if( m_X > 320 ) {
        m_X = -16;
    }
    else if( m_X < -16 ) {
        m_X = 320;
    }

    m_Y += m_VY;

    if( m_Y > 200 ) {
        m_Y = -16;
    }
    else if( m_Y < -16 ) {
        m_Y = 200;
    }

    if( m_AIState == SHOOT ) {
        Projectile* projectile;
        if( current_time - m_LastLaunchTime >= c_MinLaunchTime ) {
            m_LastLaunchTime = current_time;
            projectile = projectile_pool->GetFreeProjectile();

            if( projectile != NULL ) {
                projectile->Launch( m_X, m_Y, m_DX, m_DY );
                }
            }
        }
}

void EnemyShip::AIStub() {
    m_AIStateTTL -= diff_time;
    if( m_AIStateTTL <= 0 ) {
        // for now get a random AI state.
        m_AIState = (FSM_STUB)(rand() % 5);
        m_AIStateTTL = c_AIStateTime;
    }
}
```

These functions are all the same as the functions defined in our `player_ship.cpp` file, except for the `Move` function. We have added a new function, `AIStub`. Here is the code in the `AIStub` function:

```
void EnemyShip::AIStub() {
    m_AIStateTTL -= diff_time;

    if( m_AIStateTTL <= 0 ) {
        // for now get a random AI state.
        m_AIState = (FSM_STUB)(rand() % 5);
        m_AIStateTTL = c_AIStateTime;
    }
}
```

This function is meant to be temporary. We will eventually define a real AI for our enemy spaceship. Right now, this function uses `m_AIStateTTL` to count down a fixed number of milliseconds until it reaches or goes below 0. At this point, it randomly sets a new AI state based on one of the values in the enumeration we defined earlier called `FSM_STUB`. We have also made some modifications to the `Move()` function that we created for the player ship:

```
void EnemyShip::Move() {
    AIStub();

    if( m_AIState == TURN_LEFT ) {
        RotateLeft();
    }
    if( m_AIState == TURN_RIGHT ) {
        RotateRight();
    }
    if( m_AIState == ACCELERATE ) {
        Accelerate();
    }
    if( m_AIState == DECELERATE ) {
        Decelerate();
    }
    CapVelocity();
     m_X += m_VX;

    if( m_X > 320 ) {
        m_X = -16;
    }
    else if( m_X < -16 ) {
        m_X = 320;
    }
    m_Y += m_VY;
```

```
        if( m_Y > 200 ) {
            m_Y = -16;
        }
        else if( m_Y < -16 ) {
            m_Y = 200;
        }

        if( m_AIState == SHOOT ) {
            Projectile* projectile;
            if( current_time - m_LastLaunchTime >= c_MinLaunchTime ) {
                m_LastLaunchTime = current_time;
                projectile = projectile_pool->GetFreeProjectile();

                if( projectile != NULL ) {
                    projectile->Launch( m_X, m_Y, m_DX, m_DY );
                }
            }
        }
    }
}
```

I have taken the code from our `PlayerShip::Move` function and made some modifications to it. At the beginning of this new function, we have added a call to the `AIStub` function. This function is a stand-in for our future AI. Instead of looking at our keyboard input as we did for the player ship, the enemy ship will look at the AI state and choose to rotate left, rotate right, accelerate, decelerate, or shoot. That is not real AI, it is just the ship doing random things, but it allows us to get an idea of what the ship will look like when it has real AI, and it will allow us to add more functionality later, such as collision detection.

Compiling game_objects.html

Now that we have built all of these game objects, we no longer have everything inside a single file. We will need to include several CPP files and compile them all into a single output file we will call `game_objects.html`. Because we have moved from the world of C to C++, we will be using em++ to indicate that the files we are compiling are C++ files and not C files. That is not strictly necessary, because Emscripten will figure out that we are compiling with C++ when it receives files with the `.cpp` extension as input. We are also telling the compiler explicitly the version of C++ we are using when we pass in the -std=c++17 flag. Go ahead and compile the `game_objects.html` file with the following em++ command:

```
em++ main.cpp enemy_ship.cpp player_ship.cpp projectile.cpp
projectile_pool.cpp -std=c++17 --preload-file sprites -s USE_WEBGL2=1 -s
USE_SDL=2 -s USE_SDL_IMAGE=2 -s SDL2_IMAGE_FORMATS=["png"] -o
game_objects.html
```

Now that we have our `game_objects.html` file compiled use a web server to serve the files and open it in a browser, it should look like this:

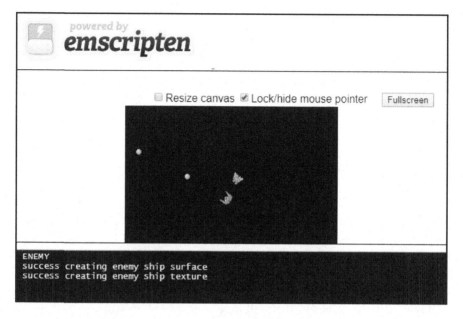

A screenshot of game_objects.html

 Do not forget that you must run WebAssembly apps using a web server, or with `emrun`. If you would like to run your WebAssembly app using `emrun`, you must compile it with the `--emrun` flag. The web browser requires a web server to stream the WebAssembly module. If you attempt to open an HTML page that uses WebAssembly in a browser directly from your hard drive, that WebAssembly module will not load.

You can move your spaceship around the canvas with the arrow keys, and fire a projectile with the spacebar. The enemy ship will move around the canvas shooting randomly.

 If you are having problems building this app, or any of the other apps in this book, please remember you can contact me on Twitter, `https://twitter.com/battagline/`, using the Twitter handle `@battagline` to ask questions. I am happy to help.

Summary

In this chapter, we learned how to create a basic game framework. We learned what a game loop is and how we create one for WebAssembly using Emscripten. We learned about game objects and created classes to define our player's spaceship, an enemy spaceship, and projectiles. We learned about object pooling, and how we can use an object pool to recycle objects in memory so that we do not need to create and destroy new objects in memory continually. We used this knowledge to create an object pool for our projectiles. We also created an AI stub for our enemy spaceship that gave that object random behavior, and we created functions that let our player and enemy shoot at each other while our projectiles pass harmlessly through the spaceships.

By the end of the next chapter, we will add collision detection; this will allow our projectiles to destroy the spaceships they hit, and add an animation sequence that will show a ship being destroyed when it is hit by one of the projectiles.

Collision Detection 7

Right now, our spaceships can fly around and shoot at each other, but nothing happens.

Collision detection is used in the vast majority of video games to determine whether game objects intersect. There are a large number of methods for detecting collisions between different game objects. Various methods can work better in different situations. There is also a trade-off between the amount of computation time and how accurate our collision detection will be.

 You will need to include several images in your build to make this project work. Make sure you include the `/Chapter07/sprites/` folder from the project's GitHub. If you haven't yet downloaded the GitHub project, you can get it online here: `https://github.com/PacktPublishing/Hands-On-Game-Development-with-WebAssembly`.

In this chapter, we will discuss the following:

- Collision detection
- Collider objects
- Types of colliders
- Adding colliders to our game objects

Types of 2D collision detection

I could write an entire book on the kinds of 2D collision detection available to us, let alone the number available for collision detection in 3D. I have written several TypeScript tutorials on how to use different detection techniques, both basic and sophisticated at `https://www.embed.com/typescript-games/basic-collision-detection.html`, but, in this book, we will stick to using a combination of some of the more basic collision techniques.

Circle collision detection

The most basic kind of collision detection is **circle** or **distance** collision detection. If we treat all of our colliders like little circles with a radius and a position, we can calculate the distance between the two locations and see whether that distance is less than the sum of our radii. This form of collision detection is high-speed, but precision is limited. If you look at the projectile in our game, this method works pretty well. Our spaceships, on the other hand, don't fit neatly into a circle. We can adjust the radius of our circle collider on any given ship to give slightly different results. When circle collision detection works, it can be very efficient:

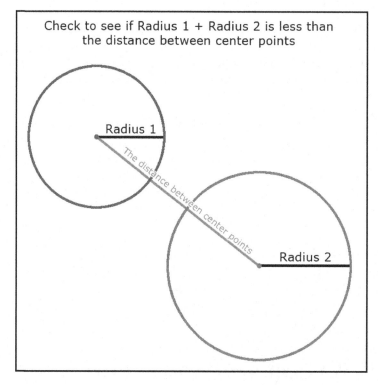

Circle collision hit test

Rectangle collision detection

Rectangle collision detection is another fast collision detection method. In many cases, it may be faster than circle collision detection. A rectangle collider is defined by an *x* and a *y* coordinate that is the position of the top left corner of our rectangle, as well as a width and a height. Detecting a rectangle collision is pretty straightforward. We look for an overlap on the *x* axis between the two rectangles. If there is an overlap on the *x* axis, we then look for an overlap on the *y* axis. If we have an overlap on both axes, there is a collision. This technique works pretty well for a lot of old-school video games. Several classic games released on the Nintendo Entertainment System used this method of collision detection. In the game we are writing, we are rotating our sprites, so using traditional non-oriented collision detection will not be useful for us.

A short refresher on trigonometry

At this point, our collision detection algorithms start to get a lot more complicated. You may remember some of the concepts from your high school trigonometry class, but some basic trigonometry is very important for many collision detection algorithms. Even our circle collision detection that we discussed earlier relies on the Pythagorean theorem, so, in reality, unless you are doing simple non-oriented rectangle collision detection, at least a tiny amount of trigonometry is required. Trigonometry is the study of triangles in mathematics. Most games use what's called a **Cartesian coordinate system**. If you're not familiar with that phrase, *Cartesian coordinate system* means we have a grid with an *x* and a *y* coordinate (for a 2D game).

The word *Cartesian* means Rene Descartes invented it—the "*I think; therefore, I am*" guy who had a lot of great ideas in mathematics and a lot of stupid ideas in philosophy (ghost in the machine...yuck!).

There are a few key concepts we have to remember from our trigonometry classes in high school, and they all have to do with right triangles. A right triangle is a triangle with a 90-degree angle in it. That is a handy thing when you're working with a Cartesian coordinate system because your *x* and *y* axes happen to form a right angle so any line between two points that do not share either an *x* or a *y* coordinate could be considered the hypotenuse (long side) of a right triangle. There are a few ratios we also need to remember; they are as follows:

- *Sine - Y / Hypotenuse*
- *Cosine - X / Hypotenuse*
- *Tangent - Y / X*

Do you remember SOHCAHTOA? (Pronounced "*Sock-Ah-Toe-Ah*")

That was meant to remind you of the following versions of the trigonometry ratios:

- *Sine - Opposite / Hypotenuse*
- *Cosine - Adjacent / Hypotenuse*
- *Tangent - Opposite / Adjacent*

In this formulation, the *opposite* side of the triangle is the y axis, and the adjacent side of the triangle is the x axis. If you remember SOHCAHTOA, you may have an easier time remembering these ratios. If not, just open this book back up or use Google:

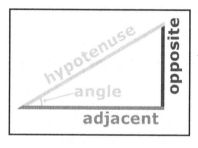

SOHCAHTOA

Some people have been taught the phrase "*Some Old Horse Came A-Hoppin' Through Our Alley.*" I'm not sure if that is helpful. I find it more difficult to remember than SOHCAHTOA, but that's a matter of opinion. So, if imagining a horse that hops like a rabbit around some city's back alley is your bag, then, by all means, use that instead.

You may remember earlier in this book we used the angle the ship was rotated with the `sin` and `cos` math library functions to figure out how fast our ship was moving on the x axis and the y axis. Those functions return the ratio for a given angle.

Another concept we need to know is the **dot product** between two **unit vectors**. A unit vector is a vector with a length of 1. The dot product between two unit vectors is just the cosine of the angle between those two unit vectors. The closer the dot products are to 1, the closer the angle between the two vectors is to 0 degrees. If the dot product is close to 0, the angles between the two vectors are close to 90 degrees, and if the dot product between the two angles is close to -1, the angle between the two vectors is near 180 degrees. Dot products between different vectors are very useful in both collision detection and in-game physics. Refer to the following diagram:

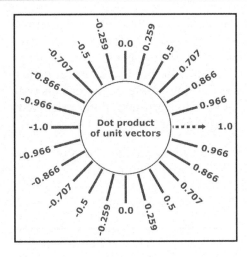

The dot product of two normalized vectors

Line collision detection

So, the first thing we need to do is talk about the difference between a line and a line segment. We define a line using two points. That line continues after the points to infinity. A line segment terminates at the two points and does not continue indefinitely. Two lines that are not parallel will always intersect somewhere. Two non-parallel line segments may or may not intersect.

For the most part, in games, we are interested in knowing whether two line segments intersect:

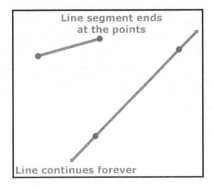

Line versus line segment

It is relatively easy to determine whether a line intersects with a line segment. All you have to do is see whether the two points of the line segments are on opposite sides of your line. Since a line is infinite, that means your line segment has to intersect with your line somewhere. If you want to find out whether two line segments intersect, you can do it in two stages. First, find out whether line segment A intersects with an infinite line B. If they do intersect, then find out whether line segment B intersects with the infinite line A. If this is true in both cases, the line segments intersect.

So, the next question is, how do we know mathematically whether two points are on the opposite sides of a line? To do that, we are going to use the previously discussed dot product and something called a **vector normal**. A vector normal is just a 90-degree rotated version of your vector. See the following diagram:

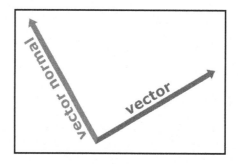

A vector and that vector's normal

We also need the vector that has an origin at the same point but has a direction aiming at point 1 of our line segment. If the dot product of those two vectors is a positive value, that means the point is on the same side of the line as the normalized vector. If the dot product is a negative value, that means the point is on the opposite side of the line to our normal vector. If the line segment intersects, that means one point has a positive dot product and the other side has a negative dot product. Since multiplying two negative numbers and two positive numbers both give you a positive result and multiplying a negative and a positive number gives you a negative result, multiply the two dot products together and see whether the resulting value is negative. If it is, the line segment intersects with the line:

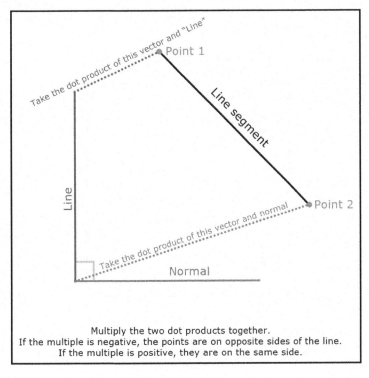

Take the dot product of this vector and "Line"

Point 1

Line segment

Line

Take the dot product of this vector and normal

Point 2

Normal

Multiply the two dot products together.
If the multiple is negative, the points are on opposite sides of the line.
If the multiple is positive, they are on the same side.

Determining whether two points are on the opposite side of a line

Compound colliders

A **compound collider** is when a game object uses multiple colliders to determine whether there was a collision. We are going to use compound circle colliders on our ship to improve the accuracy of our ship collision detection while still providing the increased speed of using circle colliders. We will cover our player's ship and our enemy ship with three circles. Our projectiles are a circle shape, so using a circle for those is entirely natural. There is no reason you need to limit compound colliders to using only one shape of collider. Internally, a compound collider could mix circle colliders with rectangle colliders or any other type you like.

The following diagram shows a hypothetical compound collider made up of a circle and two rectangle colliders:

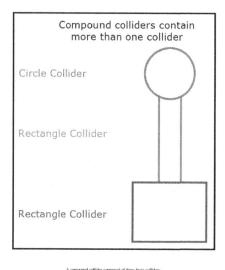

A compound collider composed of three basic colliders

In the next section, we will learn how to implement a basic circle collision detection algorithm.

Implementing circle collision detection

We are going to start by implementing circle collision detection because it is the fastest collision detection method available. It also fits well with our projectiles, which will be the most common kind of collider in our game. It will not do a great job on our ships, but later, we can improve that situation by implementing a compound collider that will use multiple circle colliders for each spaceship instead of just one. Because we only have two spaceships, this will give us the best of both worlds in our collision detection: the speed of circle collision detection, along with the accuracy of some of our better collision detection methods.

Let's start by adding a `Collider` class definition into our `game.hpp` file and creating a new `collider.cpp` file where we can define the functions used by our `Collider` class. Here's what our new `Collider` class will look like in the `game.hpp` file:

```
class Collider {
    public:
        double m_X;
```

```
        double m_Y;
        double m_Radius;

        Collider(double radius);

        bool HitTest( Collider *collider );
};
```

Here is the code we are putting in the `collider.cpp` file:

```
#include "game.hpp"
Collider::Collider(double radius) {
    m_Radius = radius;
}

bool Collider::HitTest( Collider *collider ) {
    double dist_x = m_X - collider->m_X;
    double dist_y = m_Y - collider->m_Y;
    double radius = m_Radius + collider->m_Radius;

    if( dist_x * dist_x + dist_y * dist_y <= radius * radius ) {
        return true;
    }
    return false;
}
```

The `Collider` class is a pretty simple circle collider. As we discussed earlier, a circle collider has an *x* and a *y* coordinate and a radius. The `HitTest` function does a pretty simple distance test to see whether the two circles are close enough to touch each other. We do this by squaring the *x* distance and squaring the *y* distance between the two colliders, which gives us the distance squared between the two points. We could take the square root to determine the actual distance, but a square root is a relatively slow function to perform, and it's much faster to square the sum of the radii to compare.

We will also need to talk about class inheritance briefly. If you look back at our code from earlier, we have a `PlayerShip` class and an `EnemyShip` class. These classes share most of their attributes. They all have *x* and *y* coordinates, *x* and *y* velocity, and many other attributes that are identical. Many of the functions use the same code copied and pasted. Instead of having this code defined twice, let's go back and create a `Ship` class that has all of the features that are common to our `PlayerShip` and `EnemyShip` classes. Then, we can refactor our `EnemyShip` and `PlayerShip` classes to inherit from our `Ship` class. Here is our new `Ship` class definition that we are adding to `game.hpp`:

```
class Ship: public Collider {
    public:
        Uint32 m_LastLaunchTime;
```

```
        const int c_Width = 16;
        const int c_Height = 16;
        SDL_Texture *m_SpriteTexture;
        Ship();
        float m_Rotation;
        float m_DX;
        float m_DY;
        float m_VX;
        float m_VY;

        void RotateLeft();
        void RotateRight();
        void Accelerate();
        void Decelerate();
        void CapVelocity();
        virtual void Move() = 0;
        void Render();
    };
```

The first line, `Ship class: public Collider`, tells us that `Ship` will inherit all of the public and protected members of the `Collider` class. We are doing this because we would like to be able to perform a hit test. The `Collider` class also now defines the `m_X` and `m_Y` attribute variables that keep track of the *x* and *y* coordinates of our object. We have moved everything common to our `EnemyShip` and `PlayerShip` classes into the `Ship` class. You will notice that we have one virtual function, `virtual void Move() = 0;`. This line tells us that we will have a `Move` function in all classes that inherit from `Ship`, but we will need to define `Move` inside those classes instead of directly in the `Ship` class. That makes `Ship` an **abstract class**, which means that we cannot create an instance of `Ship`, but, instead, it is a class from which other classes will inherit.

Class inheritance, abstract classes, and virtual functions are all a part of a style of programming known as **Object-Oriented Programming (OOP)**. C++ was created in 1979 by Bjarne Stroustrup to add OOP to the C programming language. If you're not familiar with OOP, there are hundreds of books that go into great detail on this topic. I will only be able to cover it in a cursory manner in this book.

Next, we are going to modify the `PlayerShip` and `EnemyShip` classes in the `game.hpp` file to remove all of the methods and attributes we have moved into the parent `Ship` class. We will also modify these classes so that they inherit from `Ship`. Here is the new version of the class definitions:

```
class PlayerShip: public Ship {
    public:
        const char* c_SpriteFile = "sprites/Franchise.png";
```

```
        const Uint32 c_MinLaunchTime = 300;
        PlayerShip();
        void Move();
};

class EnemyShip: public Ship {
    public:
        const char* c_SpriteFile = "sprites/BirdOfAnger.png";
        const Uint32 c_MinLaunchTime = 300;
        const int c_AIStateTime = 2000;
        FSM_STUB m_AIState;
        int m_AIStateTTL;

        EnemyShip();
        void AIStub();
        void Move();
};
```

Now, we need to add a `ship.cpp` file and define all of the methods that will be common to `EnemyShip` and `PlayerShip`. These methods were in both `PlayerShip` and `EnemyShip` previously, but now we can have them all in one place. Here is what the `ship.cpp` file looks like:

```
#include "game.hpp"

Ship::Ship() : Collider(8.0) {
    m_Rotation = PI;
    m_DX = 0.0;
    m_DY = 1.0;
    m_VX = 0.0;
    m_VY = 0.0;
    m_LastLaunchTime = current_time;
}

void Ship::RotateLeft() {
    m_Rotation -= delta_time;

    if( m_Rotation < 0.0 ) {
        m_Rotation += TWO_PI;
    }
    m_DX = sin(m_Rotation);
    m_DY = -cos(m_Rotation);
}

void Ship::RotateRight() {
    m_Rotation += delta_time;

    if( m_Rotation >= TWO_PI ) {
```

```
            m_Rotation -= TWO_PI;
        }
        m_DX = sin(m_Rotation);
        m_DY = -cos(m_Rotation);
    }

    void Ship::Accelerate() {
        m_VX += m_DX * delta_time;
        m_VY += m_DY * delta_time;
    }

    void Ship::Decelerate() {
        m_VX -= (m_DX * delta_time) / 2.0;
        m_VY -= (m_DY * delta_time) / 2.0;
    }
    void Ship::CapVelocity() {
        double vel = sqrt( m_VX * m_VX + m_VY * m_VY );

        if( vel > MAX_VELOCITY ) {
            m_VX /= vel;
            m_VY /= vel;

            m_VX *= MAX_VELOCITY;
            m_VY *= MAX_VELOCITY;
        }
    }
    void Ship::Render() {
        dest.x = (int)m_X;
        dest.y = (int)m_Y;
        dest.w = c_Width;
        dest.h = c_Height;

        double degrees = (m_Rotation / PI) * 180.0;

        int return_code = SDL_RenderCopyEx( renderer, m_SpriteTexture,
                                            NULL, &dest,
                                            degrees, NULL, SDL_FLIP_NONE );

        if( return_code != 0 ) {
            printf("failed to render image: %s\n", IMG_GetError() );
        }
    }
```

The only real difference between the versions of these classes that were in the
player_ship.cpp and the enemy_ship.cpp files are that, instead of PlayerShip:: or
EnemyShip:: in front of each of the function definitions, we now have Ship:: in front of
the function definitions.

Next, we are going to need to modify `player_ship.cpp` and `enemy_ship.cpp` by removing all of the functions that we now have defined inside the `ship.cpp` file. Let's take a look at what the `enemy_ship.cpp` file looks like broken into two parts. The first part is the `#include` of our `game.hpp` file and the `EnemyShip` constructor function:

```cpp
#include "game.hpp"

EnemyShip::EnemyShip() {
    m_X = 60.0;
    m_Y = 50.0;
    m_Rotation = PI;
    m_DX = 0.0;
    m_DY = 1.0;
    m_VX = 0.0;
    m_VY = 0.0;
    m_LastLaunchTime = current_time;

    SDL_Surface *temp_surface = IMG_Load( c_SpriteFile );

    if( !temp_surface ) {
        printf("failed to load image: %s\n", IMG_GetError() );
        return;
    }
    else {
        printf("success creating enemy ship surface\n");
    }
    m_SpriteTexture = SDL_CreateTextureFromSurface( renderer,
    temp_surface );

    if( !m_SpriteTexture ) {
        printf("failed to create texture: %s\n", IMG_GetError() );
        return;
    }
    else {
        printf("success creating enemy ship texture\n");
    }

    SDL_FreeSurface( temp_surface );
}
```

In the second part of our `enemy_ship.cpp` file we have the `Move` and `AIStub` functions:

```cpp
void EnemyShip::Move() {
    AIStub();

    if( m_AIState == TURN_LEFT ) {
```

```
        RotateLeft();
    }

    if( m_AIState == TURN_RIGHT ) {
        RotateRight();
    }

    if( m_AIState == ACCELERATE ) {
        Accelerate();
    }

    if( m_AIState == DECELERATE ) {
        Decelerate();
    }

    CapVelocity();
    m_X += m_VX;

    if( m_X > 320 ) {
        m_X = -16;
    }
    else if( m_X < -16 ) {
        m_X = 320;
    }

    m_Y += m_VY;

    if( m_Y > 200 ) {
        m_Y = -16;
    }
    else if( m_Y < -16 ) {
        m_Y = 200;
    }

    if( m_AIState == SHOOT ) {
        Projectile* projectile;

        if( current_time - m_LastLaunchTime >= c_MinLaunchTime ) {
            m_LastLaunchTime = current_time;
            projectile = projectile_pool->GetFreeProjectile();

            if( projectile != NULL ) {
                projectile->Launch( m_X, m_Y, m_DX, m_DY );
            }
        }
    }
}
```

```
void EnemyShip::AIStub() {
    m_AIStateTTL -= diff_time;

    if( m_AIStateTTL <= 0 ) {
        // for now get a random AI state.
        m_AIState = (FSM_STUB)(rand() % 5);
        m_AIStateTTL = c_AIStateTime;
    }
}
```

Now that we have seen what is in the enemy_ship.cpp file, let's take a look at what the new player_ship.cpp file looks like:

```
#include "game.hpp"
PlayerShip::PlayerShip() {
    m_X = 160.0;
    m_Y = 100.0;
    SDL_Surface *temp_surface = IMG_Load( c_SpriteFile );

    if( !temp_surface ) {
        printf("failed to load image: %s\n", IMG_GetError() );
        return;
    }

    m_SpriteTexture = SDL_CreateTextureFromSurface( renderer,
    temp_surface );

    if( !m_SpriteTexture ) {
        printf("failed to create texture: %s\n", IMG_GetError() );
        return;
    }

    SDL_FreeSurface( temp_surface );
}

void PlayerShip::Move() {
    current_time = SDL_GetTicks();
    diff_time = current_time - last_time;
    delta_time = (double)diff_time / 1000.0;
    last_time = current_time;

    if( left_key_down ) {
        RotateLeft();
    }

    if( right_key_down ) {
        RotateRight();
    }
```

```
        if( up_key_down ) {
            Accelerate();
        }

        if( down_key_down ) {
            Decelerate();
        }

        CapVelocity();
        m_X += m_VX;

        if( m_X > 320 ) {
            m_X = -16;
        }
        else if( m_X < -16 ) {
            m_X = 320;
        }
        m_Y += m_VY;

        if( m_Y > 200 ) {
            m_Y = -16;
        }
        else if( m_Y < -16 ) {
            m_Y = 200;
        }

        if( space_key_down ) {
            Projectile* projectile;

            if( current_time - m_LastLaunchTime >= c_MinLaunchTime ) {
                m_LastLaunchTime = current_time;
                projectile = projectile_pool->GetFreeProjectile();
                if( projectile != NULL ) {
                    projectile->Launch( m_X, m_Y, m_DX, m_DY );
                }
            }
        }
    }
```

Next, let's modify the Move function in our ProjectilePool class so that, every time it moves a Projectile, it also tests to see whether it hit one of our ships:

```
void ProjectilePool::MoveProjectiles() {
    Projectile* projectile;
    std::vector<Projectile*>::iterator it;
    for( it = m_ProjectileList.begin(); it != m_ProjectileList.end();
        it++ ) {
        projectile = *it;
```

```
    if( projectile->m_Active ) {
        projectile->Move();
        if( projectile->HitTest( player ) ) {
            printf("hit player\n");
        }
        if( projectile->HitTest( enemy ) ) {
            printf("hit enemy\n");
        }
    }
}
}
```

For right now, we are only going to print to the console when either the player or the enemy collides with a projectile. That will tell us whether our collision detection is working correctly. In later sections, we will add animations to destroy our ships when they collide with the projectile.

There is one last change we need to make to the Launch function on our Projectile class. When we launch a projectile from our ships, we give the projectile an x and a y position and an *x* and *y* velocity based on the direction the ship was facing. We need to take that direction and move the starting point of the projectile. That is to prevent the projectile from hitting the ship that launched it by moving it out of the collision detection circle for the ship:

```
void Projectile::Launch(double x, double y, double dx, double dy) {
    m_X = x + dx * 9;
    m_Y = y + dy * 9;
    m_VX = velocity * dx;
    m_VY = velocity * dy;
    m_TTL = alive_time;
    m_Active = true;
}
```

In the next section, we will detect when our ship collides with a projectile and run an explosion animation.

Destroying a spaceship on collision

Now that we are detecting collisions between the projectiles and the spaceships, it would be nice to do something more interesting than printing a line to the console. It would be nice to have a little explosion animation for our projectiles and our ships when they hit something. We can add an animation associated with each of these objects as they are destroyed.

Instead of loading multiple sprites for each frame of the animation as we did in a previous chapter, I'm going to introduce the concept of **sprite sheets**. Instead of loading a single projectile frame and a single ship frame for each of our spaceships, we will load a sprite sheet for each that includes not only the undamaged version of each but a destruction sequence that we will animate through when any of these objects are destroyed.

Having three different sprite sheets in this example is done for convenience only. When you decide how to pack your sprite sheets for production, there are several considerations that you must take into account. You will most likely want to break out your sprite sheets based on when you will need them. You may have a series of sprites you need that are common to all levels of the game. You may choose to break out the sprites based on the level. You also need to take into consideration that, for performance reasons WebGL requires power-of-2 sized sprite files. That may impact your decisions concerning what sprites to pack into what sprite sheets. You may also consider purchasing a tool such as Texture Packer to pack sprites for you more quickly than you could do by hand.

We have created three sprite sheets to replace the three sprites we were using. These Sprites are `FranchiseExp.png` to replace `Franchise.png`, `BirdOfAngerExp.png` to replace `BirdOfAnger.png`, and `ProjectileExp.png` to replace `Projectile.png`. We are going to need to make some tweaks to the `Projectile` class, `Ship` class, `EnemyShip` class, `PlayerShip`, and the `ProjectilePool` class, as well as the `game_loop` function.

We are going to start by modifying the game loop to keep track of the game's timing data. We must remove some code from the `PlayerShip::Move` function inside the `player_ship.cpp` file. This code existed from Chapter 4, *Sprite Animations in WebAssembly with SDL*, where we discussed the basics of animating a sprite by animating `PlayerShip`. We must delete the following code from the first several lines of `PlayerShip::Move`:

```
current_time = SDL_GetTicks();
diff_time = current_time - last_time;
delta_time = (double)diff_time / 1000.0;
last_time = current_time;
```

This code gets the current time and calculates all of our time-related information we use for speed adjustments and animation timing. We probably should have moved this code to the game loop a few chapters ago, but better late than never. The following is the code for the new `game_loop` function in `main.cpp`:

```
void game_loop() {
    current_time = SDL_GetTicks();
    diff_time = current_time - last_time;
    delta_time = (double)diff_time / 1000.0;
    last_time = current_time;
    input();
```

```
        move();
        render();
    }
```

Strictly speaking, we did not have to make this change, but it makes more sense to have the game timing code within the game loop. Now that we have changed our game loop, we are going to modify the `Projectile` class. Here are the changes to the class definition we must make from within the `game.hpp` file:

```
class Projectile: public Collider {
    public:
        const char* c_SpriteFile = "sprites/ProjectileExp.png";
        const int c_Width = 16;
        const int c_Height = 16;
        const double velocity = 6.0;
        const double alive_time = 2000;
        SDL_Texture *m_SpriteTexture;
        SDL_Rect src = {.x = 0, .y = 0, .w = 16, .h = 16 };
        Uint32 m_CurrentFrame = 0;
        int m_NextFrameTime;
        bool m_Active;
        float m_TTL;
        float m_VX;
        float m_VY;

        Projectile();
        void Move();
        void Render();
        void Launch(float x, float y, float dx, float dy);
};
```

We need to modify the `c_SpriteFile` variable to point to the new sprite sheet PNG file instead of the single sprite file. We need to increase the size of its width and height. To make space for the explosion, we will make all frames in the sprite sheet 16 x 16 instead of 8 x 8. We also need a source rectangle. When each sprite has used an entire file, we could pass in `null` to `SDL_RenderCopy`, and the function would render the entire contents of the sprite file. Now we only want to render one frame, so we need a rectangle that will start at 0,0 and render the width and height of 16. The sprite sheets we have created are **horizontal strip sprite sheets**, meaning that every frame is laid out in order and placed horizontally. To render a different frame of our animation, we will only need to modify the `.x` value inside our source rectangle. The final attribute we added is to the public section and is the `m_CurrentFrame` attribute. That tracks which frame in the animation we are currently on. We will keep our current frame at 0 when we are not rendering the explosion animation.

Next, we will need to modify a few functions on the `Projectile` class. These functions are the `Projectile::Move` function and the `Projectile::Render` function inside of the `projectile.cpp` file. Here is the new version of the `Projectile::Move` function:

```
void Projectile::Move() {
    if( m_CurrentFrame > 0 ) {
        m_NextFrameTime -= diff_time;
        if( m_NextFrameTime <= 0 ) {
            ++m_CurrentFrame;
            m_NextFrameTime = ms_per_frame;
            if( m_CurrentFrame >= 4 ) {
                m_Active = false;
                m_CurrentFrame = 0;
                return;
            }
        }
        return;
    }
    m_X += m_VX;
    m_Y += m_VY;
    m_TTL -= diff_time;
    if( m_TTL < 0 ) {
        m_Active = false;
        m_TTL = 0;
    }
}
```

The top section of the `Move` function is all new. If the current frame is not 0, we will run through the animation until it ends and then deactivate our projectile, sending it back to the projectile pool. We do this by subtracting the time since the app last ran the game loop. That is the value stored in the `diff_time` global variable. The `m_NextFrameTime` attribute variable stores the number of milliseconds until we switch to the next frame in our series. Once the values are below 0, we increment our current frame and reset `m_NextFrameTime` to the number of milliseconds we want between each new frame of our animation. Now that we have incremented the current animation frame, we can check to see whether it is greater than or equal to the frame number of the last frame in this animation (in this case, 4). If so, we need to deactivate the projectile and reset the current frame to 0.

Now, that we have made the changes we need to make to the `Move()` function, here are the changes we must make to the `Projectile::Render()` function:

```
void Projectile::Render() {
    dest.x = m_X + 8;
    dest.y = m_Y + 8;
    dest.w = c_Width;
    dest.h = c_Height;
```

```
    src.x = 16 * m_CurrentFrame;
    int return_val = SDL_RenderCopy( renderer, m_SpriteTexture,
                                     &src, &dest );
    if( return_val != 0 ) {
        printf("SDL_Init failed: %s\n", SDL_GetError());
    }
}
```

The first change to the `Render` function is the addition of the `src` rectangle to the `SDL_RenderCopy` call, as well as setting its *x* value immediately above that call. Each frame in our sprite sheet is 16 pixels wide, so setting the *x* value to `16 * m_CurrentFrame` will select a different 16 x 16 sprite from the sprite sheet. The width and height of that rectangle will always be 16, and the *y* value will always be 0 because we placed the sprites into this sprite sheet as a horizontal strip.

Now we are going to make some modifications to the `Ship` class definitions inside the `game.hpp` file:

```
class Ship: public Collider {
    public:
        Uint32 m_LastLaunchTime;
        const int c_Width = 32;
        const int c_Height = 32;
        SDL_Texture *m_SpriteTexture;
        SDL_Rect src = {.x = 0, .y = 0, .w = 32, .h = 32 };
        bool m_Alive = true;
        Uint32 m_CurrentFrame = 0;
        int m_NextFrameTime;

        float m_Rotation;
        float m_DX;
        float m_DY;
        float m_VX;
        float m_VY;

        void RotateLeft();
        void RotateRight();
        void Accelerate();
        void Decelerate();
        void CapVelocity();

        virtual void Move() = 0;
        Ship();
        void Render();
};
```

We modified the width and height constants to reflect the new sprite size of 32 x 32 pixels as it appears in our sprite sheet. We also must add a source rectangle to the `Projectile` class. Inside our public attributes section, we have added a few variables to track the alive or dead status of the ship, (`m_Alive`); the current frame the game is rendering, (`m_CurrentFrame`); and the time in milliseconds until we render the next frame, (`m_NextFrameTime`). Next, we will make the necessary modifications to the ship.cpp file. We need to modify the `Ship::Render` function:

```cpp
void Ship::Render() {
    if( m_Alive == false ) {
        return;
    }
    dest.x = (int)m_X;
    dest.y = (int)m_Y;
    dest.w = c_Width;
    dest.h = c_Height;

    src.x = 32 * m_CurrentFrame;
    float degrees = (m_Rotation / PI) * 180.0;
    int return_code = SDL_RenderCopyEx( renderer, m_SpriteTexture,
                            &src, &dest,
                            degrees, NULL, SDL_FLIP_NONE );
    if( return_code != 0 ) {
        printf("failed to render image: %s\n", IMG_GetError() );
    }
}
```

At the top of the function, we have added code to check to see whether the ship is currently alive. If it is not, we do not want to render the ship, so we return. Later on, we set the source rectangle *x* value to 32 times the current frame with the line: `src.x = 32 * m_CurrentFrame;`. That changes our render to render a different 32 x 32 block of pixels from our sprite sheet based on the frame we want to render. Lastly, we must pass that `src` rectangle into the call to `SDL_RenderCopyEx`.

Now that we have modified the `Ship` class, we will change the `EnemyShip` class definition and the `PlayerShip` class definition to use our sprite sheet PNG files instead of the old single sprite files. Here are the modifications to those two class definitions inside the game.hpp file:

```cpp
class PlayerShip: public Ship {
    public:
        const char* c_SpriteFile = "sprites/FranchiseExp.png";
        const Uint32 c_MinLaunchTime = 300;
        PlayerShip();
        void Move();
```

```
};

class EnemyShip: public Ship {
    public:
        const char* c_SpriteFile = "sprites/BirdOfAngerExp.png";
        const Uint32 c_MinLaunchTime = 300;
        const int c_AIStateTime = 2000;

        FSM_STUB m_AIState;
        int m_AIStateTTL;

        EnemyShip();
        void AIStub();
        void Move();
};
```

The only changes made to these class definitions are to the values of the `c_SpriteFile` constant in each class. The `c_SpriteFile` constant in the `PlayerShip` class was modified from `"sprites/Franchise.png"` to `"sprites/FranchiseExp.png"`, and the `c_SpriteFile` constant in `EnemyShip` was modified from `"sprites/BirdOfAnger.png"` to `"sprites/BirdOfAngerExp.png"`. Now that we have made that change, these classes will use the sprite sheet `.png` files instead of the original sprite files.

Now that we have modified the definitions for these classes, we must change the `Move` functions for each of them. First, we will revise the `EnemyShip::Move` function inside the `enemy_ship.cpp` file:

```
void EnemyShip::Move() {
    if( m_Alive == false ) {
        return;
    }
    AIStub();

    if( m_AIState == TURN_LEFT ) {
        RotateLeft();
    }
    if( m_AIState == TURN_RIGHT ) {
        RotateRight();
    }
    if( m_AIState == ACCELERATE ) {
        Accelerate();
    }
    if( m_AIState == DECELERATE ) {
        Decelerate();
    }
```

```
        if( m_CurrentFrame > 0 ) {
            m_NextFrameTime -= diff_time;

            if( m_NextFrameTime <= 0 ) {
                m_NextFrameTime = ms_per_frame;
                if( ++m_CurrentFrame >= 8 ) {
                    m_Alive = false;
                    return;
                }
            }
        }
    }
    CapVelocity();

    m_X += m_VX;

    if( m_X > 320 ) {
        m_X = -16;
    }
    else if( m_X < -16 ) {
        m_X = 320;
    }

    m_Y += m_VY;

    if( m_Y > 200 ) {
        m_Y = -16;
    }
    else if( m_Y < -16 ) {
        m_Y = 200;
    }

    if( m_AIState == SHOOT ) {
        Projectile* projectile;
        if( current_time - m_LastLaunchTime >= c_MinLaunchTime ) {
            m_LastLaunchTime = current_time;
            projectile = projectile_pool->GetFreeProjectile();

            if( projectile != NULL ) {
                projectile->Launch( m_X, m_Y, m_DX, m_DY );
            }
        }
    }
}
```

There are two places where the code must be changed. First, we do not want to do any of the `Move` function's work if the enemy ship is not alive, so we added this check at the beginning of the function to return if the ship is not alive:

```
if( m_Alive == false ) {
    return;
}
```

Next, we needed to add the code to check whether we needed to run the death animation. We do this if the current frame is greater than 0. The code in this section is similar to what we did for the projectile to run its death animation. We subtract the time between frames, (`diff_time`), from the next frame time, (`m_NextFrameTime`), to determine whether we need to increment the frame. When this value drops below 0, the frame is ready to change by incrementing `m_CurrentFrame`, and we reset the `m_NextFrameTime` countdown timer by setting it to the number of milliseconds we want between each frame, (`ms_per_frame`). If our current frame hits the end of our frame sprite sheet, (`++m_CurrentFrame >= 8`), then we set the enemy ship to no longer be alive, (`m_Alive = false`). This is shown here:

```
if( m_CurrentFrame > 0 ) {
    m_NextFrameTime -= diff_time;
    if( m_NextFrameTime <= 0 ) {
        m_NextFrameTime = ms_per_frame;
        if( ++m_CurrentFrame >= 8 ) {
            m_Alive = false;
            return;
        }
    }
}
```

Now, we will make the same changes to the `PlayerShip::Move` function within the `player_ship.cpp` file:

```
void PlayerShip::Move() {
    if( m_Alive == false ) {
        return;
    }
    if( left_key_down ) {
        RotateLeft();
    }
    if( right_key_down ) {
        RotateRight();
    }
    if( up_key_down ) {
        Accelerate();
    }
```

```
        if( down_key_down ) {
            Decelerate();
        }
        if( m_CurrentFrame > 0 ) {
            m_NextFrameTime -= diff_time;
            if( m_NextFrameTime <= 0 ) {
                m_NextFrameTime = ms_per_frame;
                if( ++m_CurrentFrame >= 8 ) {
                    m_Alive = false;
                    return;
                }
            }
        }
        CapVelocity();
        m_X += m_VX;

        if( m_X > 320 ) {
            m_X = -16;
        }
        else if( m_X < -16 ) {
            m_X = 320;
        }

        m_Y += m_VY;

        if( m_Y > 200 ) {
            m_Y = -16;
        }
        else if( m_Y < -16 ) {
            m_Y = 200;
        }

        if( space_key_down ) {
            Projectile* projectile;
            if( current_time - m_LastLaunchTime >= c_MinLaunchTime ) {
                m_LastLaunchTime = current_time;
                projectile = projectile_pool->GetFreeProjectile();
                if( projectile != NULL ) {
                    projectile->Launch( m_X, m_Y, m_DX, m_DY );
                }
            }
        }
    }
```

Just like in our `EnemyShip::Move` functions, we add a check to see whether the player is alive with the following code:

```
if( m_Alive == false ) {
    return;
}
```

And we also add some code to run the death animation if our current frame is greater than 0:

```
if( m_CurrentFrame > 0 ) {
    m_NextFrameTime -= diff_time;
    if( m_NextFrameTime <= 0 ) {
        m_NextFrameTime = ms_per_frame;
        if( ++m_CurrentFrame >= 8 ) {
            m_Alive = false;
            return;
        }
    }
}
```

The last thing we need to do is modify the collision detection code we added earlier to the `ProjectilePool::MoveProjectiles` function to run the death animation for a ship and a projectile if the two collide. Here is the new version of `ProjectilePool::MoveProjectiles` inside of the `projectile_pool.cpp` file:

```
void ProjectilePool::MoveProjectiles() {
    Projectile* projectile;
    std::vector<Projectile*>::iterator it;
    for( it = m_ProjectileList.begin(); it != m_ProjectileList.end(); it++
) {
        projectile = *it;
        if( projectile->m_Active ) {
            projectile->Move();
            if( projectile->m_CurrentFrame == 0 &&
                player->m_CurrentFrame == 0 &&
                projectile->HitTest( player ) ) {

                player->m_CurrentFrame = 1;
                player->m_NextFrameTime = ms_per_frame;
                projectile->m_CurrentFrame = 1;
                projectile->m_NextFrameTime = ms_per_frame;
            }
            if( projectile->m_CurrentFrame == 0 &&
                enemy->m_CurrentFrame == 0 &&
                projectile->HitTest( enemy ) ) {
```

```
                    enemy->m_CurrentFrame = 1;
                    enemy->m_NextFrameTime = ms_per_frame;
                    projectile->m_CurrentFrame = 1;
                    projectile->m_NextFrameTime = ms_per_frame;
                }
            }
        }
    }
```

Inside of this code, every time we move a projectile, we do a hit test against that projectile and the player as well as a hit test between that projectile and the enemy. If either the ship or the projectile is running its death animation (`m_CurrentFrame == 0` is false), then we do not need to run the hit test because the ship or the projectile has already been destroyed. If the hit test returns true, then we need to set the current frame of both the projectile and the ship to 1 to begin the destruction animation. We also need to set the next frame time to the number of milliseconds until the frame changes.

Now that we have added all of this new code, the ship and the enemy ship will run an explosion animation that destroys the ship when hit. The projectiles will also explode instead of just disappearing. The circle colliders are fast but not very precise. In the *Implementing compound circle colliders* section, we will learn the modifications we need to make to use multiple circle colliders on a single ship. That will give us collisions that look more accurate than simple circles.

Pointers in memory

WebAssembly's memory model piggybacks on the asm.js memory model, which uses a large typed `ArrayBuffer` to hold all of the raw bytes to be manipulated by the module. A JavaScript call to `WebAssembly.Memory` sets up the module's memory buffer in 64 KB **pages**.

 A *page* is a block of linear data that is the smallest unit of data that can be allocated by an operating system, or, in the case of WebAssembly, a virtual machine. For more information on memory pages, see the Wikipedia Page: `https://en.wikipedia.org/wiki/Page_%28computer_memory%29`.

A WebAssembly module can only access data from within this `ArrayBuffer`. That prevents malicious attacks from WebAssembly that create a pointer to a memory address outside the browser's sandbox. Because of this design, WebAssembly's memory model is just as safe as JavaScript.

In the next section, we will be using C++ pointers in our `collider` object. If you are a JavaScript developer, you may not be familiar with **pointers**. A pointer is a variable that holds a memory location instead of the value directly. Let's look at a little bit of code:

```
int VAR1 = 1;
int* POINTER = &VAR1;
```

In this code, we have created a `VAR1` variable and given it a value of 1. In the second line, we use `int*` to create a pointer called `POINTER`. We then initialize that pointer to the address of `VAR1` using the `&` character, which, in C++, is known as the **address of operator**. This operator gives us the address of the `VAR1` that we declared earlier. If we then want to change `VAR1`, we can do so using the pointer instead of directly, as shown here:

```
*POINTER = 2;
 printf("VAR1=%d\n", VAR1); // prints out "VAR1=2"
```

Putting the `*` in front of `POINTER` tells C++ to set the value in the memory address where `POINTER` is pointing; `*` when used in this way is called the **dereference operator**.

 If you would like to learn more about pointers in C++ and how they work, the following article goes into a good deal of detail on the subject: `http://www.cplusplus.com/doc/tutorial/pointers/`.

In the next section, we will implement compound circle colliders for collision detection on our spaceships.

Implementing compound circle colliders

Now that our collision detection is working, and we have our ships and projectiles exploding on a collision, let's see how we can make our collision detection better. We chose circle collision detection for two reasons: the collision algorithm is fast, and it is simple. We could do better, however, by merely adding more circles to each ship. That will increase our collision detection time by a factor of *n*, where *n* is the average number of circles we have on each ship. That is because the only collision detection we do is between the projectiles and the ships. Even so, we don't want to go overboard with the number of circles we choose to use for each ship.

For the player ship, the front of the spaceship is covered well by the basic circle. However, we could get much better coverage of the back of the player's spaceship by adding a circle to each side:

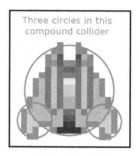

Our player ship compound collider

The enemy ship is the opposite. The back of that spaceship is covered pretty well by a default circle, but the front could use some better coverage, so, for the enemy ship, we will add some additional circles in front:

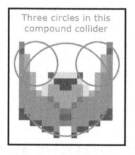

Our enemy ship compound collider

The first thing we need to do is change the `Collider` class to include information from the parent of our collider. Here is the new version of the `Collider` class definition inside our `game.hpp` file:

```
class Collider {
    public:
        float* m_ParentRotation;
        float* m_ParentX;
        float* m_ParentY;
        float m_X;
        float m_Y;
        float m_Radius;
```

```
bool CCHitTest( Collider* collider );
void SetParentInformation( double* rotation, double* x, double*
                           y );
Collider(double radius);
bool HitTest( Collider *collider );
};
```

We have added three-pointers to attributes of the parent of our `Collider` class. These will
point to the *x* and *y* coordinates, as well as the `Rotation` of the collider's parent, which will
either be the enemy ship, the player ship, or `NULL`. We will initialize those values to `NULL` in
our constructor, and if the value is null, we will not modify the behavior of our collider. If,
however, those values are set to something else, we will call the `CCHitTest` function to
determine whether there is a collision. This version of the hit test will adjust the position of
the collider to be relative to its parent's position and rotation before doing the collision test.
Now that we have made the changes to the collider's definition, we will make changes to
the functions inside the `collider.cpp` file to support the new compound colliders.

The first thing to do is modify our constructor to initialize the new pointers to `NULL`:

```
Collider::Collider(double radius) {
    m_ParentRotation = NULL;
    m_ParentX = NULL;
    m_ParentY = NULL;
    m_Radius = radius;
}
```

We have a new function to add to our `collider.cpp` file, the `CCHitTest` function, which
will be our compound collider hit test. This version of the hit test will adjust the *x* and *y*
coordinates of our collider to be relative to the position and rotation of our parent ship:

```
bool Collider::CCHitTest( Collider* collider ) {
    float sine = sin(*m_ParentRotation);
    float cosine = cos(*m_ParentRotation);
    float rx = m_X * cosine - m_Y * sine;
    float ry = m_X * sine + m_Y * cosine;
    float dist_x = (*m_ParentX + rx) - collider->m_X;
    float dist_y = (*m_ParentY + ry) - collider->m_Y;
    float radius = m_Radius + collider->m_Radius;

    if( dist_x * dist_x + dist_y * dist_y <= radius * radius ) {
        return true;
    }
    return false;
}
```

The first thing this function does is take the sine and cosine of the parent's rotation and use that rotation to get a rotated version of *x* and *y* in the variables, rx and ry. We then adjust that rotated *x* and *y* position by the parent's *x* and *y* position, before calculating the distance between the two collider *x* and *y* positions. After we add this new CCHitTest function, we need to modify the HitTest function to call this version of the hit test if the parent values are set. Here is the latest version of HitTest:

```
bool Collider::HitTest( Collider *collider ) {
    if( m_ParentRotation != NULL && m_ParentX != NULL && m_ParentY !=
NULL ) {
        return CCHitTest( collider );
    }

    float dist_x = m_X - collider->m_X;
    float dist_y = m_Y - collider->m_Y;
    float radius = m_Radius + collider->m_Radius;

    if( dist_x * dist_x + dist_y * dist_y <= radius * radius ) {
        return true;
    }
    return false;
}
```

We have created a function to set all of these values called SetParentInformation. Here is the function definition:

```
void Collider::SetParentInformation( float* rotation, float* x, float* y )
{
    m_ParentRotation = rotation;
    m_ParentX = x;
    m_ParentY = y;
}
```

To take advantage of these new kinds of colliders, we need to add a new vector of colliders into the Ship class. The following is the new class definition for Ship in the game.hpp file:

```
class Ship : public Collider {
    public:
        Uint32 m_LastLaunchTime;
        const int c_Width = 32;
        const int c_Height = 32;

        SDL_Texture *m_SpriteTexture;
        SDL_Rect src = {.x = 0, .y = 0, .w = 32, .h = 32 };
        std::vector<Collider*> m_Colliders;
        bool m_Alive = true;
        Uint32 m_CurrentFrame = 0;
```

```
        int m_NextFrameTime;
        float m_Rotation;
        float m_DX;
        float m_DY;
        float m_VX;
        float m_VY;

        void RotateLeft();
        void RotateRight();
        void Accelerate();
        void Decelerate();
        void CapVelocity();
        virtual void Move() = 0;
        Ship();
        void Render();
        bool CompoundHitTest( Collider* collider );
};
```

There are two differences between this version and the previous version of the Ship class. The first is the addition of the m_Colliders vector attribute:

```
    std::vector<Collider*> m_Colliders;
```

The second change is the new CompoundHitTest function added at the bottom of the class:

```
    bool CompoundHitTest( Collider* collider );
```

For the change to our class, we will need to add a new function to our ship.cpp file:

```
bool Ship::CompoundHitTest( Collider* collider ) {
    Collider* col;
    std::vector<Collider*>::iterator it;
    for( it = m_Colliders.begin(); it != m_Colliders.end(); it++ ) {
        col = *it;
        if( col->HitTest(collider) ) {
            return true;
        }
    }
    return false;
}
```

This `CompoundHitTest` function is a pretty simple function that loops over all of our additional colliders and performs a hit test on them. This line creates a vector of collider pointers. We will now modify our `EnemyShip` and `PlayerShip` constructors to add some colliders into this vector. First, we will add some new lines to the `EnemyShip` constructor inside the `enemy_ship.cpp` file:

```
EnemyShip::EnemyShip() {
    m_X = 60.0;
    m_Y = 50.0;
    m_Rotation = PI;
    m_DX = 0.0;
    m_DY = 1.0;
    m_VX = 0.0;
    m_VY = 0.0;
    m_AIStateTTL = c_AIStateTime;
    m_Alive = true;
    m_LastLaunchTime = current_time;

    Collider* temp_collider = new Collider(2.0);
    temp_collider->SetParentInformation( &(this->m_Rotation),
                                         &(this->m_X), &(this->m_Y) );
    temp_collider->m_X = -6.0;
    temp_collider->m_Y = -6.0;
    m_Colliders.push_back( temp_collider );
    temp_collider = new Collider(2.0);
    temp_collider->SetParentInformation( &(this->m_Rotation),
                                         &(this->m_X), &(this->m_Y) );
    temp_collider->m_X = 6.0;
    temp_collider->m_Y = -6.0;
    m_Colliders.push_back( temp_collider );

    SDL_Surface *temp_surface = IMG_Load( c_SpriteFile );

    if( !temp_surface ) {
        printf("failed to load image: %s\n", IMG_GetError() );
        return;
    }
    else {
        printf("success creating enemy ship surface\n");
    }
    m_SpriteTexture = SDL_CreateTextureFromSurface( renderer,
    temp_surface );
    if( !m_SpriteTexture ) {
        printf("failed to create texture: %s\n", IMG_GetError() );
        return;
    }
    else {
```

```
        printf("success creating enemy ship texture\n");
    }
    SDL_FreeSurface( temp_surface );
}
```

The code that we added creates new colliders and sets the parent information for those colliders as pointers to the *x* and *y* coordinates, as well as the radius to the addresses of those values inside of this object. We set the m_X and m_Y values for this collider relative to the position of this object, and then we push the new colliders into the m_Colliders vector attribute:

```
Collider* temp_collider = new Collider(2.0);
temp_collider->SetParentInformation( &(this->m_Rotation),
                                &(this->m_X), &(this->m_Y) );
temp_collider->m_X = -6.0;
temp_collider->m_Y = -6.0;
m_Colliders.push_back( temp_collider );
temp_collider = new Collider(2.0);
temp_collider->SetParentInformation( &(this->m_Rotation),
                                &(this->m_X), &(this->m_Y) );
temp_collider->m_X = 6.0;
temp_collider->m_Y = -6.0;
m_Colliders.push_back( temp_collider );
```

We will now do something similar for the PlayerShip constructor inside the player_ship.cpp file:

```
PlayerShip::PlayerShip() {
    m_X = 160.0;
    m_Y = 100.0;
    SDL_Surface *temp_surface = IMG_Load( c_SpriteFile );

    Collider* temp_collider = new Collider(3.0);
    temp_collider->SetParentInformation( &(this->m_Rotation),
                                    &(this->m_X), &(this->m_Y) );
    temp_collider->m_X = -6.0;
    temp_collider->m_Y = 6.0;
    m_Colliders.push_back( temp_collider );
    temp_collider = new Collider(3.0);
    temp_collider->SetParentInformation( &(this->m_Rotation),
                                    &(this->m_X), &(this->m_Y) );
    temp_collider->m_X = 6.0;
    temp_collider->m_Y = 6.0;
    m_Colliders.push_back( temp_collider );

    if( !temp_surface ) {
        printf("failed to load image: %s\n", IMG_GetError() );
```

```
            return;
        }
    m_SpriteTexture = SDL_CreateTextureFromSurface( renderer,
    temp_surface );

    if( !m_SpriteTexture ) {
        printf("failed to create texture: %s\n", IMG_GetError() );
        return;
    }
    SDL_FreeSurface( temp_surface );
}
```

Now, we have to change our projectile pool to run the collision detection on these new compound colliders in our ships. Here is the modified version of the MoveProjectiles function inside the projectile_pool.cpp file:

```
void ProjectilePool::MoveProjectiles() {
    Projectile* projectile;
    std::vector<Projectile*>::iterator it;
    for( it = m_ProjectileList.begin(); it != m_ProjectileList.end();
        it++ ) {
        projectile = *it;
        if( projectile->m_Active ) {
            projectile->Move();
            if( projectile->m_CurrentFrame == 0 &&
                player->m_CurrentFrame == 0 &&
                ( projectile->HitTest( player ) ||
                  player->CompoundHitTest( projectile ) ) ) {
                player->m_CurrentFrame = 1;
                player->m_NextFrameTime = ms_per_frame;
                projectile->m_CurrentFrame = 1;
                projectile->m_NextFrameTime = ms_per_frame;
            }
            if( projectile->m_CurrentFrame == 0 &&
                enemy->m_CurrentFrame == 0 &&
                ( projectile->HitTest( enemy ) ||
                  enemy->CompoundHitTest( projectile ) ) ) {
                enemy->m_CurrentFrame = 1;
                enemy->m_NextFrameTime = ms_per_frame;
                projectile->m_CurrentFrame = 1;
                projectile->m_NextFrameTime = ms_per_frame;
            }
        }
    }
}
```

Because we continue to inherit `Collider` in our `Ship` class, we still will perform a regular hit test on our player and enemy ships. We have added a call to `CompoundHitTest` in our `Ship` class that loops over our `m_Colliders` vector and performs a collision hit test on each of the colliders in that vector.

Our compound collider solution is not generalized, and, for the most part, neither is our collision detection. We are only detecting collisions between our ships and our projectiles. We are not currently performing any collision detection between our ships. To have a generalized approach to collision detection, we would need to implement spacial segmenting. That would prevent the number of collision checks from growing exponentially with each additional collider added to our game.

Compiling collider.html

The command we use to compile our `collider.html` file is similar to our compile command in the last chapter. We will need to add a new `collider.cpp` file into the command line, but other than that it should be the same. Here is the command you use to compile `collider.html`:

```
em++ main.cpp collider.cpp ship.cpp enemy_ship.cpp player_ship.cpp
projectile.cpp projectile_pool.cpp -std=c++17 --preload-file sprites -s
USE_WEBGL2=1 -s USE_SDL=2 -s USE_SDL_IMAGE=2 -s SDL2_IMAGE_FORMATS=["png"]
-o collider.html
```

Now that we have `collider.html` compiled, we can serve it from our web server of choice, or run it with `emrun`, and load it into a web browser. Here is what it looks like:

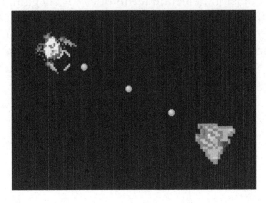

The enemy spaceship explodes when hit by a projectile

Please remember that you must run WebAssembly apps using a web server, or with emrun. If you would like to run your WebAssembly app using emrun, you must compile it with the --emrun flag. The web browser requires a web server to stream the WebAssembly module. If you attempt to open an HTML page that uses WebAssembly in a browser directly from your hard drive, that WebAssembly module will not load.

I did not take a screenshot of the entire browser as I have in previous screenshots of the game because I wanted to zoom in on the player ship destroying the enemy ship. As you can see, we now have colliders that can detect when a projectile collides with a spaceship and can destroy that spaceship when the collision happens by running an explosion animation.

Summary

Circle colliders are what we need right now. They are fast and efficient, and, for a simple game such as this, you might be able to get away with not doing anything more sophisticated. We added in a compound collider to demonstrate how this simple modification could significantly increase the accuracy of your collider. We will need to add more collision detection methods later in this book. In the future, we will be adding asteroids and a star to our game, and we will be creating an **AI** (**Artificial Intelligence**) agent to navigate our game and attack our player. This agent will eventually need to know whether it has a line of sight with the player so that line collision detection will become more important. Our agent will also want to quickly scan the area close to it to see whether there are any asteroids it must avoid. For this feature, we will be using rectangle collision.

There are many types of collision detection techniques for 2D games, and we have only scratched the surface in this chapter. We learned how to implement some basic circle colliders and compound colliders, and we added code that detects collisions between the projectiles in our game and the player and enemy spaceships. These kinds of colliders are fast and relatively easy to implement, but they are not without their drawbacks.

One drawback you may notice with simple colliders such as the ones we have implemented is that, if two objects pass each other with a high enough relative velocity, it is possible they could pass through each other without colliding. That is because our objects have a new position calculated every frame, and they do not continuously move from point A to point B. If it takes one frame to move from point A to point B, the object effectively teleports between the two points. If there was a second object in between those two points, but we are not colliding with that object when at either point A or point B, the object collision is missed. That should not be a problem in our game because we will be keeping our maximum object velocities relatively low. It is, however, something to keep in mind when writing your games.

In the next chapter, we will be building a tool to help us to configure **particle systems**.

8
Basic Particle System

A *particle system* is a graphics technique where we emit a large number of sprites from an *emitter* and have those sprites go through a life cycle where they change in a variety of ways. We build some randomness into our sprite life cycle to create a wide range of interesting effects such as explosions, sparks, snow, dust, fire, engine exhaust, and so on. Some particle effects can interact with their environment. In our game, we are going to use particle effects to create nice-looking engine exhaust and ship explosion effects.

 For this chapter, you will need to include several images in your build to make this project work. Make sure you include the /Chapter08/sprites/ folder from the project's GitHub. If you haven't yet downloaded the GitHub project, you can get it online here: https://github.com/PacktPublishing/Hands-On-Game-Develop.

This chapter and the beginning of the next one are going to feel like a digression at first. We will be spending a lot of time in the following two chapters working on something other than our game. If you are interested in particle systems, I promise it will be worth it. When you create a particle system, you spend a lot of time tweaking them and playing with them to get them to look right. To do this directly within the game will result in a lot of compiling and testing. What we need is a tool where we can configure and test a particle system before we add it to our game. This chapter and half of the next chapter are dedicated to building this tool. If you are not interested in learning how to build the tool, you can skim the text in this chapter, and download and compile the tool from GitHub. If you are as interested in learning how JavaScript, HTML, and WebAssembly can interact in an application, this chapter and the first half of Chapter 9, *Improved Particle Systems*, are a good tutorial for learning how to write an application and not just a game with WebAssembly.

In this chapter, we're going to cover the following topics:

- A brief introduction to SVG
- Trigonometry again?
- Adding the JavaScript
- The simple particle emitter tool
- The Point class
- The Particle Class
- The Emitter Class
- WebAssembly interface functions
- Compiling and testing the particle emitter

Adding to the virtual file system

This section is going to be a brief digression from *particle systems* because I would like to take the time to create a *particle system design tool*, which will require that we add files to the WebAssembly virtual file system. We are going to add an input element with a type of file that we can use to load an image into the virtual file system. We will need to check the file we are loading to verify it is a .png file, and if it is, we will draw and move the image around on the canvas using WebAssembly and SDL.

 Emscripten does not create a virtual file system by default. Because we will need to use a virtual file system that will not initially have anything inside of it, we will need to pass the following flag to em++ to force Emscripten to build a virtual filesystem: -s FORCE_FILESYSTEM=1.

The first thing we will do is copy canvas_shell.html from Chapter 2, *HTML5 and WebAssembly*, and use it to create a new shell file we will call upload_shell.html. We will need to add some code into the JavaScript that will handle file loads and insert that file into the WebAssembly virtual file system. We also need to add an HTML input element of file type that will not display until the Module object has finished loading. In the following code, we have the new shell file:

```
<!doctype html><html lang="en-us">
<head><meta charset="utf-8"><meta http-equiv="Content-Type"
content="text/html; charset=utf-8">
    <title>Upload Shell</title>
    <link href="upload.css" rel="stylesheet" type="text/css">
</head>
```

```html
<body>
    <canvas id="canvas" width="800" height="600"
     oncontextmenu="event.preventDefault()"></canvas>
    <textarea class="em_textarea" id="output" rows="8"></textarea>
    <script type='text/javascript'>
        var canvas = null;
        var ctx = null;
        function ShowFileInput()
            {document.getElementById("file_input_label")
            .style.display="block";}
        var Module = {
            preRun: [],
            postRun: [ShowFileInput],
            print: (function() {
                var element = document.getElementById('output');
                if (element) element.value = '';
                return function(text) {
                    if (arguments.length > 1)
                    text=Array.prototype.slice.call(arguments).join('
                    ');
                    console.log(text);
                    if (element) {
                        element.value += text + "\n";
                        element.scrollTop = element.scrollHeight;
                } }; })(),
    printErr: function(text) {
        if (arguments.length > 1)
        text=Array.prototype.slice.call(arguments).join(' ');
        if (0) { dump(text + '\n'); }
        else { console.error(text); } },
    canvas: (function() {
        var canvas = document.getElementById('canvas');
        canvas.addEventListener("webglcontextlost", function(e) {
        alert('WebGL context lost. You will need to reload the page.');
        e.preventDefault(); }, false);
        return canvas; })(),
    setStatus: function(text) {
        if (!Module.setStatus.last) Module.setStatus.last = { time:
            Date.now(), text: '' };
        if (text === Module.setStatus.last.text) return;
        var m = text.match(/([^(]+)\(((\d+(\.\d+)?)\/(\d+)\)/);
        var now = Date.now();
        if (m && now - Module.setStatus.last.time < 30) return;
        Module.setStatus.last.time = now;
        Module.setStatus.last.text = text;
        if (m) { text = m[1]; }
        console.log("status: " + text);
    },
```

```
            totalDependencies: 0,
            monitorRunDependencies: function(left) {
                this.totalDependencies = Math.max(this.totalDependencies,left);
                Module.setStatus(left ? 'Preparing... (' +
                (this.totalDependencies-left) + '/' +
                 this.totalDependencies + ')' : 'All downloads complete.'); }
        };
        Module.setStatus('Downloading...');
        window.onerror = function() {
            Module.setStatus('Exception thrown, see JavaScript console');
            Module.setStatus = function(text) { if (text) Module.printErr('[post-
        exception status] ' + text); };
        };
        function handleFiles(files) {
            var file_count = 0;
            for (var i = 0; i < files.length; i++) {
                if (files[i].type.match(/image.png/)) {
                    var file = files[i];
                    console.log("file name=" + file.name);
                    var file_name = file.name;
                    var fr = new FileReader();
                    fr.onload = function (file) {
                        var data = new Uint8Array(fr.result);
                        Module.FS_createDataFile('/', file_name, data, true,
                        true, true);
                        Module.ccall('add_image', 'undefined', ["string"],
                        [file_name]);
                    };
                    fr.readAsArrayBuffer(files[i]);
                }
            }
        }
        </script>
        <input type="file" id="file_input" onchange="handleFiles(this.files)" />
        <label for="file_input" id="file_input_label">Upload .png</label>
        {{{ SCRIPT }}}
        </body></html>
```

In the header, the only changes we are making are to the title, and the style sheet:

```
<title>Upload Shell</title>
<link href="upload.css" rel="stylesheet" type="text/css">
```

In the `body` tag, we are leaving the `canvas` and `textarea` elements alone, but there are significant changes to the JavaScript. The first thing we will do to the JavaScript is to add a `ShowFileInput` function to display the `file_input_label` element, which starts as hidden by our CSS. You can see it in the following code snippet:

```
function ShowFileInput() {
    document.getElementById("file_input_label").style.display = "block";
}

var Module = {
    preRun: [],
    postRun: [ShowFileInput],
```

Notice that we have added a call to this function in our `postRun` array so that it runs after the module is loaded. That is to make sure no one loads an image file before the `Module` object has loaded and our page can handle it. Aside from the addition of `ShowFileInput` to the `postRun` array, the `Module` object is unchanged. After our `Module` object code, we added a `handleFiles` function that is called by our file input element when the user picks a new file to load. Here is the code for that function:

```
function handleFiles(files) {
    var file_count = 0;
    for (var i = 0; i < files.length; i++) {
        if (files[i].type.match(/image.png/)) {
            var file = files[i];
            var file_name = file.name;
            var fr = new FileReader();
            fr.onload = function (file) {
                var data = new Uint8Array(fr.result);
                Module.FS_createDataFile('/', file_name, data, true,
                true, true);
                Module.ccall('add_image', 'undefined', ["string"],
                [file_name]);
            };
            fr.readAsArrayBuffer(files[i]);
        }
    }
}
```

You will notice that the function is designed to handle multiple files at once by looping over the `files` parameter passed into `handleFiles`. The first thing we will do is check to see if the image file type is PNG. When we compile the WebAssembly, we need to tell it what image file types SDL will handle. The PNG format should be all you need, but it is not difficult to add other types here.

If you do not want to check for PNG files specifically, you can leave out the .png part of the match string and later add additional file types into the compile command-line parameters. If the file is an image/png type, we put the filename into its variable, file_name, and create a FileReader object. We then define the function that runs when the FileReader loads the file:

```
fr.onload = function (file) {
    var data = new Uint8Array(fr.result);
    Module.FS_createDataFile('/', file_name, data, true, true, true);
    Module.ccall('add_image', 'undefined', ["string"], [file_name]);
};
```

This function takes in the data as an 8-bit unsigned integer array and then passes it into the Module function, FS_createDataFile. This function takes as its parameters a string that is the parent directory '/' of our file, the filename, file_name, the data we read from our file, followed by canRead, canWrite, and canOwn, which should all be set to true because we would like to be able to have our WebAssembly read, write, and own this file. We then use Module.ccall to call a function defined in our WebAssembly called add_image that will take the filename so that our WebAssembly can render this image to the HTML canvas using SDL. After we define the function that tells the FileReader what to do when a file is loaded, we have to instruct the FileReader to go ahead and read in the loaded file as an ArrayBuffer:

```
fr.readAsArrayBuffer(files[i]);
```

After the JavaScript, we added a file input element and a label to go along with it, as shown here:

```
<input type="file" id="file_input" onchange="handleFiles(this.files)" />
<label for="file_input" id="file_input_label">Upload .png</label>
```

The label is purely for styling. Styling an input file element is not a straightforward thing in CSS. We will go over how to do that in a little bit. Before discussing the CSS, I would like to go over the WebAssembly C code that we will use to load and render this image using SDL. The following code will go inside of a file we have named upload.c:

```
#include <emscripten.h>
#include <stdlib.h>
#include <SDL2/SDL.h>
#include <SDL2/SDL_image.h>

SDL_Window *window;
SDL_Renderer *renderer;
char* fileName;
SDL_Texture *sprite_texture = NULL;
```

```c
SDL_Rect dest = {.x = 160, .y = 100, .w = 16, .h = 16 };

int sprite_x = 0;
int sprite_y = 0;

void add_image(char* file_name) {
    SDL_Surface *temp_surface = IMG_Load( file_name );

    if( !temp_surface ) {
        printf("failed to load image: %s\n", IMG_GetError() );
        return;
    }
    sprite_texture = SDL_CreateTextureFromSurface( renderer,
    temp_surface );
    SDL_FreeSurface( temp_surface );
    SDL_QueryTexture( sprite_texture,
                        NULL, NULL,
                        &dest.w, &dest.h );
}

void show_animation() {
    if( sprite_texture == NULL ) {
        return;
    }

    SDL_SetRenderDrawColor( renderer, 0, 0, 0, 255 );
    SDL_RenderClear( renderer );

    sprite_x += 2;
    sprite_y++;

    if( sprite_x >= 800 ) {
        sprite_x = -dest.w;
    }

    if( sprite_y >= 600 ) {
        sprite_y = -dest.h;
    }
    dest.x = sprite_x;
    dest.y = sprite_y;

    SDL_RenderCopy( renderer, sprite_texture, NULL, &dest );
    SDL_RenderPresent( renderer );
}

int main() {
    printf("Enter Main\n");
    SDL_Init( SDL_INIT_VIDEO );
```

```
    int return_val = SDL_CreateWindowAndRenderer( 800, 600, 0, &window,
    &renderer );

    if( return_val != 0 ) {
        printf("Error creating renderer %d: %s\n", return_val,
        IMG_GetError() );
         return 0;
    }
    emscripten_set_main_loop(show_animation, 0, 0);
    printf("Exit Main\n");
    return 1;
}
```

There are three functions we have defined inside of our new `upload.c` file. The first function is the `add_image` function. This function takes in a `char*` string that represents the file we have just loaded into the WebAssembly virtual file system. We use SDL to load the image into a surface, and then we use that surface to create a texture we will use to render the image we loaded. The second function is `show_animation`, which we use to move the image around the canvas. The third is the `main` function, which always gets run when the module is loaded, so we use it to initialize our SDL.

Let's take a quick look at the `add_image` function:

```
void add_image(char* file_name) {
    SDL_Surface *temp_surface = IMG_Load( file_name );

    if( !temp_surface ) {
        printf("failed to load image: %s\n", IMG_GetError() );
        return;
    }
    sprite_texture = SDL_CreateTextureFromSurface( renderer,
    temp_surface );
    SDL_FreeSurface( temp_surface );
    SDL_QueryTexture( sprite_texture,
                      NULL, NULL,
                      &dest.w, &dest.h );
}
```

The first thing we do in the `add_image` function is use the `file_name` parameter we passed in to load an image into an `SDL_Surface` object pointer, using the `IMG_Load` function that is a part of the `SDL_image` library:

```
    SDL_Surface *temp_surface = IMG_Load( file_name );
```

If the load fails, we print an error message and return from the function:

```
if( !temp_surface ) {
    printf("failed to load image: %s\n", IMG_GetError() );
    return;
}
```

If it does not fail, we use the surface to create a texture that we will be able to render in the frame animation. Then, we free the surface because we no longer need it:

```
sprite_texture = SDL_CreateTextureFromSurface( renderer, temp_surface
);
SDL_FreeSurface( temp_surface );
```

The final thing we do is use the SDL_QueryTexture function to get the image's width and height, and load those values into the dest rectangle:

```
SDL_QueryTexture( sprite_texture,
                  NULL, NULL,
                  &dest.w, &dest.h );
```

The show_animation function is similar to other game loops we have written in the past. It should run every frame, and as long as a sprite texture is loaded, it should clear the canvas, increment the sprite's x and y values, and then render the sprite to the canvas:

```
void show_animation() {
    if( sprite_texture == NULL ) {
        return;
    }

    SDL_SetRenderDrawColor( renderer, 0, 0, 0, 255 );
    SDL_RenderClear( renderer );
    sprite_x += 2;
    sprite_y++;

    if( sprite_x >= 800 ) {
        sprite_x = -dest.w;
    }
    if( sprite_y >= 600 ) {
        sprite_y = -dest.h;
    }

    dest.x = sprite_x;
    dest.y = sprite_y;
    SDL_RenderCopy( renderer, sprite_texture, NULL, &dest );
    SDL_RenderPresent( renderer );
}
```

The first thing we do in `show_animation` is to check if the `sprite_texture` is still `NULL`. If it is, the user has not loaded a PNG file yet so we can not render anything:

```
if( sprite_texture == NULL ) {
    return;
}
```

The next thing we will do is clear the canvas with the color black:

```
SDL_SetRenderDrawColor( renderer, 0, 0, 0, 255 );
SDL_RenderClear( renderer );
```

Then, we will increment the sprite's x and y coordinates and use those values to set the `dest` (destination) rectangle:

```
sprite_x += 2;
sprite_y++;
if( sprite_x >= 800 ) {
    sprite_x = -dest.w;
}
if( sprite_y >= 600 ) {
    sprite_y = -dest.h;
}
dest.x = sprite_x;
dest.y = sprite_y;
```

Finally, we render the sprite to the back buffer, and then move the back buffer to the canvas:

```
SDL_RenderCopy( renderer, sprite_texture, NULL, &dest );
SDL_RenderPresent( renderer );
```

The final function in `upload.c` is the `main` function, which gets called when the module is loaded. This function is used for initialization purposes and looks like this:

```
int main() {
    printf("Enter Main\n");
    SDL_Init( SDL_INIT_VIDEO );
    int return_val = SDL_CreateWindowAndRenderer( 800, 600, 0, &window,
    &renderer );

    if( return_val != 0 ) {
        printf("Error creating renderer %d: %s\n", return_val,
        IMG_GetError() );
        return 0;
    }

    emscripten_set_main_loop(show_animation, 0, 0);
```

```
        printf("Exit Main\n");
        return 1;
}
```

It calls a few SDL functions to initialize our SDL renderer:

```
SDL_Init( SDL_INIT_VIDEO );
int return_val = SDL_CreateWindowAndRenderer( 800, 600, 0, &window,
&renderer );

if( return_val != 0 ) {
    printf("Error creating renderer %d: %s\n", return_val,
    IMG_GetError() );
    return 0;
}
```

Then, it sets up the show_animation function to run every time we render a frame:

```
emscripten_set_main_loop(show_animation, 0, 0);
```

The final thing we will do is set up a CSS file to display the HTML in our shell file correctly. Here are the contents of the new upload.css file:

```
body {
    margin-top: 20px;
}
#output {
    background-color: darkslategray;
    color: white;
    font-size: 16px;
    padding: 10px;
    margin-left: auto;
    margin-right: auto;
    display: block;
    width: 780px;
}
#canvas {
    width: 800px;
    height: 600px;
    margin-left: auto;
    margin-right: auto;
    display: block;
    background-color: black;
    margin-bottom: 20px;
}
[type="file"] {
    height: 0;
    overflow: hidden;
```

```
        width: 0;
        display: none;
    }

    [type="file"] + label {
        background: orangered;
        border-radius: 5px;
        color: white;
        display: none;
        font-size: 20px;
        font-family: Verdana, Geneva, Tahoma, sans-serif;
        text-align: center;
        margin-top: 10px;
        margin-bottom: 10px;
        margin-left: auto;
        margin-right: auto;
        width: 130px;
        padding: 10px 50px;
        transition: all 0.2s;
        vertical-align: middle;
    }
    [type="file"] + label:hover {
        background-color: orange;
    }
```

The first few classes, `body`, `#output`, and `#canvas`, are not much different from the version of those classes we had in previous CSS files, so we do not need to go into any detail on those. After those classes is a CSS class that looks a little different:

```
[type="file"] {
 height: 0;
 overflow: hidden;
 width: 0;
 display: none;
 }
```

That defines the look of an `input` element that has a type of `file`. For some reason, using CSS to style a file input element is not very straightforward. Instead of styling the element directly, we will hide the element with the `display: none;` attribute and then create a styled label, like this:

```
[type="file"] + label {
    background: orangered;
    border-radius: 5px;
    color: white;
    display: none;
    font-size: 20px;
```

```
        font-family: Verdana, Geneva, Tahoma, sans-serif;
        text-align: center;
        margin-top: 10px;
        margin-bottom: 10px;
        margin-left: auto;
        margin-right: auto;
        width: 130px;
        padding: 10px 50px;
        transition: all 0.2s;
        vertical-align: middle;
}
[type="file"] + label:hover {
        background-color: orange;
}
```

That is why, in the HTML, we have a label element immediately after our input file element. You may notice that our label also has set the display to none. That is so that the user can not use the element to upload a PNG file until after the Module object is loaded. If you look back to the JavaScript inside of our HTML shell file, we called the following code on postRun so that the label becomes visible after our Module is loaded:

```
function ShowFileInput() {
    document.getElementById("file_input_label").style.display =
    "block";
}
```

Now, we should have an app that can load an image into the WebAssembly virtual file system. In the next several sections, we will expand this app to configure and test a simple particle emitter.

A brief introduction to SVG

SVG stands for *Scalable Vector Graphics* and is an alternative to the immediate-mode raster graphics rendering that takes place in the HTML canvas. SVG is an XML-based graphics rendering language and should look at least somewhat familiar to anyone familiar with HTML. An SVG tag can be placed right inside of the HTML and accessed like any other DOM node. Because we are writing a tool for configuring particle emitter data, we will be adding SVG into our app for data visualization purposes.

Vector versus raster graphics

As a game developer, you may not be familiar with *vector graphics*. When we render computer graphics, no matter what format we use, they will need to be *rasterized* into a grid of pixels before the game displays them on a computer screen. Working with raster graphics is working with our images on the pixel level. Vector graphics, on the other hand, involves dealing with graphics at a different level of abstraction where we are working with lines, points, and curves. In the end, a vector-based graphics engine still must figure out how the lines, points, and curves it is dealing with are converted to pixels, but working with vector graphics is not without its benefits. They are as follows:

- Vector graphics can be cleanly scaled
- Vector graphics allow for smaller downloads
- Vector graphics can easily be modified at runtime

One of the sweet spots for using vector graphics on the web is for *data visualization*. This book is not about SVG or data visualization, and SVG is not currently fast enough to be used for game rendering for most applications. It is, however, a useful tool when you want to render graphical aids to go along with data on a website. We will be adding a little SVG into our particle emitter configuration tool as a visual aid to help the user see the direction the emitter is configured to emit particles. Because we are using this as a visual aid, it is not strictly necessary to have it inside of our app.

The first thing we will do is add a few tags to our HTML. We need an SVG tag to set up an area we can use to draw our vector circle graphic. We also need a couple of input values that allow us to enter two angles with values in degrees. These two input fields will take the minimum and maximum angles to emit a particle. When we have this working, it will give some direction to our particle emission. Here is the HTML code we need to add to our `body` tag:

```
<svg id="pie" width="200" height="200" viewBox="-1 -1 2 2"></svg>
<br/>
<div style="margin-left: auto; margin-right: auto">
<span class="label">min angle:</span>
<input type="number" id="min_angle" max="359" min="-90" step="1"
 value="-20" class="em_input"><br/>
<span class="label">max angle:</span>
<input type="number" id="max_angle" max="360" min="0" step="1"
 value="20" class="em_input"><br/>
</div>
```

We have set the `id` to pie in the `svg` tag. That will allow us to modify the values inside of this tag with lines and arcs later. We have given it a height and width of 200 pixels.

The `viewbox` is set to -1 -1 2 2. This says that the top-left coordinate of our SVG drawing area is set to coordinate -1, -1. The second two numbers, 2 2, are the width and height in the drawing space of the SVG drawing area. That means that our drawing space will go from coordinates -1, -1 in the top-left corner to 1, 1 in the bottom right. That will make it easy to deal with sine and cosine values when we need to calculate our angles.

Trigonometry again?

OMG yes, there is more *trigonometry*. I have already covered basic trigonometry in, Chapter 7, *Collision Detection*, but believe it or not, trigonometry is really useful in game development. Trigonometry happens to be very useful for particle systems and we will be using SVG and some trig to build a little pie chart we can use to visualize the direction of our particle emitter. So, let's take a second to quickly review things one more time:

- *Sine = Opposite/Hypotenuse (SOH)*
- *Cosine = Adjacent/Hypotenuse (CAH)*
- *Tangent = Opposite/Adjacent (TOA)*

Remember the word SOHCAHTOA?

If we are using a 2D Cartesian coordinate system (spoiler alert, we are) the *opposite* edge in our scenario is just the Y coordinate, and the *adjacent* edge is the X coordinate. So, in terms of a 2D Cartesian coordinate system, our ratios look like this:

- *Sine = Y/Circle Radius*
- *Cosine = X/Circle Radius*
- *Tangent = Y/X*

If you are calling a function in the JavaScript math library such as `cos` (for cosine) or `sin` (for sine), you usually pass in an angle measured in radians. You would get back the ratio, which if you are dealing with a *unit circle* (circle with a radius of 1), gives you the X value for cosine and the Y value for sine. So most of the time, all you need to remember is this:

- If you want the Y coordinate, use sine
- If you want the X coordinate, use cosine

We used this earlier to figure out the direction and velocity of our ship. We will use it later to get the direction and velocity of our particles given an angle. And, we are going to use it right now to figure out how to draw the SVG chart that shows us at what angle we will emit our particles.

We are taking in two different angles to get a range of angles to emit particles. Because we want our angles to overlap the angle 0 degrees, we have to allow the `min_angle` to go negative. Our minimum angle can go from -90 degrees to 359 degrees, and the max angle can go from 0 degrees to 360 degrees.

I prefer to measure angles in degrees instead of radians. Math functions typically use radians, so if you are more comfortable in using radians in your interface, you can save yourself the trouble of running the conversion. Radians is a measurement of angle based on a *unit circle*. A *unit circle* has a circumference of 2π. If you measure an angle in radians, you are determining your angle based on how far around the *unit circle* you would have to walk to get to that point. So, if you walked from one side of your *unit circle* to the opposite side, you would have to walk a distance of π. Therefore π (in radians) = 180 degrees. If you wanted an angle one-quarter of the circle, you would have to walk a distance of $\pi / 2$ around your circle, so $\pi / 2 = 90$ *degrees*. I still find a 360-degree circle more intuitive because we spent a lot more time learning about degrees when I was in school. Radians were mentioned as an afterthought. If this had not been the case, I am sure I would find measuring my angle in terms of a *unit circle* to make a lot more sense.

The idea of a 360-degree circle is only intuitive because they drilled it into us when we were in school. The only reason we have this model of a circle is that we inherited it from the ancient Babylonians who used a base 60 mathematical system, which is also the reason we have 60 seconds in a minute and 60 minutes in an hour.

Later, we will be using SVG and some trig to draw a little pie chart that represents the direction particles will be emitted from our particle system. We need this directionality to create our engine exhaust particle emitter:

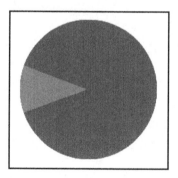

Figure 8.1: Our SVG pie chart

In the next section, we will be implementing our SVG pie chart using JavaScript.

Adding the JavaScript

Now that we have discussed a little of the trigonometry necessary to draw our SVG chart, let me step through the JavaScript we need to add to make our code work:

```
<script>
    document.getElementById("min_angle").onchange = function() {
        var min_angle = Number(this.value);
        var max_angle = Number(document.getElementById
                        ("max_angle").value);

        if( min_angle >= max_angle ) {
            max_angle = min_angle + 1;
            document.getElementById("max_angle").value = max_angle;
        }

        if( min_angle < this.min ) {
            min_angle = this.min;
            this.value = min_angle;
        }
        SetPie( min_angle / 180 * Math.PI, max_angle / 180 * Math.PI );
    }

    document.getElementById("max_angle").onchange = function() {
        var min_angle = Number(document.getElementById
                        ("min_angle").value);
        var max_angle = Number(this.value);

        if( min_angle >= max_angle ) {
            min_angle = max_angle - 1;
            document.getElementById("min_angle").value = min_angle;
        }

        if( max_angle > this.max ) {
            max_angle = this.max;
            this.value = max_angle;
        }

        SetPie( min_angle / 180 * Math.PI, max_angle / 180 * Math.PI );
    }

    function SetPie( start_angle, end_angle ) {
        const svg = document.getElementById('pie');
        const start_x = Math.cos( start_angle );
        const start_y = Math.sin( start_angle );

        const end_x = Math.cos( end_angle );
```

```
        const end_y = Math.sin( end_angle );
        var arc_flag_1 = 0;
        var arc_flag_2 = 0;

        if( end_angle - start_angle <= 3.14) {
            arc_flag_1 = 0;
            arc_flag_2 = 1;
        }
        else {
            arc_flag_1 = 1;
            arc_flag_2 = 0;
        }

        const path_data_1 =
            `M 0 0 L ${start_x} ${start_y} A 1 1 0 ${arc_flag_1} 1
            ${end_x} ${end_y} L 0 0`;

        const path_1 = document.createElementNS
        ('http://www.w3.org/2000/svg', 'path');
        path_1.setAttribute('d', path_data_1);
        path_1.setAttribute('fill', 'red');
        svg.appendChild(path_1);

        const path_data_2 =
            `M 0 0 L ${end_x} ${end_y} A 1 1 0 ${arc_flag_2} 1
            ${start_x} ${start_y} L 0 0`;

        const path_2 =
        document.createElementNS('http://www.w3.org/2000/svg', 'path');
        path_2.setAttribute('d', path_data_2);
        path_2.setAttribute('fill', 'blue');
        svg.appendChild(path_2);
    }

    SetPie( Number(document.getElementById("min_angle").value) / 180 *
            Math.PI,
    Number(document.getElementById("max_angle").value) / 180 * Math.PI );
</script>
```

Even though it is the last function in this code, I would like to begin by explaining the SetPie function, which is used to set the SVG pie chart that shows the emission angle range in red that the user has entered. Way back when we set up the SVG tag, we set the viewport to go from x and y values of −1 to 1. That is great, because using Math.cos and Math.sin will give us the values of the *X* and *Y* coordinates for the *unit circle*, which has a radius of 1 and so those values will also run from −1 to 1.

We use `document.getElementById('pie')` to grab the `svg` element from the DOM so we can modify it based on a change to the angle values. Next, we get the x and y coordinates on a unit circle with the `Math.cos` and `Math.sin` functions, respectively. We then do the same thing to get the ending x and y coordinates using the `end_angle`:

```
const end_x = Math.cos( end_angle );
const end_y = Math.sin( end_angle );
```

What we need to do in SVG is draw two paths. The first path will be drawn in red and will represent the angle where the particle system emitter will emit particles. The second path will be drawn in blue and will represent the part of our emission circle where we will not emit particles. When we draw an SVG arc, we give the arc two points and tell it with a flag if we need to take the long way (obtuse angle) or the short way (acute angle) around the circle. We do this by checking to see if the emission angle is less than π and set a flag that will go into our SVG based on this:

```
if( end_angle - start_angle <= 3.14) {
    arc_flag_1 = 0;
    arc_flag_2 = 1;
}
else {
    arc_flag_1 = 1;
    arc_flag_2 = 0;
}
```

Now, we need to define the path data and put it into the SVG path object. The following code sets the path data for the portion of our emitter in which we emit our particles:

```
const path_data_1 = `M 0 0 L ${start_x} ${start_y} A 1 1 0 ${arc_flag_1} 1
${end_x} ${end_y} L 0 0`;

const path_1 = document.createElementNS('http://www.w3.org/2000/svg',
                                        'path');
path_1.setAttribute('d', path_data_1);
path_1.setAttribute('fill', 'red');
svg.appendChild(path_1);
```

A series of commands define path data in SVG. If you look at the definition of `path_data_1`, it begins with `M 0 0`, which tells SVG to move the cursor to position `0, 0` without drawing. The next command is `L ${start_x} ${start_y}`. Because we are using a string template literal, `${start_x}` and `${start_y}` are replaced with the values in the `start_x` and `start_y` variables. This command draws a line from the current location we have moved to in the previous step (`0,0`) to the coordinates `start_x` and `start_y`. The next command in our path is the `Arc` command and begins with A: `A 1 1 0 ${arc_flag_1} 1 ${end_x} ${end_y}`.

The first two parameters, 1 1, are the x and y radius of an ellipse. Because we want a unit circle, both of these values are 1. The 0 that follows is an *X*-axis rotation that SVG uses when drawing an ellipse. Because we are drawing a circle, we set this to 0. The value after that is `${arc_flag_1}`. That is used to set the *large arc flag*, which tells SVG if we are drawing the obtuse arc (we set the value to 1) or the acute arc (we set the value to 0). The value after this is the *sweep flag*. This flag determines if we are drawing in the clockwise (value is 1) or counter-clockwise (value is 0) direction. We always want to draw in the clockwise direction, so this value is going to be 1. The last two parameters in our *arc* command are `${end_x}` `${end_y}`. These values are the end position of our arc, which we had determined earlier by getting the cosine and sine of our ending angle. After we have completed our arc, we finish our shape by drawing a line back to the 0,0 coordinate using the `L 0 0` line command.

After we have drawn the emission angle in red, we cover the remainder of the circle in blue with a second path by drawing from the ending position to the starting position.

In the next section, we are going to build a simple particle emitter configuration tool.

The simple particle emitter tool

Now that we have created a simple web app that can upload a PNG image file to the WebAssembly *virtual file system*, and an SVG chart to display the emission direction of the particles, we are going to add a simple particle system configuration tool. For this first version of our particle system configuration tool, we are going to keep the number of configurable values small. Later, we will add more features to our particle system tool, but for the moment this is the list of parameters we will be able to use to configure a particle emitter:

- Image file
- Minimum emission angle
- Maximum emission angle
- Maximum particles
- Particle lifetime in milliseconds
- Particle acceleration (or deceleration)
- Alpha fade (will the particles fade out over time?)
- Emission rate (number of particles to emit per second)
- X position (emitter x coordinate)

- Y position (emitter y coordinate)
- Radius (how far from the emitter's position can we create a particle?)
- Minimum starting velocity
- Maximum starting velocity

That will let us create a very basic particle emitter. We will improve this emitter in the next section, but we need to start somewhere. I do not plan on discussing any of the CSS we have added to enhance the look of this tool. The first thing I want to do is cover the HTML that will go into the new shell file, which we are calling `basic_particle_shell.html`. We need to add some HTML `input` fields to take in all of the configurable values we discussed previously. We will also need a button to update the emitter once we have written in our changes.

Add the following code into the `<body>` tag in our new shell file:

```
<div class="container">
    <svg id="pie" width="200" height="200" viewBox="-1 -1 2 2"></svg>
    <br/>
    <div style="margin-left: auto; margin-right: auto">
        <span class="label">min angle:</span>
        <input type="number" id="min_angle" max="359" min="-90"
         step="1" value="-20" class="em_input">
        <br/>
        <span class="label">max angle:</span>
        <input type="number" id="max_angle" max="360" min="0" step="1"
         value="20" class="em_input">
        <br/>
    </div>
    <span class="label">max particles:</span>
    <input type="number" id="max_particles" max="10000" min="10"
            step="10" value="100" class="em_input">
    <br/>
    <span class="label">life time:</span>
    <input type="number" id="lifetime" max="10000" min="10"
            step="10" value="1000" class="em_input"><br/>
    <span class="label">acceleration:</span>

    <input type="number" id="acceleration" max="2.0" min="0.0"
                        step="0.1" value="1.0" class="em_input"><br/>
    <label class="ccontainer"><span class="label">alpha fade:</span>
        <input type="checkbox" checked="checked">
        <span class="checkmark"></span>
    </label>
    <br/>
    <span class="label">emission rate:</span>
    <input type="number" id="emission_rate" max="100" min="1" step="1"
```

```
            value="20" class="em_input">
        <br/>

        <span class="label">x position:</span>
        <input type="number" id="x_pos" max="800" min="0" step="1"
         value="400" class="em_input">
        <br/>
        <span class="label">y position:</span>
        <input type="number" id="y_pos" max="600" min="0" step="1"
         value="300" class="em_input">
        <br/>
        <span class="label">radius:</span>
        <input type="number" id="radius" max="500" min="0" step="1"
         value="20" class="em_input">
        <br/>

        <span class="label">min start vel:</span>
        <input type="number" id="min_starting_vel" max="9.9" min="0.0"
                        step="0.1" value="1.0" class="em_input"><br/>
        <span class="label">max start vel:</span>
        <input type="number" id="max_starting_vel" max="10.0" min="0.0"
                        step="0.1" value="2.0" class="em_input"><br/>

    <div class="input_box">
        <button id="update_btn" class="em_button"
         onclick="UpdateClick()">Update Emitter</button>
    </div>
</div>
```

The CSS file styles this container to appear on the left side of the web page. The user can load an image into the virtual file system as they could previously, but this time all of the values in these input fields are used to create a particle emitter. The user can modify these settings and click the **Update Emitter** button to update the values used by the emitter. That will allow the user to test some basic emitter settings.

 The code inside of the main function will need to be added to prevent the SDL Event handler from intercepting the keyboard events and preventing the default behavior inside of these input elements. We will cover that code a little later.

Now that I have shown you the HTML elements that must be added to allow us to configure a particle system, let's step through the JavaScript code that will enable us to pass these values into the WebAssembly module. Here is what that JavaScript code looks like:

```
<script type='text/javascript'>
 var canvas = null;
 var ctx = null;
 var ready = false;
    var image_added = false;
    function ShowFileInput() {
        document.getElementById("file_input_label").style.display =
        "block";
        ready = true;
    }
    function UpdateClick() {
        if( ready == false || image_added == false ) { return; }
        var max_particles = Number(document.getElementById
                            ("max_particles").value);
        var min_angle = Number(document.getElementById
                            ("min_angle").value) / 180 * Math.PI;
        var max_angle = Number(document.getElementById
                            ("max_angle").value) / 180 * Math.PI
        var particle_lifetime = Number(document.getElementById
                            ("lifetime").value);
        var acceleration = Number(document.getElementById
                            ("acceleration").value);
        var alpha_fade = Boolean(document.getElementById
                            ("alpha_fade").checked);
        var emission_rate = Number(document.getElementById
                            ("emission_rate").value);
        var x_pos = Number(document.getElementById("x_pos").value);
        var y_pos = Number(document.getElementById("y_pos").value);
        var radius = Number(document.getElementById("radius").value);
        var min_starting_velocity = Number(document.getElementById
                            ("min_starting_vel").value);
        var max_starting_velocity = Number(document.getElementById
                            ("max_starting_vel").value);
        Module.ccall('update_emitter', 'undefined',
        ["number","number","number","number", "number","bool",
        "number","number","number","number","number","number"],

        [max_particles,min_angle,max_angle,particle_lifetime,
         acceleration,alpha_fade,min_starting_velocity,
         max_starting_velocity,emission_rate,x_pos ,y_pos,radius]);
        }
        var Module = {
            preRun: [],
            postRun: [ShowFileInput],
```

```
        print: (function() {
            var element = document.getElementById('output');
            if (element) element.value = '';
            return function(text) {
                if (arguments.length > 1) text =
                Array.prototype.slice.call(arguments).join(' ');
                console.log(text);
                if (element) {
                    element.value += text + "\n";
                    element.scrollTop = element.scrollHeight;
                }
            }; })(),
    printErr: function(text) {
        if (arguments.length > 1) text =
        Array.prototype.slice.call(arguments).join(' ');
        if (0) { dump(text + '\n'); }
        else { console.error(text); }
    },
    canvas: (function() {
        var canvas = document.getElementById('canvas');
        canvas.addEventListener("webglcontextlost", function(e) {
            alert('WebGL context lost. You will need to reload the
                    page.');
            e.preventDefault();},false);
        return canvas; })(),
    setStatus: function(text) {
        if (!Module.setStatus.last) Module.setStatus.last={ time:
            Date.now(), text: '' };
        if (text === Module.setStatus.last.text) return;
        var m = text.match(/([^(]+)\(((\d+(\.\d+)?)\/(\d+)\))/);
        var now = Date.now();
        if (m && now - Module.setStatus.last.time < 30) return;
        Module.setStatus.last.time = now;
        Module.setStatus.last.text = text;
        if(m) { text = m[1]; }
        console.log("status: " + text); },
    totalDependencies: 0,
    monitorRunDependencies: function(left) {
        this.totalDependencies = Math.max(this.totalDependencies,
                                    left);
        Module.setStatus(left?'Preparing... (' +
                    (this.totalDependencies-left) +
            '/' + this.totalDependencies + ')' :
            'All downloads complete.');
    } };
Module.setStatus('Downloading...');
window.onerror = function() {
    Module.setStatus('Exception thrown, see JavaScript console');
```

```
     Module.setStatus = function(text) {
         if (text) Module.printErr('[post-exception status] ' +
                                   text);
     }; };
function handleFiles(files) {
  var file_count = 0;
  for (var i = 0; i < files.length; i++) {
      if (files[i].type.match(/image.png/)) {
          var file = files[i];
          var file_name = file.name;
          var fr = new FileReader();
          fr.onload = function(file) {
            var data = new Uint8Array(fr.result);
            Module.FS_createDataFile('/', file_name, data,
                                     true, true, true);
            var max_particles = Number(document.getElementById
                             ("max_particles").value);
            var min_angle = Number(document.getElementById
                             ("min_angle").value) / 180 *
                             Math.PI;
            var max_angle = Number(document.getElementById
                             ("max_angle").value) / 180 *
                             Math.PI
            var particle_lifetime = Number(document.getElementById
                                ("lifetime").value);
            var acceleration = Number(document.getElementById
                             ("acceleration").value);
            var alpha_fade = Boolean(document.getElementById
                             ("alpha_fade").checked);
            var emission_rate = Number(document.getElementById
                             ("emission_rate").value);
            var x_pos = Number(document.getElementById
                       ("x_pos").value);
            var y_pos = Number(document.getElementById
                       ("y_pos").value);
            var radius = Number(document.getElementById
                       ("radius").value);
            var min_starting_velocity = Number(document.getElementById
                                      ("min_starting_vel").value);
            var max_starting_velocity = Number(document.getElementById
                                      ("max_starting_vel").value);
            Module.ccall('add_emitter','undefined',
            ["string","number", "number", "number", "number",
             "number", "bool",   "number", "number","number",
             "number", "number", "number"],
            [file_name, max_particles, min_angle, max_angle,
            particle_lifetime, acceleration, alpha_fade,
            min_starting_velocity, max_starting_velocity,
```

```
                    emission_rate, x_pos, y_pos, radius]);
                image_added = true; };
            fr.readAsArrayBuffer(files[i]);
} } }
</script>
```

Most of the `Module` code is unmodified, but we have added several functions and some new variables. We have added a global `ready` variable that is set to `false` when initialized. This flag will be set to `true` when the `Module` is loaded. As it was in the previous section, `ShowFileInput` runs after the `Module` is loaded using the `postRun` array. We have tweaked this code to set the `ready` flag that we mentioned earlier:

```
function ShowFileInput() {
    document.getElementById("file_input_label").style.display = "block";
    ready = true;
}
```

In an earlier section, we created a `handleFiles` function that loaded a file into our WebAssembly virtual file system. We now need to modify that function to call a function, `add_emitter`, that we will need to define inside of our C++ code. We will call this function, passing in all of the values we have defined in the HTML input elements. Here is what that function looks like:

```
function handleFiles(files) {
    var file_count = 0;
    for (var i = 0; i < files.length; i++) {
        if (files[i].type.match(/image.png/)) {
            var file = files[i];
            var file_name = file.name;
            var fr = new FileReader();
            fr.onload = function (file) {
                var data = new Uint8Array(fr.result);
                Module.FS_createDataFile('/', file_name, data, true,
                                true, true);
                var max_particles = Number(document.getElementById(
                                "max_particles").value);
                var min_angle = Number(document.getElementById
                                ("min_angle").value) / 180 * Math.PI;
                var max_angle = Number(document.getElementById
                                ("max_angle").value) / 180 * Math.PI
                var particle_lifetime = Number(document.getElementById
                                ("lifetime").value);
                var acceleration = Number(document.getElementById
                                ("acceleration").value);
                var alpha_fade = Boolean(document.getElementById
                                ("alpha_fade").checked);
                var emission_rate = Number(document.getElementById
```

```
                                          ("emission_rate").value);
                var x_pos = Number(document.getElementById
                               ("x_pos").value);
                var y_pos = Number(document.getElementById
                               ("y_pos").value);
                var radius = Number(document.getElementById
                                ("radius").value);
            var min_starting_velocity = Number(document.getElementById
                                           ("min_starting_vel").value);
            var max_starting_velocity = Number(document.getElementById
                                            ("max_starting_vel").value);
                Module.ccall('add_emitter', 'undefined', ["string",
                "number", "number", "number",
                "number", "number", "bool",
                "number", "number",
                "number", "number", "number", "number"],
                [file_name, max_particles,
                min_angle, max_angle,
                particle_lifetime, acceleration, alpha_fade,
                min_starting_velocity, max_starting_velocity,
                emission_rate, x_pos, y_pos, radius]);
                image_added = true;
            };
            fr.readAsArrayBuffer(files[i]);
        }
    }
}
```

The `FileReader` code, and the call to `Module.FS_createDataFile` from the previous iteration of this function, is still here. In addition to that, we use `document.getElementById` to grab the HTML elements and store the value of those elements into a set of variables:

```
var max_particles = Number(document.getElementById
                      ("max_particles").value);
var min_angle = Number(document.getElementById("min_angle").value) /
             180 * Math.PI;
var max_angle = Number(document.getElementById("max_angle").value) /
             180 * Math.PI
var particle_lifetime = Number(document.getElementById
                          ("lifetime").value);
var acceleration = Number(document.getElementById
                     ("acceleration").value);
var alpha_fade = Boolean(document.getElementById
                   ("alpha_fade").checked);
var emission_rate = Number(document.getElementById
                      ("emission_rate").value);
var x_pos = Number(document.getElementById("x_pos").value);
```

```
var y_pos = Number(document.getElementById("y_pos").value);
var radius = Number(document.getElementById("radius").value);
var min_starting_velocity = Number(document.getElementById
                            ("min_starting_vel").value);
var max_starting_velocity = Number(document.getElementById
                            ("max_starting_vel").value);
```

Many of these values need to be explicitly coerced into numbers using the `Number` coercion function. The `alpha_fade` variable must be coerced into a `Boolean` value. Now that we have all of these values inside of variables, we can use `Module.ccall` to call the C++ function, `add_emitter`, passing in all of these values:

```
Module.ccall('add_emitter', 'undefined', ["string", "number", "number",
        "number",
        "number", "number", "bool",
        "number", "number",
        "number", "number", "number", "number"],
        [file_name, max_particles, min_angle, max_angle,
        particle_lifetime, acceleration, alpha_fade,
        min_starting_velocity, max_starting_velocity,
        emission_rate, x_pos, y_pos, radius]);
```

At the very end of this, we set the `image_added` flag to `true`. We will not allow the user to update an emitter unless a call to `add_emitter` has created it. We have also added a new function, `UpdateClick`, that we will call whenever someone clicks the **Update Emitter** button, assuming that they have already created an emitter. Here is what the code in that function looks like:

```
function UpdateClick() {
    if( ready == false || image_added == false ) {
        return;
    }
    var max_particles = Number(document.getElementById
                        ("max_particles").value);
    var min_angle = Number(document.getElementById("min_angle").value)
                    / 180 * Math.PI;
    var max_angle = Number(document.getElementById("max_angle").value)
                    / 180 * Math.PI
    var particle_lifetime = Number(document.getElementById
                            ("lifetime").value);
    var acceleration = Number(document.getElementById
                        ("acceleration").value);
    var alpha_fade = Boolean(document.getElementById
                    ("alpha_fade").checked);
    var emission_rate = Number(document.getElementById
                        ("emission_rate").value);
    var x_pos = Number(document.getElementById("x_pos").value);
```

```
var y_pos = Number(document.getElementById("y_pos").value);
var radius = Number(document.getElementById("radius").value);
var min_starting_velocity = Number(document.getElementById
                          ("min_starting_vel").value);
var max_starting_velocity = Number(document.getElementById
                          ("max_starting_vel").value);

Module.ccall('update_emitter', 'undefined', ["number", "number",
             "number",
             "number", "number", "bool",
             "number", "number",
             "number", "number", "number", "number"],
             [max_particles, min_angle, max_angle,
             particle_lifetime, acceleration, alpha_fade,
             min_starting_velocity, max_starting_velocity,
             emission_rate, x_pos, y_pos, radius]);
}
```

The first thing we do is make sure that the Module object is loaded, and that we created the emitter. If either of these has not happened, we do not want to run this code, so we must return:

```
if( ready == false || image_added == false ) {
    return;
}
```

The remainder of this code is similar to the code we added to handleFiles. First, we grab all of the HTML elements and coerce the values in them into the appropriate data types to pass into our call to the C++ function:

```
var max_particles = Number(document.getElementById
                     ("max_particles").value);
var min_angle = Number(document.getElementById("min_angle").value) /
              180 * Math.PI;
var max_angle = Number(document.getElementById("max_angle").value) /
              180 * Math.PI
var particle_lifetime = Number(document.getElementById
                         ("lifetime").value);
var acceleration = Number(document.getElementById
                     ("acceleration").value);
var alpha_fade = Boolean(document.getElementById
                    ("alpha_fade").checked);
var emission_rate = Number(document.getElementById
                     ("emission_rate").value);
var x_pos = Number(document.getElementById("x_pos").value);
var y_pos = Number(document.getElementById("y_pos").value);
var radius = Number(document.getElementById("radius").value);
var min_starting_velocity = Number(document.getElementById
```

```
                                        ("min_starting_vel").value);
    var max_starting_velocity = Number(document.getElementById
                                        ("max_starting_vel").value);
```

After getting all of the values from the input elements, we use those values to call the `update_emitter` C++ function, passing in those values:

```
Module.ccall('update_emitter', 'undefined', ["number", "number",
            "number",
            "number", "number", "bool",
            "number", "number",
            "number", "number", "number", "number"],
            [max_particles, min_angle, max_angle,
            particle_lifetime, acceleration, alpha_fade,
            min_starting_velocity, max_starting_velocity,
            emission_rate, x_pos, y_pos, radius]);
```

In the next section, we will be implementing a `Point` class to track game object positions.

The Point class

In previous chapters, we have dealt with the 2D X and Y coordinates directly in our classes. I want to add a little bit of functionality that deals with our X and Y coordinates. For this, we are going to need to define a new class called `Point`. Eventually, `Point` will do more than what we are using it for here. But for right now, I would like to be able to create a `Point` object and be able to `Rotate` that point by an angle. Here is the class definition for `Point` that we have added to the `game.hpp` file:

```
class Point {
    public:
        float x;
        float y;
        Point();
        Point( float X, float Y );
        Point operator=(const Point& p);
        void Rotate( float radians );
};
```

The first several functions and the `operator=` are pretty straightforward. They set the x and y attributes either through a constructor or by using a line of code such as `point_1 = point_2;`. The last function, `Rotate`, is the entire reason we created this class. Its job is to take the *X* and *Y* coordinates and rotate them around the point 0, 0. Here is the code that gets that done:

```
void Point::Rotate( float radians ) {
    float sine = sin(radians);
    float cosine = cos(radians);
    float rx = x * cosine - y * sine;
    float ry = x * sine + y * cosine;
    x = rx;
    y = ry;
}
```

This `Rotate` function will eventually be used all over the game. For right now, we will use it to define the velocities of our particles based on the emission angles.

The Particle class

The `Particle` class is the class we will use to represent the individual particles that are emitted by our particle system. The `Particles` class will need to be created with a constructor and later updated with an `Update` function used to modify the defining attributes of the particle. There will be a `Spawn` function used to activate the `Particle`, a `Move` function to move the particle through its life cycle eventually deactivating it, and a `Render` function that will perform the SDL rendering tasks required to draw the particle to the canvas. Here is what the `Particle` class looks like in our `game.hpp` file:

```
class Particle {
    public:
        bool m_active;
        bool m_alpha_fade;
        SDL_Texture *m_sprite_texture;
        int m_ttl;
        Uint32 m_life_time;
        float m_acceleration;
        float m_alpha;
        Point m_position;
        Point m_velocity;
        SDL_Rect m_dest = {.x = 0, .y = 0, .w = 0, .h = 0 };
        Particle( SDL_Texture *sprite, Uint32 life_time, float
        acceleration, bool alpha_fade, int width, int height );
        void Update( Uint32 life_time, float acceleration,
```

```
                                bool alpha_fade );
                void Spawn( float x, float y, float velocity_x, float
                velocity_y, float alpha );
                void Move();
                void Render();
        };
```

We will define the functions associated with the `Particle` class inside of the `particle.cpp` file. At the top of this file, we have defined a constructor and an `Update` function. We call the `Update` function whenever the user clicks the **Update Emitter** button on the web page. That will update all of the particles to use the new values for their lifetime, acceleration, and alpha fade. Here is what the code to these first two functions looks like:

```
Particle::Particle( SDL_Texture *sprite_texture, Uint32 life_time,
                    float acceleration, bool alpha_fade,
                    int width, int height ) {
    m_sprite_texture = sprite_texture;
    m_life_time = life_time;
    m_acceleration = acceleration;
    m_alpha_fade = alpha_fade;
    m_dest.w = width;
    m_dest.h = height;
    m_active = false;
}
void Particle::Update( Uint32 life_time, float acceleration, bool
                       alpha_fade ) {
    m_life_time = life_time;
    m_acceleration = acceleration;
    m_alpha_fade = alpha_fade;
    m_active = false;
}
```

The `Spawn` function is called by the `Emitter` whenever it needs to emit a particle. The `Emitter` checks that the particle it is emitting has an active flag set to `false`. The values passed into `Spawn`, such as the *X* and *Y* coordinates, the velocity x and y values, and the starting alpha value, are all calculated by the `Emitter` when it emits a new particle. Here is what the code looks like:

```
void Particle::Spawn( float x, float y, float velocity_x,
                      float velocity_y, float alpha ) {
    m_position.x = x;
    m_dest.x = (int)m_position.x;
    m_position.y = y;
    m_dest.y = (int)m_position.y;
    m_velocity.x = velocity_x;
```

```
    m_velocity.y = velocity_y;
    m_alpha = alpha;
    m_active = true;
    m_ttl = m_life_time;
}
```

The `Move` function of every active particle is called once per frame by the emitter, and is where the particle calculates its new position, alpha, and determines if it is still active based on how long it has been alive. Here is what the code looks like:

```
void Particle::Move() {
    float acc_adjusted = 1.0f;
    if( m_acceleration < 1.0f ) {
        acc_adjusted = 1.0f - m_acceleration;
        acc_adjusted *= delta_time;
        acc_adjusted = 1.0f - acc_adjusted;
    }
    else if( m_acceleration > 1.0f ) {
        acc_adjusted = m_acceleration - 1.0f;
        acc_adjusted *= delta_time;
        acc_adjusted += 1.0f;
    }
    m_velocity.x *= acc_adjusted;
    m_velocity.y *= acc_adjusted;
    m_position.x += m_velocity.x;
    m_position.y += m_velocity.y;
    m_dest.x = (int)m_position.x;
    m_dest.y = (int)m_position.y;

    if( m_alpha_fade == true ) {
        m_alpha = 255.0 * (float)m_ttl / (float)m_life_time;
        if( m_alpha < 0 ) {
            m_alpha = 0;
        }
    }
    else {
        m_alpha = 255.0;
    }
    m_ttl -= diff_time;
    if( m_ttl <= 0 ) {
        m_active = false;
    }
}
```

Finally, the `Render` function makes calls to the SDL functions that set the alpha value for the particle and then copies that particle to the renderer:

```
void Particle::Render() {
    SDL_SetTextureAlphaMod(m_sprite_texture, (Uint8)m_alpha );
    SDL_RenderCopy( renderer, m_sprite_texture, NULL, &m_dest );
}
```

In the next section, we will discuss the `Emitter` class and the code we will need to make that class work.

The Emitter class

The `Emitter` class manages a pool of particles and is where the loaded sprite texture that the particles use to render themselves resides. Our emitters will only be circular. It is possible to define emitters with many different possible shapes, but for our game, a circle-shaped emitter will work fine. Right now, our `Emitter` class is going to be pretty basic. In later sections, we will add some new features, but right now I want to create a very basic particle system. Here is what the class definition looks like in the `game.hpp` file:

```
class Emitter {
    public:
        SDL_Texture *m_sprite_texture;
        std::vector<Particle*> m_particle_pool;
        int m_sprite_width;
        int m_sprite_height;
        Uint32 m_max_particles;
        Uint32 m_emission_rate;
        Uint32 m_emission_time_ms;
        int m_next_emission;
        float m_max_angle;
        float m_min_angle;
        float m_radius;
        float m_min_starting_velocity;
        float m_max_starting_velocity;
        Point m_position;
        Emitter(char* sprite_file, int max_particles, float min_angle,
                float max_angle,
                Uint32 particle_lifetime, float acceleration, bool
                alpha_fade,
                float min_starting_velocity, float
                max_starting_velocity,
                Uint32 emission_rate, int x_pos, int y_pos, float
                radius );
        void Update(int max_particles, float min_angle, float
```

```
            max_angle,
                    Uint32 particle_lifetime, float acceleration, bool
                    alpha_fade,
                    float min_starting_velocity, float
                    max_starting_velocity,
                    Uint32 emission_rate, int x_pos, int y_pos, float
                    radius );
        void Move();
        Particle* GetFreeParticle();
};
```

The attributes inside this class mirror the HTML input elements we created earlier in this chapter. These values get set either when the `Emitter` is created using the constructor, or when the user clicks the update button, which calls the `Update` function. The `Move` function will be called once per frame, and will move then render all of the particles that are active inside the particle pool. It will also determine if a new particle should be emitted by calling the `Spawn` function on a free particle.

We will define all of these functions within the `emitter.cpp` file. Here is what the `Emitter` constructor and `Update` functions look like inside of the `emitter.cpp` file:

```
Emitter::Emitter(char* sprite_file, int max_particles, float min_angle,
float max_angle, Uint32 particle_lifetime, float acceleration, bool
alpha_fade, float min_starting_velocity, float max_starting_velocity,
Uint32 emission_rate, int x_pos, int y_pos, float radius ) {

    if( min_starting_velocity > max_starting_velocity ) {
        m_min_starting_velocity = max_starting_velocity;
        m_max_starting_velocity = min_starting_velocity;
    }
    else {
        m_min_starting_velocity = min_starting_velocity;
        m_max_starting_velocity = max_starting_velocity;
    }
    SDL_Surface *temp_surface = IMG_Load( sprite_file );

    if( !temp_surface ) {
        printf("failed to load image: %s\n", IMG_GetError() );
        return;
    }
    m_sprite_texture = SDL_CreateTextureFromSurface( renderer,
    temp_surface );
    SDL_FreeSurface( temp_surface );
    SDL_QueryTexture( m_sprite_texture,
                NULL, NULL, &m_sprite_width, &m_sprite_height );
    m_max_particles = max_particles;
```

```
        for( int i = 0; i < m_max_particles; i++ ) {
            m_particle_pool.push_back(
                new Particle( m_sprite_texture, particle_lifetime,
                acceleration, alpha_fade, m_sprite_width, m_sprite_height )
            );
        }
        m_max_angle = max_angle;
        m_min_angle = min_angle;
        m_radius = radius;
        m_position.x = (float)x_pos;
        m_position.y = (float)y_pos;
        m_emission_rate = emission_rate;
        m_emission_time_ms = 1000 / m_emission_rate;
        m_next_emission = 0;
}

void Emitter::Update(int max_particles, float min_angle, float
                     max_angle, Uint32 particle_lifetime, float
                     acceleration, bool alpha_fade,
                     float min_starting_velocity, float
                     max_starting_velocity, Uint32 emission_rate, int
                     x_pos, int y_pos, float radius ) {
    if( min_starting_velocity > max_starting_velocity ) {
        m_min_starting_velocity = max_starting_velocity;
        m_max_starting_velocity = min_starting_velocity;
    }
    else {
        m_min_starting_velocity = min_starting_velocity;
        m_max_starting_velocity = max_starting_velocity;
    }
    m_max_particles = max_particles;
    m_min_angle = min_angle;
    m_max_angle = max_angle;
    m_emission_rate = emission_rate;
    m_position.x = (float)x_pos;
    m_position.y = (float)y_pos;
    m_radius = radius;

    if( m_particle_pool.size() > m_max_particles ) {
        m_particle_pool.resize( m_max_particles );
    }
    else if( m_max_particles > m_particle_pool.size() ) {
        while( m_max_particles > m_particle_pool.size() ) {
            m_particle_pool.push_back(
                new Particle( m_sprite_texture, particle_lifetime,
                acceleration, alpha_fade, m_sprite_width,
                m_sprite_height )
            );
```

```
            }
        }

        Particle* particle;
        std::vector<Particle*>::iterator it;
        for( it = m_particle_pool.begin(); it != m_particle_pool.end();
            it++ ) {
            particle = *it;
            particle->Update( particle_lifetime, acceleration, alpha_fade );
        }
    }
```

Both of these functions set the attributes of the Emitter class and set up the particle pool based on the max_particles value passed into these functions. The GetFreeParticle function is called by the Move function to get a particle from the particle pool that is not currently active. The Move function first figures out if it needs to emit a new particle, and if it does, calls the GetFreeParticle function to grab an inactive particle, and then uses the attributes of the Emitter to set the values to use when spawning a particle. It will loop over all of the particles in the pool, and if the particle is active, it will Move and then Render that particle:

```
Particle* Emitter::GetFreeParticle() {
    Particle* particle;
    std::vector<Particle*>::iterator it;
    for( it = m_particle_pool.begin(); it != m_particle_pool.end();
        it++ ) {
        particle = *it;
        if( particle->m_active == false ) {
            return particle;
        }
    }
    return NULL;
}

void Emitter::Move() {
    Particle* particle;
    std::vector<Particle*>::iterator it;
    static int count = 0;
    m_next_emission -= diff_time;
    if( m_next_emission <= 0 ) {
        m_next_emission = m_emission_time_ms;
        particle = GetFreeParticle();
        if( particle != NULL ) {
            float rand_vel = (rand() %
                (int)((m_max_starting_velocity -
                    m_min_starting_velocity) * 1000)) / 1000.0f;
            Point spawn_point;
```

```
                    spawn_point.x = (float)(rand() % (int)(m_radius * 1000)) /
                    1000.0;
                    Point velocity_point;
                    velocity_point.x = (float)(rand() %
                        (int)((m_max_starting_velocity + rand_vel) * 1000)) /
                        1000.0;
                    int angle_int = (int)((m_max_angle - m_min_angle) *
                    1000.0);
                    float add_angle = (float)(rand() % angle_int) /1000.0f;
                    float angle = m_min_angle + add_angle;
                    velocity_point.Rotate(angle);
                    angle = (float)(rand() % 62832) / 10000.0;
                    spawn_point.Rotate( angle );
                    spawn_point.x += m_position.x;
                    spawn_point.y += m_position.y;
                    particle->Spawn(spawn_point.x, spawn_point.y,
                    velocity_point.x, velocity_point.y, 255.0f );
                }
        }
        for( it = m_particle_pool.begin(); it != m_particle_pool.end();
            it++ ) {
            particle = *it;
            if( particle->m_active ) {
                particle->Move();
                particle->Render();
            }
        }
    }
}
```

We will compile these classes into our WebAssembly module, but they will not be used to interact directly with the JavaScript we defined earlier. For that, we are going to need to define some functions in a new file that we will discuss in the next section.

WebAssembly interface functions

We need to define the functions that will interact with our JavaScript. We also need to define some global variables that will be used by several of our classes. Here is the code from the new basic_particle.cpp file:

```
#include "game.hpp"
#include <emscripten/bind.h>
SDL_Window *window;
SDL_Renderer *renderer;
char* fileName;
Emitter* emitter = NULL;
```

```
Uint32 last_time = 0;
Uint32 current_time = 0;
Uint32 diff_time = 0;
float delta_time = 0.0f;
extern "C"
    EMSCRIPTEN_KEEPALIVE
    void add_emitter(char* file_name, int max_particles, float
    min_angle, float max_angle, Uint32 particle_lifetime, float
    acceleration, bool alpha_fade, float min_starting_velocity, float
    kmax_starting_velocity, Uint32 emission_rate, float x_pos, float
    y_pos, float radius) {
        if( emitter != NULL ) {
            delete emitter;
        }
        emitter = new Emitter(file_name, max_particles, min_angle,
                              max_angle, particle_lifetime,
                              acceleration, alpha_fade,
                              min_starting_velocity,
                              max_starting_velocity,
                              emission_rate, x_pos, y_pos, radius );
    }
extern "C"
    EMSCRIPTEN_KEEPALIVE
    void update_emitter(int max_particles, float min_angle, float
    max_angle, Uint32 particle_lifetime, float acceleration, bool
    alpha_fade, float min_starting_velocity, float
    max_starting_velocity, Uint32 emission_rate, float x_pos, float
    y_pos, float radius ) {
        if( emitter == NULL ) {
            return;
        }
        emitter->Update(max_particles, min_angle, max_angle,
                        particle_lifetime, acceleration, alpha_fade,
                        min_starting_velocity, max_starting_velocity,
                        emission_rate, x_pos, y_pos, radius );
    }
    void show_emission() {
        current_time = SDL_GetTicks();
        delta_time = (double)(current_time - last_time) / 1000.0;
        diff_time = current_time - last_time;
        last_time = current_time;
        if( emitter == NULL ) {
            return;
        }
        SDL_SetRenderDrawColor( renderer, 0, 0, 0, 255 );
        SDL_RenderClear( renderer );
        emitter->Move();
        SDL_RenderPresent( renderer );
```

```
    }
int main() {
    printf("Enter Main\n");
    SDL_Init( SDL_INIT_VIDEO );
    int return_val = SDL_CreateWindowAndRenderer( 800, 600, 0,
    &window, &renderer );
    SDL_EventState(SDL_TEXTINPUT, SDL_DISABLE);
    SDL_EventState(SDL_KEYDOWN, SDL_DISABLE);
    SDL_EventState(SDL_KEYUP, SDL_DISABLE);
    if( return_val != 0 ) {
        printf("Error creating renderer %d: %s\n", return_val,
        IMG_GetError() );
        return 0;
    }
    last_time = SDL_GetTicks();
    emscripten_set_main_loop(show_emission, 0, 0);
    printf("Exit Main\n");
    return 1;
}
```

The first two global variables are SDL_Window and SDL_Renderer. We need these as global objects (particularly the renderer) so that they can be used to render our textures to the canvas:

```
SDL_Window *window;
SDL_Renderer *renderer;
```

After that, we have our emitter. Right now, we are only supporting a single emitter. In later versions, we will want to have several emitters that we have configured:

```
Emitter* emitter = NULL;
```

The remaining global variables are all related to keeping track of time between frames in both milliseconds (diff_time) and terms of fractions of a second (delta_time). The last_time and current_time variables are primarily used to calculate those other two time-related variables. Here is what the definitions look like in the code:

```
Uint32 last_time = 0;
Uint32 current_time = 0;
Uint32 diff_time = 0;
float delta_time = 0.0f;
```

After we define our global variables, it is time to define the functions that will interact with our JavaScript. The first one of these functions is `add_emitter`. That is a simple function that looks to see if an emitter has been defined and, if it has, delete it. Then, it creates a new emitter with the values that were passed into this function from the JavaScript using the values that were inside of the HTML input elements at the time. Here is what the function looks like:

```
extern "C"
    EMSCRIPTEN_KEEPALIVE
    void add_emitter(char* file_name, int max_particles, float
    min_angle, float max_angle, Uint32 particle_lifetime, float
    acceleration, bool alpha_fade, float min_starting_velocity, float
    max_starting_velocity, Uint32 emission_rate, float x_pos, float
    y_pos, float radius) {
        if( emitter != NULL ) {
            delete emitter;
        }
        emitter = new Emitter(file_name, max_particles, min_angle,
        max_angle, particle_lifetime, acceleration, alpha_fade,
        min_starting_velocity, max_starting_velocity,
        emission_rate, x_pos, y_pos, radius );
    }
```

You may have noticed these two lines that precede the definition of the `add_emitter` function:

```
extern "C"
    EMSCRIPTEN_KEEPALIVE
```

We need those lines to prevent *name mangling* and *dead code elimination*. If you've never heard those terms before, let me explain.

C++ name mangling

The first of these lines, `extern "C"`, tells the compiler that this is a C function and instructs it not to use C++ *name mangling* on that function. If you are not familiar with C++ name mangling, the basics of it are this: C++ supports function overloading. In other words, you can have multiple functions with the same name that have different parameters. C++ will call the correct function based on the parameters that are getting passed into that function. Because of this functionality, C++ will *mangle* the names as it compiles them, giving each function a different name during the compilation process. Because I am now using C++ and I am no longer using C, these functions I would like to be called from JavaScript are subject to this name mangling process. The `extern "C"` directive tells the C++ compiler that these are C functions, and to please not mangle the names so that I can call them externally from my JavaScript.

Dead code elimination

By default, Emscripten uses *dead code elimination* to remove any function that you are not calling from somewhere inside of your C++ code. In most instances, this is a good thing. You do not want unused code taking up space inside of your WebAssembly module. That creates a problem when there is a function that exists to be called from the JavaScript, but not from inside of the C++ code. The Emscripten compiler sees that nothing is calling this function, and eliminates it. `EMSCRIPTEN_KEEPALIVE` tells the Emscripten compiler not to remove this code because you would like to call it from an external source.

Updating the emitter

After the `add_emitter` code, the next function that is set up for an external call is `update_emitter`. This function first checks to see if there is a defined emitter, and if so, calls an update function that updates all of the attributes on the emitter to the values passed in from the HTML input elements. Here is what the code looks like:

```
extern "C"
    EMSCRIPTEN_KEEPALIVE
    void update_emitter(int max_particles, float min_angle, float
    max_angle, Uint32 particle_lifetime, float acceleration, bool
    alpha_fade, float min_starting_velocity, float
    max_starting_velocity, Uint32 emission_rate, float x_pos, float
    y_pos, float radius ) {
        if( emitter == NULL ) {
            return;
        }
```

```
emitter->Update(max_particles, min_angle, max_angle,
                particle_lifetime, acceleration, alpha_fade,
                min_starting_velocity, max_starting_velocity,
                emission_rate, x_pos, y_pos, radius );
}
```

The looping function

The next function, show_emission, is the function that would be our game loop if this app were a game. This function gets called for every frame rendered and is responsible for the setting of timer values, preparing our SDL to render, and calling the emitter Move function, which will move and render all of the particles in our particle system:

```
void show_emission() {
    current_time = SDL_GetTicks();
    delta_time = (double)(current_time - last_time) / 1000.0;
    diff_time = current_time - last_time;
    last_time = current_time;

    if( emitter == NULL ) {
        return;
    }
    SDL_SetRenderDrawColor( renderer, 0, 0, 0, 255 );
    SDL_RenderClear( renderer );
    emitter->Move();
    SDL_RenderPresent( renderer );
}
```

The first few lines calculate the delta_time and diff_time global variables, which are used by the particles to adjust the movement of the particles based on the frame rate:

```
current_time = SDL_GetTicks();
delta_time = (double)(current_time - last_time) / 1000.0;
diff_time = current_time - last_time;
last_time = current_time;
```

If the emitter has not been set, we do not want to render anything, so we return:

```
if( emitter == NULL ) {
    return;
}
```

If the emitter exists, we need to clear out the renderer using a black color:

```
SDL_SetRenderDrawColor( renderer, 0, 0, 0, 255 );
SDL_RenderClear( renderer );
```

After that, we call the emitter Move function, which both moves all the particles and copies the sprite texture to the appropriate position in the renderer. Then, we call the SDL_RenderPresent function, to render to the HTML canvas element:

```
emitter->Move();
SDL_RenderPresent( renderer );
```

Initialization

The final function is the main function, which is called automatically when the WebAssembly module is loaded:

```
int main() {
    SDL_Init( SDL_INIT_VIDEO );
    int return_val = SDL_CreateWindowAndRenderer( 800, 600, 0, &window,
                                                  &renderer );
    if( return_val != 0 ) {
        printf("Error creating renderer %d: %s\n", return_val,
            IMG_GetError() );
        return 0;
    }
    SDL_EventState(SDL_TEXTINPUT, SDL_DISABLE);
    SDL_EventState(SDL_KEYDOWN, SDL_DISABLE);
    SDL_EventState(SDL_KEYUP, SDL_DISABLE);
    last_time = SDL_GetTicks();
    emscripten_set_main_loop(show_emission, 0, 0);
    return 1;
}
```

The first couple of lines initialize our SDL:

```
SDL_Init( SDL_INIT_VIDEO );
int return_val = SDL_CreateWindowAndRenderer( 800, 600, 0, &window,
                                              &renderer );
```

After that, the next several lines are used to disable the SDL text input and keyboard events. These lines prevent SDL from capturing the keyboard input we need to set the input values inside of our HTML elements. In most games, we would not want these lines, because we would prefer these events to be captured so that we could manage our game input from within our WebAssembly module. But, if we want our app to work, and we want our users to be able to change our HTML input, we must have these lines in our code:

```
SDL_EventState(SDL_TEXTINPUT, SDL_DISABLE);
SDL_EventState(SDL_KEYDOWN, SDL_DISABLE);
SDL_EventState(SDL_KEYUP, SDL_DISABLE);
```

The next line gets the starting clock value for the `last_time` global variable:

```
last_time = SDL_GetTicks();
```

The last line in this function prior to the return is used to set up our loop function. Our loop function will be called every time a frame is rendered:

```
emscripten_set_main_loop(show_emission, 0, 0);
```

In the next section, we will compile and test an early version of our emitter configuration tool.

Compiling and testing the particle emitter

Wow, that was a lot of code. Okay, now that we have everything that we need in our particle emitter config tool, we need to take the time to compile and test it. After we test this version, we can use this same call to em++ to test the advanced version we will start building in the next section.

Run this command at the command line:

```
em++ emitter.cpp particle.cpp point.cpp basic_particle.cpp -o particle.html
-std=c++17 --shell-file basic_particle_shell.html -s NO_EXIT_RUNTIME=1 -s
USE_WEBGL2=1 -s USE_SDL=2 -s USE_SDL_IMAGE=2 -s SDL2_IMAGE_FORMATS=["png"]
-s NO_EXIT_RUNTIME=1 -s EXPORTED_FUNCTIONS="['_add_emitter',
'_update_emitter', '_main']" -s EXTRA_EXPORTED_RUNTIME_METHODS="['cwrap',
'ccall']" -s FORCE_FILESYSTEM=1
```

Your particle emitter configuration tool should look like this:

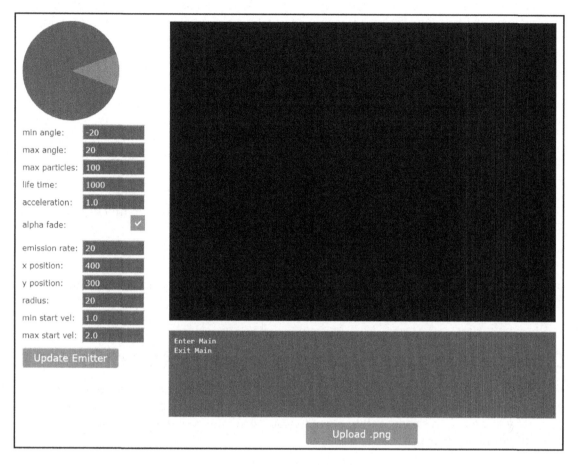

Figure 8.2: Screenshot of the particle system configuration tool

 Do not forget that you must run WebAssembly apps using a web server, or with emrun. If you would like to run your WebAssembly app using emrun, you must compile it with the --emrun flag. The web browser requires a web server to stream the We1bAssembly module. If you attempt to open an HTML page that uses WebAssembly in a browser directly from your hard drive, that WebAssembly module will not load.

Use this interface to upload a .png image file and play around with the numbers we have in the fields on the left. We do not yet have enough values to make an excellent particle emitter, but you can get a feel for the basics with what we currently have.

Summary

In this chapter, we learned how to create a basic particle emitter configuration tool. We covered how to force Emscripten to create a virtual file system when there are no files loaded into it at application startup. We learned how we could load an image from our user's computer into the browser's virtual file system, and added functionality to allow us to upload a `.png` image file. We covered some basics of SVG, discussed the differences between vector and raster graphics, and learned how we would use SVG to draw pie charts for our configuration tool. We covered some basic trigonometry that was useful in this chapter, and will only become more useful in later chapters. We created a new HTML shell file that interacts with our WebAssembly, to help us configure a new particle system for our game. We created a `Point`, `Particle`, and `Emitter` class in a WebAssembly module that we are using for the emitter, which we will eventually use inside of our game. Finally, we learned about C++ name mangling, dead code elimination, and the circumstances where we must avoid them when writing Emscripten code.

In the next chapter, we will improve our *particle emitter configuration tool*. By the end of the chapter, we will use it to configure effects in our game such as explosions, solar flares, and spaceship exhaust plumes. The tool can be used to play around with different effects, and get a feeling for how they look before we add that effect into our game. Finally, we will take the values we used in our configuration tool and use them as a starting point for configuring the particle effects in our game.

Improved Particle Systems

9

The *particle system* we developed in the previous chapter was a good start, but the effects you can create with it are rather bland. Our particles do not rotate or scale, they are not animated, and they are relatively consistent in the way they look over time.

 For this chapter, you will need to include several images in your build to make this project work. Make sure that you include the /Chapter09/sprites/ folder from this project's GitHub repository. If you would like to build the particle system tool from GitHub, the source for the tool is located in the /Chapter09/advanced-particle-tool/ folder. If you haven't downloaded the GitHub project yet, you can get it online here: https://github.com/PacktPublishing/Hands-On-Game-Develop.

If we want the most out of our particle system, we are going to need to add more features to it. In this chapter, we will be adding the following additional features:

- Particle scale over its lifetime
- Particle rotation
- Animated particles
- Color change over time
- Support for particle bursts
- Support for looping and non-looping emitters

Modifying our HTML shell file

The first thing we need to do is add some new inputs into the HTML shell file. We are going to copy the `basic_particle_shell.html` file to a new shell file that we will call `advanced_particle_shell.html`. We will be adding a second container class `div` element and a lot of new inputs to the HTML portion of the shell file between the original container and the `canvas` element. Here is what that new container element looks like:

```html
<div class="container">
<div class="empty_box"> </div><br/>
<span class="label">min start scale:</span>
<input type="number" id="min_starting_scale" max="9.9" min="0.1" step="0.1"
value="1.0" class="em_input"><br/>
<span class="label">max start scale:</span>
<input type="number" id="max_starting_scale" max="10.0" min="0.2"
step="0.1" value="2.0" class="em_input"><br/>
<span class="label">min end scale:</span>
<input type="number" id="min_end_scale" max="9.9" min="0.1" step="0.1"
value="1.0" class="em_input">
<br/>
<span class="label">max end scale:</span>
<input type="number" id="max_end_scale" max="10.0" min="0.2" step="0.1"
value="2.0" class="em_input">
<br/>
<span class="label">start color:</span>
<input type="color" id="start_color" value="#ffffff"
class="color_input"><br/>
<span class="label">end color:</span>
<input type="color" id="end_color" value="#ffffff"
class="color_input"><br/>
<span class="label">burst time pct:</span>
<input type="number" id="burst_time" max="1.0" min="0.0" step="0.05"
value="0.0" class="em_input">
<br/>
<span class="label">burst particles:</span>
<input type="number" id="burst_particles" max="100" min="0" step="1"
value="0" class="em_input">
<br/>
<label class="ccontainer"><span class="label">loop:</span>
    <input type="checkbox" id="loop" checked="checked">
    <span class="checkmark"></span>
</label>
<br/>
<label class="ccontainer"><span class="label">align rotation:</span>
    <input type="checkbox" id="align_rotation" checked="checked">
    <span class="checkmark"></span>
</label>
```

```
<br/>
<span class="label">emit time ms:</span>
<input type="number" id="emit_time" max="10000" min="100" step="100"
value="1000" class="em_input">
<br/>
<span class="label">animation frames:</span>
<input type="number" id="animation_frames" max="64" min="1" step="1"
value="1" class="em_input">
<br/>
<div class="input_box">
<button id="update_btn" class="em_button" onclick="UpdateClick()">Update
Emitter</button>
</div>
</div>
```

Scaling values

Scaling a sprite means modifying that sprite's size by some multiple of its original size. For example, if we scale a 16 x 16 sprite by a scaling value of 2.0, the sprite will render to the canvas as a 32 x 32 image. This new container starts with four input elements, as well as their labels, which tell the particle system how to scale the particles over their lifetimes. The min_starting_scale and max_starting_scale elements are the starting range scale of the particles. If you want the particle to always start with a scale of 1.0 (1 to 1 scale with the .png image size), you should put 1.0 in both of these fields. The actual starting scale value will be a randomly chosen value that falls between the two values you put in those fields. We haven't added any checks in this interface to verify that max is larger than min, so make sure that max is the same value or larger than the min value or this will break the emitter. The next two input elements are min_end_scale and max_end_scale. Like the starting scale values, the actual ending scale will be a randomly chosen value that falls between the two values we put in these fields. At any given point in a particle's lifetime, it will have a scale that is a value interpolated between the scale value assigned to the start of that particle's lifetime and the scale value at the end. So, if I start with a scale value of 1.0 and end with a scale value of 3.0, when the lifetime of the particle is half over, the scale value of the particle will be 2.0.

Here is what those elements look like in the HTML file:

```
<span class="label">min start scale:</span>
<input type="number" id="min_starting_scale" max="9.9" min="0.1" step="0.1"
value="1.0" class="em_input"><br/>
<span class="label">max start scale:</span>
<input type="number" id="max_starting_scale" max="10.0" min="0.2"
step="0.1" value="2.0" class="em_input"><br/>
<span class="label">min end scale:</span>
<input type="number" id="min_end_scale" max="9.9" min="0.1" step="0.1"
value="1.0" class="em_input">
<br/>
<span class="label">max end scale:</span>
<input type="number" id="max_end_scale" max="10.0" min="0.2" step="0.1"
value="2.0" class="em_input">
<br/>
```

Color-blending values

SDL has a function called `SDL_SetTextureColorMod` that is capable of modifying the red, green, and blue color channels of a texture. This function can only reduce color channel values, so using these values works best on grayscale images. The next two inputs in the HTML are `start_color` and `end_color`. These values will be used to modify the color channels of the particle over its lifetime. Each color channel (red, green, and blue) interpolated over the lifetime of the particle.

Here is what those elements look like in the HTML file:

```
<span class="label">start color:</span>
<input type="color" id="start_color" value="#ffffff"
class="color_input"><br/>
<span class="label">end color:</span>
<input type="color" id="end_color" value="#ffffff"
class="color_input"><br/>
```

Particle burst

Up until this point, the particle systems we have worked with have emitted a consistent stream of particles. We may want a point in time within the lifetime of our particle system when a burst of particles is emitted all at once. The next two input elements are `burst_time` and `burst_particles`. The `burst_time` element allows values from `0.0` to `1.0`. This number represents the portion of the way through the particle emitter's lifetime at which the burst will occur. A value of `0.0` would mean that the burst would happen at the very beginning of the emitter's life cycle, `1.0` would occur at the very end, and `0.5` would occur halfway between. After the `burst_time` element is the `burst_particles` element. This element contains the number of particles that are emitted in the burst. Before adjusting this so that it's a large number, make sure that you set the `max_particles` input element to a value that can accommodate the burst. For instance, if you have a particle emitter that emits `20` particles per second and you have a maximum number of particles that is also `20` particles, adding a burst of any size will not be noticeable because there will not be enough inactive particles left in the particle pool for the burst to use.

Here is what those elements look like in the HTML file:

```
<span class="label">burst time pct:</span>
<input type="number" id="burst_time" max="1.0" min="0.0" step="0.05"
value="0.0" class="em_input">
<br/>
<span class="label">burst particles:</span>
<input type="number" id="burst_particles" max="100" min="0" step="1"
value="0" class="em_input">
<br/>
```

Looping the emitter

Some emitters execute for a fixed time and then stop when that time has expired. An example of this kind of emitter is an explosion. Once an explosion effect has finished, we want it to end. A different type of emitter might loop, it would continue to execute until some other code stops the emitter. An example of this kind of emitter is our spaceship's engine exhaust. As long as our spaceship is accelerating, we would like to see a trail of particles being emitted out of the back of it. The next element in the HTML is a loop checkbox element. If clicked, the emitter will continue emitting, even after its lifetime is over. If there is a burst associated with this emitter, that burst will occur each time the emitter passes through that part of its loop.

Here is what the input element will look like in the HTML:

```
<label class="ccontainer"><span class="label">loop:</span>
<input type="checkbox" id="loop" checked="checked">
<span class="checkmark"></span>
</label>
<br/>
```

Aligning particle rotation

Rotation can improve many particle effects. We are forced to pick and choose the values we want to use for the particle system in our project because, frankly, I could write an entire book on particle systems. Instead of having rotation value ranges, like we did earlier for the particle's scale, we are going to have a single flag that allows the user to choose whether the particle system is going to align its rotation with the emission velocity vector. I find this to be a pleasant effect. The user will make this decision with an id="align_rotation" checkbox.

Here is what the HTML code looks like:

```
<label class="ccontainer"><span class="label">align rotation:</span>
 <input type="checkbox" id="align_rotation" checked="checked">
 <span class="checkmark"></span>
 </label>
 <br/>
```

Emission time

The *emission time* is the amount of time in milliseconds that our particle emitter will run for before it stops running, or loops if the user has ticked the loop checkbox. If the particle system loops, this value will only be noticeable for particle systems with a burst. This will cause the burst to happen each time the particle system goes through the loop.

The HTML code is as follows:

```
<span class="label">emit time ms:</span>
<input type="number" id="emit_time" max="10000" min="100" step="100"
value="1000" class="em_input"><br/>
```

Animation frames

If we want to create a particle with a multi-frame animation, we can add the number of frames here. This feature assumes a *horizontal strip sprite sheet* and will divide the loaded image file evenly on the *x* axis. When this value is 1, there is no animation because there is only a single frame. The frame time for the animation will be evenly divided across the individual particle's time to live. In other words, if you have a ten-frame animation and the particle lifetime is 1,000 milliseconds, each frame of the animation will display for 100 milliseconds (1,000/10).

Here are the HTML elements:

```
<span class="label">animation frames:</span>
<input type="number" id="animation_frames" max="64" min="1" step="1"
value="1" class="em_input"><br/>
```

Now that we have defined our HTML, let's take a look at the JavaScript portion of our code.

Modifying the JavaScript

The tool we are creating operates outside of the game we have been working on for several chapters now. Because of this, we are working on a new HTML shell file, and we will be writing a lot of JavaScript to integrate our user interface with the WebAssembly classes we will drop into our game later. Let's take the time to walk through all of the JavaScript functions we will need to add to our new HTML shell file.

The JavaScript UpdateClick function

After we have modified the HTML, the next thing we need to do is modify the `UpdateClick()` JavaScript function to allow it to grab the new values out of the HTML elements and pass those values into the `Module.ccall` function call to `update_emitter`.

Here is the new version of the `UpdateClick` function in its entirety:

```
function UpdateClick() {
    if( ready == false || image_added == false ) {
        return;
    }
    var max_particles = Number(document.getElementById
                        ("max_particles").value);
    var min_angle = Number(document.getElementById
                    ("min_angle").value) / 180 * Math.PI;
```

```
var max_angle = Number(document.getElementById
                ("max_angle").value) / 180 * Math.PI
var particle_lifetime = Number(document.getElementById
                          ("lifetime").value);
var acceleration = Number(document.getElementById
                    ("acceleration").value);
var alpha_fade = Boolean(document.getElementById
                  ("alpha_fade").checked);
var emission_rate = Number(document.getElementById
                     ("emission_rate").value);
var x_pos = Number(document.getElementById
            ("x_pos").value);
var y_pos = Number(document.getElementById
            ("y_pos").value);
var radius = Number(document.getElementById
              ("radius").value);
var min_starting_velocity = Number(document.getElementById
                            ("min_starting_vel").value);
var max_starting_velocity = Number(document.getElementById
                            ("max_starting_vel").value);

/* NEW INPUT PARAMETERS */
var min_start_scale = Number(document.getElementById
                      ("min_starting_scale").value);
var max_start_scale = Number(document.getElementById
                      ("max_starting_scale").value);
var min_end_scale = Number(document.getElementById
                    ("min_end_scale").value);
var max_end_scale = Number(document.getElementById
                    ("max_end_scale").value);
var start_color_str = document.getElementById
                      ("start_color").value.substr(1, 7);
var start_color = parseInt(start_color_str, 16);
var end_color_str = document.getElementById
                    ("end_color").value.substr(1, 7);
var end_color = parseInt(end_color_str, 16);
var burst_time = Number(document.getElementById
                  ("burst_time").value);
var burst_particles = Number(document.getElementById
                       ("burst_particles").value);
var loop = Boolean(document.getElementById
           ("loop").checked);
var align_rotation = Boolean(document.getElementById
                      ("align_rotation").checked);
var emit_time = Number(document.getElementById
                 ("emit_time").value);
var animation_frames = Number(document.getElementById
                        ("animation_frames").value);
```

```
Module.ccall('update_emitter', 'undefined', ["number", "number",
"number", "number", "number", "bool", "number", "number",
"number", "number", "number", "number",
/* new parameters */
"number", "number", "number", "number", "number", "number",
"number", "number", "bool", "bool", "number"],
[max_particles, min_angle, max_angle, particle_lifetime,
acceleration, alpha_fade, min_starting_velocity,
max_starting_velocity, emission_rate, x_pos, y_pos, radius,
/* new parameters */
min_start_scale, max_start_scale, min_end_scale, max_end_scale,
start_color, end_color, burst_time, burst_particles,
loop, align_rotation, emit_time, animation_frames]);
}
```

As you can see, we have added new local variables into this JavaScript function that will store the values that we take from our new HTML elements. Retrieving the scaling values and coercing them into numbers to pass into `update_emitter` should look pretty familiar by now. Here is that code:

```
var min_start_scale = Number(document.getElementById
                            ("min_starting_scale").value);
var max_start_scale = Number(document.getElementById
                            ("max_starting_scale").value);
var min_end_scale = Number(document.getElementById
                            ("min_end_scale").value);
var max_end_scale = Number(document.getElementById
                            ("max_end_scale").value);
```

Coercing color values

In JavaScript, variable coercion is the process of turning one variable type into a different variable type. Because JavaScript is a weakly typed language, coercion is a little different from typecasting, which is analogous to variable coercion in strongly typed languages such as C and C++.

The process of coercing our color values into `Integer` values is a two-step process. The values in these elements are strings that start with the # character, followed by a six-digit hexadecimal number. The first thing we need to do is remove that starting # character, as it will prevent us from parsing that string into an integer. We do this with a simple `substr` to get a substring (part of a string) of the value inside of the element.

Here is what that looks like for start_color:

```
var start_color_str = document.getElementById
                        ("start_color").value.substr(1, 7);
```

We know that the string will always be seven characters long, but we only want the last six characters. We now have a hexadecimal representation of the starting color, but it is still a string variable. Now, we need to coerce this into an Integer value, and we have to tell the parseInt function to use base 16 (hexadecimal), so we will pass the value 16 into parseInt as a second parameter:

```
var start_color = parseInt(start_color_str, 16);
```

Now that we have coerced start_color into an integer, we will do the same for end_color:

```
var end_color_str = document.getElementById
                      ("end_color").value.substr(1, 7);
var end_color = parseInt(end_color_str, 16);
```

Additional variable coercions

After the start_color and end_color coercions, the remaining coercions we must perform should feel familiar. We coerce the values in burst_time, burst_particles, emit_time, and animation_frames into Number variables. We coerce the checked values from loop and align_rotation into Boolean variables.

Here is the remainder of the coercion code:

```
var burst_time = Number(document.getElementById
                    ("burst_time").value);
var burst_particles = Number(document.getElementById
                          ("burst_particles").value);
var loop = Boolean(document.getElementById
              ("loop").checked);
var align_rotation = Boolean(document.getElementById
                        ("align_rotation").checked);
var emit_time = Number(document.getElementById
                    ("emit_time").value);
var animation_frames = Number(document.getElementById
                          ("animation_frames").value);
```

Finally, we need to add the variable types and the new variables into our `Module.ccall` call to `update_emitter` in our WebAssembly module:

```
Module.ccall('update_emitter', 'undefined', ["number", "number",
"number", "number", "number", "bool",
                            "number", "number", "number",
"number", "number","number",
                                    /* new parameters */
                                     "number", "number",
                                     "number", "number",
                                     "number", "number",
                                     "number", "number",
                                     "bool", "bool", "number"],
                                    [max_particles, min_angle,
                                     max_angle,
                                     particle_lifetime,
                                     acceleration, alpha_fade,
                                     min_starting_velocity,
                                     max_starting_velocity,
                                     emission_rate, x_pos,
                                     y_pos, radius,
                                    /* new parameters */
                                     min_start_scale,
                                     max_start_scale,
                                     min_end_scale,
                                     max_end_scale,
                                     start_color, end_color,
                                     burst_time,
                                     burst_particles,
                                     loop, align_rotation,
                                     emit_time,
                                     animation_frames
                                    ]);
```

Modifying the handleFiles function

The last changes we need to make to our HTML shell file are modifications to the `handleFiles` function. These modifications effectively mirror the changes to the `UpdateClick` function. As you step through the code, you will see the same coercion replicated inside of `handleFiles`, and the `Module.ccall` to `add_emitter` will be updated with the same new parameter types and parameters. Here is the code for the latest version of the `handleFiles` function:

```
function handleFiles(files) {
    var file_count = 0;
```

```
for (var i = 0; i < files.length; i++) {
    if (files[i].type.match(/image.png/)) {
        var file = files[i];
        var file_name = file.name;
        var fr = new FileReader();
        fr.onload = function (file) {
            var data = new Uint8Array(fr.result);
            Module.FS_createDataFile('/', file_name, data, true, true,
            true);
            var max_particles = Number(document.getElementById
                                ("max_particles").value);
            var min_angle = Number(document.getElementById
                        ("min_angle").value) / 180 * Math.PI;
            var max_angle = Number(document.getElementById
                        ("max_angle").value) / 180 * Math.PI
            var particle_lifetime = Number(document.getElementById
                                ("lifetime").value);
            var acceleration = Number(document.getElementById
                        ("acceleration").value);
            var alpha_fade = Boolean(document.getElementById
                        ("alpha_fade").checked);
            var emission_rate = Number(document.getElementById
                                ("emission_rate").value);
            var x_pos = Number(document.getElementById
                        ("x_pos").value);
            var y_pos = Number(document.getElementById
                        ("y_pos").value);
            var radius = Number(document.getElementById
                        ("radius").value);
            var min_starting_velocity = Number(document.getElementById
                                    ("min_starting_vel").value);
            var max_starting_velocity = Number(document.getElementById
                                    ("max_starting_vel").value);

            /* NEW INPUT PARAMETERS */
            var min_start_scale = Number(document.getElementById
                                ("min_starting_scale").value);
            var max_start_scale = Number(document.getElementById
                                ("max_starting_scale").value);
            var min_end_scale = Number(document.getElementById
                                ("min_end_scale").value);
            var max_end_scale = Number(document.getElementById
                                ("max_end_scale").value);
            var start_color_str = document.getElementById
                                ("start_color").value.substr(1, 7);
            var start_color = parseInt(start_color_str, 16);
            var end_color_str = document.getElementById
                                ("end_color").value.substr(1, 7);
```

```
        var end_color = parseInt(end_color_str, 16);
        var burst_time = Number(document.getElementById
                        ("burst_time").value);
        var burst_particles = Number(document.getElementById
                            ("burst_particles").value);
        var loop = Boolean(document.getElementById
                    ("loop").checked);
        var align_rotation = Boolean(document.getElementById
                            ("align_rotation").checked);
        var emit_time = Number(document.getElementById
                        ("emit_time").value);
        var animation_frames = Number(document.getElementById
                            ("animation_frames").value);

        Module.ccall('add_emitter', 'undefined',
        ["string","number", "number", "number",
        "number","number","bool","number","number",
        "number", "number", "number","number",
        /* new parameters */
        "number", "number", "number",
        "number", "number", "number", "number",
        "number","bool", "bool", "number"],
            file_name,max_particles,min_angle,max_angle,
            particle_lifetime,acceleration,alpha_fade,
            min_starting_velocity,max_starting_velocity,
            emission_rate, x_pos,y_pos,radius,
            /* new parameters */
            min_start_scale,max_start_scale,min_end_scale,
            max_end_scale,start_color,end_color,
            burst_time,burst_particles,loop,
            align_rotation,emit_time,animation_frames ]);
        image_added = true;
    };
    fr.readAsArrayBuffer(files[i]); }}}
```

Now that we have our JavaScript code, we can begin making our changes to the
WebAssembly module.

Modifying the Particle class

Now that we have added the changes to our HTML shell file, we need to make some changes to our WebAssembly module to support these new parameters. We are going to work our way from the bottom up, starting with the `Particle` class. This class is not only useful for the tool we are building to design particle systems, but it is one of a few classes that, once we have completed it, we will be able to pull into our game, allowing us to add some beautiful looking effects.

Here is what the particle class definition looks like inside the `game.hpp` file:

```
class Particle {
    public:
        bool m_active;
        bool m_alpha_fade;
        bool m_color_mod;
        bool m_align_rotation;
        float m_rotation;

        Uint8 m_start_red;
        Uint8 m_start_green;
        Uint8 m_start_blue;

        Uint8 m_end_red;
        Uint8 m_end_green;
        Uint8 m_end_blue;

        Uint8 m_current_red;
        Uint8 m_current_green;
        Uint8 m_current_blue;

        SDL_Texture *m_sprite_texture;
        int m_ttl;

        Uint32 m_life_time;
        Uint32 m_animation_frames;
        Uint32 m_current_frame;
        Uint32 m_next_frame_ms;

        float m_acceleration;
        float m_alpha;
        float m_width;
        float m_height;
        float m_start_scale;
        float m_end_scale;
        float m_current_scale;
```

```
    Point m_position;
    Point m_velocity;

    SDL_Rect m_dest = {.x = 0, .y = 0, .w = 0, .h = 0 };
    SDL_Rect m_src = {.x = 0, .y = 0, .w = 0, .h = 0 };

    Particle( SDL_Texture *sprite, Uint32 life_time, float
    acceleration,
                bool alpha_fade, int width, int height, bool
                align_rotation,
                Uint32 start_color,
                Uint32 end_color,
                Uint32 animation_frames );
    void Update( Uint32 life_time, float acceleration,
                bool alpha_fade, bool align_rotation,
                Uint32 start_color, Uint32 end_color,
                Uint32 animation_frames );

    void Spawn( float x, float y, float velocity_x, float
        velocity_y,
                float start_scale, float end_scale, float rotation );

    void Move();
    void Render();
};
```

New attributes

We are going to walk through the new attributes that were added to the `Particle` class definition and briefly discuss what each new attribute does. The first attribute that we added was `bool m_color_mod`. In our HTML, we don't have a checkbox for this value, so you may be wondering why there is one here. The reason is performance. If the user doesn't want a color modification, a call to `SDL_SetTextureColorMod` is a waste. If we have two white values passed into the `Particle` object, no interpolation or call to modify the value is necessary. We could check the start and end color each time to see if their values are `0xffffff`, but I felt that adding this flag would make the check clearer.

Aligning rotation attributes

The `m_align_rotation` flag that follows is simply the flag we passed in from the checkbox. If this value is `true`, the particle will rotate itself to point in the direction it is moving. The `m_rotation` floating-point variable follows that. The attribute variable that holds the angle of the particle will be rotated based on the direction in which the particle is moving. Here is what these values look like in our code:

```
bool m_align_rotation;
float m_rotation;
```

Color attributes

The color mod flag I mentioned earlier makes the check on the next set of values a lot easier. Our hexadecimal color value that represented the red, green, and blue values in our HTML needed to be passed in as an integer so that it could be broken down into three 8-bit channels. Here is what those 8-bit color variables look like in the code:

```
Uint8 m_start_red;
Uint8 m_start_green;
Uint8 m_start_blue;

Uint8 m_end_red;
Uint8 m_end_green;
Uint8 m_end_blue;

Uint8 m_current_red;
Uint8 m_current_green;
Uint8 m_current_blue;
```

You will notice that these are all 8-bit unsigned integer variables that are declared with `Uint8`. When SDL performs color modification, it doesn't take in RGB values as a single variable; instead, it takes the values broken down into three 8-bit variables representing each of the individual channels. The `m_start_(color)` variable and the `m_end_(color)` variable will be interpolated based on the particle lifetime to get the `m_current_(color)` variable, which will be passed in as the channels to SDL when we do the color modification. Because we will be passing these values in as a single color variable from the JavaScript, the `Particle` constructor and the `Update` functions will need to perform bitwise operations to set these individual channel variables.

Animation attributes

The next set of new attributes are all related to the new frame animation functionality in our `Particle`. Here are those attributes in the code:

```
Uint32 m_animation_frames;
Uint32 m_current_frame;
Uint32 m_next_frame_ms;
```

The first attribute, `m_animation_frames`, is the value that's passed indirectly from the JavaScript. It tells the `Particle` class how many frames are in the sprite texture when it renders that texture to the canvas. The second attribute, `m_current_frame`, is used by the `Particle` class to keep track of which frame it should currently be rendering. The final attribute variable, `m_next_frame_ms`, tells the particle how many milliseconds are left before it must increment its current frame to display the next frame in the sequence.

Size and scale attributes

The next batch of attributes have to do with the size and scale of our particle. In the previous version of this code, we handled width and height in the `m_dest` rectangle. That is no longer practical, because the width and height (`w` and `h`) attributes of this rectangle will need to be modified to account for our current scale. Here are the new variables as they appear in the code:

```
float m_width;
float m_height;

float m_start_scale;
float m_end_scale;
float m_current_scale;
```

The `m_width` and `m_height` attributes are now required to keep track of the original width and height of the particle, which haven been adjusted by the scale.

The `m_start_scale` and `m_end_scale` attributes are values that are randomly picked between the `max` and `min` values we defined in the JavaScript.

The `m_current_scale` attribute is the current scale that's used when calculating the `m_dest.w` and `m_dest.h` values when we render the particle. The current scale will be a value interpolated between the `m_start_scale` and `m_end_scale` attributes.

The source rectangle attribute

In the previous version of the code, we didn't have frame-animated particles. Because of this, we didn't need to declare a source rectangle. If you want to render the entire texture to the canvas, you can pass in NULL in place of a source rectangle in the call to SDL_RenderCopy, which was what we were doing. Now that we have frame animations, we will pass in the location and the dimension of the part of the texture we render to the canvas. Because of this, we need to define a source rectangle attribute:

```
SDL_Rect m_src = {.x = 0,  .y = 0,  .w = 0,  .h = 0 };
```

Additional constructor parameters

Now that we have walked through all the new attributes, we will briefly discuss the changes that are required by the signatures of our functions. The Particle class constructor must add some new parameters that will support our align rotation, color modification, and frame animation functionality. Here is what the new signature for the constructor looks like:

```
Particle( SDL_Texture *sprite, Uint32 life_time, float acceleration,
          bool alpha_fade, int width, int height, bool align_rotation,
          Uint32 start_color,
          Uint32 end_color,
          Uint32 animation_frames );
```

The boolean value called align_rotation tells the constructor to align the particle's rotation with the direction it is moving in. The start_color and end_color parameters are the color modification values if we are using the new color modification feature of our particle system. The last parameter, animation_frames, tells the particle system whether or not it is using a frame animation system, and if so, how many frames it will use.

The Update function's parameters

The modifications to the signature for the Update function mirrors the changes we need to make to the constructor. There are a total of four new parameters that are used to influence the align rotation, the color modification system, and the frame animation system.

Here is what the new `Update` function signature looks like:

```
void Update( Uint32 life_time, float acceleration,
             bool alpha_fade, bool align_rotation,
             Uint32 start_color, Uint32 end_color,
             Uint32 m_animation_frames );
```

The Spawn function's parameters

The last function signature that will need to be modified is the `Spawn` function. New values will be required to allow the `Emitter` to set the scale and rotation values when we spawn an individual particle. The `float start_scale` and `float end_scale` parameters are used to set the starting and ending scale multipliers when we generate the particle. The last parameter that's added is `float rotation`, which represents the angle the particle is moving based on the *x* and *y* velocities of this particular particle. The following is the new version of the function:

```
void Spawn( float x, float y, float velocity_x, float velocity_y,
            float start_scale, float end_scale, float rotation );
```

Changes to particle.cpp

The next set of changes we need to make to our `Particle` class are all changes to the functions we defined in the `particle.cpp` file. It is challenging to keep track of the changes made to these functions, so rather than discuss these changes, I will walk you through everything that is happening in each of the functions we discuss.

Particle constructor logic

The logic in the new `Particle` constructor adds a lot of code to set the stage for our new features. Here is what the latest version of the function looks like:

```
Particle::Particle( SDL_Texture *sprite_texture, Uint32 life_time,
                    float acceleration, bool alpha_fade, int width,
                    int height, bool align_rotation,
                    Uint32 start_color, Uint32 end_color,
                    Uint32 animation_frames ) {

    if( start_color != 0xffffff || end_color != 0xffffff ) {
        m_color_mod = true;
        m_start_red = (Uint8)(start_color >> 16);
```

```
        m_start_green = (Uint8)(start_color >> 8);
        m_start_blue = (Uint8)(start_color);

        m_end_red = (Uint8)(end_color >> 16);
        m_end_green = (Uint8)(end_color >> 8);
        m_end_blue = (Uint8)(end_color);

        m_current_red = m_start_red;
        m_current_green = m_start_green;
        m_current_blue = m_start_blue;
    }
    else {
        m_color_mod = false;

        m_start_red = (Uint8)255;
        m_start_green = (Uint8)255;
        m_start_blue = (Uint8)255;

        m_end_red = (Uint8)255;
        m_end_green = (Uint8)255;
        m_end_blue = (Uint8)255;

        m_current_red = m_start_red;
        m_current_green = m_start_green;
        m_current_blue = m_start_blue;
    }
    m_align_rotation = align_rotation;
    m_animation_frames = animation_frames;
    m_sprite_texture = sprite_texture;
    m_life_time = life_time;
    m_acceleration = acceleration;
    m_alpha_fade = alpha_fade;
    m_width = (float)width;
    m_height = (float)height;

    m_src.w = m_dest.w = (int)((float)width / (float)m_animation_frames);
    m_src.h = m_dest.h = height;

    m_next_frame_ms = m_life_time / m_animation_frames;
    m_current_frame = 0;
    m_active = false;
}
```

The first large batch of this code is used to set up the 8-bit color channels at the beginning and the end of our particle's lifetime. If either the starting color or the ending color is not `0xffffff` (white), we will set up the starting and ending color channels using the >> operator (bit shift). Here is the code that sets the starting channels:

```
m_start_red = (Uint8)(start_color >> 16);
m_start_green = (Uint8)(start_color >> 8);
m_start_blue = (Uint8)(start_color);
```

If you aren't familiar with the right bit shift operator >>, it takes an integer on the left-hand side of the operator and shifts the number of bits on the right-hand side of the operator. For example, a binary value of 15 (0000 1111) that's shifted to the right by two bits will return a new value of 3 (0000 0011). When we shift to the right, any bits shifted to the right-hand side are lost, and bits with a value of 0 are moved in from the left-hand side:

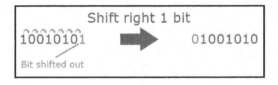

Figure 9.1: Example of a right bit shift

If we have an RGB integer that comes in, each channel takes up 1 byte or 8 bits. So, if R = **9**, G = **8**, and B = **7**, our integer value in hexadecimal would look like this: ff090807. If we want to get to the R-value, we need to shift off the two bytes on the right-hand side of this 4 byte integer. Each byte is 8 bits, so we would take our RGB and use the >> operator to shift it by 16 bits. We would then have the value `09`, which we could use to set our 8 bit red channel. When we do the green channel, we want the second byte from the right so that we can shift off 8 bits. Now, in our 4 byte integer, we would have 00000908. Because we are moving this into an 8 bit integer, all the data not in the rightmost byte is lost in the assignment, so we end up with `08` in our green channel. Finally, the blue channel value is already in the rightmost byte. All we need to do with that is cast it to an 8 bit integer, so we lose all of the data that is not in the blue channel. The following is a diagram of the 32 bit color:

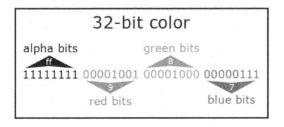

Figure 9.2: Color bits in a 32-bit integer

We have to perform this same bit of magic on the end color channels:

```
m_end_red = (Uint8)(end_color >> 16);
m_end_green = (Uint8)(end_color >> 8);
m_end_blue = (Uint8)(end_color);
```

The last thing we will do is set the current color channels to the starting color channels. We do this to create our particles with the colors' starting values.

If both the starting and ending colors are white, we want to set the color mod flag to `false`, so we will not attempt to modify the color on this particle. We will initialize all the color channels to 255. Here is the code that does this:

```
else {
    m_color_mod = false;
    m_start_red = (Uint8)255;
    m_start_green = (Uint8)255;
    m_start_blue = (Uint8)255;

    m_end_red = (Uint8)255;
    m_end_green = (Uint8)255;
    m_end_blue = (Uint8)255;

    m_current_red = m_start_red;
    m_current_green = m_start_green;
    m_current_blue = m_start_blue;
}
```

After the code for managing the color modification is some initialization code, which sets the attribute variables in this object from the parameters passed into the constructor:

```
m_align_rotation = align_rotation;
m_animation_frames = animation_frames;
m_sprite_texture = sprite_texture;
m_life_time = life_time;
m_acceleration = acceleration;
m_alpha_fade = alpha_fade;

m_width = (float)width;
m_height = (float)height;
```

Then, we set the source and destination rectangles based on the height and width passed in, as well as the number of animation frames for the particle:

```
m_src.w = m_dest.w = (int)((float)width / (float)m_animation_frames);
m_src.h = m_dest.h = height;
```

The last two lines of code initialize the current frame to 0 and our active flag to `false`. All animations start on frame 0, and a new particle is not active until it's spawned.

Here are the last few lines of code:

```
m_current_frame = 0;
m_active = false;
```

Particle Update logic

The `Particle` class' `Update` function is run on each of the particles that were created by a previous PNG file upload. This function updates most of the values set in the constructor. The only exception is that the width and height dimensions of the particle must stay the same. This is because the constructor set these values based on the dimensions of the image file that was uploaded. I don't feel the need to step through each part of this function, because of how similar it is to the constructor that we just walked through. Take a moment to look over the code to see how similar it is:

```
void Particle::Update( Uint32 life_time, float acceleration,
                       bool alpha_fade, bool align_rotation,
                       Uint32 start_color, Uint32 end_color,
                       Uint32 animation_frames ) {
    if( start_color != 0xffffff || end_color != 0xffffff ) {
        m_color_mod = true;

        m_start_red = (Uint8)(start_color >> 16);
        m_start_green = (Uint8)(start_color >> 8);
        m_start_blue = (Uint8)(start_color);

        m_end_red = (Uint8)(end_color >> 16);
        m_end_green = (Uint8)(end_color >> 8);
        m_end_blue = (Uint8)(end_color);

        m_current_red = m_start_red;
        m_current_green = m_start_green;
        m_current_blue = m_start_blue;
    }
    else {
        m_color_mod = false;

        m_start_red = (Uint8)255;
        m_start_green = (Uint8)255;
        m_start_blue = (Uint8)255;

        m_end_red = (Uint8)255;
```

```
            m_end_green = (Uint8)255;
            m_end_blue = (Uint8)255;

            m_current_red = m_start_red;
            m_current_green = m_start_green;
            m_current_blue = m_start_blue;
        }

        m_align_rotation = align_rotation;
        m_life_time = life_time;
        m_acceleration = acceleration;
        m_alpha_fade = alpha_fade;
        m_active = false;

        m_current_frame = 0;
        m_animation_frames = animation_frames;
        m_next_frame_ms = m_life_time / m_animation_frames;;

        m_src.w = m_dest.w = (int)((float)m_width / (float)m_animation_frames);
        m_src.h = m_dest.h = m_height;
    }
```

Particle Spawn function

The Particle class' Spawn function is run by the Emitter whenever it needs to emit a
new particle. When the emitter hits its next particle emission time, it searches through the
particle pool, looking for a particle that is marked as not active. If it finds a particle, it calls
the Spawn function on that particle, which activates the particle and sets several values
specific to its run. All of the values that are passed into Spawn are changed by
the Emitter every time the particle is emitted. Here is what the code for this function looks
like:

```
    void Particle::Spawn( float x, float y,
                          float velocity_x, float velocity_y,
                          float start_scale, float end_scale,
                          float rotation ) {
        m_position.x = x;
        m_dest.x = (int)m_position.x;
        m_position.y = y;
        m_dest.y = (int)m_position.y;

        m_velocity.x = velocity_x;
        m_velocity.y = velocity_y;
        m_alpha = 255.0;
        m_active = true;
```

```
m_ttl = m_life_time;
m_rotation = rotation;

m_current_red = m_start_red;
m_current_green = m_start_green;
m_current_blue = m_start_blue;

m_current_scale = m_start_scale = start_scale;
m_end_scale = end_scale;

m_current_frame = 0;
m_next_frame_ms = m_life_time / m_animation_frames;
}
```

Almost everything that's done in this function is initialization and is pretty straightforward. The first four lines initialize the position attribute (m_position), as well as the position with the destination rectangle (m_dest). Then, the velocity is set. The alpha always begins at 255. The particle is activated, the time to live variable is activated, and the rotation is set. Color channels are reinitialized, the scale is initialized, and the current frame and the time to the next frame are set.

Particle Move function

The Particle class' Move function is the function that not only changes the render position of the particle, but also adjusts all of the interpolated values between the beginning and the end of the particle's life. Let's step through the code:

```
void Particle::Move() {
    float time_pct = 1.0 - (float)m_ttl / (float)m_life_time;
    m_current_frame = (int)(time_pct * (float)m_animation_frames);
    float acc_adjusted = 1.0f;

    if( m_acceleration < 1.0f ) {
        acc_adjusted = 1.0f - m_acceleration;
        acc_adjusted *= delta_time;
        acc_adjusted = 1.0f - acc_adjusted;
    }
    else if( m_acceleration > 1.0f ) {
        acc_adjusted = m_acceleration - 1.0f;
        acc_adjusted *= delta_time;
        acc_adjusted += 1.0f;
    }
    m_velocity.x *= acc_adjusted;
    m_velocity.y *= acc_adjusted;
```

```
m_position.x += m_velocity.x * delta_time;
m_position.y += m_velocity.y * delta_time;

m_dest.x = (int)m_position.x;
m_dest.y = (int)m_position.y;

if( m_alpha_fade == true ) {
    m_alpha = 255.0 * (1.0 - time_pct);
    if( m_alpha < 0 ) {
        m_alpha = 0;
    }
}
else {
    m_alpha = 255.0;
}
if( m_color_mod == true ) {
    m_current_red = m_start_red + (Uint8)(( m_end_red - m_start_red
    ) *
    time_pct);
    m_current_green = m_start_green + (Uint8)(( m_end_green -
    m_start_green ) *
    time_pct);
    m_current_blue = m_start_blue + (Uint8)(( m_end_blue -
    m_start_blue ) *
    time_pct);
}

m_current_scale = m_start_scale + (m_end_scale - m_start_scale) *
time_pct;
m_dest.w = (int)(m_src.w * m_current_scale);
m_dest.h = (int)(m_src.h * m_current_scale);
m_ttl -= diff_time;

if( m_ttl <= 0 ) {
    m_active = false;
}
else {
    m_src.x = (int)(m_src.w * m_current_frame);
}
}
```

The first line of the Move function calculates time_pct. That is a floating-point value that ranges from 0.0-1.0. This variable starts with a value of 0.0 when the particle has just been spawned and hits 1.0 when the particle is ready to be deactivated. It gives us a floating-point value indicating where we are in the lifespan of this particle:

```
float time_pct = 1.0 - (float)m_ttl / (float)m_life_time;
```

The `m_ttl` attribute is the time to live for this particle in milliseconds, and `m_life_time` is the total lifespan of the particle. This value is useful for doing all of our interpolated value calculations inside of this `Move` function.

The following line returns the current frame, based on the value that is in `time_pct`:

```
m_current_frame = (int)(time_pct * (float)m_animation_frames);
```

After that, several lines adjust the x and y velocity of the particle based on the acceleration value:

```
float acc_adjusted = 1.0f;

if( m_acceleration < 1.0f ) {
    acc_adjusted = 1.0f - m_acceleration;
    acc_adjusted *= delta_time;
    acc_adjusted = 1.0f - acc_adjusted;
}
else if( m_acceleration > 1.0f ) {
    acc_adjusted = m_acceleration - 1.0f;
    acc_adjusted *= delta_time;
    acc_adjusted += 1.0f;
}

m_velocity.x *= acc_adjusted;
m_velocity.y *= acc_adjusted;
```

We need to set the `acc_adjusted` variable to a modified version of the `m_acceleration` variable based on the fraction of a second (`delta_time`) that has elapsed. After changing the `m_velocity` values, we need to use those velocity values to modify the position of the particle:

```
m_position.x += m_velocity.x * delta_time;
m_position.y += m_velocity.y * delta_time;

m_dest.x = (int)m_position.x;
m_dest.y = (int)m_position.y;
```

If the `m_alpha_fade` variable is `true`, the code will modify the alpha value, interpolating it to 0 by the time the `time_pct` value becomes `1.0`. If the `m_alpha_fade` flag is not set, the alpha value is set to `255` (full opacity). Here is the code:

```
if( m_alpha_fade == true ) {
    m_alpha = 255.0 * (1.0 - time_pct);
    if( m_alpha < 0 ) {
        m_alpha = 0;
    }
```

```
    }
    else {
        m_alpha = 255.0;
    }
```

If the `m_color_mod` flag is `true`, we need to use `time_pct` to interpolate between the starting channel color value and the ending channel color value in order to find the current channel color value:

```
if( m_color_mod == true ) {
    m_current_red = m_start_red + (Uint8)(( m_end_red - m_start_red ) *
    time_pct);
    m_current_green = m_start_green + (Uint8)(( m_end_green -
    m_start_green ) * time_pct);
    m_current_blue = m_start_blue + (Uint8)(( m_end_blue - m_start_blue
    ) * time_pct);
}
```

After finding the interpolated value for each of the color channels, we need to use `time_pct` to interpolate the current scale. Then, we set our destination width and destination height based on that current scale value, and the dimensions of the source rectangle:

```
m_current_scale = m_start_scale + (m_end_scale - m_start_scale) * time_pct;
m_dest.w = (int)(m_src.w * m_current_scale);
m_dest.h = (int)(m_src.h * m_current_scale);
```

The last thing we will do is decrease the `m_ttl` variable (time to live) by `diff_time` (time since the previous frame render). If the time to live drops to or below 0, we deactivate the particle, make it available in the particle pool, and stop it from rendering. If there is still some time to live, we set the `m_src.x` (source rectangle *x* value) to the proper location for the frame we want to render:

```
m_ttl -= diff_time;
if( m_ttl <= 0 ) {
    m_active = false;
}
else {
    m_src.x = (int)(m_src.w * m_current_frame);
}
```

Particle Render function

The final function in our `Particle` class is the `Render` function. The `Emitter` class calls this function for every active particle in the particle pool. The function sets the alpha and color channel values on the sprite texture used by the particle. It then checks the `m_align_rotation` flag to see if the texture needs to be copied to the back buffer using `SDL_RenderCopy` or `SDL_RederCopyEx`. The difference between these two render calls is that `SDL_RenderCopyEx` allows the copy to be rotated or flipped. Both of these functions use the `m_src` rectangle to determine a rectangle inside of the texture to copy. Both use the `m_dest` rectangle to determine the destination in the back buffer, where we copy our texture data:

```
void Particle::Render() {

    SDL_SetTextureAlphaMod(m_sprite_texture,
                           (Uint8)m_alpha );

    if( m_color_mod == true ) {
        SDL_SetTextureColorMod(m_sprite_texture,
        m_current_red,
        m_current_green,
        m_current_blue );
    }

    if( m_align_rotation == true ) {
        SDL_RenderCopyEx( renderer, m_sprite_texture, &m_src, &m_dest,
                          m_rotation, NULL, SDL_FLIP_NONE );
    }
    else {
        SDL_RenderCopy( renderer, m_sprite_texture, &m_src, &m_dest );
    }
}
```

In the next section, we will discuss how to modify our `Emitter` class to accommodate our improvements.

Modifying the Emitter class

As I mentioned earlier, when we discussed the `Emitter` class, it manages and emits particles. In a typical particle system, you may have many emitters. In our game, we will eventually allow for multiple emitters, but in this tool, we will keep to a single emitter for simplicity. We have four functions defined in the `Emitter` class, and we will be changing three of them. The only function that will not require a change is the `GetFreeParticle` function. If you don't remember, `GetFreeParticle` loops through `m_particle_pool` (the particle pool attribute) looking for particles that are not marked as active (`particle->m_active == false`). If it finds one, it returns that particle. If not, it returns `null`.

The Emitter constructor function

The code for the `Emitter` constructor will need to change to allow us to set the attributes that are required to support the new particle system functionality. The following is the code for the new `Emitter` constructor:

```
Emitter::Emitter(char* sprite_file, int max_particles, float min_angle,
        float max_angle, Uint32 particle_lifetime,
        float acceleration, bool alpha_fade,
        float min_starting_velocity, float max_starting_velocity,
        Uint32 emission_rate, int x_pos, int y_pos, float radius,
        float min_start_scale, float max_start_scale,
        float min_end_scale, float max_end_scale,
        Uint32 start_color, Uint32 end_color,
        float burst_time_pct, Uint32 burst_particles,
        bool loop, bool align_rotation, Uint32 emit_time_ms,
        Uint32 animation_frames ) {
    m_start_color = start_color;
    m_end_color = end_color;
    m_active = true;
    if( min_starting_velocity > max_starting_velocity ) {
        m_min_starting_velocity = max_starting_velocity;
        m_max_starting_velocity = min_starting_velocity;
    }
    else {
        m_min_starting_velocity = min_starting_velocity;
        m_max_starting_velocity = max_starting_velocity;
    }
    SDL_Surface *temp_surface = IMG_Load( sprite_file );
    if( !temp_surface ) {
        printf("failed to load image: %s\n", IMG_GetError() );
        return;
```

```
    }
    m_sprite_texture = SDL_CreateTextureFromSurface( renderer, temp_surface
    );
    SDL_FreeSurface( temp_surface );
    SDL_QueryTexture( m_sprite_texture,
                        NULL, NULL,
                        &m_sprite_width, &m_sprite_height );
    m_max_particles = max_particles;
    for( int i = 0; i < m_max_particles; i++ ) {
        m_particle_pool.push_back(
            new Particle( m_sprite_texture, particle_lifetime,
                        acceleration, alpha_fade, m_sprite_width,
                        m_sprite_height, align_rotation,
                        m_start_color, m_end_color,
                        animation_frames )
            );
    }
    m_max_angle = max_angle;
    m_min_angle = min_angle;
    m_radius = radius;
    m_position.x = (float)x_pos;
    m_position.y = (float)y_pos;
    m_emission_rate = emission_rate;
    m_emission_time_ms = 1000 / m_emission_rate;
    m_next_emission = 0;
    /* new values */
    m_min_start_scale = min_start_scale;
    m_max_start_scale = max_start_scale;
    m_min_end_scale = min_end_scale;
    m_max_end_scale = max_end_scale;

    m_loop = loop;
    m_align_rotation = align_rotation;
    m_emit_loop_ms = emit_time_ms;
    m_ttl = m_emit_loop_ms;
    m_animation_frames = animation_frames;
    m_burst_time_pct = burst_time_pct;
    m_burst_particles = burst_particles;
    m_has_burst = false;
}
```

Enough of this code has changed that I feel it makes sense to walk through the entire function. The first two lines set the color attribute, and then activate the emitter by setting m_active to true. We set this active flag to true when an emitter is created or updated. If it is a looping emitter, the active flag will remain on indefinitely. If Emitter does not loop, the emitter will stop emitting when it reaches the end of its emit time, as set by the emit_time_ms parameter.

The next thing we do is set the minimum and maximum starting velocities. We have a little code in `Emitter` that makes sure that `max_starting_velocity` is greater than `min_starting_velocity`, but when we move this code into the game, we may choose to just set the values to whatever works well. Here is the code:

```
if( min_starting_velocity > max_starting_velocity ) {
    m_min_starting_velocity = max_starting_velocity;
    m_max_starting_velocity = min_starting_velocity;
}
else {
    m_min_starting_velocity = min_starting_velocity;
    m_max_starting_velocity = max_starting_velocity;
}
```

After we set the velocities, an SDL surface is created using a `sprite_file` string, which is the location of the file we have loaded into the WebAssembly virtual filesystem. If that file is not in the virtual filesystem, we print out an error message and exit the constructor:

```
SDL_Surface *temp_surface = IMG_Load( sprite_file );

if( !temp_surface ) {
    printf("failed to load image: %s\n", IMG_GetError() );
    return;
}
```

After creating the surface from the image file, we use that surface to create an SDL texture called `m_sprite_texture`, and then we use `SDL_FreeSurface` to destroy the memory that was used by the surface because it is no longer needed now that we have a texture. Then, we call `SDL_QueryTexture` to retrieve the width and the height of the sprite texture and use them to set the `Emitter` attributes `m_sprite_width` and `m_sprite_height`. Here is the code:

```
m_sprite_texture = SDL_CreateTextureFromSurface( renderer, temp_surface );
SDL_FreeSurface( temp_surface );
SDL_QueryTexture( m_sprite_texture,
                  NULL, NULL,
                  &m_sprite_width, &m_sprite_height );
```

The next thing we need to do is set the `m_max_particles` attribute and use that variable to initialize the particle pool. A `for` loop is used to push new particles to the back of the `std::vector` variable, `m_particle_pool`:

```
m_max_particles = max_particles;
for( int i = 0; i < m_max_particles; i++ ) {
    m_particle_pool.push_back(
        new Particle( m_sprite_texture, particle_lifetime, acceleration,
```

```
                          alpha_fade, m_sprite_width, m_sprite_height,
                          align_rotation,
                          m_start_color, m_end_color, animation_frames )
        );
    }
```

After setting up the particle pool, we use the parameters to set the emitter's attributes for the old and the new particle system values:

```
m_max_angle = max_angle;
m_min_angle = min_angle;
m_radius = radius;
m_position.x = (float)x_pos;
m_position.y = (float)y_pos;
m_emission_rate = emission_rate;
m_emission_time_ms = 1000 / m_emission_rate;
m_next_emission = 0;

/* new values */
m_min_start_scale = min_start_scale;
m_max_start_scale = max_start_scale;
m_min_end_scale = min_end_scale;
m_max_end_scale = max_end_scale;

m_loop = loop;
m_align_rotation = align_rotation;
m_emit_loop_ms = emit_time_ms;
m_ttl = m_emit_loop_ms;
m_animation_frames = animation_frames;
m_burst_time_pct = burst_time_pct;
m_burst_particles = burst_particles;
m_has_burst = false;
```

Emitter update logic

The Update function of Emitter is similar to the constructor, but runs when Emitter already exists and needs to be updated. This function begins by setting all of the attribute variables on our Emitter:

```
if( min_starting_velocity > max_starting_velocity ) {
    m_min_starting_velocity = max_starting_velocity;
    m_max_starting_velocity = min_starting_velocity;
}
else {
    m_min_starting_velocity = min_starting_velocity;
    m_max_starting_velocity = max_starting_velocity;
```

```
    }
    m_active = true;
    m_has_burst = false;
    m_max_particles = max_particles;
    m_min_angle = min_angle;
    m_max_angle = max_angle;
    m_emission_rate = emission_rate;
    m_emission_time_ms = 1000 / m_emission_rate;
    m_position.x = (float)x_pos;
    m_position.y = (float)y_pos;
    m_radius = radius;
    /* new values */
    m_min_start_scale = min_start_scale;
    m_max_start_scale = max_start_scale;
    m_min_end_scale = min_end_scale;
    m_max_end_scale = max_end_scale;
    m_start_color = start_color;
    m_end_color = end_color;
    m_burst_time_pct = burst_time_pct;
    m_burst_particles = burst_particles;
    m_loop = loop;
    m_align_rotation = align_rotation;
    m_emit_loop_ms = emit_time_ms;
    m_ttl = m_emit_loop_ms;
    m_animation_frames = animation_frames;
```

After we set the attribute variables, we may need to either increase or decrease the size of the `m_particle_pool` vector (the particle pool). If the number of particles in our pool is greater than the new maximum number of particles, we can shrink the particle pool with a simple resize. If the particle pool is too small, we will need to loop over the code that creates new particles and adds those particles to the pool. We do this until the size of the pool matches the new maximum number of particles. Here is the code that does that:

```
    if( m_particle_pool.size() > m_max_particles ) {
        m_particle_pool.resize( m_max_particles );
    }
    else if( m_max_particles > m_particle_pool.size() ) {
        while( m_max_particles > m_particle_pool.size() ) {
            m_particle_pool.push_back(
                new Particle( m_sprite_texture, particle_lifetime,
                              acceleration, alpha_fade, m_sprite_width,
                              m_sprite_height, m_align_rotation,
                              m_start_color, m_end_color,
                              m_animation_frames )
            );
        }
    }
```

Now that we have resized the particle pool, we need to loop over every particle inside of that pool and run the `Update` function on each particle to make sure that every particle updates with the new attribute values. Here is the code:

```
Particle* particle;
std::vector<Particle*>::iterator it;
for( it = m_particle_pool.begin(); it != m_particle_pool.end(); it++ ) {
    particle = *it;
    particle->Update( particle_lifetime, acceleration, alpha_fade,
    m_align_rotation, m_start_color, m_end_color, m_animation_frames );
}
```

Emitter Move function

The final emitter function we need to update is the `Emitter::Move` function. This function determines whether it emits any new particles this frame, and if so, how many. It also uses randomization to pick many of the starting values of these particles, within the ranges passed in from our HTML. After spawning any new particles, the function will loop over the particle pool, moving and rendering any particles that are currently active. Here is the full code for this function:

```
void Emitter::Move() {
    Particle* particle;
    std::vector<Particle*>::iterator it;
    if( m_active == true ) {
        m_next_emission -= diff_time;
        m_ttl -= diff_time;
        if( m_ttl <= 0 ) {
            if( m_loop ) {
                m_ttl = m_emit_loop_ms;
                m_has_burst = false;
            }
            else {
                m_active = false;
            }
        }
        if( m_burst_particles > 0 && m_has_burst == false ) {
            if( (float)m_ttl / (float)m_emit_loop_ms <= 1.0 -
            m_burst_time_pct ) {
                m_has_burst = true;
                m_next_emission -= m_burst_particles * m_emission_time_ms;
            }
        }
        while( m_next_emission <= 0 ) {
            m_next_emission += m_emission_time_ms;
```

```
                    particle = GetFreeParticle();
                    if( particle != NULL ) {
                        Point spawn_point;
                        spawn_point.x = get_random_float( 0.0, m_radius );
                        Point velocity_point;
                        velocity_point.x = get_random_float(
                        m_min_starting_velocity, m_max_starting_velocity );
                        float angle = get_random_float( m_min_angle, m_max_angle );
                        float start_scale = get_random_float( m_min_start_scale,
                        m_max_start_scale );
                        float end_scale = get_random_float( m_min_end_scale,
                        m_max_end_scale );
                        spawn_point.x += m_position.x;
                        spawn_point.y += m_position.y;
                        particle->Spawn(spawn_point.x, spawn_point.y,
                        velocity_point.x, velocity_point.y,
                                    start_scale, end_scale,
                                    (int)(angle / 3.14159 * 180.0 + 360.0)
                                    % 360 );
                    }
                    else {
                        m_next_emission = m_emission_time_ms;
                    }
                }
            }
        for( it = m_particle_pool.begin(); it != m_particle_pool.end(); it++ )
    {
            particle = *it;
            if( particle->m_active ) {
                particle->Move();
                particle->Render();
            }
        }
    }
}
```

We will break this code into two parts to make it easier to understand. The first part of the Move function is responsible for spawning new particles when necessary. The second portion is responsible for moving and rendering any existing active particles. The particle spawning portion of this code is only run if m_active (the active flag) is true. The second part will run either way. When an emitter is deactivated, we don't want all of the particles that have been spawned by the emitter to disappear suddenly. Instead, we would like all the particles to continue to be moved and rendered until they have all been deactivated.

We are now going to walk through the code in smaller chunks to explain everything:

```
if( m_active == true ) {
    m_next_emission -= diff_time;
```

```
    m_ttl -= diff_time;
    if( m_ttl <= 0 ) {
        if( m_loop ) {
            m_ttl = m_emit_loop_ms;
            m_has_burst = false;
        }
        else {
            m_active = false;
        }
    }
```

This first chunk of code checks the m_active attribute variable to make sure that the emitter is currently active. If it isn't, we can skip over the part of this function that spawns new particles. The next thing we do is subtract diff_time from the m_next_emission attribute. When the m_next_emission attribute hits or goes below 0, another particle will spawn. We also subtract diff_time from m_ttl, which is the time to live attribute. Immediately after subtracting from m_ttl, we check the value in m_ttl to see if it is less than or equal to 0. If time to live drops below 0, we need to check to see whether this is a looping emitter by looking at the m_loop attribute. If it is a looping emitter, we reset the time to live variable, and we set the m_has_burst flag to false. If this is not a looping emitter, we deactivate the emitter by setting m_active to false.

The following chunk of code has to do with emitting bursts of particles using the new burst feature:

```
    if( m_burst_particles > 0 && m_has_burst == false ) {
        if( (float)m_ttl / (float)m_emit_loop_ms <= 1.0 - m_burst_time_pct ) {
            m_has_burst = true;
            m_next_emission -= m_burst_particles * m_emission_time_ms;
        }
    }
```

The burst particle feature is new to our *advanced particle system*. We are using a nested if statement here. We could have put && on the end of the first if and done this with one if statement, but I wanted to separate conditions to make it easier to understand. The outer if statement first checks to see if the m_burst_particles attribute (the number of burst particles) is greater than 0. If it is, then this emitter uses the burst system and will need to create a burst of particles at the proper burst time. The next check in this outer if statement is to check if the burst has already run in this emitter. Because of the way we have designed this burst system, there can only be one burst per emission loop. So, if the m_has_burst attribute is true, then a burst will not run.

Moving on to the inner loop, we need to check to see whether we have passed the burst time for our emission. The m_burst_time_pct attribute holds a value between 0.0 and 1.0 that represents the decimal percentage of time through the emission at which the particle burst happens. The m_ttl variable holds the time to live in milliseconds for the emitter. If we divide m_ttl by m_emit_loop_ms (the emit time in milliseconds), we get an emit time countdown from 1.0 to 0.0, where 0.0 means the emission is complete. The m_burst_time_pct variable goes in the other direction. A value of 0.6 means that the burst happens 60% of the way through our emission. Because the other side of this if statement is a countdown and the burst time counts up, we need to subtract m_burst_time_pct from 1.0 to make a proper comparison. If (float)m_ttl / (float)m_emit_loop_ms is less than 1.0 - m_burst_time_pct, then we are ready for the burst. To make the burst happen, we first set m_has_burst = true. This will prevent the burst from happening multiple times in the same emission. We then subtract the number of burst particles, multiplied by the emission time in milliseconds, from m_next_emission.

The following few lines of code enter a while loop that emits particles as long as the next emission time is less than 0. In the previous version of this code, we had an if statement here instead of a loop. This limited our particle system to emit no more than one particle per frame. That may work for some simple particle systems without a burst mode, but once you add a burst, you need to be able to emit many particles in a single frame. Let's take a look at this:

```
while( m_next_emission <= 0 ) {
    m_next_emission += m_emission_time_ms;
    particle = GetFreeParticle();
    if( particle != NULL ) {
```

The while loop checks to see whether m_next_emission is less than or equal to 0. The line immediately after that adds m_emission_time_ms to the next emission. The effect of this is that if we had subtracted a large number from m_next_emission (like we did in our burst), this loop would allow us to emit multiple particles in a single run of our Move function. This means we can emit numerous particles in a single frame. What we do immediately after the addition to m_next_emission is get a free particle from our particle pool by making a call to GetFreeParticle. If we make the maximum number of particles too small, GetFreeParticle might run out of particles we can use and return NULL. If this is the case, we need to skip all of the steps that emit a new particle, which is why there is the if statement, which checks for a NULL particle.

Once we know that we can spawn a particle, we need to grab a bunch of random values inside of the ranges we set in the HTML file. The C/C++ `rand()` function returns a random integer number. Most of the values we need are floating points. We will need to write a simple function called `get_random_float`. This function gets a random floating-point number with three decimal precision that falls between a min and a max value passed into it. We chose three-decimal precision based on our needs for this game. The function can be modified for higher precision if that is necessary later.

Here is the code that gets random values for use with the newly spawned particle:

```
Point spawn_point;
spawn_point.x = get_random_float( 0.0, m_radius );
Point velocity_point;
velocity_point.x = get_random_float( m_min_starting_velocity,
m_max_starting_velocity );
float angle = get_random_float( m_min_angle, m_max_angle );
float start_scale = get_random_float( m_min_start_scale, m_max_start_scale
);
float end_scale = get_random_float( m_min_end_scale, m_max_end_scale );
```

The random values we get here are the distance from our emitter at which we will generate the particle, the velocity of the particle, the particle directional angle, and the starting and ending scale values. Because we would like the particle that is spawned at a given angle from the center of our emitter to also have the same directional velocity, we have assigned a random number to only the *x* values of `spawn_point` and `velocity_point`. We are going to use the same angle we generated randomly earlier to rotate both of those points. Here is the rotation code for those points:

```
velocity_point.Rotate(angle);
spawn_point.Rotate( angle );
```

We generate the spawn points with a position relative to an origin of 0, 0. Because our emitter is probably not at 0, 0, we need to adjust the position of the spawn point by the values in the `m_position` point. Here is the code we use to do that:

```
spawn_point.x += m_position.x;
spawn_point.y += m_position.y;
```

The last thing we do is spawn the particle with the values we randomly generated:

```
particle->Spawn(spawn_point.x, spawn_point.y, velocity_point.x,
                velocity_point.y,
                start_scale, end_scale,
                (int)(angle / 3.14159 * 180.0 + 360.0) % 360 );
```

Now that the function has completed spawning the particles for the current frame, the function will need to loop over the particle pool looking for active particles to move and render:

```
for( it = m_particle_pool.begin(); it != m_particle_pool.end(); it++ ) {
    particle = *it;
    if( particle->m_active ) {
        particle->Move();
        particle->Render();
    }
}
```

In the next section, we will update the C++/WebAssembly functions we are calling from our JavaScript.

External functions

The *advanced particle system* we are writing has two external functions that can be called from the JavaScript in our app. These functions, `add_emitter`, and `update_emitter`, are called to either insert or modify the particle system in the WebAssembly module. The `advanced_particle.cpp` file contains these functions, as well as the `main` function, which is called when the `Module` is loaded, and the `show_emission` function, which is called once per frame render. We will not need to modify the `main` and the `show_emission` functions from what we created for the basic particle system earlier in this chapter. We will, however, need to add the additional parameters we put into our JavaScript code to `add_emitter` and `update_emitter`. Also, we have created a utility function called `get_random_float`, which we use when spawning particles. Because this file contains all of our other C-style functions, I feel that `advanced_particle.cpp` is the best place to put this function as well.

Random floating-point numbers

Let's start by discussing the new `get_random_float` function. Here is the code:

```
float get_random_float( float min, float max ) {
    int int_min = (int)(min * 1000);
    int int_max = (int)(max * 1000);
    if( int_min > int_max ) {
        int temp = int_max;
        int_max = int_min;
        int_min = temp;
```

```
    }
    int int_diff = int_max - int_min;
    int int_rand = (int_diff == 0) ? 0 : rand() % int_diff;
    int_rand += int_min;
    return (float)int_rand / 1000.0;
}
```

The `%` (modulo operator) is used to make the random integer value between 0 and whatever value you use after `%`. The modulo operator is a remainder operator. It returns the remainder of a division operation. For example, `13 % 10` would return 3, as would `23 % 10`. Taking `% 10` of any number will always result in a number between 0 and 9. Modulo is useful in conjunction with `rand()` because it will result in a random number between 0 and the value after `%`. So, `rand() % 10` will result in a random number between 0 and 9.

The `get_random_float` function takes in a minimum and maximum float value and generates a random number within that range. The first two lines take those float values, multiply them by 1,000, and cast them to an integer. Because `rand()` only works with integers, we need to simulate a precision value. Multiplying by 1,000 gives us three-decimal precision. If, for instance, we want to generate a random number between 1.125 and 1.725, both of those values would be multiplied by 1,000, and we would use `rand()` to generate a random value between 1,125 and 1,175:

```
int int_min = (int)(min * 1000);
int int_max = (int)(max * 1000);
```

Once again, `rand()` only generates random integers, and using the `%` (modulo operator) alongside `rand()` will give you a number between 0 and the number that follows `%`. Because of this, we want to know the difference between our `int_min` and `int_max` values. If we subtract `int_min` from `int_max`, we will get a number that is this difference. We could potentially be thrown off if the calling code accidentally passes in a value for max that is smaller than the value for `int_min`, so we need a little bit of code to check whether `max` is smaller than `min`, and if it is, we need to switch those two values. Here is that `if` statement code:

```
if( int_min > int_max ) {
    int temp = int_max;
    int_max = int_min;
    int_min = temp;
}
```

Now, we can go ahead and get the difference between the two:

```
int int_diff = int_max - int_min;
```

In the following line of code, we get a random value between 0 and the value in `int_diff`. We are using the `?:` (ternary operator) to make sure that `int_diff` is not 0 before we execute `rand() % int_diff`. The reason for this is that `%` is a division remainder operator, so, like dividing by 0, executing `% 0` results in an exception. If there is no difference between our minimum and maximum values, we will return the minimum value. So, by using the ternary operator, we can set `int_rand` to 0 if `int_diff` is 0. Here's the code:

```
int int_rand = (int_diff == 0) ? 0 : rand() % int_diff;
```

Then, we add `int_min` to `int_rand`, and we have a random value between the `int_min` and `int_max` values:

```
int_rand += int_min;
```

The last thing we need to do is cast `int_rand` to a `float` and divide it by `1000.0`. This will return a floating-point value that falls between the `min` and `max` floating-point values that are passed into the function:

```
return (float)int_rand / 1000.0;
```

Adding an emitter

The `add_emitter` function is a pass-through that checks to see if there is an existing emitter and deletes it if there is. It then creates a new `Emitter` object, passing in all of the values we set in our HTML and passed through in JavaScript. The changes we need to make include adding the new parameters into the signature of the `add_emitter` function, and adding those same new parameters into the call to the `Emitter` constructor. In both the function signature and the constructor call, we will add a `/* new parameters */` comment that shows where old parameters end and the new ones begin. Here is the new code:

```
extern "C"
    EMSCRIPTEN_KEEPALIVE
    void add_emitter(char* file_name, int max_particles, float min_angle,
        float max_angle,
        Uint32 particle_lifetime, float acceleration, bool alpha_fade,
        float min_starting_velocity, float max_starting_velocity,
        Uint32 emission_rate, float x_pos, float y_pos, float radius,
        /* new parameters */
        float min_start_scale, float max_start_scale,
        float min_end_scale, float max_end_scale,
        Uint32 start_color, Uint32 end_color,
        float burst_time_pct, Uint32 burst_particles,
```

```
        bool loop, bool align_rotation, Uint32 emit_time_ms,
        Uint32 animation_frames ) {
    if( emitter != NULL ) {
        delete emitter;
    }

    emitter = new Emitter(file_name, max_particles, min_angle,
            max_angle,
            particle_lifetime, acceleration, alpha_fade,
            min_starting_velocity, max_starting_velocity,
            emission_rate, x_pos, y_pos, radius,
            /* new parameters */
            min_start_scale, max_start_scale,
            min_end_scale, max_end_scale,
            start_color, end_color,
            burst_time_pct, burst_particles,
            loop, align_rotation, emit_time_ms,
            animation_frames
            );
}
```

Updating an emitter

The changes we made to the update_emitter function mirror those made in
the add_emitter function. The primary differences between add_emitter and
update_emitter are that update_emitter will not run if there is not an existing emitter,
and instead of calling the Emitter constructor to create a new Emitter, it calls an existing
emitter's Update function. The Update function passes in all of the new values and most of
the old ones (except for char* file_name). Just like with the changes we made to
the add_emitter function, we have placed a /* new parameters */ comment in the
function signature and the call to the emitter Update function to show where the new
parameters have been added. Here is the code:

```
extern "C"
    EMSCRIPTEN_KEEPALIVE
    void update_emitter(int max_particles, float min_angle,
        float max_angle,
        Uint32 particle_lifetime, float acceleration, bool alpha_fade,
        float min_starting_velocity, float max_starting_velocity,
        Uint32 emission_rate, float x_pos, float y_pos, float radius,
        /* new parameters */
        float min_start_scale, float max_start_scale,
        float min_end_scale, float max_end_scale,
        Uint32 start_color, Uint32 end_color,
        float burst_time_pct, Uint32 burst_particles,
```

```
            bool loop, bool align_rotation, Uint32 emit_time_ms,
            Uint32 animation_frames ) {
            if( emitter == NULL ) {
                    return;
            }
            emitter->Update(max_particles, min_angle, max_angle,
                    particle_lifetime, acceleration, alpha_fade,
                    min_starting_velocity, max_starting_velocity,
                    emission_rate, x_pos, y_pos, radius,
                    /* new parameters */
                    min_start_scale, max_start_scale,
                    min_end_scale, max_end_scale,
                    start_color, end_color,
                    burst_time_pct, burst_particles,
                    loop, align_rotation, emit_time_ms,
                    animation_frames
            );
        }
```

In the next section, we will configure our *advance particle system tool* to create a new *particle emitter*.

Configuring the particle emitter

At this point, you may be wondering when we are going to get back to writing the game. We built this *particle emitter configuration tool* for a few reasons. First of all, it is difficult to configure a particle system in compiled code. If we wanted to test a configuration for an emitter, we would need to recompile our values with every test, or we would need to write a data loader, and rerun the game after making configuration changes. Creating a tool that allows us to test different emitter configurations allows for faster (and more interesting) particle system creation.

HTML shell and WebAssembly module interaction

I also had an ulterior motive for creating a particle system configuration tool. It is possible that some of you may not be reading this book to learn game programming, per se. You may have purchased this book as a fun way to learn more about WebAssembly. Writing this tool was a fun way to learn more about the interaction between a WebAssembly module and the HTML and JavaScript that drives that module.

Compiling and running the new tool

Now that we have all the parameters we would like, it is time to recompile the updated version of the configuration tool and start designing some particle systems.

 If you are building this from the GitHub project, you will need to run this compile command from the /Chapter09/advanced-particle-tool/ directory.

First, run the following on the command line to compile the new configuration tool:

```
em++ emitter.cpp particle.cpp point.cpp advanced_particle.cpp -o
particle.html -std=c++17 --shell-file advanced_particle_shell.html -s
NO_EXIT_RUNTIME=1 -s USE_WEBGL2=1 -s USE_SDL=2 -s USE_SDL_IMAGE=2 -s
SDL2_IMAGE_FORMATS=["png"] -s NO_EXIT_RUNTIME=1 -s
EXPORTED_FUNCTIONS="['_add_emitter', '_update_emitter', '_main']" -s
EXTRA_EXPORTED_RUNTIME_METHODS="['cwrap', 'ccall']" -s FORCE_FILESYSTEM=1
```

Open the web page in emrun or a web browser (if you are running a web server). It will look something like this:

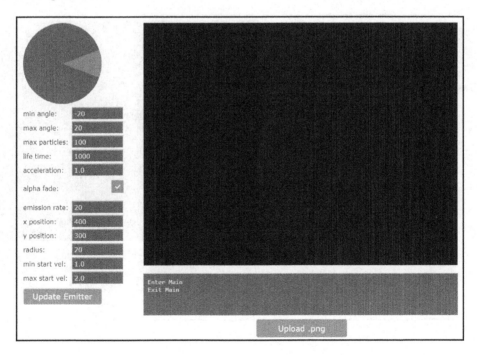

Figure 9.3: Screenshot of our particle system configuration tool

We are going to start with a simple exhaust emitter. Make the following changes to the HTML values and click the **Upload .png** button:

- **min angle: -10**
- **max angle: 10**
- **max particles: 500**
- **emission rate: 50**
- **radius: 0.5**
- **min start vel: 100.0**
- **max start vel: 150.0**
- **burst time: 0.7**
- **burst particles: 40**
- **animation frames: 6**

When you have clicked the **Upload .png** button, navigate to the `ProjectileExpOrange.png` file in the image directory and open it.

Here is a screenshot of what the config tool looks like with our exhaust particle emitter:

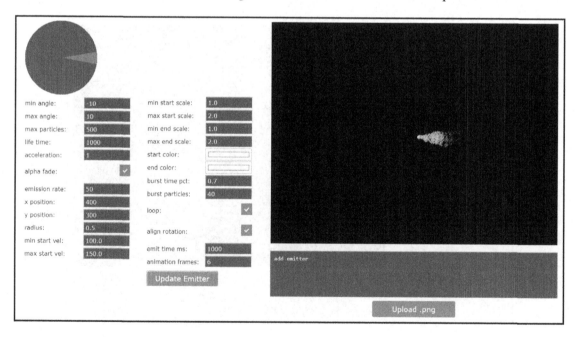

Figure 9.4: Engine exhaust configuration

I would encourage you to play around with the values until you get something you like. Whenever you change the values on the left-hand side of the page, you will need to click the **Update Emitter** button to see that new value reflected in the particle system on the right-hand side of the web page.

Creating a particle emitter

Now that we have an exhaust particle system, we are going to start adding the particle system code into the game to add some nice particle effects. I would like to have a particle system for the player and enemy ship exhaust. I would also like to add a particle system effect on top of the animated explosion we have to make it stand out.

The first thing we are going to do is copy the `particle.cpp` and `emitter.cpp` files into the main `Chapter09` directory. After that, we will need to add those class definitions to the `game.hpp` file, as well as to the `get_random_float` function prototype.

Changes to game.hpp

The first set of changes we need to make are to the `game.hpp` file. We need to add an `Emitter` class definition, a `Particle` class definition, and an external function prototype for `get_random_float`. We also need to add some new attributes to the `Ship` class. Here is the line we must add for the `get_random_float` prototype:

```
extern float get_random_float( float min, float max );
```

Adding the Particle class definition

The definition for the `Particle` class that we must add to `game.hpp` is the same definition that we have for our advanced configuration tool. Because it is the same, we will not walk through what everything in the class does. If you don't remember, please feel free to go back to the previous chapter as a reference. Here is the class definition code for `Particle` that we'll be adding to `game.hpp`:

```
class Particle {
    public:
        bool m_active;
        bool m_alpha_fade;
        bool m_color_mod;
        bool m_align_rotation;
```

```
Uint8 m_start_red;
Uint8 m_start_green;
Uint8 m_start_blue;

Uint8 m_end_red;
Uint8 m_end_green;
Uint8 m_end_blue;

Uint8 m_current_red;
Uint8 m_current_green;
Uint8 m_current_blue;

SDL_Texture *m_sprite_texture;
int m_ttl;

Uint32 m_life_time;
Uint32 m_animation_frames;
Uint32 m_current_frame;

Uint32 m_next_frame_ms;
float m_rotation;
float m_acceleration;
float m_alpha;

float m_width;
float m_height;

float m_start_scale;
float m_end_scale;
float m_current_scale;

Point m_position;
Point m_velocity;
SDL_Rect m_dest = {.x = 0,  .y = 0,  .w = 0,  .h = 0 };
SDL_Rect m_src = {.x = 0,  .y = 0,  .w = 0,  .h = 0 };

Particle( SDL_Texture *sprite, Uint32 life_time, float
          acceleration,
          bool alpha_fade, int width, int height, bool
          align_rotation,
          Uint32 start_color,
          Uint32 end_color,
          Uint32 animation_frames );

void Update( Uint32 life_time, float acceleration,
          bool alpha_fade, bool align_rotation,
          Uint32 start_color, Uint32 end_color,
          Uint32 m_animation_frames );
```

```
        void Spawn( float x, float y, float velocity_x, float velocity_y,
                float start_scale, float end_scale, float rotation );
        void Move();
        void Render();
};
```

Emitter class definition

The Emitter class has a few additional attributes we have added that help
the Emitter position itself relative to the game objects. There is a Run function that we do
not need in the particle emitter configuration tool, but we will need it in the game code so
that we can trigger the Emitter at any time. The Update function inside of
Emitter and Particle are not necessary inside of the game, but we are going to leave
them in there in order to not complicate the changes. The Emscripten dead code elimination
logic should remove that code when it compiles the game anyway. Here is the new code for
the Emitter class definition that we need to add to games.hpp:

```
class Emitter {
    public:
        bool m_loop;
        bool m_align_rotation;
        bool m_active;
        bool m_has_burst;

        SDL_Texture *m_sprite_texture;
        std::vector<Particle*> m_particle_pool;
        int m_sprite_width;
        int m_sprite_height;
        int m_ttl;

        // added ----------------------------
        int m_x_adjustment = 0;
        int m_y_adjustment = 0;
        // ----------------------------------

        Uint32 m_max_particles;
        Uint32 m_emission_rate;
        Uint32 m_emission_time_ms;

        Uint32 m_start_color;
        Uint32 m_end_color;

        Uint32 m_burst_particles;
        Uint32 m_emit_loop_ms;
        Uint32 m_animation_frames;
```

```
int m_next_emission;

float* m_parent_rotation;

float m_max_angle;
float m_min_angle;
float m_radius;
float m_min_starting_velocity;
float m_max_starting_velocity;

float m_min_start_scale;
float m_max_start_scale;
float m_min_end_scale;
float m_max_end_scale;
float m_min_start_rotation;
float m_max_start_rotation;
float m_burst_time_pct;

// added ----------------------------
float* m_parent_rotation_ptr;
float* m_parent_x_ptr;
float* m_parent_y_ptr;
// ----------------------------------

Point m_position;

Emitter(char* sprite_file, int max_particles, float min_angle,
        float max_angle,
        Uint32 particle_lifetime, float acceleration,
        bool alpha_fade,
        float min_starting_velocity, float max_starting_velocity,
        Uint32 emission_rate, int x_pos, int y_pos, float radius,
        float min_start_scale, float max_start_scale,
        float min_end_scale, float max_end_scale,
        Uint32 start_color, Uint32 end_color,
        float burst_time_pct, Uint32 burst_particles,
        bool loop, bool align_rotation,
        Uint32 emit_time_ms, Uint32 animation_frames );

void Update(int max_particles, float min_angle, float max_angle,
        Uint32 particle_lifetime, float acceleration, bool alpha_fade,
        float min_starting_velocity, float max_starting_velocity,
        Uint32 emission_rate, int x_pos, int y_pos, float radius,
        float min_start_scale, float max_start_scale,
        float min_end_scale, float max_end_scale,
        Uint32 start_color, Uint32 end_color,
        float burst_time_pct, Uint32 burst_particles,
        bool loop, bool align_rotation, Uint32 emit_time_ms,
```

```
                  Uint32 animation_frames );

          void Move();
          Particle* GetFreeParticle();

          void Run(); // added
  };
```

The code we added to the particle system configuration tool is surrounded by comments labeled `added`. Let me walk through what each of these new attributes and the new function does. Here are the first two added attributes:

```
int m_x_adjustment = 0;
int m_y_adjustment = 0;
```

These two values are adjustments, and are used to modify the position at which the emitter spawns particles. These variables are useful for small adjustments to particle positions relative to the position of an object the emitter is following. Here are the following three attributes that we have added:

```
float* m_parent_rotation_ptr;
float* m_parent_x_ptr;
float* m_parent_y_ptr;
```

These are pointers to the x, y, and rotational attributes of a parent object. If we set `Emitter->m_parent_rotation_ptr = &m_Rotation`, for instance, that pointer will point to the rotation of our parent object, and we will be able to access that value inside of our `Emitter` to adjust the rotation. The same holds true for `m_parent_x_ptr` and `m_parent_y_ptr`.

Finally, we have added a `Run` function:

```
void Run();
```

This function allows a particle emitter, that is not looping, to be restarted. We will be using this for the `Explosion` emitter that we added to the `Ship` class.

Changes to emitter.cpp

Now that we have walked through the changes that we need to make to `game.hpp`, we are going to walk through all of the changes that we will make to the `emitter.cpp` file, function by function.

Changes to the constructor function

There are two changes to be made to the constructor function. First, we'll add some
initialization at the top that initializes all of the new pointers to NULL. We do not need these
pointers in every emitter, so we can check against NULL to see when they are or are not
used. Further down, we will modify the values that are passed into the constructors from
degrees to radians. Here is what the function looks like:

```
Emitter::Emitter(char* sprite_file, int max_particles, float min_angle,
                float max_angle,
                Uint32 particle_lifetime, float acceleration, bool
                alpha_fade,
                float min_starting_velocity, float max_starting_velocity,
                Uint32 emission_rate, int x_pos, int y_pos, float radius,
                float min_start_scale, float max_start_scale,
                float min_end_scale, float max_end_scale,
                Uint32 start_color, Uint32 end_color,
                float burst_time_pct, Uint32 burst_particles,
                bool loop, bool align_rotation, Uint32 emit_time_ms, Uint32
                animation_frames ) {
    // added ----------------------------
    m_parent_rotation_ptr = NULL;
    m_parent_x_ptr = NULL;
    m_parent_y_ptr = NULL;
    // ----------------------------------
    m_start_color = start_color;
    m_end_color = end_color;
    m_active = true;

    if( min_starting_velocity > max_starting_velocity ) {
        m_min_starting_velocity = max_starting_velocity;
        m_max_starting_velocity = min_starting_velocity;
    }
    else {
        m_min_starting_velocity = min_starting_velocity;
        m_max_starting_velocity = max_starting_velocity;
    }
    SDL_Surface *temp_surface = IMG_Load( sprite_file );

    if( !temp_surface ) {
        printf("failed to load image: %s\n", IMG_GetError() );
        printf("failed sprite file: %s\n", sprite_file );
        return;
    }
    m_sprite_texture = SDL_CreateTextureFromSurface( renderer, temp_surface
    );
    SDL_FreeSurface( temp_surface );
```

```
        SDL_QueryTexture( m_sprite_texture,
                          NULL, NULL,
                          &m_sprite_width, &m_sprite_height );
                          m_max_particles = max_particles;

    for( int i = 0; i < m_max_particles; i++ ) {
        m_particle_pool.push_back(
            new Particle( m_sprite_texture, particle_lifetime,
            acceleration,
                          alpha_fade, m_sprite_width, m_sprite_height,
                          align_rotation,
                          m_start_color, m_end_color, animation_frames )
            );
    }

    // modified -----------------------------
    m_min_angle = (min_angle+90) / 180 * 3.14159;
    m_max_angle = (max_angle+90) / 180 * 3.14159;
    // -------------------------------------

    m_radius = radius;
    m_position.x = (float)x_pos;
    m_position.y = (float)y_pos;
    m_emission_rate = emission_rate;
    m_emission_time_ms = 1000 / m_emission_rate;
    m_next_emission = 0;
    m_min_start_scale = min_start_scale;
    m_max_start_scale = max_start_scale;
    m_min_end_scale = min_end_scale;
    m_max_end_scale = max_end_scale;

    m_loop = loop;
    m_align_rotation = align_rotation;
    m_emit_loop_ms = emit_time_ms;
    m_ttl = m_emit_loop_ms;

    m_animation_frames = animation_frames;
    m_burst_time_pct = burst_time_pct;
    m_burst_particles = burst_particles;
    m_has_burst = false;
}
```

The first changes are at the very top of this function, and set our new pointer attributes
to NULL:

```
m_parent_rotation_ptr = NULL;
m_parent_x_ptr = NULL;
m_parent_y_ptr = NULL;
```

Later, we will check to see if these pointers are NULL, and if not, we will use
m_parent_rotation_ptr to adjust the rotation angle of this emitter. We will use
m_parent_x_ptr to change the x coordinate of the emitter, and we will use
m_parent_y_ptr to adjust the y coordinate of this emitter. After that, we have the code
that modifies the passed in minimum and maximum angles from degrees to radians:

```
m_min_angle = (min_angle+90) / 180 * 3.14159;
m_max_angle = (max_angle+90) / 180 * 3.14159;
```

The real reason we need to do this is that we are hardcoding the values we pass into the
emitter. If we created a data loader, we could have done this conversion when the data
loaded up. But, because we are taking these values straight out of our *particle emitter
configuration tool* and hardcoding the values right into the call to the new emitter, we will
either have to remember to do the conversion ourselves every time we change these values,
or we will have to do it from within the constructor and the Update function.

Changes to the Update function

The Update function is not likely to ever be called inside our game. Emscripten's dead code
removal process should eliminate it. However, we haven't removed it from
the Emitter class. If you think you may ever call this, you might want to change
the m_min_angle and m_max_angle initialization to convert from degrees into radians,
like we did in the constructor:

```
m_min_angle = (min_angle+90) / 180 * 3.14159;
m_max_angle = (max_angle+90) / 180 * 3.14159;
```

Adding a Run function

In the particle system configuration tool, we didn't need a Run function because calling
the Update function would run Emitter. The Update function is far too cumbersome to
use inside our game. It uses a large number of configuration variables that we may not
have access to when we call the function. All we want to do is set the emitter to active, reset
the time to live, and the burst flag. Instead of calling Update, we create a small Run
function to do what we need:

```
void Emitter::Run() {
    m_active = true;
    m_ttl = m_emit_loop_ms;
    m_has_burst = false;
}
```

Setting m_active to true makes the emitter active so that it can spawn new particles when calling the Move function. Resetting m_ttl to m_emit_loop_ms makes sure that the time to live does not automatically shut the emitter down the next time it calls the Move function. Setting m_has_burst = false makes sure that, if there is a particle burst that must occur somewhere in the emission, it will run.

Changes to the Move function

The new version of the Move function will need to be able to modify its position based on a parent position and rotate its defined position based on the parent's rotation. It will also need to be able to make minor adjustments using m_x_adjustment and m_y_adjustment. Here is the new version of Move in its entirety:

```
void Emitter::Move() {
 Particle* particle;
 std::vector<Particle*>::iterator it;
    if( m_active == true ) {
        m_next_emission -= diff_time;
        m_ttl -= diff_time;
        if( m_ttl <= 0 ) {
            if( m_loop ) {
                m_ttl = m_emit_loop_ms;
                m_has_burst = false;
            }
            else { m_active = false; }
        }
        if( m_burst_particles > 0 && m_has_burst == false ) {
            if( (float)m_ttl / (float)m_emit_loop_ms <= 1.0 -
                m_burst_time_pct ) {
                m_has_burst = true;
                m_next_emission -= m_burst_particles * m_emission_time_ms;
            }
        }
        while( m_next_emission <= 0 ) {
            m_next_emission += m_emission_time_ms;
            particle = GetFreeParticle();
            if( particle != NULL ) {
                Point spawn_point, velocity_point, rotated_position;
                spawn_point.x = get_random_float( 0.0, m_radius );
                velocity_point.x =
                get_random_float(m_min_starting_velocity,
                m_max_starting_velocity);
                float angle = get_random_float( m_min_angle,m_max_angle );
                float start_scale = get_random_float(m_min_start_scale,
                m_max_start_scale);
```

```
            float end_scale = get_random_float( m_min_end_scale,
            m_max_end_scale );
            if( m_parent_rotation_ptr != NULL ) {
                angle += *m_parent_rotation_ptr;
                rotated_position = m_position;
                rotated_position.Rotate( *m_parent_rotation_ptr );
            }
            velocity_point.Rotate(angle);
            spawn_point.Rotate( angle );

            if( m_parent_rotation_ptr == NULL ) {
                spawn_point.x += m_position.x;
                spawn_point.y += m_position.y;
                if( m_parent_x_ptr != NULL ) { spawn_point.x +=
                *m_parent_x_ptr; }
                if( m_parent_y_ptr != NULL ) { spawn_point.y +=
                *m_parent_y_ptr; }
            }
            else {
                spawn_point.x += rotated_position.x;
                spawn_point.y += rotated_position.y;
                if( m_parent_x_ptr != NULL ) { spawn_point.x +=
                *m_parent_x_ptr; }
                if( m_parent_y_ptr != NULL ) { spawn_point.y +=
                *m_parent_y_ptr; }
            }
            spawn_point.x += m_x_adjustment;
            spawn_point.y += m_y_adjustment;
            particle->Spawn(spawn_point.x,
            spawn_point.y,velocity_point.x, velocity_point.y,
                start_scale, end_scale, (int)(angle / 3.14159 * 180.0 +
                360.0) % 360 );
        }
        else {
            m_next_emission = m_emission_time_ms;
        }
    }
}
}
for( it = m_particle_pool.begin(); it != m_particle_pool.end(); it++ )
{
    particle = *it;
    if( particle->m_active ) {
        particle->Move();
        particle->Render();
    }
}
}
```

Most of this code is the same as it was in earlier versions. Let's walk through the differences. First, we need to rotate this entire particle system if there is a rotated parent object. We will use this for the exhaust particle system that we will be adding to the spaceship objects. This exhaust has to be positioned relative to the spaceship. To do that, we need to take the position and rotate it. We also need to add the parent's rotation to the existing emission angle. Here is the new code:

```
Point rotated_position;

if( m_parent_rotation_ptr != NULL ) {
    angle += *m_parent_rotation_ptr;
    rotated_position = m_position;
    rotated_position.Rotate( *m_parent_rotation_ptr );
}
```

At the top, we create a new `Point` object called `rotated_position`. If the `m_parent_rotation_ptr` is not `NULL`, we add that value to the emission angle we calculated earlier. We will copy the values of `m_position` into `rotated_position` and `Rotate` that position by the parent's rotation. Later, we will check whether `m_parent_rotation_ptr` is not `NULL`, and if not, we will use `rotated_position` relative to the parent object's position to calculate the location of the emitter. The following is an `if` statement that checks whether `m_parent_rotation_ptr` == `NULL`. If it is null, the first part of this `if` block does what would have been done earlier. Here is the code:

```
if( m_parent_rotation_ptr == NULL ) {
    spawn_point.x += m_position.x;
    spawn_point.y += m_position.y;
}
```

Because the `if` statement was checking whether `m_parent_rotation_ptr` == `NULL`, we don't want to use the rotated version of the particle system's position. That block defaulted to using the `m_position` attribute unmodified. If `m_parent_rotation_ptr` is not `NULL`, we will run the following `else` block:

```
else {
    spawn_point.x += rotated_position.x;
    spawn_point.y += rotated_position.y;
}
```

This code uses a rotated version of `m_position`. Next, we want to see whether `m_parent_x_ptr` and `m_parent_y_ptr` are not NULL. If they aren't, then we need to add the parent's position to the `spawn_point` using these values. Here is that piece of code:

```
if( m_parent_x_ptr != NULL ) {
    spawn_point.x += *m_parent_x_ptr;
}
if( m_parent_y_ptr != NULL ) {
    spawn_point.y += *m_parent_y_ptr;
}
```

The final piece of code we will add to the `Move` function is the micro adjustment to the spawn point. Sometimes, particle systems need a little bit of tweaking before rotation to have them look just right. Therefore, we add the following:

```
spawn_point.x += m_x_adjustment;
spawn_point.y += m_y_adjustment;
```

The values of `m_x_adjustment` and `m_y_adjustment` default to 0, so if you want to use these values, they will need to be set sometime after creating the emitter.

Changes to ship.cpp

The next thing we are going to do is modify the `ship.cpp` file to make use of two new particle emitters. We want a particle emitter for the ship's exhaust, and one to improve the ship's explosion. We are going to need to make changes to the `Ship` class' constructor, the `Ship` class' `Acceleration` function, and the `Ship` class' `Render` function.

The Ship class' constructor function

The `Ship` class' constructor function has changed most of the functions inside of the `Ship` class. We are not only initializing new attributes – we also need to set the parent and adjustment values on the emitters. Here is the new code for the constructor:

```
Ship::Ship() : Collider(8.0) {
    m_Rotation = PI;
    m_DX = 0.0;
    m_DY = 1.0;
    m_VX = 0.0;
    m_VY = 0.0;
    m_LastLaunchTime = current_time;
    m_Accelerating = false;
```

```
m_Exhaust = new Emitter((char*)"/sprites/ProjectileExpOrange.png", 200,
                    -10, 10,
                    400, 1.0, true,
                    0.1, 0.1,
                    30, 0, 12, 0.5,
                    0.5, 1.0,
                    0.5, 1.0,
                    0xffffff, 0xffffff,
                    0.7, 10,
                    true, true,
                    1000, 6 );

m_Exhaust->m_parent_rotation_ptr = &m_Rotation;
m_Exhaust->m_parent_x_ptr = &m_X;
m_Exhaust->m_parent_y_ptr = &m_Y;
m_Exhaust->m_x_adjustment = 10;
m_Exhaust->m_y_adjustment = 10;
m_Exhaust->m_active = false;
m_Explode = new Emitter((char*)"/sprites/Explode.png", 100,
                    0, 360,
                    1000, 0.3, false,
                    20.0, 40.0,
                    10, 0, 0, 5,
                    1.0, 2.0,
                    1.0, 2.0,
                    0xffffff, 0xffffff,
                    0.0, 10,
                    false, false,
                    800, 8 );
m_Explode->m_parent_rotation_ptr = &m_Rotation;
m_Explode->m_parent_x_ptr = &m_X;
m_Explode->m_parent_y_ptr = &m_Y;
m_Explode->m_active = false;
}
```

The first several lines haven't changed from the old version. The new changes start when we initialize m_Accelerating to false. After that, we set up the exhaust emitter, first creating a new emitter, then setting the parent values and the adjustment values, and finally, we set it to inactive:

```
m_Exhaust = new Emitter((char*)"/sprites/ProjectileExpOrange.png", 200,
                    -10, 10,
                    400, 1.0, true,
                    0.1, 0.1,
                    30, 0, 12, 0.5,
                    0.5, 1.0,
                    0.5, 1.0,
                    0xffffff, 0xffffff,
```

```
                        0.7, 10,
                        true, true,
                        1000, 6 );

    m_Exhaust->m_parent_rotation_ptr = &m_Rotation;
    m_Exhaust->m_parent_x_ptr = &m_X;
    m_Exhaust->m_parent_y_ptr = &m_Y;
    m_Exhaust->m_x_adjustment = 10;
    m_Exhaust->m_y_adjustment = 10;
    m_Exhaust->m_active = false;
```

All of those values that are passed into the `Emitter` function come straight from the *particle system configuration tool*. We have to add them manually into our function call. If we were working on a large project, this would not be very scalable. We would probably have the configuration tool create some sort of data file (for example, JSON or XML). But for expediency, we have simply hardcoded these values based on what we had inside of the configuration tool. Unfortunately, the values are not in the same order that they appear inside of the tool. You will need to look at the signature of the `Emitter` constructor to make sure that you put the values in the right place:

```
Emitter(char* sprite_file, int max_particles, float min_angle, float
max_angle,
        Uint32 particle_lifetime, float acceleration, bool alpha_fade,
        float min_starting_velocity, float max_starting_velocity,
        Uint32 emission_rate, int x_pos, int y_pos, float radius,
        float min_start_scale, float max_start_scale,
        float min_end_scale, float max_end_scale,
        Uint32 start_color, Uint32 end_color,
        float burst_time_pct, Uint32 burst_particles,
        bool loop, bool align_rotation, Uint32 emit_time_ms, Uint32
        animation_frames );
```

The first parameter, `sprite_file`, is the location of your file in the virtual filesystem. That file is not automatically included in your project. You will need to make sure that it is in the right location. We put the file in the `sprites` directory and use the following flag when we run Emscripten:

```
--preload-file sprites
```

After creating our `Exhaust` emitter, we create an `Explosion` emitter with the following code:

```
m_Explode = new Emitter((char*)"/sprites/Explode.png", 100,
                        0, 360,
                        1000, 0.3, false,
                        20.0, 40.0,
```

```
                          10, 0, 0, 5,
                          1.0, 2.0,
                          1.0, 2.0,
                          0xffffff, 0xffffff,
                          0.0, 10,
                          false, false,
                          800, 8 );

    m_Explode->m_parent_rotation_ptr = &m_Rotation;
    m_Explode->m_parent_x_ptr = &m_X;
    m_Explode->m_parent_y_ptr = &m_Y;
    m_Explode->m_active = false;
```

The creation of the m_Explode emitter is similar to the m_Exhaust emitter, but we have different values that we pass into the emitter based on what we created in the *particle emitter configuration tool*:

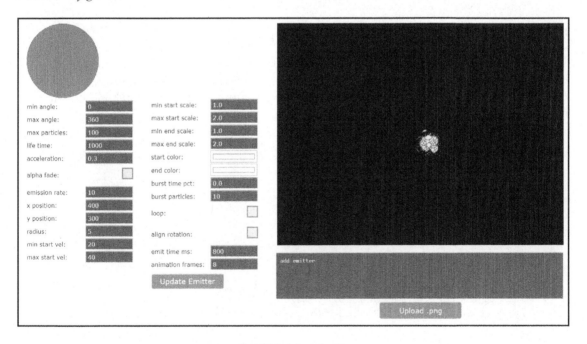

Figure 9.5: Explosion configuration

As with the m_Exhaust emitter, we will need to set all of the parent pointer variables and deactivate the emitter. Unlike m_Exhaust, we won't need to make fine adjustments using the m_x_adjustment and m_y_adjustment attributes.

The Ship class' Acceleration function

We want to run the exhaust emitter only when the ship is accelerating. To do this, we will need to set a flag inside of our ship's `Accelerate` function. Here is the new version of the acceleration function:

```
void Ship::Accelerate() {
    m_Accelerating = true; // added line
    m_VX += m_DX * delta_time;
    m_VY += m_DY * delta_time;
}
```

The only change is the addition of the line at the beginning, which sets m_Accelerating to true. When we are rendering the ship, we can check this flag and start or stop the emitter based on the value inside it.

The Ship class' Render function

The final changes to the Ship class are in the ship's Render function. Inside this function, we will need to add code that moves and renders the two new particle systems, as well as code that will turn the exhaust on if the ship is accelerating, and off if it isn't. Here is the new version of the function:

```
void Ship::Render() {
    if( m_Alive == false ) {
        return;
    }
    m_Exhaust->Move();
    m_Explode->Move();
    dest.x = (int)m_X;
    dest.y = (int)m_Y;
    dest.w = c_Width;
    dest.h = c_Height;
    src.x = 32 * m_CurrentFrame;
    float degrees = (m_Rotation / PI) * 180.0;
    int return_code = SDL_RenderCopyEx( renderer, m_SpriteTexture,
                                        &src, &dest,
                                        degrees, NULL, SDL_FLIP_NONE );
    if( return_code != 0 ) {
        printf("failed to render image: %s\n", IMG_GetError() );
    }

    if( m_Accelerating == false ) {
        m_Exhaust->m_active = false;
    }
```

```
    else {
        m_Exhaust->m_active = true;
    }
    m_Accelerating = false;
}
```

Take a look at the first block of added code, near the top:

```
m_Exhaust->Move();
m_Explode->Move();
```

The call to the Move function on an emitter both moves and renders all of the particles inside of the particle system. It also spawns new particles if it is time for the emitter to do that. At the very end of the function, there is code to handle the exhaust emitter:

```
if( m_Accelerating == false ) {
    m_Exhaust->m_active = false;
}
else {
    m_Exhaust->m_active = true;
}
m_Accelerating = false;
```

This code checks to see if the m_Accelerating flag is false. If it is, we deactivate the exhaust emitter. If the ship is accelerating, we set the m_active flag to true. We don't make a call to the Run function, because we are doing this every frame, and we don't want to start the *time to live* over on that emitter every time we loop. The last line sets m_Accelerating to false. We do this because we don't have anywhere in our code that detects when a ship stops accelerating. If the ship is accelerating, that flag will be set back to true before we get to this point in the code. If not, it will stay set to false.

Changes to projectile_pool.cpp

We don't need to change a lot inside of the ProjectilePool class. In fact, we only need to make two changes to one function. The MoveProjectiles function inside of the ProjectilePool class performs all of the collision detection between projectiles and our two ships. If a ship is destroyed, we run the m_Explode particle emitter on that ship. That will require two new lines of code inside of the hit test condition for each of the ships. Here is the new version of the MoveProjectiles function:

```
void ProjectilePool::MoveProjectiles() {
    Projectile* projectile;
    std::vector<Projectile*>::iterator it;
    for( it = m_ProjectileList.begin(); it != m_ProjectileList.end(); it++
```

```
        ) {
                projectile = *it;
                if( projectile->m_Active ) {
                    projectile->Move();
                    if( projectile->m_CurrentFrame == 0 &&
                        player->m_CurrentFrame == 0 &&
                        ( projectile->HitTest( player ) ||
                            player->CompoundHitTest( projectile ) ) ) {
                        player->m_CurrentFrame = 1;
                        player->m_NextFrameTime = ms_per_frame;
                        player->m_Explode->Run(); // added
                        projectile->m_CurrentFrame = 1;
                        projectile->m_NextFrameTime = ms_per_frame;
                    }
                    if( projectile->m_CurrentFrame == 0 &&
                        enemy->m_CurrentFrame == 0 &&
                        ( projectile->HitTest( enemy ) ||
                            enemy->CompoundHitTest( projectile ) ) ) {
                        enemy->m_CurrentFrame = 1;
                        enemy->m_NextFrameTime = ms_per_frame;
                        enemy->m_Explode->Run(); // added
                        projectile->m_CurrentFrame = 1;
                        projectile->m_NextFrameTime = ms_per_frame;
                    }
                }
            }
        }
    }
```

The two lines of code I have added are for the calls
to `player->m_Explode->Run();` and `enemy->m_Explode->Run();`. These lines execute
when the player's ship or the enemy ship collides with one of the projectiles and is
destroyed.

Changes to main.cpp

The last change we need to make in order to add exhaust and explosion particle systems is
to the `main.cpp` file. This change requires the addition of a single
function, `get_random_float`. We discussed this function earlier. It is a way for our
particle emitter to get random floating-point values that fall between a minimum and a
maximum value. Here is the code:

```
float get_random_float( float min, float max ) {
    int int_min = (int)(min * 1000);
    int int_max = (int)(max * 1000);
    if( int_min > int_max ) {
```

```
        int temp = int_max;
        int_max = int_min;
        int_min = temp;
    }
    int int_diff = int_max - int_min;
    int int_rand = (int_diff == 0) ? 0 : rand() % int_diff;
    int_rand += int_min;
    return (float)int_rand / 1000.0;
}
```

Compiling the new particle_system.html file

Now that we have made all the necessary changes to our files, we can go ahead and use
Emscripten to compile and test the new version of the game.

 If you are building this from the GitHub project, you will need to run this
compile command from the /Chapter09/ directory. The previous
compile was done from inside the /Chapter09/advanced-particle-
tool/ directory, so make sure that you are in the right place when you
run this command; otherwise, it won't have the files it needs to build the
game.

Execute the following command from the command line:

```
em++ collider.cpp emitter.cpp enemy_ship.cpp particle.cpp player_ship.cpp
point.cpp projectile_pool.cpp projectile.cpp ship.cpp main.cpp -o
particle_system.html --preload-file sprites -std=c++17 -s USE_WEBGL2=1 -s
USE_SDL=2 -s USE_SDL_IMAGE=2 -s SDL2_IMAGE_FORMATS=["png"] -s
USE_SDL_IMAGE=2 -s SDL2_IMAGE_FORMATS=["png"]
```

Taking it further

We will not be writing a data export tool for configuration. This chapter is too long as it is.
When you are creating particle systems, you can spend a near infinite amount of time
tweaking them to your liking. Particle systems can have a tremendous number of
configuration parameters. You can even have Bézier curves for movement, rotation, and
scaling. Some advanced particle systems have particles that emit other particles. There is no
limit to the complexity that we can add to a particle system, but there is a limit to the
number of pages I can have in this book, so I encourage you to take this system and add to
it until you get the results you want.

Summary

Congratulations! You have made it through a very long, information-packed chapter. In the last two chapters, we discussed what particle systems are and why they are used. We learned how to add files to, and how to access, the WebAssembly virtual filesystem. We learned how to create more advanced interactions between the HTML shell file and the WebAssembly module. We then constructed a more advanced particle emitter configuration tool with a lot more functionality. After constructing some nice looking particle systems in the tool, we took the data and code and used it to construct two new particle emitters inside the game we have been building.

In the next chapter, we will be discussing and building AI for our enemy spaceship.

10
AI and Steering Behaviors

The game we have been writing is loosely based on the computer game *Spacewar!* If you are not familiar with *Spacewar!*, it was the first computer game ever written. It originally ran on a PDP-1 owned by MIT and was written by an MIT student named Steve Russel, in 1962. Back then, just getting a computer to display graphical output was difficult enough. *Spacewar!*, as well as many other early game systems such as *Pong*, were designed to be played by more than one person. That was because programming a computer to behave like a human was a very difficult thing. That is still somewhat true today, although more processing power and data allows modern **Artificial Intelligence (AI)** algorithms to behave much more intelligently than they have in the past.

Because our game is a single-player web game, we do not have the benefit of using a second human intelligence to power our enemy spaceship. Before this chapter, we used an AI stub to allow our enemy spaceship to move and shoot randomly around our gameplay area. That might have worked for us up to this point, but now we want our player to feel threatened by the enemy ship. It should be intelligent enough to fight and kill our player in one-on-one combat.

 You will need to include several images in your build to make this project work. Make sure you include the /Chapter10/sprites/ folder from the project's GitHub. If you haven't yet downloaded the GitHub project, you can get it online at: https://github.com/PacktPublishing/Hands-On-Game-Development-with-WebAssembly.

In this chapter, we will be doing the following:

- Introducing the concept of AI and Game AI
- Adding obstacles to the game for avoidance AI (and increasing the canvas size)
- Adding new collision detection for a line of sight
- Introducing the concept of a **Finite State Machine (FSM)**
- Introducing the concept of **autonomous agents**
- Introducing the concept of **steering behaviors**
- Adding force fields to our game
- Using FSMs and steering behaviors to create an AI
- Tuning our AI to allow the enemy spaceship to navigate obstacles

What is Game AI?

Many early video games avoided AI because it was a very challenging problem with the hardware available at the time. For example, *Space Invaders*, *Galaga*, and *Galaxian* all had aliens that moved in specific non-intelligent patterns. Early Atari games were either two-player games (*Pong*) or had the player interact with a non-intelligent environment (*Breakout*). One early and successful attempt at a game with AI was *PAC-MAN*. Each ghost in *PAC-MAN* had a different personality and would behave a little differently in the same circumstances. *PAC-MAN* also used a simple **Finite State Machine (FSM)**. That is a type of AI where the AI behaves differently under different environmental circumstances. If the player ate a *power pellet* in *PAC-MAN*, the ghosts would all turn blue and suddenly become edible in a *hunter-becomes-the-hunted* reversal of fortune. While the ghosts could be eaten, it would have been easier for the programmers to have those ghosts continue to hunt down *PAC-MAN*, as they did before. That would make the ghosts look either stupid or suicidal, which is the kind of behavior we would like to avoid when writing an AI.

In 1950, the mathematical and computer genius Alan Turing proposed a benchmark for AI that he called "the imitation game," but it would later become known as *the Turing test*. He proposed a game having human players interacting with humans and computers through a text-based interface. If a computer could convince a human that they were interacting with another human and not a computer, that computer should be considered to be intelligent. Personally, I feel as if we passed this threshold a long time ago. But when machines threaten human intelligence, humans like to move the goal posts.

In 1964, Joseph Weizenbaum of MIT wrote a chatbot named ELIZA. ELIZA pretended to be a psychotherapist at the other end of a chat system. ELIZA managed to fool quite a few people into believing it was a real psychotherapist, which is probably as much a commentary on psychotherapy as it is on human intelligence. Anyone looking for a chatbot would easily be able to tell ELIZA was not human, but Joesph Weizenbaum was quite disturbed by the number of people willing to pour their heart out to ELIZA as if she were a real person.

The Loebner prize is an annual Turing test competition, where a series of judges who are AI experts have yet to be fooled by a chatbot. Today, many programs routinely fool people into thinking they are humans. I would argue that needing a human expert to determine whether an AI has passed the Turing test is moving the goalposts significantly from where Alan Turing initially set them. I believe if we had a large sample of non-experts that were fooled by a chatbot, we should consider that chatbot to be intelligent, but I digress.

My point in bringing up the Turing test is that a Game AI needs to pass a modified form of the Turing test. When you write a Game AI, your goal is to convince the player that they are not playing a game against a total loser. All Game AIs are, more or less, lame. For the time being, we will not be able to create a Game AI version of IBM's Watson (the AI that defeated Ken Jennings in Jeopardy). Like everything in a computer game, we need to learn to work within the constraints of the system. And for a web-based game, those constraints may be significant.

Remember, it is OK to cheat, but don't get caught. Many Game AIs cheat. An RTS may be able to see through the fog of war. An AI poker player may be able to peak at the player's cards. One way we are going to cheat is to allow our enemy spaceship to accelerate in directions that are not allowed for the player. The key to cheating with a Game AI is to make sure that the behavior or movement does not look unnatural. Many years ago, I wrote an online version of the card game Spades, playable at `https://www.icardgames.com/spades.html`. The player's partner AI is allowed to peak at everyone's cards. One common complaint I get is that the player's partner will frequently trump the player's high card. That is because the AI is looking not at who is currently winning the trick, but whether the player that will follow him can win the trick if he does not play a higher card than the one the player lead with. Not realizing this behavior is helping them, I get many frustrated complaints from players about the partner trumping their card. This is an example of a case where the player is actually doing better because of the AI but leaves with the impression that the AI is making stupid choices. My point is, Game AI is all about impression. Remember what the AI host said in the HBO television show *Westworld*, when one of the characters asked her if she was real: "If you can't tell, does it really matter?"

Autonomous agents versus top-down AI

In 1986, Craig Reynolds created a well-regarded AI program called *Boids* (a combination of bird and droids). This program created a fascinating bird-like flocking behavior, where little triangles moved around the screen in ways that remind the observer of flocking birds or fish. When the environment had obstacles, the boids broke up to steer around the obstacles and rejoin later. A collision between two flocks will usually end up in the flocks joining up and moving on. The Boids algorithm is an implementation of autonomous agents for AI. Each individual boid makes decisions based on a few simple rules and its immediate environment. That results in what is called **emergent behavior**, which is behavior that looks as if it was designed from the top down, but is not. The irony is that a top-down-implemented AI frequently looks less intelligent than allowing the individual agents to make their own decisions. It's a little like the old Soviet top-down command-and-control economy, versus a capitalist economy where individuals make decisions based on their immediate environment. In games, as in economics, you can also have a mixed system, where a top-down AI can send messages to autonomous agents giving them new goals or instructions. In the game we are writing, we have a single enemy spaceship, so the decision to manage AI from the top down or through autonomous agents does not really matter much, but because you may choose to expand the game in the future to support multiple enemies and their AIs, our agent will manage itself autonomously.

What is an FSM?

FSMs are very common in games. As I mentioned before, PAC-MAN was an early game that had an AI with more than one state. The ghosts could be in a *hunt* or a *flee* state based on a global condition flipped when PAC-MAN would eat a large dot on the screen, commonly known as a **power pellet**. A specific state in an FSM can be either a global condition or, in the case of a **finite state automaton**, could be a state that is specific to any *autonomous agent* within the game. Managing behaviors or state transitions could be as simple as using a switch statement, or they could be more complicated systems that load and unload AI modules when different states are triggered. A state may choose when a transition to a different state occurs, or state transitions could be managed by the game from the top down.

The FSM we will be writing for this game will be very basic. It will be a simple switch that will perform different behaviors based on the current state. The enemy ship's position relative to the player and whether there is an unobstructed line of sight between them will be used to determine the transitions between states. Our FSM will have four basic states:

1. WANDER
2. APPROACH
3. ATTACK
4. FLEE

The conditions for entering these states are as follows: If the enemy ship does not have an unobstructed path to the player ship, it enters a WANDER state where it wanders around the gameplay area checking periodically for a line of sight path to the player. Once there is a line-of-sight path to the player, the enemy ship will enter an APPROACH state, where it will attempt to get close enough to the player ship to attack it. Once the player is close enough, it enters the ATTACK state, where it fires on the player ship. If the player ship gets too close to the enemy ship, the enemy will FLEE, attempting to increase the distance between itself and the player ship.

Introducing steering behaviors

Steering behaviors are a force-based approach to navigation toward, or away from, specific points while avoiding obstacles. It was originally discussed in a presentation by Craig Reynolds (the *Boids* guy) at the **Game Developer's Conference (GDC)** in 1999, and the original paper discussing steering behaviors can be found online at `https://www.red3d.com/cwr/steer/gdc99/`. Unlike pathfinding algorithms such as the A* or Dijkstra's algorithms, steering behaviors are tactical in nature. They involve a goal position and forces drawing the autonomous agent toward its goal, while simultaneously pushing the agent away from obstacles you would like it to avoid. In the case of our game, the enemy spaceship is our autonomous agent that will be using the steering behaviors. It will be in pursuit of the player spaceship while avoiding obstacles including asteroids, projectiles, and the star in the center of the gameplay area. We will be discussing several steering behaviors in detail in the next few sections.

The seek behavior

The **seek steering behavior** is a force that points the agent (the enemy ship) at the desired target and moves the agent in the direction of that target. This behavior attempts to hit a maximum velocity and reach its target in the minimum amount of time. The seek behavior assumes that the position it is seeking is static and is not subject to change over time. This diagram shows what the seek behavior looks like:

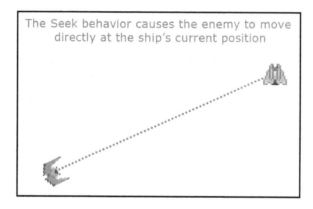

The seek behavior

The flee behavior

Flee is a steering behavior that is the opposite of seek behavior. This behavior takes a position or game object and attempts to get as far away from it as possible.

Fleeing is the behavior you demonstrate when chased by a bear. Your only goal is to put as much distance between you and the current location of that bear as you can. So, the next time a bear chases you, stop for a moment and think, *"Wow, my brain is currently implementing a version of the autonomous agent steering behavior known as* flee." Or you could keep running. The choice is yours. Take a look at the next diagram:

An artist's rendering of a bear eating the reader

You can program the flee behavior by negating the direction of the seek behavior. In other words, if the seek behavior produces a direction vector force of 1,1, the flee steering behavior would produce a direction vector force of -1,-1. This diagram depicts flee behavior:

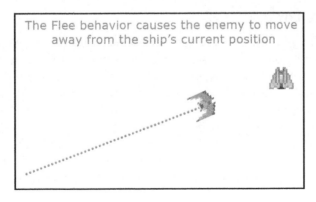

The flee behavior

The arrival behavior

The problem with the seek steering behavior is that it won't be satisfied until the agent reaches its target position. The other problem is that because it tries to reach that position at maximum speed, it will almost always overshoot it, resulting in oscillation around the desired destination. The **arrival steering behavior** allows the seek behavior to end gracefully by beginning to decelerate when it is in an **arrival range** of the target. As long as the target destination is within the desired range, the arrival behavior will reduce movement toward the seek position. The following diagram depicts the arrival behavior:

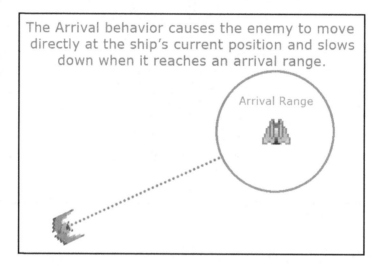

The arrival behavior

The pursuit behavior

We build the **pursuit behavior** on top of the seek behavior. Where the seek behavior is looking to reach a static point, the pursuit behavior assumes that the target is moving. Because our agent (the enemy ship) wishes to track down and destroy the player, which is usually moving, we will be using the pursuit steering behavior. The pursuit behavior looks at the velocity of the target. Instead of heading directly for the target's current position, it attempts to locate an intercept point where it predicts the target will be. Seek reminds me a little of a children's soccer team. All the kids run to where the ball is, not where the ball will be. Because of this, everyone on the soccer field runs as one large unit up and down the field. Someday, they will grow up and incorporate the pursuit steering behavior into their soccer strategy.

The next diagram depicts the pursuit behavior:

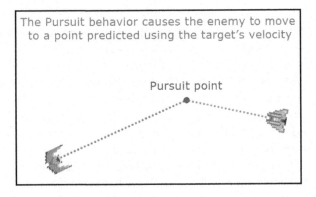

The pursuit behavior

The evade behavior

Evade is to *pursuit* as *flee* is to *seek*. Like pursuit, the **evade steering behavior** is attempting to determine where the obstacle you are avoiding will be, and moves as far away from that point as possible. In other words, it takes the same point we found in the pursuit behavior and then runs away from that point. The next diagram depicts the evade behavior:

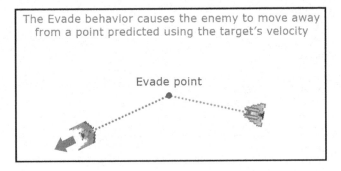

The evade behavior

Obstacle avoidance

Obstacle avoidance differs from the flee and evade behaviors in that an obstacle may potentially be in the path of our agent as it attempts to seek out a new location. Flee and evade cause us to try to move as far away as possible from the location of the object or the position we are fleeing, whereas obstacle avoidance is more about avoiding a collision with an obstacle on the way to a target. In the case of our game, obstacles to be avoided include asteroids, projectiles, and the star in the center of the game screen. Obstacle avoidance usually involves only seeking to avoid the most threatening (nearest) obstacle. Our agent has a given lookahead distance that looks in the direction it is moving. If a line between its current position and the maximum lookahead in the direction it is moving collides with an object, obstacle avoidance requires we adjust our direction. The area we avoid should be larger than the collision detection area for the obstacle to give us a buffer to avoid, especially because the asteroids and projectiles are moving in the game.

The next diagram depicts obstacle avoidance:

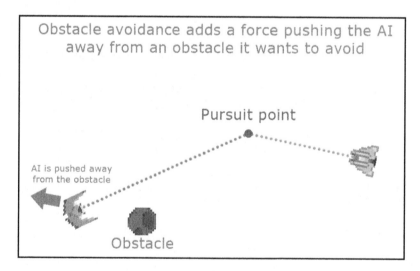

Obstacle avoidance

The wander behavior

Wander is a state in which the agent is moving somewhat randomly around the game screen. Causing the direction of the enemy spaceship to rotate every frame randomly would result in very erratic behavior. Instead, there should be a random number of milliseconds (200-2,000) where the spaceship maintains its current direction. When the ship has gone the random number of milliseconds, it should randomly choose to turn left or turn right, but should have a biased chance of turning in the same direction it did the previous time, with that bias decreasing each time it chooses the same direction after the initial choice. That will give the wandering behavior a little more consistency and appear a little less jittery.

See how the wander behavior chooses a point at random and moves toward it:

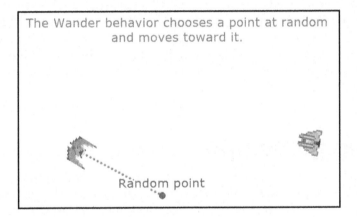

Demonstrating the wander behavior

Combining forces

Our earlier discussion of the reader using the flee behavior to escape a bear was oversimplified. It assumes you are fleeing that bear in a large open field. If you are running from a bear in the woods, you will both need to avoid running into the trees and get yourself as far away from that bear as you can. You have to blend these two activities seamlessly, or get eaten by that bear. If we want the enemy ship to pursue or flee from the player ship, and avoid obstacles at the same time, we are going to need to combine steering forces. The highest priority always has to be avoiding obstacles. If you run into a tree while fleeing that bear, he's still going to end up eating you. The general strategy our steering behavior will implement is finding a line-of-sight vector with the player ship. There are several opportunities we have to find a line of sight, because of the way our game level wraps around on itself. If that line of sight is longer than a chosen distance, we will wander until our distance is short enough that we can pursue the player while shooting at him. While we are wandering, we will want to combine any wandering force with forces that help the enemy ship avoid hitting asteroids or the star. Once we are in pursuit, we will want to continue to avoid obstacles. There will be a large arrival area where our ship will slow to a stop and fire in the direction of the player. Once the player closes in a specific range, our ship will flee.

Modifying game.hpp

Before we get too far into our new code, I want to make some quick changes to the game.hpp file to add some functionality we will be using later in this chapter. The first thing I want to add near the top of the game.hpp file is a few macros that will let us quickly convert from an angle in degrees to radians, and also from radians to degrees. I find myself doing this a lot when using SDL because SDL, for some reason, wants rotations in degrees, and every other library out there uses radians. So, let's go ahead and add the following two lines of code somewhere near the top of the game.hpp file:

```
#define DEG_TO_RAD(deg) ((float)deg/180.0)*3.14159
#define RAD_TO_DEG(rad) ((float)rad*180.0)/3.14159
```

We will be changing the size of our canvas from 320 x 200 to 800 x 600. To make this easy to switch later, let's go ahead and define a few macros we will use for the canvas width and height and put those somewhere near the top of the game.hpp file:

```
#define CANVAS_WIDTH 800
#define CANVAS_HEIGHT 600
```

The `rand()` function, used in C and C++ to get a random number, can only be used to return an integer. I will be adding a function to get a random number that falls between minimum and maximum floating-point values, so I will need to add an external reference to that function to our `game.hpp` file:

```
extern float get_random_float( float min, float max );
```

We are also starting to need circular references in our classes. The `FiniteStateMachine` class will need a reference to the `EnemyShip` class, and the `EnemyShip` class will need a reference to the `FiniteStateMachine` class. Unfortunately, we need to define one of these classes before the other. In the past, we have been able to define our classes in a specific order to avoid this problem, but now we will need a group of class declarations before any of our class definitions. That will allow the compiler to know that a class will be defined before the definition. Add this block of class declarations somewhere near the top of the `game.hpp` file:

```
class Ship;
class Particle;
class Emitter;
class Collider;
class Asteroid;
class Star;
class PlayerShip;
class EnemyShip;
class Projectile;
class ProjectilePool;
class FiniteStateMachine;
```

We will add an enumeration to keep track of our FSM states. As I mentioned earlier, there are four states in our FSM: APPROACH, ATTACK, FLEE, and WANDER. We will define these states in an enumeration called `FSM_STATE`:

```
enum FSM_STATE {
    APPROACH = 0,
    ATTACK = 1,
    FLEE = 2,
    WANDER = 3
};
```

One of the first classes we defined in `game.hpp` was the `Point` class. This class has *x* and *y* attributes and a few useful functions such as `Rotate`. We are going to need to greatly expand the use of this class and what it can do. So much so, that calling it *point* is no longer accurate. I would prefer to call this class *vector*, because we will be using it for vector mathematics from now on. The only problem I have with this name is that it might be confusing because we are using the `std::vector` to handle array-like data in our code. Because of this, I have decided we will call this class `Vector2D`. We will be greatly expanding the functionality of this class to include a function that will normalize the vector (that is, change its magnitude to 1). We need two functions that will determine the magnitude and the square magnitude of the vector. We will need a function that will project the vector on to another vector (to help us in the line-of-sight collision detection). We will need to be able to find the dot product of two vectors. We will also need to be able to find the rotation of a given vector. In addition to these new functions, we will overload operators on our vectors to allow us to add vectors, subtract vectors, and multiply and divide vectors by a scalar value.

Go ahead and delete the `Point` class definition, and replace that code with the new `Vector2D` class definition:

```
class Vector2D {
    public:
        float x;
        float y;

        Vector2D();
        Vector2D( float X, float Y );

        void Rotate( float radians );
        void Normalize();
        float MagSQ();
        float Magnitude();
        Vector2D Project( Vector2D &onto );
        float Dot(Vector2D &vec);
        float FindRotation();

        Vector2D operator=(const Vector2D &vec);
        Vector2D operator*(const float &scalar);
        void operator+=(const Vector2D &vec);
        void operator-=(const Vector2D &vec);
        void operator*=(const float &scalar);
        void operator/=(const float &scalar);
};
```

Our new collision detection will also need a `Range` class. A range represents a range of values between a minimum and a maximum. We can add two ranges together. We can find the overlap between the two ranges. We can extend a range by a given scalar value, or we can clamp a value to fall inside a given range. Here is what the new `Range` class definition looks like:

```
class Range {
    public:
        float min;
        float max;

        Range();
        Range( float min_val, float max_val );

        void operator+=(const Range& range);
        Range operator+(const Range& range);
        Range operator=(const Range& range);

        bool Overlap( Range &other );
        void Sort();
        void Extend( float ex );
        float Clamp( float value );
};
```

If you scroll down to the `Collider` class, we will be adding a few new functions and a few new attributes. I want to use our `Collider` class to support new steering behaviors. So, we will need some steering-specific attributes:

```
float m_SteeringRadius;
float m_SteeringRadiusSQ;
```

`m_SteeringRadius` is a new attribute that is a multiple of `m_Radius`. For steering purposes, we want to make sure that the sizes of the objects we want to avoid is smaller than the object's collision area. That creates an additional margin for our steering behavior that will help us to avoid these objects. The `m_SteeringRadiusSQ` attribute is the square of the steering radius. That will keep us from having to square the steering radius for collision checks over and over again.

We will also need to add the declarations of the following functions:

```
bool SteeringLineTest( Vector2D &p1, Vector2D &p2 );
bool SteeringRectTest( Vector2D &start_point, Vector2D &end_point );
void WrapPosition();
```

The `SteeringLineTest` and `SteeringRecTest` functions will differ from a real line and rectangle collision test. The steering rectangle test (`SterringRectTest`) will be used to limit the number of objects we must test for object avoidance purposes. We only want our AI to worry about objects that are within a box around the enemy ship that is 200 x 200 pixels. That will be useful if we have a large number of objects to test. To keep this test fast, we will be checking against the objects in that box as if they are points and will not take the object's radius into account. The `SteeringLineTest` function will be testing to see whether the steering radius of this collider hits a line defined by two points in the test.

In our game, we have not added a hit point system. A single collision with an asteroid or projectile results in instant death. That makes the game really short. To increase the game time, we will be adding shields to our ship. These shields will cause the player or enemy to be invulnerable for as long as the shields are active. While you use the shields, they will slowly turn from green to red, and at some point, they will stop working. That will all depend on the amount of time that you have used the shields during the given game to encourage the player to use the shields only when needed. Here is what the `Shield` class definition will look like:

```
class Shield : public Collider {
    public:
        bool m_Active;
        int m_ttl;
        int m_NextFrame;
        Uint32 m_CurrentFrame;
        Ship* m_Ship;
        SDL_Texture *m_SpriteTexture;

        SDL_Rect m_src = {.x = 0, .y = 0, .w = 32, .h = 32 };
        SDL_Rect m_dest = {.x = 0, .y = 0, .w = 32, .h = 32 };

        Shield( Ship* ship, const char* sprite_file );

        void Move();
        void Render();
        bool Activate();
        void Deactivate();
};
```

After the `Shield` class definition, we will need to add a class definition for our `Asteroid` class. Unlike the Atari game *Asteroids*, we cannot destroy these asteroids by shooting them. They are meant to be obstacles, but we will (for the moment) allow the asteroids to be destroyed if the player crashes into them with their shields active. They will move slowly around the game screen and provide obstacles for the player and the enemy AI to navigate during gameplay. Here is the code:

```
class Asteroid : public Collider {
    public:
        SDL_Texture *m_SpriteTexture;
        SDL_Rect m_src = { .x = 0, .y = 0, .w = 16, .h = 16 };
        SDL_Rect m_dest = { .x = 0, .y = 0, .w = 0, .h = 0 };

        bool m_Alive;
        Uint32 m_CurrentFrame = 0;
        int m_NextFrameTime;
        float m_Rotation;

        Vector2D m_Direction;
        Vector2D m_Velocity;

        Emitter* m_Explode;
        Emitter* m_Chunks;

        Asteroid( float x, float y,
                  float velocity,
                  float rotation );

        void Move();
        void Render();
        void Explode();
};
```

We will also be adding a big star to the center of the gameplay area. That is similar to the black hole that was in the center of the game *Spacewar!*, which we are loosely basing our game on. This star will eventually provide gravitational attraction to make the game a bit more challenging. We will be animating a star image and adding some solar flares using particle emitters:

```
class Star : public Collider {
    public:
        SDL_Texture *m_SpriteTexture;
        SDL_Rect m_src = { .x = 0, .y = 0, .w = 64, .h = 64 };
        SDL_Rect m_dest = { .x = 0, .y = 0, .w = 64, .h = 64 };

        std::vector<Emitter*> m_FlareList;
        Uint32 m_CurrentFrame = 0;
```

```
        int m_NextFrameTime;

        Star();

        void Move();
        void Render();
    };
```

Now we can make a few modifications to our `Ship` class. Here is what it will look like once we finish:

```
class Ship : public Collider {
    public:
        const float c_Acceleration = 10.0f;
        const float c_MaxVelocity = 50.0f;
        const int c_AliveTime = 2000;
        const Uint32 c_MinLaunchTime = 300;
        const int c_Width = 32;
        const int c_Height = 32;

        bool m_Accelerating = false;
        Uint32 m_LastLaunchTime;
        SDL_Texture *m_SpriteTexture;
        SDL_Rect src = {.x = 0, .y = 0, .w = 32, .h = 32 };

        Emitter* m_Explode;
        Emitter* m_Exhaust;
        Shield* m_Shield;
        std::vector<Collider*> m_Colliders;

        bool m_Alive = true;
        Uint32 m_CurrentFrame = 0;
        int m_NextFrameTime;
        float m_Rotation;

        Vector2D m_Direction;
        Vector2D m_Velocity;

        void RotateLeft();
        void RotateRight();
        void Accelerate();
        void Decelerate();
        void CapVelocity();
        void Shoot();
        virtual void Move() = 0;
        Ship();
        void Render();
```

```
        bool CompoundHitTest( Collider* collider );
};
```

The first thing we will do is add the `m_Shield` attribute, which is a pointer to a `Shield` object:

```
Shield* m_Shield;
```

After that, we use separate variables for the *x* direction and *y* direction, as well as different variables for the *x* velocity and *y* velocity, like this:

```
double m_DX;    // x-direction variable
double m_DY;    // y-direction variable
double m_VX;    // x-velocity variable
double m_VY;    // y-velocity variable
```

Let's remove all of that code and swap it for some `Vector2D` objects, representing the direction vector and the velocity vector, like this:

```
Vector2D m_Direction;
Vector2D m_Velocity;
```

Finally, to prevent code duplication between our enemy ship and our player ship, we will add a `Shoot()` function that will fire a projectile from the ship:

```
void Shoot();
```

The next class we need to modify is our `EnemyShip` class. We need to add a string with the filename of our `Shield` sprite. We also need to remove our old `AIStub()` function and replace it with a pointer to our FSM. Here is what the new version of the `EnemyShip` class looks like:

```
class EnemyShip: public Ship {
    public:
        const char* c_SpriteFile = "/sprites/BirdOfAngerExp.png";
        const char* c_ShieldSpriteFile = "/sprites/shield-bird.png";
        const int c_AIStateTime = 2000;
        int m_AIStateTTL;
        FiniteStateMachine* m_FSM;

        EnemyShip();
        void Move();
};
```

A significant new class we will be adding is the `FiniteStateMachine` class. This class will be doing all of the AI's heavy lifting. Here is the class definition that you must add to `game.hpp`:

```
class FiniteStateMachine {
    public:
        const float c_AttackDistSq = 40000.0;
        const float c_FleeDistSq = 2500.0;
        const int c_MinRandomTurnMS = 100;
        const int c_RandTurnMS = 3000;
        const int c_ShieldDist = 20;
        const int c_AvoidDist = 80;
        const int c_StarAvoidDistSQ = 20000;
        const int c_ObstacleAvoidForce = 150;
        const int c_StarAvoidForce = 120;

        FSM_STATE m_CurrentState;
        EnemyShip* m_Ship;
        bool m_HasLOS;
        bool m_LastTurnLeft;
        int m_SameTurnPct;
        int m_NextTurnMS;
        int m_CheckCycle;
        float m_DesiredRotation;
        float m_PlayerDistSQ;

        FiniteStateMachine(EnemyShip* ship);

        void SeekState(Vector2D &seek_point);
        void FleeState(Vector2D &flee_point);
        void WanderState();
        void AttackState();
        void AvoidForce();
        bool ShieldCheck();
        bool LOSCheck();
        Vector2D PredictPosition();
        float GetPlayerDistSq();
        void Move();
};
```

At the top of this class definition are nine constants:

```
const float c_AttackDistSq = 40000.0;
const float c_FleeDistSq = 2500.0;
const int c_MinRandomTurnMS = 100;
const int c_RandTurnMS = 3000;
const int c_ShieldDist = 20;
const int c_AvoidDist = 80;
const int c_StarAvoidDistSQ = 20000;
const int c_ObstacleAvoidForce = 150;
const int c_StarAvoidForce = 120;
```

The first two constants, c_AttackDistSq and c_FleeDistSq, are the values used by the FSM to determine whether it will change states into either the ATTACK or FLEE states; c_MinRandomTurnMS and c_RandTurnMS are both constants used by the WANDER state to determine when the AI will next decide to change directions randomly. The c_ShieldDist constant is the distance at which an obstacle will cause the AI to turn on its shields. The c_AvoidDist constant gives us the range at which an AI makes corrective adjustments to avoid an object. The c_StarAvoidDistSQ function is the distance at which the AI will make course adjustments to avoid the star in the center of the play area. The c_ObstacleAvoidForce constant is a steering force added to the velocity of an object to help it avoid obstacles, and c_StarAvoidForce is a similar force used to avoid the star.

After the constants, we have a block of attributes that are used by the FSM to make state-based decisions:

```
FSM_STATE m_CurrentState;
EnemyShip* m_Ship;
bool m_HasLOS;
bool m_LastTurnLeft;
int m_SameTurnPct;
int m_NextTurnMS;
int m_CheckCycle;
float m_DesiredRotation;
float m_PlayerDistSQ;
```

The m_CurrentState attribute holds the current state of our FSM. The m_Ship attribute contains a pointer to the ship. Right now, this is always the single enemy ship that is in our game, but in the future, you may want to add multiple enemy ships. The m_HasLOS attribute is a boolean that keeps track of whether our ship currently has an unobstructed line of sight with the player. The m_LastTurnLeft attribute is a boolean that keeps track of the direction, in which the ship last turned while in the WANDER state. The m_SameTurnPct attribute is the percentage chance that the ship will continue turning in the same direction while in the WANDER state. The m_NextTurnMS attribute is the number of milliseconds a ship in the WANDER state will continue before making a directional heading change. The m_CheckCycle variable is used to break up the AI into performing different checks during different frame rendering cycles. If you have your AI do all the work between each frame render each time, you could potentially bog the system down. It is usually better practice to break the AI into multiple parts and only do part of the logic with each frame render. The m_DesiredRotation attribute is the desired heading of the AI, and, finally, m_PlayerDistSQ is the squared distance between the enemy ship and the player ship.

We need to modify the Projectile class to use a Vector2D to keep track of the velocity instead of two floating-point variables, m_VX and m_VY. Here is the new version of the Projectile class after the modifications:

```cpp
class Projectile: public Collider {
    public:
        const char* c_SpriteFile = "sprites/ProjectileExp.png";
        const int c_Width = 16;
        const int c_Height = 16;
        const double velocity = 6.0;
        const double alive_time = 2000;

        SDL_Texture *m_SpriteTexture;
        SDL_Rect src = {.x = 0, .y = 0, .w = 16, .h = 16 };

        Uint32 m_CurrentFrame = 0;
        int m_NextFrameTime;
        bool m_Active;
        float m_TTL;
        float m_VX;
        float m_VY;

        Projectile();
        void Move();
        void Render();
        void Launch(double x, double y, double dx, double dy);
};
```

At the end of the `game.hpp` file, we should add a few external references to our new list of asteroids, and the star that will be going in the center of the gameplay area:

```
extern std::vector<Asteroid*> asteroid_list;
extern Star* star;
```

Now that we have taken care of the modifications we need to make to our `game.hpp` file, let's get into the obstacles we are adding.

Adding obstacles to our game

Right now, we do not have anything in our game for an AI to steer around. We need to add some obstacles that can get in the way of our enemy ship. We want our enemy ship to do what it can to avoid these obstacles while attempting to approach and attack our player's spaceship. The first thing we will add is a big star right in the middle of our gameplay area. We can animate this star and add some nice particle effects for the star's corona. In the last section, we created the class definition of this star in the `game.hpp` file and it looked like this:

```
class Star : public Collider {
    public:
        SDL_Texture *m_SpriteTexture;
        SDL_Rect m_src = {.x = 0, .y = 0, .w = 64, .h = 64 };
        SDL_Rect m_dest = {.x = 0, .y = 0, .w = 64, .h = 64 };

        std::vector<Emitter*> m_FlareList;

        Uint32 m_CurrentFrame = 0;
        int m_NextFrameTime;

        Star();

        void Move();
        void Render();
};
```

We will need to create a new file called `star.cpp` to accompany this class definition. In it, we should define our constructor and the `Move` and `Render` functions. As with all of our CPP files, the first thing we do is include the `game.hpp` file:

```
#include "game.hpp"
```

After that, we have a few `#define` directives that we use to define the sprite files we will be using to render our star and the flare particle systems:

```
#define STAR_SPRITE_FILE "/sprites/rotating-star.png"
#define FLARE_FILE (char*)"/sprites/flare.png"
```

The constructor is fairly long, but a lot of it should look pretty familiar:

```
Star::Star() : Collider(32.0) {
    SDL_Surface *temp_surface = IMG_Load( STAR_SPRITE_FILE );

    if( !temp_surface ) {
        printf("failed to load image: %s\n", IMG_GetError() );
        return;
    }
    else {
        printf("success creating enemy ship surface\n");
    }
    m_SpriteTexture = SDL_CreateTextureFromSurface( renderer,
    temp_surface );

    if( !m_SpriteTexture ) {
        printf("failed to create texture: %s\n", IMG_GetError() );
        return;
    }
    else {
        printf("success creating enemy ship texture\n");
    }
    SDL_FreeSurface( temp_surface );

    m_Radius = 36;

    m_Position.x = CANVAS_WIDTH / 2;
    m_Position.y = CANVAS_HEIGHT / 2;

    m_dest.x = m_Position.x - m_Radius / 2;
    m_dest.y = m_Position.y - m_Radius / 2;

    m_FlareList.push_back(new
    Emitter(FLARE_FILE,100,160,220,1500,0.05,true,30,40, 1,
    m_Position.x+8, m_Position.y+8, 10,0.1, 0.2,0.5, 1.0,0xffffff,
    0xffffff, 0.1, 50,true, true, 4409, 1));

    m_FlareList.push_back(new
    Emitter(FLARE_FILE,100,220,280,1500,0.05,true,30,40, 1, m_Position.x+8,
    m_Position.y+8,10,0.1,0.2,0.5,1.0,0xffffff, 0xffffff, 0.0,
    50,true,true,3571, 1));
```

```
m_FlareList.push_back(new
Emitter(FLARE_FILE,100,280,360,1500,0.05,true,30,40, 1,
m_Position.x+8, m_Position.y+8, 10, 0.1, 0.2, 0.5, 1.0, 0xffffff,
0xffffff, 0.2, 50, true, true, 3989, 1));

m_FlareList.push_back(new
Emitter(FLARE_FILE,100,0,60,1500,0.05,true,30,40, 1, m_Position.x+8,
m_Position.y+8, 10, 0.1, 0.2, 0.5, 1.0, 0xffffff, 0xffffff, 0.1, 50,
true, true, 3371, 1));

m_FlareList.push_back(new
Emitter(FLARE_FILE,100,60,100,1500,0.05,true,30,40, 1, m_Position.x+8,
m_Position.y+8, 10, 0.1, 0.2, 0.5, 1.0, 0xffffff, 0xffffff, 0.3, 50,
true, true, 4637, 1));
}
```

This constructor starts by inheriting the Collider constructor passing it a radius of 32:

```
Star::Star() : Collider(32.0) {
```

It then creates a sprite texture to use when rendering the star. This part of the code should look pretty familiar:

```
SDL_Surface *temp_surface = IMG_Load( STAR_SPRITE_FILE );

if( !temp_surface ) {
    printf("failed to load image: %s\n", IMG_GetError() );
    return;
}
else {
    printf("success creating enemy ship surface\n");
}
m_SpriteTexture = SDL_CreateTextureFromSurface( renderer, temp_surface );
if( !m_SpriteTexture ) {
    printf("failed to create texture: %s\n", IMG_GetError() );
    return;
}
else {
    printf("success creating enemy ship texture\n");
}
SDL_FreeSurface( temp_surface );
```

After setting up the sprite texture, the constructor sets some of the attributes, including radius and position:

```
m_Radius = 36;
m_Position.x = CANVAS_WIDTH / 2;
m_Position.y = CANVAS_HEIGHT / 2;
m_dest.x = m_Position.x - m_Radius / 2;
m_dest.y = m_Position.y - m_Radius / 2;
```

Finally, it adds emitters to the `m_FlareList` vector. These will be some solar flare particle systems. I used the particle system configuration tool to come up with the values we are creating in these emitters. You can play with the values if you like, but I felt that these values created a nice-looking flare effect:

```
m_FlareList.push_back(new
Emitter(FLARE_FILE,100,160,220,1500,0.05,true,30,40, 1, m_Position.x+8,
m_Position.y+8, 10,0.1, 0.2,0.5, 1.0,0xffffff, 0xffffff, 0.1, 50,true,
true,4409, 1));

m_FlareList.push_back(new
Emitter(FLARE_FILE,100,220,280,1500,0.05,true,30,40, 1, m_Position.x+8,
m_Position.y+8,10,0.1,0.2,0.5,1.0,0xffffff, 0xffffff, 0.0,
50,true,true,3571, 1));

m_FlareList.push_back(new
Emitter(FLARE_FILE,100,280,360,1500,0.05,true,30,40, 1, m_Position.x+8,
m_Position.y+8, 10, 0.1, 0.2, 0.5, 1.0, 0xffffff, 0xffffff, 0.2, 50, true,
true, 3989, 1));

m_FlareList.push_back(new Emitter(FLARE_FILE,100,0,60,1500,0.05,true,30,40,
1, m_Position.x+8, m_Position.y+8, 10, 0.1, 0.2, 0.5, 1.0, 0xffffff,
0xffffff, 0.1, 50, true, true, 3371, 1));

m_FlareList.push_back(new
Emitter(FLARE_FILE,100,60,100,1500,0.05,true,30,40, 1, m_Position.x+8,
m_Position.y+8, 10, 0.1, 0.2, 0.5, 1.0, 0xffffff, 0xffffff, 0.3, 50, true,
true, 4637, 1));
```

The star's `Move` function is pretty simple. It cycles through the eight frames of the star's animation sequence:

```
void Star::Move() {
    m_NextFrameTime -= diff_time;
    if( m_NextFrameTime <= 0 ) {
        ++m_CurrentFrame;
        m_NextFrameTime = ms_per_frame;
        if( m_CurrentFrame >= 8 ) {
            m_CurrentFrame = 0;
        }
    }
}
```

The star's `Render` function is a little bit more complicated because it needs to loop over the flare emitters, and move them before it renders the star's sprite texture:

```
void Star::Render() {
    Emitter* flare;
    std::vector<Emitter*>::iterator it;

    for( it = m_FlareList.begin(); it != m_FlareList.end(); it++ ) {
        flare = *it;
        flare->Move();
    }
    m_src.x = m_dest.w * m_CurrentFrame;

    SDL_RenderCopy( renderer, m_SpriteTexture,
                    &m_src, &m_dest );
}
```

Next, we need to define the `asteroid.cpp` file. That will hold the function definitions for our `Asteroid` class. Here is our class definition for `Asteroid` in the `games.hpp` file:

```
class Asteroid : public Collider {
    public:
        SDL_Texture *m_SpriteTexture;
        SDL_Rect m_src = { .x = 0, .y = 0, .w = 16, .h = 16 };
        SDL_Rect m_dest = { .x = 0, .y = 0, .w = 0, .h = 0 };

        bool m_Alive;
        Uint32 m_CurrentFrame = 0;
        int m_NextFrameTime;
        float m_Rotation;
        Vector2D m_Direction;
        Vector2D m_Velocity;

        Emitter* m_Explode;
```

```
            Emitter* m_Chunks;

            Asteroid( float x, float y,
                        float velocity,
                        float rotation );

            void Move();
            void Render();
            void Explode();
    };
```

Inside our `asteroid.cpp` file, we will need to define the `Asteroid` constructor, the `Move` function, the `Render` function, and the `Explode` function. At the top of the `asteroid.cpp` file, we will need to #`include` the `game.hpp` file and define the location of our asteroid sprite file in the virtual filesystem. Here are what those first few lines of code look like:

```
#include "game.hpp"
#define ASTEROID_SPRITE_FILE (char*)"/sprites/asteroid.png"
```

The first function we will define is our constructor. Here is the constructor function in its entirety:

```
Asteroid::Asteroid( float x, float y,
                        float velocity,
                        float rotation ): Collider(8.0) {
    SDL_Surface *temp_surface = IMG_Load( ADSTEROID_SPRITE_FILE );

    if( !temp_surface ) {
        printf("failed to load image: %s\n", IMG_GetError() );
        return;
    }
    else {
        printf("success creating asteroid surface\n");
    }

    m_SpriteTexture = SDL_CreateTextureFromSurface( renderer, temp_surface
);

    if( !m_SpriteTexture ) {
        printf("failed to create texture: %s\n", IMG_GetError() );
        return;
    }
    else {
        printf("success creating asteroid texture\n");
    }
    SDL_FreeSurface( temp_surface );

    m_Explode = new Emitter((char*)"/sprites/Explode.png",
```

```
        100, 0, 360,      // int max_particles, float min_angle, float
        max_angle,
        1000, 0.3, false, // Uint32 particle_lifetime, float acceleration,
        bool alpha_fade,
        20.0, 40.0,       // float min_starting_velocity, float
        max_starting_velocity,
        10, 0, 0, 5,      // Uint32 emission_rate, int x_pos, int y_pos,
        float radius,
        1.0, 2.0,         // float min_start_scale, float max_start_scale,
        1.0, 2.0,         // float min_end_scale, float max_end_scale,
        0xffffff, 0xffffff,
        0.01, 10,         // float burst_time_pct, Uint32 burst_particles,
        false, false,     // bool loop, bool align_rotation,
        800, 8 );         // Uint32 emit_time_ms, Uint32 animation_frames
m_Explode->m_parent_rotation_ptr = &m_Rotation;
m_Explode->m_parent_x_ptr = &(m_Position.x);
m_Explode->m_parent_y_ptr = &(m_Position.y);
m_Explode->m_active = false;


m_Chunks = new Emitter((char*)"/sprites/small-asteroid.png",
        40, 0, 360, // int max_particles, float min_angle, float
        max_angle,
        1000, 0.05, false, // Uint32 particle_lifetime, float
        acceleration,
        bool alpha_fade,
        80.0, 150.0, // float min_starting_velocity, float
        max_starting_velocity,
        5, 0, 0, 10, // Uint32 emission_rate, int x_pos, int y_pos,
        float radius,
        2.0, 2.0, // float min_start_scale, float max_start_scale,
        0.25, 0.5, // float min_end_scale, float max_end_scale,
        0xffffff, 0xffffff,
        0.1, 10, // float burst_time_pct, Uint32 burst_particles,
        false, true, // bool loop, bool align_rotation,
        1000, 8 ); // Uint32 emit_time_ms, Uint32 animation_frames

m_Chunks->m_parent_rotation_ptr = &m_Rotation;
m_Chunks->m_parent_x_ptr = &m_Position.x;
m_Chunks->m_parent_y_ptr = &m_Position.
m_Chunks->m_active = false;

m_Position.x = x;
m_Position.y = y;

Vector2D direction;
direction.x = 1;
direction.Rotate( rotation );
```

```
        m_Direction = direction;
        m_Velocity = m_Direction * velocity;

        m_dest.h = m_src.h = m_dest.w = m_src.w = 16;

        m_Rotation = rotation;
        m_Alive = true;
        m_CurrentFrame = 0;
        m_NextFrameTime = ms_per_frame;
    }
```

The definition of the constructor calls the parent constructor in the Collider class, passing in a radius for the Collider of 8.0:

```
Asteroid::Asteroid( float x, float y,
                    float velocity,
                    float rotation ): Collider(8.0) {
```

After that, the constructor loads and initializes the sprite texture using SDL, a process we should all be pretty familiar with by now:

```
SDL_Surface *temp_surface = IMG_Load( ADSTEROID_SPRITE_FILE );

if( !temp_surface ) {
    printf("failed to load image: %s\n", IMG_GetError() );
    return;
}
else {
    printf("success creating asteroid surface\n");
}

m_SpriteTexture = SDL_CreateTextureFromSurface( renderer, temp_surface );

if( !m_SpriteTexture ) {
    printf("failed to create texture: %s\n", IMG_GetError() );
    return;
}
else {
    printf("success creating asteroid texture\n");
}

SDL_FreeSurface( temp_surface );
```

We then define our explosion emitter. This emitter will be activated if our asteroid is destroyed:

```
m_Explode = new Emitter((char*)"/sprites/Explode.png",
    100, 0, 360, // int max_particles, float min_angle, float max_angle,
    1000, 0.3, false, // Uint32 particle_lifetime, float acceleration,
    bool alpha_fade,
    20.0, 40.0, // float min_starting_velocity, float
    max_starting_velocity,
    10, 0, 0, 5, // Uint32 emission_rate, int x_pos, int y_pos,
    float radius,
    1.0, 2.0, // float min_start_scale, float max_start_scale,
    1.0, 2.0, // float min_end_scale, float max_end_scale,
    0xffffff, 0xffffff,
    0.01, 10, // float burst_time_pct, Uint32 burst_particles,
    false, false, // bool loop, bool align_rotation,
    800, 8 ); // Uint32 emit_time_ms, Uint32 animation_frames

m_Explode->m_parent_rotation_ptr = &m_Rotation;
m_Explode->m_parent_x_ptr = &(m_Position.x);
m_Explode->m_parent_y_ptr = &(m_Position.y);
m_Explode->m_active = false;
```

After that, we create a second emitter that will shoot out little chunks of rock when our asteroid is destroyed. That is meant to compliment the m_Explosion emitter, and it will run at the same time as the asteroid explodes:

```
m_Chunks = new Emitter((char*)"/sprites/small-asteroid.png",
    40, 0, 360, // int max_particles, float min_angle, float max_angle,
    1000, 0.05, false, // Uint32 particle_lifetime, float acceleration,
    bool alpha_fade,
    80.0, 150.0, // float min_starting_velocity, float
    max_starting_velocity,
    5, 0, 0, 10, // Uint32 emission_rate, int x_pos, int y_pos,
    float radius,
    2.0, 2.0, // float min_start_scale, float max_start_scale,
    0.25, 0.5, // float min_end_scale, float max_end_scale,
    0xffffff, 0xffffff,
    0.1, 10, // float burst_time_pct, Uint32 burst_particles,
    false, true, // bool loop, bool align_rotation,
    1000, 8 ); // Uint32 emit_time_ms, Uint32 animation_frames

m_Chunks->m_parent_rotation_ptr = &m_Rotation;
m_Chunks->m_parent_x_ptr = &m_Position.x;
m_Chunks->m_parent_y_ptr = &m_Position.y;
m_Chunks->m_active = false;
```

The last several lines set the starting values for our asteroid's attributes:

```
m_Position.x = x;
m_Position.y = y;

Vector2D direction;
direction.x = 1;
direction.Rotate( rotation );

m_Direction = direction;
m_Velocity = m_Direction * velocity;
m_dest.h = m_src.h = m_dest.w = m_src.w = 16;

m_Rotation = rotation;
m_Alive = true;
m_CurrentFrame = 0;
m_NextFrameTime = ms_per_frame;
```

The next function we will be defining is the `Move` function. Here is what it looks like:

```
void Asteroid::Move() {
m_NextFrameTime -= diff_time;
if( m_NextFrameTime <= 0 ) {
    m_NextFrameTime = ms_per_frame;
    m_CurrentFrame++;
    if( m_CurrentFrame >= 8 ) {
        m_CurrentFrame = 0;
    }
}
m_Position += m_Velocity * delta_time;
WrapPosition();
}
```

The first batch of code dealing with `m_NextFrameTime` and `m_CurrentFrame` simply alternates between the sprite frames based on the amount of time that has passed:

```
m_NextFrameTime -= diff_time;
if( m_NextFrameTime <= 0 ) {
    m_NextFrameTime = ms_per_frame;
    m_CurrentFrame++;

    if( m_CurrentFrame >= 8 ) {
        m_CurrentFrame = 0;
    }
}
```

After that, we update the position based on the time delta and current velocity:

```
m_Position += m_Velocity * delta_time;
```

Finally, the `WrapPosition` function is called. This function moves our asteroid back to the right side of the screen if it went off the screen to the left, and moves it to the top if it goes off the bottom. Whenever an asteroid moves off the screen in a given direction, its position will be wrapped around to the other side of the gameplay area.

After the `Move` function, we define the `Asteroid Render` function. The complete function is shown here:

```
void Asteroid::Render() {
    m_Explode->Move();
    m_Chunks->Move();
    if( m_Alive == false ) {
        return;
    }
    m_src.x = m_dest.w * m_CurrentFrame;
    m_dest.x = m_Position.x + m_Radius / 2;
    m_dest.y = m_Position.y + m_Radius / 2;
    SDL_RenderCopyEx( renderer, m_SpriteTexture,
                      &m_src, &m_dest,
                      RAD_TO_DEG(m_Rotation), NULL, SDL_FLIP_NONE );
}
```

The first two lines move the explosion emitter and the chunks emitter. If the asteroid has not been destroyed, these functions will not do anything. If the asteroid has been destroyed, the functions will run the particle emitter. These emitters do not loop, so when their emission time is up, they will stop:

```
m_Explode->Move();
m_Chunks->Move();
```

After that, we check to see whether the asteroid is alive, and if it is not, we exit this function. The reason we do this after moving our emitters is that we must continue to run the emitter after an asteroid is destroyed:

```
if( m_Alive == false ) {
    return;
}
```

The final thing we do in this function is to render our asteroid sprite texture, a process that should look pretty familiar by now:

```
m_src.x = m_dest.w * m_CurrentFrame;
m_dest.x = m_Position.x + m_Radius / 2;
m_dest.y = m_Position.y + m_Radius / 2;
SDL_RenderCopyEx( renderer, m_SpriteTexture,
                  &m_src, &m_dest,
                  RAD_TO_DEG(m_Rotation), NULL, SDL_FLIP_NONE );
```

The last function in our `asteroid.cpp` file is the `Explode` function. This function will run when an asteroid is destroyed. The function will run our two emitters, which were designed to create an explosion effect. It will also set the asteroid's alive flag to `false`. Here is the code:

```
void Asteroid::Explode() {
    m_Explode->Run();
    m_Chunks->Run();
    m_Alive = false;
}
```

Now that we have defined our game obstacles, let's look into what it will take to create some shields for our spaceships.

Adding force fields

Currently, in our game, our spaceships are destroyed with a single collision. This ends up creating a game that is over very quickly. It would be nice to have a force field to prevent the ship's destruction when a collision is about to occur. This will also give our AI something else it can do in its bag of tricks. When the shields are up, there will be a little force-field animation surrounding the spaceship that is using it. There is a time limit to shield use. That will prevent the player or the AI from keeping the shield up for the entire game. While the shield is active, the color of the shields will transition from green to red. The closer the color gets to red, the closer the shields are to running out of power. Every time the shields get hit, the player or AI's shields will have additional time taken off them. We have already created the class definition inside of the `game.hpp` file. Here is what it looks like:

```
class Shield : public Collider {
    public:
        bool m_Active;
        int m_ttl;
        int m_NextFrame;
        Uint32 m_CurrentFrame;
```

```
            Ship* m_Ship;
            SDL_Texture *m_SpriteTexture;

            SDL_Rect m_src = { .x = 0,  .y = 0,  .w = 32,  .h = 32 };
            SDL_Rect m_dest = { .x = 0,  .y = 0,  .w = 32,  .h = 32 };

            Shield( Ship* ship, const char* sprite_file );

            void Move();
            void Render();
            bool Activate();
            void Deactivate();
    };
```

To accompany this class definition, we will need a shield.cpp file, where we can define all of the functions used by this class. The first function we will define inside our shield.cpp file is the Shield constructor function:

```
Shield::Shield( Ship* ship, const char* sprite_string ) : Collider(12.0) {
    m_Active = false;
    m_ttl = 25500;
    m_Ship = ship;
    m_CurrentFrame = 0;
    m_NextFrame = ms_per_frame;
    SDL_Surface *temp_surface = IMG_Load( sprite_string );

    if( !temp_surface ) {
        printf("failed to load image: %s\n", IMG_GetError() );
        return;
    }

    m_SpriteTexture = SDL_CreateTextureFromSurface( renderer,
    temp_surface );

    if( !m_SpriteTexture ) {
        printf("failed to create texture: %s\n", IMG_GetError() );
        return;
    }
    SDL_FreeSurface( temp_surface );
}
```

The `Shield` constructor function will call the `Collider` constructor function, with a radius of `12.0`. That is a larger radius than the ship's radius. We will want this `Collider` to be hit instead of the ship, if the shields are active. The first block of code in this constructor function sets the starting values for the attributes of this class:

```
m_Active = false;
m_ttl = 25500;
m_Ship = ship;
m_CurrentFrame = 0;
m_NextFrame = ms_per_frame;
```

Notice that we set `m_ttl` to `25500`. That is the time you can use the shield in milliseconds. That amounts to 25.5 seconds. I wanted it to be a multiple of 255, so that the green color will transition from 255 to 0, based on the time left.

Conversely, the red color will transition from 0 to 255, also based on the time left. After that, we create the shield's sprite texture in the standard way:

```
SDL_Surface *temp_surface = IMG_Load( sprite_string );

if( !temp_surface ) {
    printf("failed to load image: %s\n", IMG_GetError() );
    return;
}

m_SpriteTexture = SDL_CreateTextureFromSurface( renderer, temp_surface );

if( !m_SpriteTexture ) {
    printf("failed to create texture: %s\n", IMG_GetError() );
return;
}

SDL_FreeSurface( temp_surface );
```

After the constructor, we need to define our `Move` function:

```
void Shield::Move() {
    if( m_Active ) {
        m_NextFrame -= diff_time;
        m_ttl -= diff_time;

        if( m_NextFrame <= 0 ) {
            m_NextFrame = ms_per_frame;
            m_CurrentFrame++;

            if( m_CurrentFrame >= 6 ) {
                m_CurrentFrame = 0;
```

```
        }
    }
    if( m_ttl <= 0 ) {
        m_Active = false;
    }
  }
}
```

If the shield is not active, this function does not do anything. If it is active, the m_ttl parameter is decremented based on the number of milliseconds passed since the last frame. Then, we increment the current frame if the proper number of milliseconds has elapsed. If the shield's time left drops below 0, the shields are deactivated.

After we have defined our Move function, we will define our Render function:

```
void Shield::Render() {
    if( m_Active ) {
        int color_green = m_ttl / 100 + 1;
        int color_red = 255 - color_green;
        m_src.x = m_CurrentFrame * m_dest.w;
        m_dest.x = m_Ship->m_Position.x;
        m_dest.y = m_Ship->m_Position.y;

        SDL_SetTextureColorMod(m_SpriteTexture,
                        color_red,
                        color_green,
                        0 );

        SDL_RenderCopyEx( renderer, m_SpriteTexture,
                        &m_src, &m_dest,
                        RAD_TO_DEG(m_Ship->m_Rotation),
                        NULL, SDL_FLIP_NONE );
    }
}
```

Like the Move function, the Render function does not do anything if the active flag is false. We calculate the colors based on the time left using the following formulas:

```
int color_green = m_ttl / 100 + 1;
int color_red = 255 - color_green;
```

That will smoothly transition the color of our shields from green to red. We use a call to `SDL_SetTextureColorMod` to set the sprite texture's color:

```
SDL_SetTextureColorMod(m_SpriteTexture,
                       color_red,
                       color_green,
                       0 );
```

Everything else in the `Shield::Render` function is pretty standard and should look very familiar by now.

More collision detection

Let's take a look at the modifications we need to make to our `Collider` class. As we discussed earlier, our AI will be implementing steering behaviors. These steering behaviors will require some new attributes and functions in our `Collider` class. Here is what the new `Collider` class is going to look like:

```
class Collider {
    public:
        float* m_ParentRotation;
        float* m_ParentX;
        float* m_ParentY;
        Vector2D m_TempPoint;
        bool CCHitTest( Collider* collider );

        Vector2D m_Position;
        float m_Radius;
        float m_SteeringRadius;
        float m_SteeringRadiusSQ;

        void SetParentInformation( float* rotation, float* x, float* y );
        Collider(float radius);
        bool HitTest( Collider *collider );
        bool SteeringLineTest( Vector2D &p1, Vector2D &p2 );
        bool SteeringRectTest( Vector2D &start_point, Vector2D &end_point
        );
        void WrapPosition();
};
```

We have three new functions, two of them are for steering. One of the functions, WrapPosition(), will be used to wrap objects moving off the screen in one direction so that they reappear on the other side of the game screen. Let's open up collider.cpp and take a look. The first thing we need to change is the constructor function. Here is what the new version of the constructor looks like:

```
Collider::Collider(float radius) {
    m_ParentRotation = NULL;
    m_ParentX = NULL;
    m_ParentY = NULL;

    m_Radius = radius;
    m_SteeringRadius = m_Radius * 1.5;
    m_SteeringRadiusSQ = m_SteeringRadius * m_SteeringRadius;
}
```

The last two lines are the only modifications. You will notice that we set the m_SteeringRadius attribute to 1.5 times the m_Radius value. This additional buffer space is to prevent our enemy ship from getting too close to the asteroids, especially if they are moving. This factor effectively makes the steering behavior more wary of collisions with asteroids. The multiple of 1.5 was chosen somewhat arbitrarily because it worked well when I tested it. If you would like your AI to be less concerned with asteroid collisions and more likely to pursue the player by putting itself in danger, you could reduce this value, maybe to something like 1.1. You could also increase this value to make the AI even more wary of asteroids. Setting the value too high will result in an AI that is too timid. Setting it too low will have it pursue the player under almost any circumstance, mimicking the infamous words of Admiral David Farragut during the Battle of Mobile Bay, "*Damn the torpedoes—full speed ahead!*"

Next, we will need to add the new function, SteeringLineText, to collider.cpp. This new function will do circle-line collision detection between a line connecting our enemy ship and our player, and detect all of the asteroids and projectiles our ship could hit along that path. It is a line-of-sight test to determine whether there is a clear path to the player from our position. Circle-line collision detection is somewhat complicated, compared to circle-circle or rectangle-rectangle collision detection. I borrowed heavily from a solution I created on embed.com at the following address: https://www.embed.com/typescript-games/multiple-type-collision-detection.html.

Circle-line collision detection

The first step in determining whether a circle and line collide is the simplest: Check whether either of the endpoints of your line falls within the circle's radius. That is done by a simple distance check using the Pythagorean theorem. If the distance between one of the points and the center of our circle is less than the radius, the line is inside the circle. Here is a diagram of a point falling inside the radius of the circle:

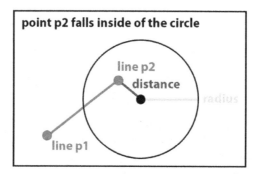

The line's p2 point falls inside the circle radius

If either point falls within the radius of the circle, we know that the line and the circle collide. If neither point falls within the radius of the circle, we are not done. Then what we will need to do is find the closest point on the line to the center of the circle. Let me digress for a moment to get a little more technical. Technically, all lines are infinite. When we have two points and draw a "line" in between those points, it is a line segment. To find the closest point between a line and our circle, we are going to need to talk about something called **vector projection**.

Vector projection

Vector projection is a little bit complicated. If you project a given vector b on to vector *a*, you get a scalar multiple of vector *a* (we will call this scalar multiple *c*), where you can add a vector perpendicular to vector *ca* to get vector *b*.

The following diagram is an example of projecting vector *b* onto vector *a*:

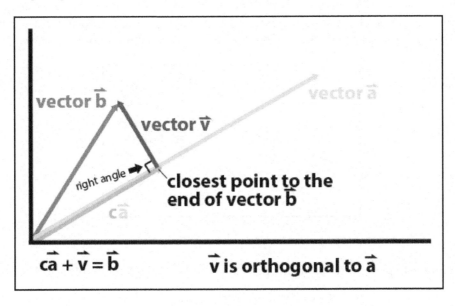

An example of projecting vector b onto vector a

Another way to look at this is that a projection of vector b on to vector a gives us the closest point to the end point of vector b that is on a line segment, as defined by any scalar multiple of vector a. You may be wondering what this has to do with detecting a collision between a circle and a line. Well, if we assume that vector b represents the position of the center point of our circle, we can figure out what the closest point on our line is to the center point of that circle. We then test for a collision between the point we found with our projection and the center of the circle. See how vector projection can be used to determine the closest point on a line to a circle in the following diagram:

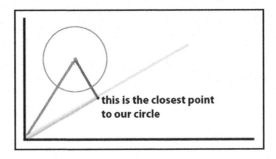

Notice that projecting the vector onto our line gives us the closest point on the line to the circle

There is another potential problem you have to look at. The projection onto vector a might give you a value for c (the scalar multiple) that is greater than 1. If this is the case, it might be that our line collides with the circle beyond our ending point. Because of this, we will also need to do some range checks to see whether we are past the end of our line:

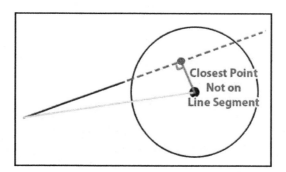

Projecting the circle's vector on to our line gives us the closest point that is passed the range of our line segment

Now that I have explained what vector projection is, let's take a look at the code:

```
bool Collider::SteeringLineTest( Vector2D &start, Vector2D &end ) {
    if( m_Active == false ) {
        return false;
    }
    Vector2D dist = start;
    dist -= m_Position;
    if( m_SteeringRadiusSQ > dist.MagSQ() ) {
        return true;
    }
    dist = end;
    dist -= m_Position;

    if( m_SteeringRadiusSQ > dist.MagSQ() ) {
        return true;
    }
    dist = end;
    dist -= start;

    Vector2D circle_vec = m_Position;
    circle_vec -= start;

    Vector2D near_point = circle_vec.Project( dist );
    near_point += start;

    Vector2D temp_vector = near_point;
    circle_vec += start;
```

```
    temp_vector -= circle_vec;

    Range x_range;
    x_range.min = start.x;
    x_range.max = end.x;
    x_range.Sort();
    Range y_range;
    y_range.min = start.y;
    y_range.max = end.y;
    y_range.Sort();

    if ((x_range.min <= near_point.x && near_point.x <= x_range.max &&
         y_range.min <= near_point.y && near_point.y <= y_range.max) ==
         false) {
        return false;
    }
    if( temp_vector.MagSQ() < m_SteeringRadiusSQ ) {
        return true;
    }
    return false;
}
```

As we discussed earlier, the first thing we do is test the start and end point distance to the location of this `Collider` object. If the distance squared is less than the steering radius squared for either of the points, we know that the line collides with our steering radius:

```
if( m_Active == false ) {
    return false;
}

Vector2D dist = start;
dist -= m_Position;

if( m_SteeringRadiusSQ > dist.MagSQ() ) {
    return true;
}

dist = end;
dist -= m_Position;
if( m_SteeringRadiusSQ > dist.MagSQ() ) {
    return true;
}
```

If neither point falls inside the circle, we will need to test against the projection. We will need to turn the line segment into a vector that goes through the origin. To do this, we will need to subtract the starting point from the ending point, and we will also need to adjust the position of the circle by the same amount:

```
dist = end;
dist -= start;

Vector2D circle_vec = m_Position;
circle_vec -= start;

Vector2D near_point = circle_vec.Project( dist );
near_point += start;

Vector2D temp_vector = near_point;
circle_vec += start;
temp_vector -= circle_vec;
```

We need to make sure that the point closest to the collider is still on the line segment. That can be done with a simple range test against the starting and ending x and y values. If both the x and y coordinates fall into our range, we know that the point must lie somewhere on the line segment. If it does not, we know that the line does not collide with the circle:

```
Range x_range;
x_range.min = start.x;
x_range.max = end.x;
x_range.Sort();

Range y_range;
y_range.min = start.y;
y_range.max = end.y;
y_range.Sort();

if ((x_range.min <= near_point.x && near_point.x <= x_range.max &&
     y_range.min <= near_point.y && near_point.y <= y_range.max) == false)
{
    return false;
}
```

If we have not returned with a `false` value at this point, we know what the nearest point to the collider is on our line segment. Now we can test the distance from that point to our collider to see whether it is close enough to collide with our steering radius; if it is, we return `true`, and if it is not, we return `false`:

```
if( m_SteeringRadiusSQ > dist.MagSQ() ) {
    return true;
```

```
    }
    return false;
```

The Vector2D class

I mentioned earlier that we needed to scrap our old `Point` class in favor of something that has a lot more functionality. The new `Vector2D` class will add several new functions to the `Point` class we were using earlier. Let's take another look at the function definition we have inside our `game.hpp` file:

```cpp
class Vector2D {
    public:
        float x;
        float y;

        Vector2D();
        Vector2D( float X, float Y );

        void Rotate( float radians );
        void Normalize();
        float MagSQ();
        float Magnitude();

        Vector2D Project( Vector2D &onto );
        float Dot(Vector2D &vec);
        float FindAngle();

        Vector2D operator=(const Vector2D &vec);
        Vector2D operator*(const float &scalar);
        void operator+=(const Vector2D &vec);
        void operator-=(const Vector2D &vec);
        void operator*=(const float &scalar);
        void operator/=(const float &scalar);
};
```

Unlike points, vectors have a magnitude. Because it is faster to calculate, we will also add a squared magnitude, `MagSQ`, function. Vectors can be normalized, which means they can be modified to have a magnitude of 1. We discussed vector projection earlier, and we have created a `Project` function to allow us to do that. Finding the dot product of two vectors is a very useful operation in games. The dot product of two normalized vectors is a scalar value that ranges between 1 and -1, depending on the angle between those two vectors. The value is 1 if the vectors point in the same direction, -1 if they point in the opposite direction, and 0 if the two vectors are perpendicular to each other.

The dot product of two normalized vectors is the same as the cosine of the angle between those two normalized vectors. Getting the dot product of any two vectors, *a* and *b*, gives you the (magnitude of *a*) * (magnitude of *b*) * cosine (angle between *a* and *b*). The reason we normalize these vectors first is to set the magnitude of *a* and the magnitude of *b* to 1, which causes our normalized dot product to return the cosine of the angle between vectors *a* and *b*.

We will also add a `FindAngle` function that will tell us the directional angle of this function. We will overload many operators to allow for easier vector manipulation.

Let's take a look at `vector.cpp` in its entirety:

```
#include "game.hpp"

Vector2D::Vector2D( float X, float Y ) {
    x = X;
    y = Y;
}
Vector2D::Vector2D() {
    y = x = 0.0;
}
Vector2D Vector2D::operator=(const Vector2D& p) {
    x = p.x;
    y = p.y;
    return *this;
}
void Vector2D::operator+=(const Vector2D& p) {
    x += p.x;
    y += p.y;
}
void Vector2D::operator-=(const Vector2D& p) {
    x -= p.x;
    y -= p.y;
}
void Vector2D::operator*=(const float& scalar) {
    x *= scalar;
    y *= scalar;
}
void Vector2D::operator/=(const float& scalar) {
    x /= scalar;
    y /= scalar;
}
Vector2D Vector2D::operator*(const float& scalar) {
    Vector2D vec = *this;
    vec *= scalar;
    return vec;
```

```
}
void Vector2D::Rotate( float radians ) {
    float sine = sin(radians);
    float cosine = cos(radians);
    float rx = x * cosine - y * sine;
    float ry = x * sine + y * cosine;
    x = rx;
    y = ry;
}
void Vector2D::Normalize() {
    float mag = Magnitude();
    x /= mag;
    y /= mag;
}
Vector2D Vector2D::Project(Vector2D &onto) {
    Vector2D proj = *this;
    float proj_dot_onto = proj.Dot(onto);
    proj *= proj_dot_onto;
    return proj;
}
float Vector2D::Dot(Vector2D &vec) {
    Vector2D this_norm;
    this_norm = *this;
    this_norm.Normalize();
    Vector2D vec_norm;
    vec_norm = vec;
    vec_norm.Normalize();

    return this_norm.x * vec_norm.x + this_norm.y * vec_norm.y;
}
float Vector2D::FindAngle() {
    if( x == 0.0 && y == 0.0 ) {
        return 0.0;
    }
    Vector2D this_norm;
    this_norm = *this;
    this_norm.Normalize();
    return atan2( this_norm.y, this_norm.x ) + PI / 2;
}
float Vector2D::MagSQ() {
    return x * x + y * y;
}
float Vector2D::Magnitude() {
    return sqrt( MagSQ() );
}
```

The first two functions are constructors, and they are essentially the same as the constructors that were in the `Point` class:

```
Vector2D::Vector2D( float X, float Y ) {
    x = X;
    y = Y;
}
Vector2D::Vector2D() {
    y = x = 0.0;
}
```

After that, we have our overloaded operators. That allows us to add, subtract, multiply, and divide vectors easily:

```
Vector2D Vector2D::operator=(const Vector2D& p) {
    x = p.x;
    y = p.y;
    return *this;
}
void Vector2D::operator+=(const Vector2D& p) {
    x += p.x;
    y += p.y;
}
void Vector2D::operator-=(const Vector2D& p) {
    x -= p.x;
    y -= p.y;
}
void Vector2D::operator*=(const float& scalar) {
    x *= scalar;
    y *= scalar;
}
void Vector2D::operator/=(const float& scalar) {
    x /= scalar;
    y /= scalar;
}
Vector2D Vector2D::operator*(const float& scalar) {
    Vector2D vec = *this;
    vec *= scalar;
    return vec;
}
```

The `Rotate` function is one of the few functions that existed on the `Point` class. It has not changed from the `Point` class version:

```
void Vector2D::Rotate( float radians ) {
    float sine = sin(radians);
    float cosine = cos(radians);
    float rx = x * cosine - y * sine;
```

```
        float ry = x * sine + y * cosine;
        x = rx;
        y = ry;
    }
```

The `Normalize` function changes the magnitude of the vector to a value of 1. It does this by determining the magnitude of the vector and dividing the *x* and *y* value by that magnitude:

```
void Vector2D::Normalize() {
    float mag = Magnitude();
    x /= mag;
    y /= mag;
}
```

The `Project` function uses the dot product of the normalized angles and multiplies that scalar value by the vector to determine the new projected vector:

```
Vector2D Vector2D::Project(Vector2D &onto) {
    Vector2D proj = *this;
    float proj_dot_onto = proj.Dot(onto);
    proj *= proj_dot_onto;
    return proj;
}
```

Our `Dot` product function is actually a dot product of the normalized vectors. That gives us information on the angle between the two vectors. We are normalizing first because we are using this dot product only in our vector projection:

```
float Vector2D::Dot(Vector2D &vec) {
    Vector2D this_norm;
    this_norm = *this;
    this_norm.Normalize();

    Vector2D vec_norm;
    vec_norm = vec;
    vec_norm.Normalize();

    return this_norm.x * vec_norm.x + this_norm.y * vec_norm.y;
}
```

The `FindAngle` function uses the inverse tangent to find the angle in radians between two vectors:

```
float Vector2D::FindAngle() {
    if( x == 0.0 && y == 0.0 ) {
        return 0.0;
```

```
        }
        Vector2D this_norm;
        this_norm = *this;
        this_norm.Normalize();
        return atan2( this_norm.y, this_norm.x ) + PI / 2;
}
```

The final two functions get the vector's magnitude and squared magnitude:

```
float Vector2D::MagSQ() {
        return x * x + y * y;
}

float Vector2D::Magnitude() {
        return sqrt( MagSQ() );
}
```

Writing an FSM

Now that we have the tools we need in our `Collider` and `Vector2D` classes, we can build our FSM. The `FiniteStateMachine` class will manage our AI. Our FSM will have four states: SEEK, FLEE, ATTACK, and WANDER. It will implement steering behaviors and add an avoid force whenever it is trying to navigate through obstacles such as asteroids. The AI will also need to check whether the enemy ship should raise or lower its shields. Let's take a second look at the definition of the `FiniteStateMachine` class as we have defined it in our `game.hpp` file:

```
class FiniteStateMachine {
    public:
        const float c_AttackDistSq = 40000.0;
        const float c_FleeDistSq = 2500.0;
        const int c_MinRandomTurnMS = 100;
        const int c_RandTurnMS = 3000;
        const int c_ShieldDist = 20;
        const int c_AvoidDist = 80;
        const int c_StarAvoidDistSQ = 20000;
        const int c_ObstacleAvoidForce = 150;
        const int c_StarAvoidForce = 120;

        FSM_STATE m_CurrentState;
        EnemyShip* m_Ship;

        bool m_HasLOS;
        bool m_LastTurnLeft;
        int m_SameTurnPct;
```

```
    int m_NextTurnMS;
    int m_CheckCycle;
    float m_DesiredRotation;
    float m_PlayerDistSQ;

    FiniteStateMachine(EnemyShip* ship);

    void SeekState(Vector2D &seek_point);
    void FleeState(Vector2D &flee_point);
    void WanderState();
    void AttackState();

    void AvoidForce();
    bool ShieldCheck();
    bool LOSCheck();

    Vector2D PredictPosition();

    float GetPlayerDistSq();
    void Move();
};
```

Now let's spend a little time going through all of the functions that we will define in our `finite_state_machine.cpp` file. The constructor function at the beginning of this file does not do anything complicated. It does some basic initialization:

```
FiniteStateMachine::FiniteStateMachine(EnemyShip* ship) {
    m_Ship = ship;
    m_CurrentState = APPROACH;
    m_HasLOS = false;
    m_DesiredRotation = 0.0;
    m_CheckCycle = 0;
    m_PlayerDistSQ = 0;
}
```

After the constructor, we have four state functions defined: `SeekState`, `FleeState`, `WanderState`, and `AttackState`. The first of these four states causes our enemy ship to seek out a specific point in our gameplay area. That point will either be calculated in our `Move` function or inside our `AttackState` function. Here is what the code looks like:

```
void FiniteStateMachine::SeekState(Vector2D &seek_point) {
    Vector2D direction = seek_point;
    direction -= m_Ship->m_Position;
    m_DesiredRotation = direction.FindAngle();
    float rotate_direction = m_Ship->m_Rotation - m_DesiredRotation;

    if( rotate_direction > PI ) {
```

```
                rotate_direction -= 2 * PI;
        }
        else if( rotate_direction < -PI ) {
                rotate_direction += 2 * PI;
        }

        if( rotate_direction < -0.05 ) {
                m_Ship->RotateRight ();
                m_Ship->RotateRight ();
        }
        else if( rotate_direction > 0.05 ) {
                m_Ship->RotateLeft ();
                m_Ship->RotateLeft ();
        }
        m_Ship->Accelerate ();
        m_Ship->Accelerate ();
        m_Ship->Accelerate ();
        m_Ship->Accelerate ();
}
```

The first thing the function does is determine what angle the ship should point at to seek out the destination point:

```
Vector2D direction = seek_point;
direction -= m_Ship->m_Position;
m_DesiredRotation = direction.FindAngle ();
float rotate_direction = m_Ship->m_Rotation - m_DesiredRotation;

if( rotate_direction > PI ) {
    rotate_direction -= 2 * PI;
}
else if( rotate_direction < -PI ) {
    rotate_direction += 2 * PI;
}
```

Based on the `rotate_direction` value we calculated, the AI makes a decision to rotate the ship left or right:

```
if( rotate_direction < -0.05 ) {
    m_Ship->RotateRight ();
    m_Ship->RotateRight ();
}
else if( rotate_direction > 0.05 ) {
    m_Ship->RotateLeft ();
    m_Ship->RotateLeft ();
}
```

You may be wondering why there are two calls to `RotateRight()` and `RotateLeft()`. Well, that is a bit of AI cheating. I want the enemy spaceship to rotate and accelerate faster than the player, so we call the `Rotate` functions twice and the `Accelerate` function four times. The amount of cheating you do depends on personal preference, and how obvious your cheating is. Generally speaking, you want your AI to be challenging, but not too challenging. An AI that is obviously cheating will upset the player. Above all, if you cheat, make sure you don't get caught!

After the rotations, we end the function with the four calls to `Accelerate()`:

```
m_Ship->Accelerate();
m_Ship->Accelerate();
m_Ship->Accelerate();
m_Ship->Accelerate();
```

After our `SEEK` state, we need to define the function we run when we are in the `FLEE` state. The `FLEE` state is the opposite of the `SEEK` state in that the AI is trying to get as far away from the flee position as possible. We do a little less cheating in our version of the `FLEE` state, but this can be changed based on personal taste:

```
void FiniteStateMachine::FleeState(Vector2D& flee_point) {
    Vector2D direction = flee_point;
    direction -= m_Ship->m_Position;
    m_DesiredRotation = direction.FindAngle();
    float rotate_direction = m_DesiredRotation - m_Ship->m_Rotation;
    rotate_direction -= PI;

    if( rotate_direction > 0 ) {
        m_Ship->RotateRight();
    }
    else {
        m_Ship->RotateLeft();
    }
    m_Ship->Accelerate();
    m_Ship->Accelerate();
}
```

The `WANDER` state is a state in which the AI wanders around the gameplay area. This state runs if the enemy ship does not have an unobstructed line of sight to the player ship. The AI will wander around the gameplay area looking for an unobstructed path to the player. In the `WANDER` state, the ship is more likely to continue turning in the direction it turned the last time than choose a new direction. Here is the code:

```
void FiniteStateMachine::WanderState() {
    m_NextTurnMS -= delta_time;
    if( m_NextTurnMS <= 0 ) {
```

```
        bool same_turn = ( m_SameTurnPct >= rand() % 100 );
        m_NextTurnMS = c_MinRandomTurnMS + rand() % c_RandTurnMS;

        if( m_LastTurnLeft ) {
            if( same_turn ) {
                m_SameTurnPct -= 10;
                m_Ship->RotateLeft();
            }
            else {
                m_SameTurnPct = 80;
                m_Ship->RotateRight();
            }
        }
        else {
            if( same_turn ) {
                m_SameTurnPct -= 10;
                m_Ship->RotateRight();
            }
            else {
                m_SameTurnPct = 80;
                m_Ship->RotateLeft();
            }
        }
    }
    m_Ship->Accelerate();
}
```

The `Attack` state calls the `Seek` state while shooting at the player:

```
void FiniteStateMachine::AttackState() {
    Vector2D prediction = PredictPosition();
    SeekState( prediction );
    m_Ship->Shoot();
}
```

To know where to go when we seek and attack, we could point our enemy ship directly at the player's current location. It would be better if we could predict where the player's ship will be by the time we get there. We have a `PredictPosition` function that will predict where the player will be, using its current velocity. Here is our `PredictPosition` function:

```
Vector2D FiniteStateMachine::PredictPosition() {
    Vector2D dist = player->m_Position;
    dist -= m_Ship->m_Position;
    float mag = dist.Magnitude();
    Vector2D dir = player->m_Velocity;

    if( dir.MagSQ() > 0 ) {
```

```
        dir.Normalize();
    }
    dir *= (mag / 10);
    Vector2D prediction = player->m_Position;
    prediction += dir;
    return prediction;
}
```

That is only a guess, and it is imperfect. We use this function to predict both where we will seek and where we will attack. If we were seeking the player, we would probably want to predict the distance the player will move, which will be about the same as the current distance between the enemy ship and the player ship. However, it is more important that we predict where our projectiles will be when we fire them. The projectiles move quite a bit faster than our ship, so we divide the distance between the enemy ship and the player ship by a factor of 10 to make our prediction. The projectiles do not actually move 10 times as fast, but, as with many of the constant values we choose for our AI, trial and error and what looks right trump actual data. Dropping the multiple to a factor of 5 will double the distance we will lead the player ship with each shot. Making the value 20 would cut that lead in half. A value of 10 is what looked right to me when I was testing the AI, but you can tweak this number to your taste. You could even add a random factor if you like.

The AvoidForce function

The AvoidForce function is also a bit of a cheat. Steering behaviors use an avoid force to prevent autonomous agents from colliding with obstacles. If the avoid force value is set too high, it will look as if the enemy ship is magically repelled from the obstacles. If it is too low, it will crash right into them. Our AvoidForce function will look for the closest obstacle to our enemy ship and will increase the velocity of the enemy ship to steer it around any obstacles. Here is what that function looks like:

```
void FiniteStateMachine::AvoidForce() {
    Vector2D start_corner;
    Vector2D end_corner;
    Vector2D avoid_vec;
    Vector2D dist;

    float closest_square = 999999999999.0;
    float msq;
    Vector2D star_avoid;

    star_avoid.x = CANVAS_WIDTH / 2;
    star_avoid.y = CANVAS_HEIGHT / 2;
    star_avoid -= m_Ship->m_Position;
```

```
msq = star_avoid.MagSQ();
if( msq >= c_StarAvoidDistSQ ) {
    start_corner = m_Ship->m_Position;
    start_corner.x -= c_AvoidDist;
    start_corner.y -= c_AvoidDist;
    end_corner = m_Ship->m_Position;
    end_corner.x += c_AvoidDist;
    end_corner.y += c_AvoidDist;
    Asteroid* asteroid;
    std::vector<Asteroid*>::iterator it;
    int i = 0;

    for( it = asteroid_list.begin(); it != asteroid_list.end();
        it++ ) {
        asteroid = *it;
        if( asteroid->m_Active == true &&
            asteroid->SteeringRectTest( start_corner, end_corner ) ) {
            dist = asteroid->m_Position;
            dist -= m_Ship->m_Position;
            msq = dist.MagSQ();

            if( msq <= closest_square ) {
                closest_square = msq;
                avoid_vec = asteroid->m_Position;
            }
        }
    }
}

// LOOP OVER PROJECTILES
Projectile* projectile;
std::vector<Projectile*>::iterator proj_it;

for( proj_it = projectile_pool->m_ProjectileList.begin();
    proj_it != projectile_pool->m_ProjectileList.end();
    proj_it++ ) {

    projectile = *proj_it;

    if( projectile->m_Active == true &&
        projectile->SteeringRectTest( start_corner, end_corner )
        ) {

        dist = projectile->m_Position;
        dist -= m_Ship->m_Position;
        msq = dist.MagSQ();

        if( msq <= closest_square ) {
            closest_square = msq;
```

```
                        avoid_vec = projectile->m_Position;
                }
            }
        }
        if( closest_square != 999999999999.0 ) {
            avoid_vec -= m_Ship->m_Position;
            avoid_vec.Normalize();
            float rot_to_obj = avoid_vec.FindAngle();

            if( std::abs( rot_to_obj - m_Ship->m_Rotation ) < 0.75 ) {
                if( rot_to_obj >= m_Ship->m_Rotation ) {
                    m_Ship->RotateLeft();
                }
                else {
                    m_Ship->RotateRight();
                }
            }
            m_Ship->m_Velocity -= avoid_vec * delta_time *
            c_ObstacleAvoidForce;
        }
    }
    else {
        avoid_vec.x = CANVAS_WIDTH / 2;
        avoid_vec.y = CANVAS_HEIGHT / 2;
        avoid_vec -= m_Ship->m_Position;
        avoid_vec.Normalize();
        float rot_to_obj = avoid_vec.FindAngle();

        if( std::abs( rot_to_obj - m_Ship->m_Rotation ) < 0.75 ) {
            if( rot_to_obj >= m_Ship->m_Rotation ) {
                m_Ship->RotateLeft();
            }
            else {
                m_Ship->RotateRight();
            }
        }
        m_Ship->m_Velocity -= avoid_vec * delta_time * c_StarAvoidForce;
    }
}
```

Our first check in this function is how close we are to the star in the center of the gameplay area. This star is the biggest thing we need to avoid. It is the only object that will destroy us even if our shields are on, so the AI needs to be extra certain it does not hit the star. This check involves finding the squared distance between the center of the play area and the enemy spaceship, and checking that value against a constant we set in our class definition call, `c_StarAvoidDistSQ`:

```
if( msq >= c_StarAvoidDistSQ ) {
```

You can tweak the value of `c_StarAvoidDistSQ` to allow the enemy spaceship to get closer to, or stay further away from, the center of the game screen. If our enemy ship is not too close to the viewable game area, we look to see whether any obstacles are close to the spaceship:

```
if( msq >= c_StarAvoidDistSQ ) {
    start_corner = m_Ship->m_Position;
    start_corner.x -= c_AvoidDist;
    start_corner.y -= c_AvoidDist;

    end_corner = m_Ship->m_Position;
    end_corner.x += c_AvoidDist;
    end_corner.y += c_AvoidDist;

    Asteroid* asteroid;
    std::vector<Asteroid*>::iterator it;
    int i = 0;

    for( it = asteroid_list.begin(); it != asteroid_list.end(); it++ ) {
        asteroid = *it;
        if( asteroid->m_Active == true &&
            asteroid->SteeringRectTest( start_corner, end_corner ) ) {

            dist = asteroid->m_Position;
            dist -= m_Ship->m_Position;
            msq = dist.MagSQ();

            if( msq <= closest_square ) {
                closest_square = msq;
                avoid_vec = asteroid->m_Position;
            }
        }
    }
}
// LOOP OVER PROJECTILES
Projectile* projectile;
std::vector<Projectile*>::iterator proj_it;

for( proj_it = projectile_pool->m_ProjectileList.begin();
```

```
        proj_it != projectile_pool->m_ProjectileList.end(); proj_it++
        ) {

    projectile = *proj_it;

    if( projectile->m_Active == true &&
        projectile->SteeringRectTest( start_corner, end_corner
        ) ) {
        dist = projectile->m_Position;
        dist -= m_Ship->m_Position;
        msq = dist.MagSQ();

        if( msq <= closest_square ) {
            closest_square = msq;
            avoid_vec = projectile->m_Position;
        }
    }
}
if( closest_square != 999999999999.0 ) {
    avoid_vec -= m_Ship->m_Position;
    avoid_vec.Normalize();
    float rot_to_obj = avoid_vec.FindAngle();
    if( std::abs( rot_to_obj - m_Ship->m_Rotation ) < 0.75 ) {
        if( rot_to_obj >= m_Ship->m_Rotation ) {
            m_Ship->RotateLeft();
        }
        else {
            m_Ship->RotateRight();
        }
    }
    m_Ship->m_Velocity -= avoid_vec * delta_time *
    c_ObstacleAvoidForce;
}
}
```

We do a rectangle test against all of the asteroids and projectiles in our game. At the beginning of the `if` block, we set up the corners of our rectangle test:

```
start_corner = m_Ship->m_Position;
start_corner.x -= c_AvoidDist;
start_corner.y -= c_AvoidDist;

end_corner = m_Ship->m_Position;
end_corner.x += c_AvoidDist;
end_corner.y += c_AvoidDist;
```

The c_AvoidDist constant is set in the FiniteStateMachine class definition and can be changed based on your taste. Increasing the avoid distance makes the AI keep a greater distance from all the projectiles. If you set this value too high, your AI will be rather timid. Reduce the distance and the AI will tolerate flying much closer to the obstacles. If it's too low, it will frequently crash into them. After determining the values to use for our rectangle test, we loop over all of our asteroids, looking for an asteroid that is both active and within the bounds of our rectangle test:

```
Asteroid* asteroid;
std::vector<Asteroid*>::iterator it;
int i = 0;

for( it = asteroid_list.begin(); it != asteroid_list.end(); it++ )
{
    asteroid = *it;
    if( asteroid->m_Active == true &&
        asteroid->SteeringRectTest( start_corner, end_corner ) ) {

        dist = asteroid->m_Position;
        dist -= m_Ship->m_Position;
        msq = dist.MagSQ();

        if( msq <= closest_square ) {
            closest_square = msq;
            avoid_vec = asteroid->m_Position;
        }
    }
}
```

When adding avoid forces, we are only avoiding the closest obstacle. You could write a more complicated version of this, capable of adding an avoiding force for several objects within our bounding box, but avoiding the closest obstacle works reasonably well. After checking all of our asteroids, we check to see whether there is a projectile that is active and closer than the closest asteroid:

```
// LOOP OVER PROJECTILES
Projectile* projectile;
std::vector<Projectile*>::iterator proj_it;
for( proj_it = projectile_pool->m_ProjectileList.begin();
     proj_it != projectile_pool->m_ProjectileList.end(); proj_it++ ) {
    projectile = *proj_it;
    if( projectile->m_Active == true &&
        projectile->SteeringRectTest( start_corner, end_corner ) ) {
        dist = projectile->m_Position;
        dist -= m_Ship->m_Position;
        msq = dist.MagSQ();
```

```
        if( msq <= closest_square ) {
            closest_square = msq;
            avoid_vec = projectile->m_Position;
        }
    }
}
```

If we find at least one object in our bounding box, we want to both rotate our spaceship so that it moves to avoid it naturally as the player would, and we also add an avoid force, which is a bit of a cheat. The avoid force pushes our enemy spaceship away from the object based on a constant, c_ObstacleAvoidForce, that we set in our class definition. That value can be tweaked up and down. In general, I like to keep this value high, risking the player may realize that this is a cheat. You may modify the value of c_ObstacleAvoidForce based on your preferences:

```
if( closest_square != 999999999999.0 ) {
    avoid_vec -= m_Ship->m_Position;
    avoid_vec.Normalize();
    float rot_to_obj = avoid_vec.FindAngle();
    if( std::abs( rot_to_obj - m_Ship->m_Rotation ) < 0.75 ) {
        if( rot_to_obj >= m_Ship->m_Rotation ) {
            m_Ship->RotateLeft();
        }
        else {
            m_Ship->RotateRight();
        }
    }
    m_Ship->m_Velocity -= avoid_vec * delta_time * c_ObstacleAvoidForce;
}
```

The obstacle branch runs if the enemy ship is not too close to the star. If the object is too close to the star, the code jumps into the else block. This code creates an avoid force that pushes and steers the ship away from the center of the play area. It has its own constant avoid force that we set inside the class definition:

```
else {
    avoid_vec.x = CANVAS_WIDTH / 2;
    avoid_vec.y = CANVAS_HEIGHT / 2;
    avoid_vec -= m_Ship->m_Position;
    avoid_vec.Normalize();
    float rot_to_obj = avoid_vec.FindAngle();

    if( std::abs( rot_to_obj - m_Ship->m_Rotation ) < 0.75 ) {
        if( rot_to_obj >= m_Ship->m_Rotation ) {
            m_Ship->RotateLeft();
        }
        else {
```

```
                m_Ship->RotateRight();
            }
        }
        m_Ship->m_Velocity -= avoid_vec * delta_time * c_StarAvoidForce;
    }
```

The `ShieldCheck` function is similar to the avoid force function, in that it checks a bounding rectangle to see whether there is an obstacle close to our ship. It then determines whether the ship is unlikely to avoid a collision. No matter how good our steering forces, sometimes we are not able to avoid an asteroid or projectile. If this is the case, we want to raise our shields. We do not need to check whether we are close to the star because the star will kill us whether our shields are up or not, so there is no need to bother worrying about that in the `ShieldCheck` function:

```cpp
bool FiniteStateMachine::ShieldCheck() {
    Vector2D start_corner;
    Vector2D end_corner;

    start_corner = m_Ship->m_Position;
    start_corner.x -= c_ShieldDist;
    start_corner.y -= c_ShieldDist;

    end_corner = m_Ship->m_Position;
    end_corner.x += c_ShieldDist;
    end_corner.y += c_ShieldDist;

    Asteroid* asteroid;
    std::vector<Asteroid*>::iterator it;
    int i = 0;

    for( it = asteroid_list.begin(); it != asteroid_list.end(); it++ ) {
        asteroid = *it;
        if( asteroid->m_Active &&
            asteroid->SteeringRectTest( start_corner, end_corner ) ) {
            return true;
        }
    }
    // LOOP OVER PROJECTILES
    Projectile* projectile;
    std::vector<Projectile*>::iterator proj_it;

    for( proj_it = projectile_pool->m_ProjectileList.begin();
         proj_it != projectile_pool->m_ProjectileList.end(); proj_it++ ) {
        projectile = *proj_it;
        if( projectile->m_Active &&
            projectile->SteeringRectTest( start_corner, end_corner ) ) {
            return true;
```

```
            }
        }
        return false;
    }
```

Like the avoid force check, we set up a bounding rectangle around our ship with the c_ShieldDist constant. This value should be lower than the avoid force. If it is not, we will raise our shields needlessly when we could avoid the object. Just like everything else in our AI, if the value of c_ShieldDist is set too high, we will be raising our shields when we do not need to. Our shields have limited use, so this would waste shield time that we could otherwise use later. If we set the value too low, we risk hitting an obstacle that the ship is accelerating toward before we have a chance to raise the shields.

The next function, LOSCheck, is a line-of-sight check. That means that it looks to see whether a straight line could be drawn between the enemy ship and the player's ship without intersecting any obstacles. If there is a clear line of sight, this function returns true. If there is an obstacle blocking the line of sight, the function returns false:

```
bool FiniteStateMachine::LOSCheck() { // LINE OF SIGHT CHECK
    // LOOP OVER ASTEROIDS
    Asteroid* asteroid;
    std::vector<Asteroid*>::iterator it;
    int i = 0;
    for( it = asteroid_list.begin(); it != asteroid_list.end(); it++ ) {
        asteroid = *it;
        if( asteroid->SteeringLineTest( m_Ship->m_Position,
        player->m_Position ) ) {
            return false;
        }
    }

    // LOOP OVER PROJECTILES
    Projectile* projectile;
    std::vector<Projectile*>::iterator proj_it;
    for( proj_it = projectile_pool->m_ProjectileList.begin();
        proj_it != projectile_pool->m_ProjectileList.end(); proj_it++ ) {
        projectile = *proj_it;
        if( projectile->SteeringLineTest( m_Ship->m_Position,
        player->m_Position ) ) {
            return false;
        }
    }
    return true;
}
```

One thing we will frequently want to make checks against is the player's distance to the enemy ship. Because the square root is a time-consuming operation, we eliminate it by checking against a squared distance. We use the `GetPlayerDistSq` function to get the squared distance between the enemy ship and the player ship:

```
float FiniteStateMachine::GetPlayerDistSq() {
    float x_diff = m_Ship->m_Position.x - player->m_Position.x;
    float y_diff = m_Ship->m_Position.y - player->m_Position.y;
    return x_diff * x_diff + y_diff * y_diff;
}
```

The FSM's `Move` function is the function that runs our AI every frame. It performs a series of checks to determine what state the AI should be in and executes that state's function. It also checks to see whether the AI should raise or lower the spaceship's shields. Here is the function in its entirety:

```
void FiniteStateMachine::Move() {
    m_CheckCycle++;
    if( m_CheckCycle == 0 ) {
        m_HasLOS = LOSCheck();
        if( !m_HasLOS ) {
            m_CurrentState = WANDER;
        }
        float player_dist_sq = 0.0f;
    }
    else if( m_CheckCycle == 1 ) {
        if( m_HasLOS ) {
            m_PlayerDistSQ = GetPlayerDistSq();
            if( m_PlayerDistSQ <= c_FleeDistSq ) {
                m_CurrentState = FLEE;
            }
            else if( m_PlayerDistSQ <= c_AttackDistSq ) {
                m_CurrentState = ATTACK;
            }
            else {
                m_CurrentState = APPROACH;
            }
        }
    }
    else {
        AvoidForce();
        m_CheckCycle = -1;
    }
    if( ShieldCheck() ) {
        m_Ship->m_Shield->Activate();
    }
    else {
```

```
                    m_Ship->m_Shield->Deactivate();
        }
        if( m_CurrentState == APPROACH ) {
                Vector2D predict = PredictPosition();
                SeekState(predict);
        }
        else if( m_CurrentState == ATTACK ) {
                AttackState();
        }
        else if( m_CurrentState == FLEE ) {
                Vector2D predict = PredictPosition();
                FleeState(predict);
        }
        else if( m_CurrentState == WANDER ) {
                WanderState();
        }
}
```

We use the `m_CheckCycle` attribute to cycle through the different state checks we perform to reduce the burden on the CPU. That is not really necessary for an AI as simple as this one. There is only one agent in our game executing this AI, but if we ever expanded this to use multiple agents, we might set up each of those agents starting on a different cycle check number to spread out our computations. Right now, this cycle check is included for demonstration purposes:

```
m_CheckCycle++;

if( m_CheckCycle == 0 ) {
        m_HasLOS = LOSCheck();
        if( !m_HasLOS ) {
                m_CurrentState = WANDER;
        }
        float player_dist_sq = 0.0f;
}
else if( m_CheckCycle == 1 ) {
        if( m_HasLOS ) {
                m_PlayerDistSQ = GetPlayerDistSq();
                if( m_PlayerDistSQ <= c_FleeDistSq ) {
                        m_CurrentState = FLEE;
                }
                else if( m_PlayerDistSQ <= c_AttackDistSq ) {
                        m_CurrentState = ATTACK;
                }
                else {
                        m_CurrentState = APPROACH;
                }
        }
```

```
    }
    else {
        AvoidForce();
        m_CheckCycle = -1;
    }
```

As you can see, if we are on cycle 0, we run the line-of-sight check, and if we do not have a line of sight, we set the current state to WANDER. In cycle 1, we look to see whether we had a line of sight on the last frame, and if we did, we figure out whether we want to approach, flee, or attack, based on the distance between the enemy ship and the player ship. On cycle 2, we add any avoid forces and reset our check cycle attribute.

Then we perform a shield check every cycle. I initially had the shield check performed on every fourth cycle, but the enemy ship was getting hit too often when it was struck by a projectile head on. Because of this, I changed the code to perform the shield check on every cycle. That is the kind of manual tweaking you end up doing in Game AI to make it work. There is a lot of trial and error:

```
if( ShieldCheck() ) {
    m_Ship->m_Shield->Activate();
}
else {
    m_Ship->m_Shield->Deactivate();
}
```

The last few blocks of code are just a series of if and else if statements that look to see what the current state is, and calls the appropriate function based on that state:

```
if( m_CurrentState == APPROACH ) {
    Vector2D predict = PredictPosition();
    SeekState(predict);
}
else if( m_CurrentState == ATTACK ) {
    AttackState();
}
else if( m_CurrentState == FLEE ) {
    Vector2D predict = PredictPosition();
    FleeState(predict);
}
else if( m_CurrentState == WANDER ) {
    WanderState();
}
```

Compiling the ai.html file

We are now ready to compile and test our `ai.html` file. The screenshot for this version of the game will look quite a bit different than our previous version:

```
em++ asteroid.cpp collider.cpp emitter.cpp enemy_ship.cpp
finite_state_machine.cpp main.cpp particle.cpp player_ship.cpp
projectile_pool.cpp projectile.cpp range.cpp shield.cpp ship.cpp star.cpp
vector.cpp -o ai.html --preload-file sprites -std=c++17 -s USE_WEBGL2=1 -s
USE_SDL=2 -s USE_SDL_IMAGE=2 -s SDL2_IMAGE_FORMATS=["png"] -s
USE_SDL_IMAGE=2 -s SDL2_IMAGE_FORMATS=["png"]
```

The new version of the game will have a much larger canvas, with asteroids and a star in the middle. The enemy spaceship will seek out the player and attack. Here is a screenshot:

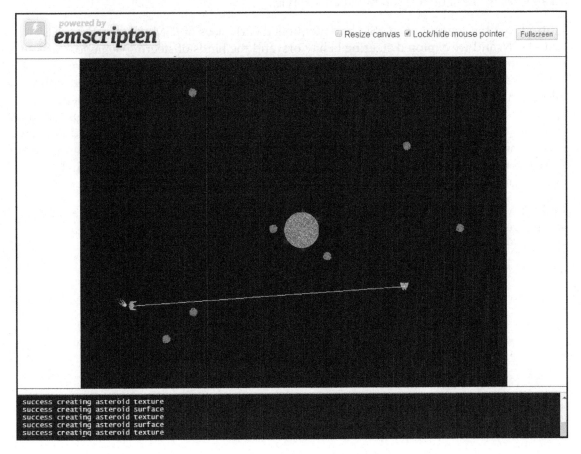

A screenshot of ai.html

Remember that you must run WebAssembly apps using a web server, or with emrun. If you would like to run your WebAssembly app using emrun, you must compile it with the --emrun flag. The web browser requires a web server to stream the WebAssembly module. If you attempt to open an HTML page that uses WebAssembly in a browser directly from your hard drive, that WebAssembly module will not load.

Summary

In this chapter, we discussed Game AI, what it is, and how it is different than academic AI. We talked about using autonomous agents versus a top-down AI, and the benefits of each AI style, as well as how we can mix the two styles.

I introduced the concept of an FSM and mentioned early uses of FSMs in games such as *PAC-MAN*, and we explored steering behaviors, and the kinds of steering behaviors we will use to direct the agent in our game. We added asteroids and a star as obstacles to our game and increased the size of our gameplay area. We added new forms of collision detection to allow our AI to determine when it has a line of sight with our player. We also added rectangle collision detection to determine whether there is an obstacle close enough for our AI to use an avoid force. We expanded our `Point` class to a `Vector2D` class and added new functionality including projection, magnitude, and dot product calculations. We wrote an FSM and used it to determine what steering forces we will be using, and under what circumstances.

In the next chapter, we will be greatly expanding the size of our level and adding a camera so that we can move our spaceship around this larger version of the gameplay area.

11
Designing a 2D Camera

Camera design is one of those things that is frequently forgotten by novice game designers. Up to this point, we have had what is called a *fixed position camera*. There is a single screen with no change in perspective. In the 1970s, almost all of the early arcade games were designed this way. The oldest game that I have found with any sort of camera was Atari's *Lunar Lander*, which was released in August 1979. *Lunar Lander* was an early vector-based game that would zoom the camera in as the lander neared the surface of the moon, and would then pan the camera out to follow your lander as it approached the surface.

In the early 1980s, more games began experimenting with the idea of a game world that was larger than a single game screen would allow. *Rally X* was a *Pac-Man*-like maze game released in 1980 by Namco, where the maze was larger than a single display. *Rally X* used a *position snap camera* (sometimes called a *locked camera*) that always kept the player's car in the center of the game screen no matter what. That is the most straightforward form of 2D scrolling camera that you can implement, and many novice game designers will create a *2D position snap camera* and then call it a day, but there are reasons why you may wish to implement a more sophisticated camera in your game.

Midway released the game *Defender* in 1981. It was a side-scrolling shooter that allowed the player to move their spaceship in either direction. Realizing that the player needed to see more of the level in the direction that the spaceship was facing, *Defender* used the first *dual-forward-focus camera*. This camera shifts the viewing area so that two-thirds of the screen is in front of the direction the player's spaceship is facing, and one third of the screen is behind. That puts more of a focus on what is currently in front of the player. The camera did not just snap back and forth between the two positions. That would have been very jarring. Instead, when the player switched directions, the camera position would smoothly transition to its new position (pretty cool for 1981).

During the 1980s, many new camera designs came into use. Konami began using an autoscrolling camera in many of their shooter games, including *Scramble*, *Gradius*, and *1942*. In 1985, Atari released *Gauntlet*, which was an early multi-player game allowing four players to be in the game at the same time. The camera in *Gauntlet* positioned itself at the average of all of the player's positions. Platformer games, such as *Super Mario Bros.*, would allow the position of the user to push the camera forward.

 You will need to include several images in your build to make this project work. Make sure you include the `/Chapter11/sprites/` folder from the project's GitHub. If you haven't yet downloaded the GitHub project, you can get it online at `https://github.com/PacktPublishing/Hands-On-Game-Development-with-WebAssembly`.

There are many great examples of 2D cameras out there if you take the time to look. We are going to focus (no pun intended) on a few 2D camera features that will be helpful for our game.

Creating a camera for our game

We are going to build our camera in several different stages. We will start with a bare-bones **locked-on camera** implementation. That will give us a good starting point from where we can add new camera features. Later, we will modify this camera to be a **projected focus camera**. A projected focus camera looks at the velocity of the player's ship and adjusts the camera so that it shows more of the gameplay area in front of the player. This technique works off the assumption that, in this game, the player is generally more focused on the gameplay in the direction the player's ship is moving. For the final version of our camera, we will add *camera attractors* to our projectiles. The idea behind this modification is that, when there are shots fired in the game, the camera should draw attention to that area of the game.

Camera for tracking player movement

The first implementation of our camera will be a locked-on camera, which will lock onto our player and follow them as they move through the area in the level. Right now, our level is the same size as our *fixed camera* at that level. Not only will we need to make our level larger, but we will also need to modify our object wrapping so that it works with our camera. The first thing that we will need to do to implement our locked-on camera is to modify our `game.hpp` file. We will be creating a `Camera` class as well as a `RenderManager` class, where we will move all of our rendering-specific code. We will also need to add some `#define` macros than define our level's height and width, because that will now be different to the canvas height and width that we have already defined. We will also be adding a few additional overloaded operators to our `Vector2D` class.

Projected focus and camera attractors

A locked-on camera is not a terrible thing, but a better camera shows more of what the player needs to see. In our game, the player is more likely to be interested in what lies ahead in the direction they are moving. A camera that looks ahead in the direction of movement is sometimes called a projected focus camera. We can look at the velocity at which our ship is currently moving, and offset our camera accordingly.

Another camera technique that we will employ is called **camera attractors**. Sometimes in games, there are objects of interest that can be used to pull/attract the focus of the camera. These create an attractive force that will pull our camera in that direction. One attractive force for our camera is the enemy ship. Another attractive force is projectiles. The enemy ship represents potential action, and projectiles represent a potential threat to our player. In this section, we will combine a projected focus with camera attractors to improve our camera positioning.

The last thing I would like to add is an arrow that points the way toward the enemy spaceship. Because the play area is now larger than the canvas, we need a hint to help us find the enemy. Without this, we may find ourselves wandering around aimlessly, which is not very fun. Another way we could have done this is with a mini-map, but, because there is only a single enemy, I felt an arrow would be easier to implement. Let's walk through the code we need to add to improve our camera and add our locating arrow.

Modifying our code

We are going to need to add several new classes for this chapter. Obviously, if we want a camera in our game, we will need to add a `Camera` class. In previous versions of the code, the rendering was done through direct calls to SDL. Because SDL does not have a camera as a part of the API, we will need to add a `RenderManager` class that will act as an intermediate step in our rendering process. This class will use the position of the camera to determine where on our canvas we will be rendering our game object. We will be increasing our gameplay area to four screens wide and four screens high. This creates a gameplay problem, because now, we will need to be able to find the enemy spaceship when we play. To solve this problem, we will need to create a locator **user interface** (**UI**) element that points an arrow in the direction of the enemy spaceship.

Modifying the game.hpp file

Let's walk through the changes we will make to our `game.hpp` file. We begin by adding a few `#define` macros:

```
#define LEVEL_WIDTH CANVAS_WIDTH*4
#define LEVEL_HEIGHT CANVAS_HEIGHT*4
```

This will define the width and height of our level to be four times as large as the width and height of our canvas. At the end of our list of classes, we should add a `Camera` class, a `Locator` class, and the `RenderManager` class, as follows:

```
class Ship;
class Particle;
class Emitter;
class Collider;
class Asteroid;
class Star;
class PlayerShip;
class EnemyShip;
class Projectile;
class ProjectilePool;
class FiniteStateMachine;
class Camera;
class RenderManager;
class Locator;
```

You will notice that the last three lines declare that a class called `Camera`, a class called `Locator`, and a class called `RenderManager` will be defined later in the code.

The Vector2D class definition

We will be expanding our `Vector2D` class definition to add an `operator+` and `operator-` overload for the + and – operators in our `Vector2D` class.

 If you are not familiar with operator overloading, these are a convenient way to allow classes to use C++ operators instead of functions. There is a good tutorial that can help if you are looking for more information that is available at `https://www.tutorialspoint.com/cplusplus/cpp_overloading.htm`.

Here is what the new definition of the `Vector2D` class looks like:

```
class Vector2D {
    public:
        float x;
        float y;

        Vector2D();
        Vector2D( float X, float Y );

        void Rotate( float radians );
        void Normalize();
        float MagSQ();
        float Magnitude();
        Vector2D Project( Vector2D &onto );
        float Dot(Vector2D &vec);
        float FindAngle();

        Vector2D operator=(const Vector2D &vec);
        Vector2D operator*(const float &scalar);
        void operator+=(const Vector2D &vec);
        void operator-=(const Vector2D &vec);
        void operator*=(const float &scalar);
        void operator/=(const float &scalar);
        Vector2D operator-(const Vector2D &vec);
        Vector2D operator+(const Vector2D &vec);
    };
```

You will notice that the last two lines of the definition are new:

```
Vector2D operator-(const Vector2D &vec);
Vector2D operator+(const Vector2D &vec);
```

The Locator class definition

The `Locator` class is a new class for a UI element that will be an arrow pointing our player in the direction of the enemy spaceship. We require a UI element to help the player find the enemy spaceship when it does not appear on the canvas. Here is what the class definition looks like:

```
class Locator {
    public:
        bool m_Active = false;
        bool m_LastActive = false;
        SDL_Texture *m_SpriteTexture;
        SDL_Rect m_dest = { .x = 0, .y = 0, .w = 32, .h = 32 };
        Vector2D m_Position;
        int m_ColorFlux;
        float m_Rotation;

        Locator();
        void SetActive();
        void Move();
        void Render();
};
```

The first two attributes are Boolean flags that have to do with the active state of the locator. The `m_Active` attribute tells us whether the locator is currently active and should be rendered. The `m_LastActive` attribute is a Boolean flag that tells us whether the locator was active the last time a frame was rendered. The next two lines are the sprite texture and the destination rectangle that will be used by the render manager to render this game object:

```
SDL_Texture *m_SpriteTexture;
SDL_Rect m_dest = { .x = 0, .y = 0, .w = 32, .h = 32 };
```

After that, we have an x and y positional value in the `m_Position` attribute, an integer that represents an RGB color value in `m_ColorFlux`, and a rotation value for the sprite in the `m_Rotation` attribute. We will be using the `m_ColorFlux` attribute to cause the color of the arrow to be redder when the enemy is close, and whiter when the enemy is further away.

The last four lines of this class definition are the class functions. There is a constructor, a function that sets the status of the locator to active, and `Move` and `Render` functions:

```
Locator();
void SetActive();
void Move();
void Render();
```

The Camera class definition

We now need to add the new `Camera` class definition. This class will be used to define our `viewport` and the position of our camera. The `Move` function will be called for every frame. Initially, `Move` will lock on to the position of our player and follow it around the level. Later, we will change this functionality to create a more dynamic camera. This is what the `Camera` class will look like:

```
class Camera {
    public:
        Vector2D m_Position;
        float m_HalfWidth;
        float m_HalfHeight;

        Camera( float width, float height );
        void Move();
};
```

The RenderManager class definition

All this time, we have been moving around our level without a background. This was fine in previous chapters, where our level fitted exactly onto the canvas element. Now, however, we are scrolling around our level with a camera. If nothing is moving in the background, it can be hard to tell whether your spaceship is moving at all. To create the illusion of movement in our game, we will need to add a background renderer. In addition to that, we want all rendering in our game to be done using the camera we just created as an offset. Because of this, we no longer want our game objects to call `SDL_RenderCopy` or `SDL_RenderCopyEx` directly. Instead, we have created a `RenderManager` class that will take responsibility for performing the rendering from within our game. We have a `RenderBackground` function that will render a starfield as a background, and we have created a `Render` function that will render our sprite textures using the camera as an offset. This is what the `RenderManager` class definition looks like:

```
class RenderManager {
    public:
        const int c_BackgroundWidth = 800;
        const int c_BackgroundHeight = 600;
        SDL_Texture *m_BackgroundTexture;
        SDL_Rect m_BackgroundDest = {.x = 0, .y = 0, .w =
        c_BackgroundWidth, .h = c_BackgroundHeight };

        RenderManager();
        void RenderBackground();
        void Render( SDL_Texture *tex, SDL_Rect *src, SDL_Rect *dest, float
```

```
            rad_rotation = 0.0, int alpha = 255, int red = 255, int green =
            255, int blue = 255 );
    };
```

The last thing we need to do in the game.hpp file is to create an external link to two new object pointers of the Camera and RenderManager types. These will be the camera and render manager objects that we will be using in this version of our game engine and are external references to variables that we will define inside our main.cpp file:

```
    extern Camera* camera;
    extern RenderManager* render_manager;
    extern Locator* locator;
```

The camera.cpp file

There are two functions we have defined in our Camera class; a constructor for our camera object, and the Move function, which we will use to follow our player object. The following is what we have in the camera.cpp file:

```
    #include "game.hpp"
    Camera::Camera( float width, float height ) {
        m_HalfWidth = width / 2;
        m_HalfHeight = height / 2;
    }

    void Camera::Move() {
        m_Position = player->m_Position;
        m_Position.x -= CANVAS_WIDTH / 2;
        m_Position.y -= CANVAS_HEIGHT / 2;
    }
```

The Camera constructor and Move functions are pretty bare bones in this implementation. The constructor sets the half width and half height of the camera based on the width and height that is passed in. The Move function sets the position of the camera to the position of the player and then shifts the position of the camera by half of the canvas width and canvas height to center the player. We have just built a starter camera and will add more functionality to it later in this chapter.

The render_manager.cpp file

We will be moving all of the calls we were making to render sprites inside our objects to the RenderManager class. We need to do this because we will be using the position of our camera to decide where on our canvas we will be rendering the sprites. We also need a function that will render our background starfield. The first few lines of our render_manager.cpp file will be including the game.hpp file and defining the virtual filesystem location of our background image:

```
#include "game.hpp"
#define BACKGROUND_SPRITE_FILE (char*)"/sprites/starfield.png"
```

After that, we will define our constructor. The constructor will be used to load our starfield.png file as an SDL_Surface object, and will then use that surface to create an SDL_Texture object that we will use to render our background:

```
RenderManager::RenderManager() {
    SDL_Surface *temp_surface = IMG_Load( BACKGROUND_SPRITE_FILE );

    if( !temp_surface ) {
        printf("failed to load image: %s\n", IMG_GetError() );
        return;
    }

    m_BackgroundTexture = SDL_CreateTextureFromSurface( renderer,
    temp_surface );

    if( !m_BackgroundTexture ) {
        printf("failed to create texture: %s\n", IMG_GetError() );
        return;
    }
    SDL_FreeSurface( temp_surface );
}
```

The RenderBackground function will need to be called at the beginning of our render() function that we have defined in the main loop. Because of this, the first two lines of RenderBackground will have two functions that we will use to clear the renderer that was previously called from the render() function in main.cpp to black:

```
SDL_SetRenderDrawColor( renderer, 0, 0, 0, 255 );
SDL_RenderClear( renderer );
```

After that, we will set up a background rectangle that will be our rendering destination. The size of `starfield.png` matches our canvas size (800 x 600), so we will need to render it four times based on the camera's position. Because this is a repeating texture, we can use a modulo operator (%) on the position of our camera to figure out how we want to offset the starfield. As an example, if we had positioned our camera at $x = 100$, $y = 200$, we would want to render the first copy of our starfield background at -100, -200. If we stopped there, we would have 100 pixels of black space on the right, and 200 pixels of black space on the bottom of our canvas. Because we would like a background in those areas, we will need three additional renders of our background. If we render our background a second time at 700, -200 (adding canvas width to the previous render's x value), we would now have a 200-pixel strip of black at the bottom of the canvas. We could then render our starfield at -100, 400 (adding canvas height to the original render's y value). That would leave us with a 100 x 200 pixel of black in the bottom corner. The fourth render would need to add the canvas width and canvas height to the original render's x and y value to fill in that corner. That is what is going on in the `RenderBackground` function that we use to render the repeating background to the canvas based on the position of the camera:

```cpp
void RenderManager::RenderBackground() {
    SDL_SetRenderDrawColor( renderer, 0, 0, 0, 255 );
    SDL_RenderClear( renderer );
    SDL_Rect background_rect = {.x = 0, .y=0, .w=CANVAS_WIDTH,
                                .h=CANVAS_HEIGHT};
    int start_x = (int)(camera->m_Position.x) % CANVAS_WIDTH;
    int start_y = (int)(camera->m_Position.y) % CANVAS_HEIGHT;
    background_rect.x -= start_x;
    background_rect.y -= start_y;
    SDL_RenderCopy( renderer, m_BackgroundTexture, NULL,
                    &background_rect );
    background_rect.x += CANVAS_WIDTH;
    SDL_RenderCopy( renderer, m_BackgroundTexture, NULL,
                    &background_rect );
    background_rect.x -= CANVAS_WIDTH;
    background_rect.y += CANVAS_HEIGHT;
    SDL_RenderCopy( renderer, m_BackgroundTexture, NULL,
                    &background_rect );
    background_rect.x += CANVAS_WIDTH;
    SDL_RenderCopy( renderer, m_BackgroundTexture, NULL,
                    &background_rect );
}
```

The last function we define in `render_manager.cpp` is our `Render` function. After defining this function, we will need to find every place where we have previously called `SDL_RenderCopy` and `SDL_RenderCopyEx` in our code, and replace those calls with calls to our render manager's `Render` function. This function will not only render our sprite based on the position of our camera, but it will also be used to set color and alpha channel modifications. Here is the code from the `Render` function in its entirety:

```
void RenderManager::Render( SDL_Texture *tex, SDL_Rect *src, SDL_Rect
*dest, float rad_rotation,int alpha, int red, int green, int blue ) {

    SDL_Rect camera_dest = *dest;
    if( camera_dest.x <= CANVAS_WIDTH &&
        camera->m_Position.x >= LEVEL_WIDTH - CANVAS_WIDTH ) {
        camera_dest.x += (float)LEVEL_WIDTH;
    }
    else if( camera_dest.x >= LEVEL_WIDTH - CANVAS_WIDTH &&
             camera->m_Position.x <= CANVAS_WIDTH ) {
        camera_dest.x -= (float)LEVEL_WIDTH;
    }
    if( camera_dest.y <= CANVAS_HEIGHT &&
        camera->m_Position.y >= LEVEL_HEIGHT - CANVAS_HEIGHT ) {
        camera_dest.y += (float)LEVEL_HEIGHT;
    }
    else if( camera_dest.y >= LEVEL_HEIGHT - CANVAS_HEIGHT &&
             camera->m_Position.y <= CANVAS_HEIGHT ) {
        camera_dest.y -= (float)LEVEL_HEIGHT;
    }
    camera_dest.x -= (int)camera->m_Position.x;
    camera_dest.y -= (int)camera->m_Position.y;

    SDL_SetTextureAlphaMod(tex,
                        (Uint8)alpha );

    SDL_SetTextureColorMod(tex,
                        (Uint8)red,
                        (Uint8)green,
                        (Uint8)blue );

    if( rad_rotation != 0.0 ) {
        float degree_rotation = RAD_TO_DEG(rad_rotation);
        SDL_RenderCopyEx( renderer, tex, src, &camera_dest,
                        degree_rotation, NULL, SDL_FLIP_NONE );
    }
    else {
        SDL_RenderCopy( renderer, tex, src, &camera_dest );
    }
}
```

The first thing this function does is create a new `SDL_Rect` object, which we will use to modify the values in the `dest` variable passed into the `Render` function. Because we have a level that wraps the *x* and *y* coordinates, we will want to render objects on the far left of our level to the right if we are on the right edge of our level. Likewise, if we are on the far-left side of our level, we will want to render objects positioned on the far-right side of our level to our right. This allows our spaceship to loop around from the left side of our level back to the right side of our level, and vice versa. The following is the code that adjusts the camera position for wrapping objects to the left and right of the level:

```
if( camera_dest.x <= CANVAS_WIDTH &&
    camera->m_Position.x >= LEVEL_WIDTH - CANVAS_WIDTH ) {
    camera_dest.x += (float)LEVEL_WIDTH;
}
else if( camera_dest.x >= LEVEL_WIDTH - CANVAS_WIDTH &&
         camera->m_Position.x <= CANVAS_WIDTH ) {
    camera_dest.x -= (float)LEVEL_WIDTH;
}
```

After this has been done, we will do something similar to allow for wrapping the position of objects at the top and the bottom of our level:

```
if( camera_dest.y <= CANVAS_HEIGHT &&
    camera->m_Position.y >= LEVEL_HEIGHT - CANVAS_HEIGHT ) {
    camera_dest.y += (float)LEVEL_HEIGHT;
}
else if( camera_dest.y >= LEVEL_HEIGHT - CANVAS_HEIGHT &&
         camera->m_Position.y <= CANVAS_HEIGHT ) {
    camera_dest.y -= (float)LEVEL_HEIGHT;
}
```

Next, we need to subtract the camera's position from the `camera_dest` *x* and *y* coordinates, and set the values for our `alpha` and `color` mod:

```
camera_dest.x -= (int)camera->m_Position.x;
camera_dest.y -= (int)camera->m_Position.y;
SDL_SetTextureAlphaMod(tex,
                (Uint8)alpha );

SDL_SetTextureColorMod(tex,
                (Uint8)red,
                (Uint8)green,
                (Uint8)blue );
```

At the end of the function, we will call `SDL_RenderCopyEx` if our sprite is rotated, and
`SDL_RenderCopy` if it is not:

```
if( rad_rotation != 0.0 ) {
    float degree_rotation = RAD_TO_DEG(rad_rotation);
    SDL_RenderCopyEx( renderer, tex, src, &camera_dest,
                      degree_rotation, NULL, SDL_FLIP_NONE );
}
else {
    SDL_RenderCopy( renderer, tex, src, &camera_dest );
}
```

Modifying main.cpp

To implement our camera, we will need to make several modifications to our `main.cpp`
file. We will need to add some new global variables for our camera, render manager, and
locator. We will need to modify our `move` function to include calls to move our camera and
our locator. We will modify our `render` function to render our background and locator.
Finally, we will need to add more initialization code to our `main` function.

New global variables

We need to create three new global variables near the beginning of our `main.cpp` file. We
will need object pointers to `RenderManager`, `Camera`, and `Locator`. This is what those
declarations look like:

```
Camera* camera;
RenderManager* render_manager;
Locator* locator;
```

Modifying the move function

We will need to modify our `move` function to move our camera and our locator object. We
will need to add the following two lines at the end of our `move` function:

```
camera->Move();
locator->Move();
```

The following is the `move` function in its entirety:

```
void move() {
    player->Move();
    enemy->Move();
    projectile_pool->MoveProjectiles();
    Asteroid* asteroid;
    std::vector<Asteroid*>::iterator it;
    int i = 0;
    for( it = asteroid_list.begin(); it != asteroid_list.end(); it++ ) {
        asteroid = *it;
        if( asteroid->m_Active ) {
            asteroid->Move();
        }
    }
    star->Move();
    camera->Move();
    locator->Move();
}
```

Modifying the render function

We will add a new line to the very beginning of the `render` function. This line will render the background starfield and move it based on the camera position:

```
render_manager->RenderBackground();
```

After that, we will need to add a line to the end of the `render` function. This line will need to come immediately before the `SDL_RenderPresent` call, which will still need to be the last line in this function:

```
locator->Render();
```

This is what the `render()` function looks like in its entirety:

```
void render() {
    render_manager->RenderBackground();
    player->Render();
    enemy->Render();
    projectile_pool->RenderProjectiles();

    Asteroid* asteroid;
    std::vector<Asteroid*>::iterator it;
    for( it = asteroid_list.begin(); it != asteroid_list.end(); it++ ) {
        asteroid = *it;
        asteroid->Render();
```

```
    }
    star->Render();
    locator->Render();

    SDL_RenderPresent( renderer );
}
```

Modifying the main function

The final modifications will be to initialization that happens in the `main` function. We will need to create new objects for the `camera`, `render_manager`, and `locator` pointers we defined earlier:

```
camera = new Camera(CANVAS_WIDTH, CANVAS_HEIGHT);
render_manager = new RenderManager();
locator = new Locator();
```

In the previous version of our code, we had seven calls to `new Asteroid` and used `asteroid_list.push_back` to push those seven new asteroids into our list of asteroids. We will now need to create far more asteroids than seven, so, instead of doing them as individual calls, we will be using a double `for` loop to create and spread out our asteroids all over the gameplay area. To do this, we will first need to remove all of those earlier calls to create and push asteroids:

```
asteroid_list.push_back( new Asteroid(
                    200, 50, 0.05,
                    DEG_TO_RAD(10) ) );
asteroid_list.push_back( new Asteroid(
                    600, 150, 0.03,
                    DEG_TO_RAD(350) ) );
asteroid_list.push_back( new Asteroid(
                    150, 500, 0.05,
                    DEG_TO_RAD(260) ) );
asteroid_list.push_back( new Asteroid(
                    450, 350, 0.01,
                    DEG_TO_RAD(295) ) );
asteroid_list.push_back( new Asteroid(
                    350, 300, 0.08,
                    DEG_TO_RAD(245) ) );
asteroid_list.push_back( new Asteroid(
                    700, 300, 0.09,
                    DEG_TO_RAD(280) ) );
asteroid_list.push_back( new Asteroid(
                    200, 450, 0.03,
                    DEG_TO_RAD(40) ) );
```

Once you have removed all of the preceding code, we will add the following code to create our new asteroids and space them semi-randomly throughout the gameplay area:

```
int asteroid_x = 0;
int asteroid_y = 0;
int angle = 0;

// SCREEN 1
for( int i_y = 0; i_y < 8; i_y++ ) {
    asteroid_y += 100;
    asteroid_y += rand() % 400;
    asteroid_x = 0;

    for( int i_x = 0; i_x < 12; i_x++ ) {
        asteroid_x += 66;
        asteroid_x += rand() % 400;
        int y_save = asteroid_y;
        asteroid_y += rand() % 400 - 200;
        angle = rand() % 359;
        asteroid_list.push_back( new Asteroid(
                    asteroid_x, asteroid_y,
                    get_random_float(0.5, 1.0),
                    DEG_TO_RAD(angle) ) );
        asteroid_y = y_save;
    }
}
```

Modifying asteroid.cpp

Now that we are using a render manager to render all of our game objects, we will need to go through our various game objects and modify them to render through the render manager instead of directly. The first file we will modify is `asteroid.cpp`.

Inside `asteroid.cpp`, we have the `Asteroid::Render()` function. In previous chapters, this function would render the asteroid sprite directly through SDL using a call to `SDL_RenderCopyEx`. Now that we have the `render_manager` object that we defined in our `main.cpp` file, we will be using that render manager to render our sprite indirectly. The `RenderManager::Render` function will use the camera to adjust the location on the canvas where the sprite will be rendered. The first modification we need to make to the `Asteroid::Render()` function is to remove the following lines:

```
SDL_RenderCopyEx( renderer, m_SpriteTexture,
            &m_src, &m_dest,
            RAD_TO_DEG(m_Rotation), NULL, SDL_FLIP_NONE );
```

After removing the call to `SDL_RenderCopyEX`, we need to add the following call to the `Render` function within the `render_manager` object:

```
render_manager->Render( m_SpriteTexture, &m_src, &m_dest, m_Rotation );
```

The new version of the `Asteroid::Render` function will now look like this:

```
void Asteroid::Render() {
    m_Explode->Move();
    m_Chunks->Move();
    if( m_Active == false ) {
        return;
    }
    m_src.x = m_dest.w * m_CurrentFrame;
    m_dest.x = m_Position.x + m_Radius / 2;
    m_dest.y = m_Position.y + m_Radius / 2;
    render_manager->Render( m_SpriteTexture, &m_src, &m_dest, m_Rotation );
}
```

Modifying collider.cpp

We will need to modify one function inside the `collider.cpp` file. The previous version of the `WrapPosition` function checked to see whether a `Collider` object moved off the canvas to one side or another, and, if it did, the function would move the collider to the opposite side. This mimicked the behavior of the classic Atari arcade game, *Asteroids*. In Atari *Asteroids*, if an asteroid or the player's spaceship moved off the screen on one side, that asteroid (or spaceship) would appear on the opposite side of the game screen. Here is the previous version of our `wrap` code:

```
void Collider::WrapPosition() {
    if( m_Position.x > CANVAS_WIDTH + m_Radius ) {
        m_Position.x = -m_Radius;
    }
    else if( m_Position.x < -m_Radius ) {
        m_Position.x = CANVAS_WIDTH;
    }

    if( m_Position.y > CANVAS_HEIGHT + m_Radius ) {
        m_Position.y = -m_Radius;
    }
    else if( m_Position.y < -m_Radius ) {
        m_Position.y = CANVAS_HEIGHT;
    }
}
```

Because our game now extends beyond a single canvas, we no longer want to wrap if an object moves off the canvas. Instead, we want to wrap the object around if it falls outside the bounds of the level. Here is the new version of the WrapPosition function:

```
void Collider::WrapPosition() {
    if( m_Position.x > LEVEL_WIDTH ) {
        m_Position.x -= LEVEL_WIDTH;
    }
    else if( m_Position.x < 0 ) {
        m_Position.x += LEVEL_WIDTH;
    }

    if( m_Position.y > LEVEL_HEIGHT ) {
        m_Position.y -= LEVEL_HEIGHT;
    }
    else if( m_Position.y < 0 ) {
        m_Position.y += LEVEL_HEIGHT;
    }
}
```

Modifying enemy_ship.cpp

A small modification to the enemy_ship.cpp file is necessary. The EnemyShip constructor function will now be setting the x and y values on the m_Position attribute. We need to set the position to 810 and 800, because the level is now much larger than the canvas size. We will set the m_Position attribute at the very top of the EnemyShip constructor. This is what the beginning of the constructor will look like after the changes:

```
EnemyShip::EnemyShip() {
    m_Position.x = 810.0;
    m_Position.y = 800.0;
```

Modifying finite_state_machine.cpp

We will need to make a small change to the `finite_state_machine.cpp` file. Inside the `FiniteStateMachine::AvoidForce()` function, there are several references to the canvas dimensions that must be changed to reference the level dimensions now that the size of our level and the size of our canvas are different. Previously, we had set the x and y attributes of the `star_avoid` variable to the following canvas-based values:

```
star_avoid.x = CANVAS_WIDTH / 2;
star_avoid.y = CANVAS_HEIGHT / 2;
```

These lines must be changed to reference `LEVEL_WIDTH` and `LEVEL_HEIGHT`:

```
star_avoid.x = LEVEL_WIDTH / 2;
star_avoid.y = LEVEL_HEIGHT / 2;
```

We must do the same thing to the `avoid_vec` variable. Here is what we had previously:

```
avoid_vec.x = CANVAS_WIDTH / 2;
avoid_vec.y = CANVAS_HEIGHT / 2;
```

That must also be changed to reference `LEVEL_WIDTH` and `LEVEL_HEIGHT`:

```
avoid_vec.x = LEVEL_WIDTH / 2;
avoid_vec.y = LEVEL_HEIGHT / 2;
```

The new version of the `FiniteState::AvoidForce` function in its entirety is as follows:

```
void FiniteStateMachine::AvoidForce() {
    Vector2D start_corner;
    Vector2D end_corner;
    Vector2D avoid_vec;
    Vector2D dist;
    float closest_square = 999999999999.0;
    float msq;
    Vector2D star_avoid;
    star_avoid.x = LEVEL_WIDTH / 2;
    star_avoid.y = LEVEL_HEIGHT / 2;
    star_avoid -= m_Ship->m_Position;
    msq = star_avoid.MagSQ();

    if( msq >= c_StarAvoidDistSQ ) {
        start_corner = m_Ship->m_Position;
        start_corner.x -= c_AvoidDist;
        start_corner.y -= c_AvoidDist;
        end_corner = m_Ship->m_Position;
        end_corner.x += c_AvoidDist;
```

```
        end_corner.y += c_AvoidDist;

        Asteroid* asteroid;
        std::vector<Asteroid*>::iterator it;

        int i = 0;
        for( it = asteroid_list.begin(); it != asteroid_list.end(); it++ )
    {
            asteroid = *it;
            if( asteroid->m_Active == true &&
                asteroid->SteeringRectTest( start_corner, end_corner ) ) {
                dist = asteroid->m_Position;
                dist -= m_Ship->m_Position;
                msq = dist.MagSQ();

                if( msq <= closest_square ) {
                    closest_square = msq;
                    avoid_vec = asteroid->m_Position;
                }
            }
        }
        // LOOP OVER PROJECTILES
        Projectile* projectile;
        std::vector<Projectile*>::iterator proj_it;

        for( proj_it = projectile_pool->m_ProjectileList.begin();
            proj_it != projectile_pool->m_ProjectileList.end(); proj_it++
    ) {
            projectile = *proj_it;
            if( projectile->m_Active == true &&
                projectile->SteeringRectTest( start_corner, end_corner ) )
    {
                dist = projectile->m_Position;
                dist -= m_Ship->m_Position;
                msq = dist.MagSQ();

                if( msq <= closest_square ) {
                    closest_square = msq;
                    avoid_vec = projectile->m_Position;
                }
            }
        }
        if( closest_square != 999999999999.0 ) {
            avoid_vec -= m_Ship->m_Position;
            avoid_vec.Normalize();
            float rot_to_obj = avoid_vec.FindAngle();
            if( std::abs( rot_to_obj - m_Ship->m_Rotation ) < 0.75 ) {
                if( rot_to_obj >= m_Ship->m_Rotation ) {
```

```
                    m_Ship->RotateLeft();
            }
            else {
                m_Ship->RotateRight();
            }
        }
        m_Ship->m_Velocity -= avoid_vec * delta_time *
        c_ObstacleAvoidForce;
    }
}
else {
    avoid_vec.x = LEVEL_WIDTH / 2;
    avoid_vec.y = LEVEL_HEIGHT / 2;
    avoid_vec -= m_Ship->m_Position;
    avoid_vec.Normalize();
    float rot_to_obj = avoid_vec.FindAngle();
    if( std::abs( rot_to_obj - m_Ship->m_Rotation ) < 0.75 ) {
        if( rot_to_obj >= m_Ship->m_Rotation ) {
            m_Ship->RotateLeft();
        }
        else {
            m_Ship->RotateRight();
        }
    }
    m_Ship->m_Velocity -= avoid_vec * delta_time * c_StarAvoidForce;
}
}
}
```

Modifying particle.cpp

We will need to modify the Render function inside the particle.cpp file to render the
particle through render_manager instead of directly through calls to SDL. The old version
of the Particle::Render function is as follows:

```
void Particle::Render() {
    SDL_SetTextureAlphaMod(m_sprite_texture,
                            (Uint8)m_alpha );

    if( m_color_mod == true ) {
        SDL_SetTextureColorMod(m_sprite_texture,
                                m_current_red,
                                m_current_green,
                                m_current_blue );
    }

    if( m_align_rotation == true ) {
```

```
        SDL_RenderCopyEx( renderer, m_sprite_texture, &m_src, &m_dest,
                        m_rotation, NULL, SDL_FLIP_NONE );
    }
    else {
        SDL_RenderCopy( renderer, m_sprite_texture, &m_src, &m_dest );
    }
}
```

The new `Particle::Render` function will make a single call to the `Render` function through the `render_manager` object:

```
void Particle::Render() {
    render_manager->Render( m_sprite_texture, &m_src, &m_dest, m_rotation,
                        m_alpha, m_current_red, m_current_green,
m_current_blue );
}
```

Modifying player_ship.cpp

We will need to make one small modification to the `player_ship.cpp` file. Like the change that we made to the `enemy_ship.cpp` file, we will need to add two lines to set the x and y values in the `m_Position` attribute.

We will need to remove the first two lines of the `PlayerShip::PlayerShip()` constructor function:

```
m_Position.x = CANVAS_WIDTH - 210.0;
m_Position.y = CANVAS_HEIGHT - 200.0;
```

These are the changes we will need to make to the `PlayerShip::PlayerShip()` constructor function:

```
PlayerShip::PlayerShip() {
    m_Position.x = LEVEL_WIDTH - 810.0;
    m_Position.y = LEVEL_HEIGHT - 800.0;
```

Modifying projectile.cpp

We will need to make a small change to the `projectile.cpp` file. As in other game objects, the `Render` function previously made calls directly to the SDL function to render the game object. Instead of making those calls to SDL, we will need to make a call through the `render_manager` object. We will need to remove the following lines from the `Projectile::Render()` function:

```
int return_val = SDL_RenderCopy( renderer, m_SpriteTexture,
                                 &src, &dest );
if( return_val != 0 ) {
    printf("SDL_Init failed: %s\n", SDL_GetError());
}
```

In place of these lines, we will need to add a call to the `Render` function on the `render_manager` object:

```
render_manager->Render( m_SpriteTexture, &src, &dest );
```

This is what the new version of the `Projectile::Render()` function will look like:

```
void Projectile::Render() {
    dest.x = m_Position.x + 8;
    dest.y = m_Position.y + 8;
    dest.w = c_Width;
    dest.h = c_Height;

    src.x = 16 * m_CurrentFrame;

    render_manager->Render( m_SpriteTexture, &src, &dest );
}
```

Modifying shield.cpp

As with many other game objects, the `Shield::Render()` function will need to be modified so that it no longer calls SDL directly and instead calls the `Render` function from the `render_manager` object. Inside the `Shield::Render()` function, we will need to remove the following calls to SDL:

```
SDL_SetTextureColorMod(m_SpriteTexture,
                       color_red,
                       color_green,
                       0 );

SDL_RenderCopyEx( renderer, m_SpriteTexture,
```

```
                              &m_src, &m_dest,
                              RAD_TO_DEG(m_Ship->m_Rotation),
                              NULL, SDL_FLIP_NONE );
```

We will be replacing these lines with a single call to `Render`:

```
render_manager->Render( m_SpriteTexture, &m_src, &m_dest,
m_Ship->m_Rotation,
                         255, color_red, color_green, 0 );
```

This is what the new version of the `Shield::Render` function looks like in its entirety:

```
void Shield::Render() {
    if( m_Active ) {
        int color_green = m_ttl / 100 + 1;
        int color_red = 255 - color_green;

        m_src.x = m_CurrentFrame * m_dest.w;

        m_dest.x = m_Ship->m_Position.x;
        m_dest.y = m_Ship->m_Position.y;
        render_manager->Render( m_SpriteTexture, &m_src, &m_dest,
m_Ship->m_Rotation,
                                255, color_red, color_green, 0 );
    }
}
```

Modifying ship.cpp

Modifying the `Render` functions within our game objects is becoming pretty routine. As in other objects where we have modified the `Render` function, we will need to remove all direct calls to SDL. Here is the code that we will need to remove from the `Render` function:

```
float degrees = (m_Rotation / PI) * 180.0;
int return_code = SDL_RenderCopyEx( renderer, m_SpriteTexture,
                                    &src, &dest,
                                    degrees, NULL, SDL_FLIP_NONE );
if( return_code != 0 ) {
    printf("failed to render image: %s\n", IMG_GetError() );
}
```

After removing these lines, we will need to add a line to call the
`render_manager->Render` function:

```
render_manager->Render( m_SpriteTexture, &src, &dest, m_Rotation );
```

Modifying star.cpp

We will need to modify two functions inside the `star.cpp` file. First, we will need to
modify the position of the star in the `Star::Star()` constructor function. In the version of
the `Star` constructor from the previous chapter, we set the position of the star to the middle
of the canvas. Now, it must be set to the middle of the level. Here are the lines that were in
the original version of the constructor:

```
m_Position.x = CANVAS_WIDTH / 2;
m_Position.y = CANVAS_HEIGHT / 2;
```

We will now change these to positions relative to `LEVEL_WIDTH` and `LEVEL_HEIGHT`
instead of `CANVAS_WIDTH` and `CANVAS_HEIGHT`:

```
m_Position.x = LEVEL_WIDTH / 2;
m_Position.y = LEVEL_HEIGHT / 2;
```

After making the preceding change to the `Star::Star` constructor function, we will need
to make a change to the `Star::Render` function. We will need to remove the call to
`SDL_RenderCopy` and replace it with a call to the `Render` function on the
`render_manager` object. This is what the previous version of the `Render` function looked
like:

```
void Star::Render() {
    Emitter* flare;
    std::vector<Emitter*>::iterator it;
    for( it = m_FlareList.begin(); it != m_FlareList.end(); it++ ) {
        flare = *it;
        flare->Move();
    }
    m_src.x = m_dest.w * m_CurrentFrame;
    SDL_RenderCopy( renderer, m_SpriteTexture,
                    &m_src, &m_dest );

}
```

We will modify it to the following:

```
void Star::Render() {
    Emitter* flare;
    std::vector<Emitter*>::iterator it;
```

```
        for( it = m_FlareList.begin(); it != m_FlareList.end(); it++ ) {
            flare = *it;
            flare->Move();
        }
        m_src.x = m_dest.w * m_CurrentFrame;
        render_manager->Render( m_SpriteTexture, &m_src, &m_dest );
    }
```

Modifying vector.cpp

We will need to add two new overloaded operators to our Vector2D class. We will need to override operator- and operator+. This code is pretty straightforward. It will use the already overloaded operator-= and operator+= to allow us to add and subtract vectors from each other. Here is the new code for those overloaded operators:

```
Vector2D Vector2D::operator-(const Vector2D &vec) {
 Vector2D return_vec = *this;
 return_vec -= vec;
 return return_vec;
}

Vector2D Vector2D::operator+(const Vector2D &vec) {
 Vector2D return_vec = *this;
 return_vec += vec;
 return return_vec;
}
```

Compiling and playing with a locked-on camera

If we compile and test what we have right now, we should be able to move around our level and see a camera that directly tracks the player's position. We should have a locator arrow that helps us to find the enemy spaceship. Here is the command-line call to Emscripten that we can use to build our project:

```
em++ asteroid.cpp camera.cpp collider.cpp emitter.cpp enemy_ship.cpp
finite_state_machine.cpp locator.cpp main.cpp particle.cpp player_ship.cpp
projectile_pool.cpp projectile.cpp range.cpp render_manager.cpp shield.cpp
ship.cpp star.cpp vector.cpp -o index.html --preload-file sprites -
std=c++17 -s USE_WEBGL2=1 -s USE_SDL=2 -s USE_SDL_IMAGE=2 -s
SDL2_IMAGE_FORMATS=["png"] -s USE_SDL_IMAGE=2 -s SDL2_IMAGE_FORMATS=["png"]
```

Run the preceding line on the Windows or Linux command prompt. After running this, serve the index.html file from a web server and open it in a browser such as Chrome or Firefox.

A more advanced camera

Our current camera is functional, but a little boring. It focuses exclusively on the player, which works all right, but could be significantly improved. For starters, as the designers of *Defender* realized, it is more important to put the focus of the camera in the direction the player is moving, instead of directly on the player. To accomplish this, we will add *projected focus* to our camera. That will look at the current velocity of the player's ship, and will move the camera forward in the direction of that velocity. There are times, however, when you may still want the focus of your camera behind the player. To help with this, we will add some camera attractors. Camera attractors are objects that draw the camera's attention toward them. If the enemy appears behind the player, it may be more important to move the camera back somewhat to help keep the enemy on screen. If the enemy is shooting at you, it may be more important to draw the cameras toward the projectiles that are heading your way.

Changes to games.hpp

The first change we need to make is to our games.hpp file. Having a camera follow our player is easy. There is not any snapping or jarring movement of the camera because the player's ship does not move that way. If we are going to use more advanced features, such as attractors and forward focus, we will need to calculate the desired position of our camera, and then transition smoothly to that position. To support this, we will need to add a m_DesiredPosition attribute to our Camera class. The following is the new line we must add:

```
Vector2D m_DesiredPosition;
```

This is what the Camera class in our games.hpp file will look like after we add it:

```
class Camera {
    public:
        Vector2D m_Position;
        Vector2D m_DesiredPosition;

        float m_HalfWidth;
        float m_HalfHeight;
```

```
        Camera( float width, float height );
        void Move();
};
```

Changes to camera.cpp

Now that we have added a desired position attribute to the class definition, we need to change our `camera.cpp` file. We need to modify the constructor to set the position of the camera to the position of the player's ship. Here are the lines we will need to add to our constructor:

```
m_Position = player->m_Position;
m_Position.x -= CANVAS_WIDTH / 2;
m_Position.y -= CANVAS_HEIGHT / 2;
```

The following is the constructor after we have added those lines:

```
Camera::Camera( float width, float height ) {
    m_HalfWidth = width / 2;
    m_HalfHeight = height / 2;

    m_Position = player->m_Position;
    m_Position.x -= CANVAS_WIDTH / 2;
    m_Position.y -= CANVAS_HEIGHT / 2;
}
```

Our `Camera::Move` function will be entirely different. You might as well remove all of the lines of code that are in the current version of `Camera::Move`, because none of them are useful anymore. Our new desired position attribute will be set at the beginning of the `Move` function, the way that the position was set previously. To do this, add the following lines to the empty version of `Camera::Move` that you created by deleting everything from that function:

```
m_DesiredPosition = player->m_Position;
m_DesiredPosition.x -= CANVAS_WIDTH / 2;
m_DesiredPosition.y -= CANVAS_HEIGHT / 2;
```

If the player is not alive, we will want our camera to settle down on this position. After the player is dead, we will not want any attractors to affect the position of the camera. Moving the player camera too much after the player dies looks a little strange, so add the following lines of code that check whether the player's ship is active and, if not, moves the position of the camera toward the desired position and, then returns from the `Move` function:

```
if( player->m_Active == false ) {
    m_Position.x = m_Position.x + (m_DesiredPosition.x - m_Position.x)
```

```
    * delta_time;
    m_Position.y = m_Position.y + (m_DesiredPosition.y - m_Position.y)
    * delta_time;
    return;
}
```

We are going to make all of the active projectiles in our game attractors. If an enemy is shooting at us, it is a threat to our ship and should therefore draw the camera's attention. If we shoot projectiles, that also indicates the direction where we are focused. We are going to use a `for` loop to loop over all of the projectiles in our game, and, if that projectile is active, we will use its position to shift the desired position of our camera. Here is the code:

```
Projectile* projectile;
std::vector<Projectile*>::iterator it;
Vector2D attractor;
for( it = projectile_pool->m_ProjectileList.begin(); it !=
projectile_pool->m_ProjectileList.end(); it++ ) {
    projectile = *it;
    if( projectile->m_Active ) {
        attractor = projectile->m_Position;
        attractor -= player->m_Position;
        attractor.Normalize();
        attractor *= 5;
        m_DesiredPosition += attractor;
    }
}
```

After using our attractors to shift the desired position of the camera, we will modify the `m_DesiredPosition` variable based on the velocity of the player's ship with the following line of code:

```
m_DesiredPosition += player->m_Velocity * 2;
```

Because our level wraps around, and if you exit from one side of the level you reappear on the opposite side, we will need to adjust the desired position of our camera to account for this. Without the following lines of code, the camera makes a sudden jarring transition when the player moves outside the level bounds on one side and reappears on the other:

```
if( abs(m_DesiredPosition.x - m_Position.x) > CANVAS_WIDTH ) {
    if( m_DesiredPosition.x > m_Position.x ) {
        m_Position.x += LEVEL_WIDTH;
    }
    else {
        m_Position.x -= LEVEL_WIDTH;
    }
}
```

```
if( abs(m_DesiredPosition.y - m_Position.y) > CANVAS_HEIGHT ) {
    if( m_DesiredPosition.y > m_Position.y ) {
        m_Position.y += LEVEL_HEIGHT;
    }
    else {
        m_Position.y -= LEVEL_HEIGHT;
    }
}
```

Finally, we will add a few lines of code to smoothly transition the camera's current position to the desired position. We use `delta_time` to make this transition take about a second. Setting our camera position directly instead of using the desired position and transitioning results in jerky movements when new attractors enter the game. Here is the transition code:

```
m_Position.x = m_Position.x + (m_DesiredPosition.x - m_Position.x) *
delta_time;
m_Position.y = m_Position.y + (m_DesiredPosition.y - m_Position.y) *
delta_time;
```

Now that we have seen all of the lines of our `Move` function separately, let's take a look at the completed new version of the function:

```
void Camera::Move() {
    m_DesiredPosition = player->m_Position;
    m_DesiredPosition.x -= CANVAS_WIDTH / 2;
    m_DesiredPosition.y -= CANVAS_HEIGHT / 2;

    if( player->m_Active == false ) {
        m_Position.x = m_Position.x + (m_DesiredPosition.x - m_Position.x)
        * delta_time;
        m_Position.y = m_Position.y + (m_DesiredPosition.y - m_Position.y)
        * delta_time;
        return;
    }

    Projectile* projectile;
    std::vector<Projectile*>::iterator it;
    Vector2D attractor;

    for( it = projectile_pool->m_ProjectileList.begin();
         it != projectile_pool->m_ProjectileList.end(); it++ ) {
        projectile = *it;
            if( projectile->m_Active ) {
            attractor = projectile->m_Position;
            attractor -= player->m_Position;
            attractor.Normalize();
            attractor *= 5;
            m_DesiredPosition += attractor;
```

```
        }
    }
    m_DesiredPosition += player->m_Velocity * 2;

    if( abs(m_DesiredPosition.x - m_Position.x) > CANVAS_WIDTH ) {
        if( m_DesiredPosition.x > m_Position.x ) {
            m_Position.x += LEVEL_WIDTH;
        }
        else {
            m_Position.x -= LEVEL_WIDTH;
        }
    }

    if( abs(m_DesiredPosition.y - m_Position.y) > CANVAS_HEIGHT ) {
        if( m_DesiredPosition.y > m_Position.y ) {
            m_Position.y += LEVEL_HEIGHT;
        }
        else {
            m_Position.y -= LEVEL_HEIGHT;
        }
    }

    m_Position.x = m_Position.x + (m_DesiredPosition.x - m_Position.x) *
    delta_time;
    m_Position.y = m_Position.y + (m_DesiredPosition.y - m_Position.y) *
    delta_time;
}
```

Compiling and playing with the advanced camera

When you have built this version, you will notice that the camera moves ahead in the direction your ship is moving. If you start shooting, it will move even further ahead. When the enemy spaceship approaches, and it shoots at you, the camera should also drift in the direction of those projectiles. As before, you can compile and test the code by entering the following line on the Windows or Linux command prompt:

```
em++ asteroid.cpp camera.cpp collider.cpp emitter.cpp enemy_ship.cpp
finite_state_machine.cpp locator.cpp main.cpp particle.cpp player_ship.cpp
projectile_pool.cpp projectile.cpp range.cpp render_manager.cpp shield.cpp
ship.cpp star.cpp vector.cpp -o camera.html --preload-file sprites -
std=c++17 -s USE_WEBGL2=1 -s USE_SDL=2 -s USE_SDL_IMAGE=2 -s
SDL2_IMAGE_FORMATS=["png"] -s USE_SDL_IMAGE=2 -s SDL2_IMAGE_FORMATS=["png"]
```

Now that we have a compiled version of our app, we should run it. The new version should look something like this:

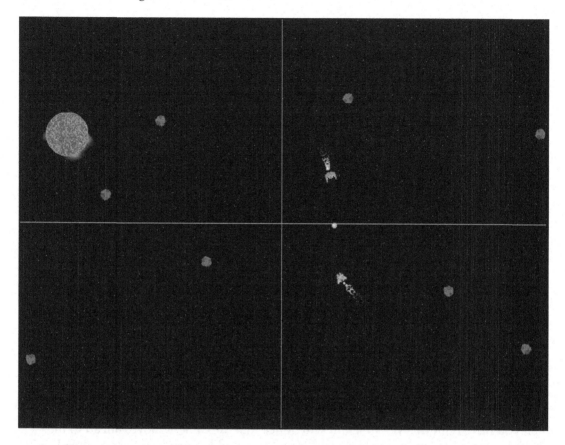

Figure 11.1: New camera version with lines added to divide the screen

As you can see, the camera is not centering the player's spaceship. The focus of the camera is primarily projected in the direction of the player ship's velocity, dragged slightly to the right and up because of the enemy ship and the projectile.

Do not forget that you must run WebAssembly apps using a web server, or with `emrun`. If you would like to run your WebAssembly app using `emrun`, you must compile it with the `--emrun` flag. The web browser requires a web server to stream the WebAssembly module. If you attempt to open an HTML page that uses WebAssembly in a browser directly from your hard drive, that WebAssembly module will not load.

Summary

We began this chapter by learning about the history of cameras in video games. The first camera we discussed is the simplest type of camera, sometimes called a locked-on camera. That is the kind of camera that tracks the location of the player exactly. After that, we learned about alternatives to a locked-on camera in 2D space, including cameras that lead the player. We talked about projected focus cameras, and how they predict the movement of the player and project the position of the camera forward based on the direction in which the player is moving. We then discussed camera attractors, and how they can draw the focus of the camera toward objects of interest. After discussing the types of cameras, we created a camera object and designed it to implement projected focus and camera attractors. We implemented a render manager and modified all of our game objects to render through the `RenderManager` class. We then created a `locator` object to help us find the enemy spaceship when it no longer appears on the canvas.

In the next chapter, we will learn how to add sound effects to our game.

12
Sound FX

The current state of sound on the web is a bit of a mess and has been for quite a while. For a long time, there were issues with loading MP3 versus OGG files based on which browser you were using. Recently, there have been issues with browsers blocking sounds that play automatically to prevent annoying audio spam. This feature in Chrome sometimes seems to create problems when playing audio in our game. I have noticed that, if Chrome does not initially play the audio, it will usually play if you reload the page. I have not had this problem on Firefox.

 You will need to include several images and audio files in your build to make this project work. Make sure that you include the `/Chapter12/sprites/` folder as well as the `/Chapter12/audio/` folder from the project's GitHub. If you haven't yet downloaded the GitHub project, you can get it online at `https://github.com/PacktPublishing/Hands-On-Game-Development-with-WebAssembly`.

Emscripten's support for audio playback is not as good as I would like it to be. On the message boards, Emscripten's defenders are quick to blame the state of audio on the web as opposed to Emscripten itself, and there is some truth to that assessment. Emscripten's FAQ claims that Emscripten supports the use of SDL1 Audio, SDL2 Audio, and OpenAL, but, in my experience, I have found that using a very limited set of SDL2 Audio provides the best outcomes. I am going to keep our use of SDL2 Audio to a minimum, using the audio queue instead of mixing sound effects. You may wish to expand on or modify what I have done here. OpenAL, in theory, should work with Emscripten, although I have not had much luck with it. Also, you may wish to look into `SDL_MixAudio` (`https://wiki.libsdl.org/SDL_MixAudio`) and `SDL_AudioStream` (`https://wiki.libsdl.org/Tutorials/AudioStream`) to improve the audio system in your game, but be aware that performance and support for streaming and mixing audio on the web may not be ready for prime time.

We will cover the following topics in this chapter:

- Where to get sound effects
- Simple audio with Emscripten
- Adding sound to our game
- Compiling and running

Where to get sound effects

There are a lot of great places to get music and sound effects online. I generated the sound effects we use in this chapter with SFXR (`http://www.drpetter.se/project_sfxr.html`), which is a tool used to generate old school 8-bit sound effects that sound like something you would hear in an NES game. These kinds of sound effects may not be to your taste. OpenGameArt.org also has a large collection of sound effects (`https://opengameart.org/art-search-advanced?keys=field_art_type_tid%5B%5D=13sort_by=countsort_order=DESC`) and music (`https://opengameart.org/art-search-advanced?keys=field_art_type_tid%5B%5D=12sort_by=countsort_order=DESC`) with a variety of open licenses, so make sure that you look over the license of any sounds or art on that website before you use it.

Simple audio with Emscripten

Before we add sound effects to our main game, I will show you how to make an audio player in the `audio.c` file to demonstrate how **SDL Audio** can be used to play sound effects in a WebAssembly application. This application will take five sound effects that we will use in our game and allow the user to press number keys one to five to play all of the chosen sound effects. I will first show you the code broken into two sections, and then I will walk you through what everything does. Here is all of the code in `audio.c` with the exception of the `main` function:

```c
#include <SDL2/SDL.h>
#include <emscripten.h>
#include <stdio.h>
#include <stdbool.h>

#define ENEMY_LASER "/audio/enemy-laser.wav"
#define PLAYER_LASER "/audio/player-laser.wav"
#define LARGE_EXPLOSION "/audio/large-explosion.wav"
#define SMALL_EXPLOSION "/audio/small-explosion.wav"
#define HIT "/audio/hit.wav"
```

```
SDL_AudioDeviceID device_id;
SDL_Window *window;
SDL_Renderer *renderer;
SDL_Event event;

struct audio_clip {
    char file_name[100];
    SDL_AudioSpec spec;
    Uint32 len;
    Uint8 *buf;
} enemy_laser_snd, player_laser_snd, small_explosion_snd,
large_explosion_snd, hit_snd;

void play_audio( struct audio_clip* clip ) {
    int success = SDL_QueueAudio(device_id, clip->buf, clip->len);
    if( success < 0 ) {
        printf("SDL_QueueAudio %s failed: %s\n", clip->file_name,
        SDL_GetError());
    }
}

void init_audio( char* file_name, struct audio_clip* clip ) {
    strcpy( clip->file_name, file_name );

    if( SDL_LoadWAV(file_name, &(clip->spec), &(clip->buf), &(clip->len))
    == NULL ) {
        printf("Failed to load wave file: %s\n", SDL_GetError());
    }
}

void input_loop() {
    if( SDL_PollEvent( &event ) ){
        if( event.type == SDL_KEYUP ) {
            switch( event.key.keysym.sym ){
                case SDLK_1:
                    printf("one key release\n");
                    play_audio(&enemy_laser_snd);
                    break;
                case SDLK_2:
                    printf("two key release\n");
                    play_audio(&player_laser_snd);
                    break;
                case SDLK_3:
                    printf("three key release\n");
                    play_audio(&small_explosion_snd);
                    break;
                case SDLK_4:
                    printf("four key release\n");
```

```
                    play_audio(&large_explosion_snd);
                    break;
                case SDLK_5:
                    printf("five key release\n");
                    play_audio(&hit_snd);
                    break;
                default:
                    printf("unknown key release\n");
                    break;
            }
        }
    }
}
```

At the end of the audio.c file we have our main function:

```
int main() {
    if((SDL_Init(SDL_INIT_VIDEO|SDL_INIT_AUDIO)==-1)) {
        printf("Could not initialize SDL: %s.\n", SDL_GetError());
        return 0;
    }

    SDL_CreateWindowAndRenderer( 320, 200, 0, &window, &renderer );

    init_audio( ENEMY_LASER, &enemy_laser_snd );
    init_audio( PLAYER_LASER, &player_laser_snd );
    init_audio( SMALL_EXPLOSION, &small_explosion_snd );
    init_audio( LARGE_EXPLOSION, &large_explosion_snd );
    init_audio( HIT, &hit_snd );

    device_id = SDL_OpenAudioDevice(NULL, 0, &(enemy_laser_snd.spec),
                                    NULL, 0);

    if (device_id == 0) {
        printf("Failed to open audio: %s\n", SDL_GetError());
    }

    SDL_PauseAudioDevice(device_id, 0);

    emscripten_set_main_loop(input_loop, 0, 0);

    return 1;
}
```

Now that you have seen the entire audio.c file, let's take a look at all of its parts. At the top of this file, we have our #include and #define macros:

```
#include <SDL2/SDL.h>
#include <emscripten.h>
#include <stdio.h>
#include <stdbool.h>

#define ENEMY_LASER "/audio/enemy-laser.wav"
#define PLAYER_LASER "/audio/player-laser.wav"
#define LARGE_EXPLOSION "/audio/large-explosion.wav"
#define SMALL_EXPLOSION "/audio/small-explosion.wav"
#define HIT "/audio/hit.wav"
```

After that, we have our SDL specific-global variables. We need an SDL_AudioDeviceID for our audio output. SDL_Window, SDL_Renderer and SDL_Event have been used in most of the earlier chapters and should be familiar by now:

```
SDL_AudioDeviceID device_id;
SDL_Window *window;
SDL_Renderer *renderer;
SDL_Event event;
```

We are working on a C program, not a C++ program, so we will be using a structure to hold our audio data instead of a class. We will create a C structure called audio_clip that will hold all of the information for the audio we will be playing in our application. This information includes a string holding the filename. It contains an SDL_AudioSpec object that holds the audio specification. It also contains the length of the audio clip and a pointer to an 8-bit data buffer, which holds the waveform data of the audio clip. After the audio_clip structure is defined, five instances of that structure are created that we will later be able to use to play these sounds:

```
struct audio_clip {
    char file_name[100];
    SDL_AudioSpec spec;
    Uint32 len;
    Uint8 *buf;
} enemy_laser_snd, player_laser_snd, small_explosion_snd,
large_explosion_snd, hit_snd;
```

After we define the `audio_clip` structure, we need to create a function to play the audio in that structure. This function calls `SDL_QueueAudio` passing in the global `device_id`, a pointer to the waveform buffer, and the length of the clip. The `device_id` is a reference to the audio device (sound card). The `clip->buf` variable is a pointer to a buffer that contains the waveform data of the `.wav` file we will be loading. The `clip->len` variable contains the length of time that the clip plays:

```
void play_audio( struct audio_clip* clip ) {
    int success = SDL_QueueAudio(device_id, clip->buf, clip->len);
    if( success < 0 ) {
        printf("SDL_QueueAudio %s failed: %s\n", clip->file_name,
        SDL_GetError());
    }
}
```

The next function we need is the function that initializes our `audio_clip` so that we can pass it into the `play_audio` function. This function sets the filename of our `audio_clip` and loads a wave file setting the `spec`, `buf`, and `len` values in our `audio_clip`. If the call to `SDL_LoadWAV` fails, we print out an error message:

```
void init_audio( char* file_name, struct audio_clip* clip ) {
    strcpy( clip->file_name, file_name );

    if( SDL_LoadWAV(file_name, &(clip->spec), &(clip->buf), &(clip-
        >len))
    == NULL ) {
        printf("Failed to load wave file: %s\n", SDL_GetError());
    }
}
```

The `input_loop` should look pretty familiar by now. The function calls the `SDL_PollEvent` and uses the event it returns to check for a keyboard key release. It checks to see which key is released. If that key is one of the number keys from one to five, a switch statement is used to call the `play_audio` function, passing in a specific `audio_clip`. The reason we are using the key release instead of the key press is to prevent the key repeat when the user holds the key down. We could easily prevent this, but I am trying to keep the code for this application as short as possible. Here is the `input_loop` code:

```
void input_loop() {
    if( SDL_PollEvent( &event ) ){
        if( event.type == SDL_KEYUP ) {
            switch( event.key.keysym.sym ){
                case SDLK_1:
                    printf("one key release\n");
                    play_audio(&enemy_laser_snd);
```

```
                break;
            case SDLK_2:
                printf("two key release\n");
                play_audio(&player_laser_snd);
                break;
            case SDLK_3:
                printf("three key release\n");
                play_audio(&small_explosion_snd);
                break;
            case SDLK_4:
                printf("four key release\n");
                play_audio(&large_explosion_snd);
                break;
            case SDLK_5:
                printf("five key release\n");
                play_audio(&hit_snd);
                break;
            default:
                printf("unknown key release\n");
                break;
            }
        }
    }
}
```

As always, the `main` function does all of the initialization for our application. In addition to the initialization that we executed in previous applications, we need a new initialization for our audio. This is what the new version of the `main` function looks like:

```
int main() {
    if((SDL_Init(SDL_INIT_VIDEO|SDL_INIT_AUDIO)==-1)) {
        printf("Could not initialize SDL: %s.\n", SDL_GetError());
        return 0;
    }
    SDL_CreateWindowAndRenderer( 320, 200, 0, &window, &renderer );
    init_audio( ENEMY_LASER, &enemy_laser_snd );
    init_audio( PLAYER_LASER, &player_laser_snd );
    init_audio( SMALL_EXPLOSION, &small_explosion_snd );
    init_audio( LARGE_EXPLOSION, &large_explosion_snd );
    init_audio( HIT, &hit_snd );

    device_id = SDL_OpenAudioDevice(NULL, 0, &(enemy_laser_snd.spec), NULL,
    0);

    if (device_id == 0) {
        printf("Failed to open audio: %s\n", SDL_GetError());
    }
    SDL_PauseAudioDevice(device_id, 0);
```

```
emscripten_set_main_loop(input_loop, 0, 0);
return 1;
}
```

The first thing we changed was our call to SDL_Init. We needed to add a flag telling SDL to initialize the audio subsystem. We did this by adding |SLD_INIT_AUDIO to the parameter we passed in, which performs a bitwise operation on the parameter with the SDL_INIT_AUDIO flag. Following the new version of SDL_Init, we will create the window and renderer, which we have done many times at this point.

The init_audio calls are all new and initialize our audio_clip structures:

```
init_audio( ENEMY_LASER, &enemy_laser_snd );
init_audio( PLAYER_LASER, &player_laser_snd );
init_audio( SMALL_EXPLOSION, &small_explosion_snd );
init_audio( LARGE_EXPLOSION, &large_explosion_snd );
init_audio( HIT, &hit_snd );
```

Next, we need to call SDL_OpenAudioDevice and retrieve a device ID. Opening an audio device requires a default spec, which informs the audio device of the quality of sound clip that you would like to play. Make sure that you pick a sound file with a quality level that is a good example of what you would like to play in your game. In our code, we chose enemy_laser_snd. We also need to call SDL_PauseAudioDevice. Whenever you create a new audio device, it is paused by default. Calling SDL_PauseAudioDevice and passing in 0 as the second parameter unpauses the audio device we just created. I found this a little confusing at first, but keep in mind that the following call to SDL_PauseAudioDevice is actually unpausing the audio clip:

```
device_id = SDL_OpenAudioDevice(NULL, 0, &(enemy_laser_snd.spec), NULL, 0);

if (device_id == 0) {
    printf("Failed to open audio: %s\n", SDL_GetError());
}

SDL_PauseAudioDevice(device_id, 0);
```

The last thing we will do before returning is set our loop to be the input_loop function we created earlier:

```
emscripten_set_main_loop(input_loop, 0, 0);
```

Now that we have our code, we should compile and test our audio.c file:

```
emcc audio.c --preload-file audio -s USE_SDL=2 -o audio.html
```

We need to preload the audio folder so that we have access to the `.wav` files in our virtual filesystem. Then, load `audio.html` in a web browser, serving the file with emrun, or with an alternative web server. When you load the application in Chrome, you may run into some minor difficulties. New versions of Chrome have added checks to prevent unrequested audio from playing to prevent some of the irritating spam that has been going around. Sometimes, this check is a little too sensitive, and this can prevent the audio in our game from running. If this happens to you, try reloading the page in the Chrome browser. Sometimes, this fixes the problem. Another way to prevent this from happening is to switch over to Firefox.

Adding sound to our game

Now that we have an understanding of how to get SDL Audio to work on the web, we can start adding sound effects to our game. We will not be using a mixer in our game, so only one sound effect will play at a time. Because of this, we will need to classify some sounds as **priority** sound effects. If a priority sound effect is triggered, the sound queue will clear, and that sound effect will run. We also want to prevent our sound queue from becoming too long, so we will clear our sound queue if there are more than two items in it. Do not fear! I will repeat all of this when we get to that part of our code.

Updating game.hpp

The first thing we will need to change is our `game.hpp` file. We need to add a new `Audio` class, as well as other new code to support audio in our game. Near the top of the `game.hpp` file, we will add a series of `#define` macros to define the location of our sound effect `.wav` files:

```
#define ENEMY_LASER (char*)"/audio/enemy-laser.wav"
#define PLAYER_LASER (char*)"/audio/player-laser.wav"
#define LARGE_EXPLOSION (char*)"/audio/large-explosion.wav"
#define SMALL_EXPLOSION (char*)"/audio/small-explosion.wav"
#define HIT (char*)"/audio/hit.wav"
```

At the top of our list of class declarations, we should add a new declaration of a class called `Audio`:

```
class Audio;
class Ship;
class Particle;
class Emitter;
class Collider;
```

```
class Asteroid;
class Star;
class PlayerShip;
class EnemyShip;
class Projectile;
class ProjectilePool;
class FiniteStateMachine;
class Camera;
class RenderManager;
class Locator;
```

We will then define the new `Audio` class, which will be very similar to the `audio_clip` structure that we used in our `audio.c` file. This class will have a filename, a spec, a length (in runtime), and a buffer. It will also have a priority flag that, when set, will give it priority over everything else that is currently in our audio queue. Finally, we will have two functions in this class; a constructor that will initialize the sound, and a `Play` function that will actually play the sound. This is what the class definition looks like:

```
class Audio {
    public:
        char FileName[100];
        SDL_AudioSpec spec;
        Uint32 len;
        Uint8 *buf;
        bool priority = false;

        Audio( char* file_name, bool priority_value );
        void Play();
};
```

Finally, we need to define some external audio related to global variables. These global variables will be references to the variables that will appear in our `main.cpp` file. Most of these are instances of the `Audio` class, which will be used in our game to play audio files. The last of these variables is a reference to our audio device:

```
extern Audio* enemy_laser_snd;
extern Audio* player_laser_snd;
extern Audio* small_explosion_snd;
extern Audio* large_explosion_snd;
extern Audio* hit_snd;
extern SDL_AudioDeviceID device_id;
```

Updating main.cpp

The first thing we need to do in our `main.cpp` file is define the audio-related global variables that we defined as external variables at the end of the `game.hpp` file:

```
SDL_AudioDeviceID device_id;

Audio* enemy_laser_snd;
Audio* player_laser_snd;
Audio* small_explosion_snd;
Audio* large_explosion_snd;
Audio* hit_snd;
```

Most of these sound effects are related to explosions that occur when there is a collision in our game. Because of this, we will be adding calls to play these sound effects throughout our `collisions` function. This is what the new version of our `collisions` function looks like:

```
void collisions() {
 Asteroid* asteroid;
 std::vector<Asteroid*>::iterator ita;
    if( player->m_CurrentFrame == 0 && player->CompoundHitTest( star ) ) {
        player->m_CurrentFrame = 1;
        player->m_NextFrameTime = ms_per_frame;
        player->m_Explode->Run(); // added
        large_explosion_snd->Play();
    }
    if( enemy->m_CurrentFrame == 0 && enemy->CompoundHitTest( star ) ) {
        enemy->m_CurrentFrame = 1;
        enemy->m_NextFrameTime = ms_per_frame;
        enemy->m_Explode->Run(); // added
        large_explosion_snd->Play();
    }
 Projectile* projectile;
 std::vector<Projectile*>::iterator it;
 for(it=projectile_pool->m_ProjectileList.begin();
        it!=projectile_pool->m_ProjectileList.end();
        it++){
        projectile = *it;
        if( projectile->m_CurrentFrame == 0 && projectile->m_Active ) {
            for( ita = asteroid_list.begin(); ita !=
                asteroid_list.end();
                  ita++ ) {
                asteroid = *ita;
                if( asteroid->m_Active ) {
                    if( asteroid->HitTest( projectile ) ) {
                        projectile->m_CurrentFrame = 1;
```

```
                              projectile->m_NextFrameTime = ms_per_frame;
                              small_explosion_snd->Play();
                          }
                      }
                  }
              if( projectile->HitTest( star ) ){
                  projectile->m_CurrentFrame = 1;
                  projectile->m_NextFrameTime = ms_per_frame;
                  small_explosion_snd->Play();
              }
              else if( player->m_CurrentFrame == 0 && ( projectile-
                      >HitTest( player ) ||
                        player->CompoundHitTest( projectile ) ) ) {
                  if( player->m_Shield->m_Active == false ) {
                      player->m_CurrentFrame = 1;
                      player->m_NextFrameTime = ms_per_frame;
                      player->m_Explode->Run();
                      large_explosion_snd->Play();
                  }
                  else { hit_snd->Play(); }
                  projectile->m_CurrentFrame = 1;
                  projectile->m_NextFrameTime = ms_per_frame;
              }
              else if( enemy->m_CurrentFrame == 0 && ( projectile-
                      >HitTest( enemy ) ||
                        enemy->CompoundHitTest( projectile ) ) ) {
                  if( enemy->m_Shield->m_Active == false ) {
                      enemy->m_CurrentFrame = 1;
                      enemy->m_NextFrameTime = ms_per_frame;
                      enemy->m_Explode->Run();
                      large_explosion_snd->Play();
                  }
                  else { hit_snd->Play(); }
                  projectile->m_CurrentFrame = 1;
                  projectile->m_NextFrameTime = ms_per_frame;
              }
          }
      }
  for( ita = asteroid_list.begin(); ita != asteroid_list.end();
       ita++ ) {
      asteroid = *ita;
      if( asteroid->m_Active ) {
          if( asteroid->HitTest( star ) ) {
              asteroid->Explode();
              small_explosion_snd->Play();
          }
      }
      else { continue; }
```

```
        if( player->m_CurrentFrame == 0 && asteroid->m_Active &&
            ( asteroid->HitTest( player ) || player->CompoundHitTest(
            asteroid ) ) ) {
            if( player->m_Shield->m_Active == false ) {
                player->m_CurrentFrame = 1;
                player->m_NextFrameTime = ms_per_frame;
                player->m_Explode->Run();
                large_explosion_snd->Play();
            }
            else {
                asteroid->Explode();
                small_explosion_snd->Play();
            }
        }
        if( enemy->m_CurrentFrame == 0 && asteroid->m_Active &&
            ( asteroid->HitTest( enemy ) || enemy->CompoundHitTest(
              asteroid ) ) ) {
            if( enemy->m_Shield->m_Active == false ) {
                enemy->m_CurrentFrame = 1;
                enemy->m_NextFrameTime = ms_per_frame;
                enemy->m_Explode->Run();
                large_explosion_snd->Play();
            }
            else {
                asteroid->Explode();
                small_explosion_snd->Play();
            }
        }
    }
  }
}
```

Sounds will now play after several explosions and collisions; for example, after the player explodes:

```
player->m_Explode->Run();
large_explosion_snd->Play();
```

Sound will also play when the enemy ship explodes:

```
enemy->m_Explode->Run();
large_explosion_snd->Play();
```

After an asteroid explodes, we will want the same effect:

```
asteroid->Explode();
small_explosion_snd->Play();
```

If an enemy shield is hit, we want to play the `hit` sound:

```
if( enemy->m_Shield->m_Active == false ) {
    enemy->m_CurrentFrame = 1;
    enemy->m_NextFrameTime = ms_per_frame;
    enemy->m_Explode->Run();
    large_explosion_snd->Play();
}
else {
    hit_snd->Play();
}
```

Similarly, if the player's shield is hit, we will, again, want to play the `hit` sound:

```
if( player->m_Shield->m_Active == false ) {
    player->m_CurrentFrame = 1;
    player->m_NextFrameTime = ms_per_frame;

    player->m_Explode->Run();
    large_explosion_snd->Play();
}
else {
    hit_snd->Play();
}
```

Finally, we need to change the `main` function to initialize our audio. Here is the entire `main` function code:

```
int main() {
    SDL_Init( SDL_INIT_VIDEO | SDL_INIT_AUDIO );
    int return_val = SDL_CreateWindowAndRenderer( CANVAS_WIDTH,
    CANVAS_HEIGHT, 0, &window, &renderer );

    if( return_val != 0 ) {
        printf("Error creating renderer %d: %s\n", return_val,
        IMG_GetError() );
        return 0;
    }

    SDL_SetRenderDrawColor( renderer, 0, 0, 0, 255 );
    SDL_RenderClear( renderer );
    last_frame_time = last_time = SDL_GetTicks();

    player = new PlayerShip();
    enemy = new EnemyShip();
    star = new Star();
    camera = new Camera(CANVAS_WIDTH, CANVAS_HEIGHT);
    render_manager = new RenderManager();
```

```
locator = new Locator();
enemy_laser_snd = new Audio(ENEMY_LASER, false);
player_laser_snd = new Audio(PLAYER_LASER, false);
small_explosion_snd = new Audio(SMALL_EXPLOSION, true);
large_explosion_snd = new Audio(LARGE_EXPLOSION, true);
hit_snd = new Audio(HIT, false);
device_id = SDL_OpenAudioDevice(NULL, 0, &(enemy_laser_snd->spec),
NULL, 0);

if (device_id == 0) {
    printf("Failed to open audio: %s\n", SDL_GetError());
}
int asteroid_x = 0;
int asteroid_y = 0;
int angle = 0;

// SCREEN 1
for( int i_y = 0; i_y < 8; i_y++ ) {
    asteroid_y += 100;
    asteroid_y += rand() % 400;
    asteroid_x = 0;
    for( int i_x = 0; i_x < 12; i_x++ ) {
        asteroid_x += 66;
        asteroid_x += rand() % 400;
        int y_save = asteroid_y;
        asteroid_y += rand() % 400 - 200;
        angle = rand() % 359;
        asteroid_list.push_back(
            new Asteroid( asteroid_x, asteroid_y,
            get_random_float(0.5, 1.0),
            DEG_TO_RAD(angle) ) );
        asteroid_y = y_save;
    }
}
projectile_pool = new ProjectilePool();
emscripten_set_main_loop(game_loop, 0, 0);
return 1;
}
```

The first change we need to make to the main function is to the SDL_Init call to include the initialization of the audio subsystem:

```
SDL_Init( SDL_INIT_VIDEO | SDL_INIT_AUDIO );
```

The other change we need to make is the addition of the new Audio objects and the call to SDL_OpenAudioDevice:

```
enemy_laser_snd = new Audio(ENEMY_LASER, false);
player_laser_snd = new Audio(PLAYER_LASER, false);
small_explosion_snd = new Audio(SMALL_EXPLOSION, true);
large_explosion_snd = new Audio(LARGE_EXPLOSION, true);
hit_snd = new Audio(HIT, false);

device_id = SDL_OpenAudioDevice(NULL, 0, &(enemy_laser_snd->spec),
NULL, 0);

if (device_id == 0) {
    printf("Failed to open audio: %s\n", SDL_GetError());
}
```

Updating ship.cpp

The ship.cpp file has one minor change to it. We are adding a call to play a sound when the ship launches a projectile. That happens in the Ship::Shoot() function. You will notice that the call to player_laser_snd->Play() occurs after the call to projectile->Launch:

```
void Ship::Shoot() {
    Projectile* projectile;
    if( current_time - m_LastLaunchTime >= c_MinLaunchTime ) {
        m_LastLaunchTime = current_time;
        projectile = projectile_pool->GetFreeProjectile();
        if( projectile != NULL ) {
            projectile->Launch( m_Position, m_Direction );
            player_laser_snd->Play();
        }
    }
}
```

The new audio.cpp file

We are adding a new audio.cpp file to implement the Audio class constructor function and the Audio class Play function. Here is the audio.cpp file in its entirety:

```
#include "game.hpp"

Audio::Audio( char* file_name, bool priority_value ) {
    strcpy( FileName, file_name );
```

```
        priority = priority_value;

        if( SDL_LoadWAV(FileName, &spec, &buf, &len) == NULL ) {
            printf("Failed to load wave file: %s\n", SDL_GetError());
        }
    }

    void Audio::Play() {
        if( priority || SDL_GetQueuedAudioSize(device_id) > 2 ) {
            SDL_ClearQueuedAudio(device_id);
        }

        int success = SDL_QueueAudio(device_id, buf, len);
        if( success < 0 ) {
            printf("SDL_QueueAudio %s failed: %s\n", FileName, SDL_GetError());
        }
    }
```

The first function in this file is the constructor for the `Audio` class. This function sets the `FileName` attribute to the value passed and sets the `priority` value. It also loads the wave file from the filename passed in and uses the `SDL_LoadWAV` file to set the `spec`, `buf`, and `len` attributes.

The `Audio::Play()` function first looks to see whether this is high-priority audio, or whether the size of the audio queue is greater than two sounds. If either of these is the case, we clear out the audio queue:

```
    if( priority || SDL_GetQueuedAudioSize(device_id) > 2 ) {
        SDL_ClearQueuedAudio(device_id);
    }
```

We are doing this because we do not want to mix the audio. We are playing the audio sequentially in a queue. If we have a priority audio clip, we want to clear out the queue so that the audio plays immediately. We also want to do this if the queue is too long. We will then call `SDL_QueueAudio` to queue up this sound to play as soon as possible:

```
    int success = SDL_QueueAudio(device_id, buf, len);
    if( success < 0 ) {
     printf("SDL_QueueAudio %s failed: %s\n", FileName, SDL_GetError());
    }
```

Now, we should be ready to compile and run our code.

Compiling and running

Now that we have made all the necessary changes to our code, we can compile and run our new code with Emscripten:

```
em++ asteroid.cpp audio.cpp camera.cpp collider.cpp emitter.cpp
enemy_ship.cpp finite_state_machine.cpp locator.cpp main.cpp particle.cpp
player_ship.cpp projectile_pool.cpp projectile.cpp range.cpp
render_manager.cpp shield.cpp ship.cpp star.cpp vector.cpp -o sound_fx.html
--preload-file audio --preload-file sprites -std=c++17 -s USE_WEBGL2=1 -s
USE_SDL=2 -s USE_SDL_IMAGE=2 -s SDL2_IMAGE_FORMATS=["png"] -s
USE_SDL_IMAGE=2 -s SDL2_IMAGE_FORMATS=["png"]
```

There are no new flags added to allow us to use the SDL Audio library. However, we need to add a new `--preload-file audio` flag to load the new `audio` directory into our virtual filesystem. Once you have compiled the new version of the game, you can run it using emrun (assuming that you included the necessary emrun flag when you compiled). If you prefer, you can choose a different web server to serve these files.

Summary

We have discussed the current (messy) state of audio on the web and have looked at the audio libraries available to Emscripten. I mentioned a few places where you can get free sound effects. We created a simple audio application using C and Emscripten that allowed us to play a series of audio files. We then added sound effects to our game, which included explosion and laser sounds. We modified our initialization code inside the `main()` function to initialize the SDL Audio subsystem. We added a new `Shoot` function to be used by our spaceships when they shoot projectiles. We also created a new `Audio` class to help us play our audio files.

In the next chapter, we will learn how we can add some physics to our game.

13
Game Physics

We already have some physics in our game. Each of our ships has a velocity and an acceleration. They also obey at least some of Newton's laws and conserve momentum. All of this was added earlier without much fanfare. Physics in computer games dates back to the original computer game, *Space War!*, which is the game that inspired the one we are currently writing. In the original version of *Space War!*, the spaceships conserved momentum, as we currently do in our game. A black hole gravitationally attracted the ships to the center of the play area. Before creating the classic game *Pong*, Nolan Bushnell created an arcade clone of *Space War!*, called *Computer Space*. *Computer Space* was not a hit like *Pong*, and Nolan Bushnell blamed Newton's laws and the public's lack of understanding of basic physics as some of the reasons for the game's commercial failure.

> *According to The Ultimate History of Video Games: from Pong to Pokemon and Beyond, by Steven Kent, "Computer Space obeys the first law—maintenance of momentum. (Bushnell is probably referring to Sir Isaac Newton's first law—objects maintain constant velocity unless acted upon by an external force.) And so that was really hard for people who didn't understand that."*
>
> *– Nolan Bushnell*

Physics is common in games, but far from universal. The kind of physics required by a game is highly dependent on the kind of game it is. There is a 3D physics library called *Bullet Physics* that has been ported, but, because it is 3D, Bullet is a rather large library for the kinds of physics we will be using in this game. Instead, we will integrate some simple Newtonian physics into our game for some extra flavor. We already have a simple implementation of Newton's first law in our game. When we accelerate our spaceship, it moves in the same direction until we either decelerate it by using the down arrow, or we *flip and burn* by turning our ship around and accelerating in the opposite direction of our current velocity.

 You will need to include several images and audio files in your build to make this project work. Make sure that you include the `/Chapter13/sprites/` folder as well as the `/Chapter13/audio/` folder from the project's GitHub. If you haven't yet downloaded the GitHub project, you can get it online at `https://github.com/PacktPublishing/Hands-On-Game-Development-with-WebAssembly`.

In this chapter, we will be applying the following aspects of physics:

- Elastic collisions between asteroids, projectiles, and spaceships.
- When our spaceships shoot, there should be a recoil (Newton's third law).
- Gravity from the star should attract the player's spaceship.

Newton's third law

Newton's third law is commonly stated as, *For every action, there is an equal and opposite reaction.* What this means is that, when object *A* exerts a force on object *B*, object *B* exerts that same force right back on object *A*. An example of this is firing a bullet from a gun. When a human holding a gun fires a bullet, the gun recoils with the same force of the bullet leaving the gun. That may sound counter-intuitive, because the bullet can kill a human, but the gun's recoil does not kill the human firing the gun. That is because the gun is significantly larger than the bullet, and Newton's first law states that $F = ma$, or force equals mass times acceleration. In other words, if the gun is 50 times larger than the bullet, then the same force will only make it accelerate to 1/50 the speed. We will be modifying our spaceship so that, whenever it shoots a projectile, it accelerates in the opposite direction of the shot based on the relative masses of the spaceship and the projectile. This will give our ship's cannon a recoil.

Chapter 13

Adding gravity

After we add the recoil to our spaceship's cannon, I would also like to add a gravitational effect on the spaceships in our game that will draw the ships toward the star when they are within a certain distance of that star. The gravitational force decreases with the square of the distance between the two objects. That is convenient because it means that we can calculate the gravitational effect with the `MagSQ` function, which runs quite a bit faster than the `Magnitude` function. I have chosen not to add a gravitational effect on the projectiles and asteroids out of personal preference. It will not be hard to add that effect if you choose to do so.

Improving collisions

We are going to improve the collisions between our spaceship and the asteroids and projectiles in the game. To simplify things, we will use elastic collisions. An elastic collision is a collision that preserves all of the kinetic energy. In reality, collisions always lose some energy to heat or friction, even ones that are close to elastic collisions, such as billiard balls. However, making our collisions perfectly elastic simplifies the math. In games, simpler math usually means faster algorithms.

For more information on elastic collisions, Wikipedia has an excellent article (`https://en.wikipedia.org/wiki/Elastic_collision`) that discusses the math we will use to implement our elastic collision function.

Modifying the code

In this section, we are going to make some changes to our game objects. We will need to add mass and elastic collisions to our `collider` class. Our star should be able to generate gravity and attract the player and enemy spaceship with a force that decreases based on the square of the distance. We will need to modify our collisions function to add elastic collisions between our spaceships, asteroids, and the projectiles.

[441]

Changing the game.hpp file

To get physics into our game, we will need to modify several class definitions and add new #define macros. Let's start by updating our game.hpp file. The first thing we need to add is #define in order to set up a constant value for our star's mass. I want to have a large constant value for the star mass that we will check against in our ElasticCollision function. If the mass of either object in our elastic collision is the same value as STAR_MASS, we do not want to accelerate that object. In reality, if you were to throw a rock into the sun, you would accelerate the sun a tiny, tiny amount in the direction you threw the rock. This amount would be so small relative to the sun that it would be undetectable. We will have a fixed value for the star's mass where any objects with a mass that size will not accelerate when hit by any objects in our game. To do this, we will need to add the following #define:

```
#define STAR_MASS 9999999
```

After adding the #define, we will need to modify our Collider class, giving it a new ElasticCollision function. This function will take in a second Collider object and use the velocity and masses of those two objects to determine what their new velocities will be. We will also need to add a mass attribute that we will name m_Mass. Finally, we need to move two attributes into our Collider class that was previously in the child classes of Collider. These variables are the 2D m_Direction and m_Velocity vectors because our elastic collision function will need this data to calculate the new velocities. This is what the new version of the Collider class looks like:

```
class Collider {
    public:
        bool m_Active;
        float* m_ParentRotation;
        float* m_ParentX;
        float* m_ParentY;
        Vector2D m_TempPoint;

        bool CCHitTest( Collider* collider );

        void ElasticCollision( Collider* collider );
        float m_Mass;
        Vector2D m_Direction;
        Vector2D m_Velocity;
        Vector2D m_Position;

        float m_Radius;
        float m_SteeringRadius;
        float m_SteeringRadiusSQ;
```

```
void SetParentInformation( float* rotation, float* x, float* y );

Collider(float radius);
bool HitTest( Collider *collider );
bool SteeringLineTest( Vector2D &p1, Vector2D &p2 );
bool SteeringRectTest( Vector2D &start_point, Vector2D
                                &end_point );
void WrapPosition();
};
```

The four lines we added are near the center of this new version of the class:

```
void ElasticCollision( Collider* collider );
float m_Mass;
Vector2D m_Direction;
Vector2D m_Velocity;
```

After adding m_Direction and m_Velocity to our Collider class, we need to remove m_Velocity from three of the child classes where we had that code in previous versions of our game. We need to remove those attributes from the Asteroid, Ship, and Projectile classes. Here are the two lines we need to remove:

```
Vector2D m_Direction;
Vector2D m_Velocity;
```

In the following code snippet, we have the Asteroid class after you have removed those two lines:

```
class Asteroid : public Collider {
    public:
        SDL_Texture *m_SpriteTexture;
        SDL_Rect m_src = {.x = 0, .y = 0, .w = 16, .h = 16 };
        SDL_Rect m_dest = {.x = 0, .y = 0, .w = 0, .h = 0 };

        Uint32 m_CurrentFrame = 0;
        int m_NextFrameTime;
        float m_Rotation;

        Emitter* m_Explode;
        Emitter* m_Chunks;

        Asteroid( float x, float y,
                    float velocity,
                    float rotation );
        void Move();
        void Render();
        void Explode();
};
```

This is what the `Ship` class will look like after you have removed those two lines:

```
class Ship : public Collider {
    public:
        const float c_Acceleration = 10.0f;
        const float c_MaxVelocity = 100.0f;
        const int c_AliveTime = 2000;
        const Uint32 c_MinLaunchTime = 300;

        bool m_Accelerating = false;
        Uint32 m_LastLaunchTime;
        const int c_Width = 32;
        const int c_Height = 32;
        SDL_Texture *m_SpriteTexture;
        SDL_Rect src = {.x = 0, .y = 0, .w = 32, .h = 32 };

        Emitter* m_Explode;
        Emitter* m_Exhaust;
        Shield* m_Shield;
        std::vector<Collider*> m_Colliders;

        Uint32 m_CurrentFrame = 0;
        int m_NextFrameTime;
        float m_Rotation;

        void RotateLeft();
        void RotateRight();
        void Accelerate();
        void Decelerate();
        void CapVelocity();
        void Shoot();
        virtual void Move() = 0;
        Ship();
        void Render();
        bool CompoundHitTest( Collider* collider );
};
```

Finally, here is what the `Projectile` class will look like after you have removed those two lines:

```
class Projectile: public Collider {
    public:
        const char* c_SpriteFile = "sprites/ProjectileExp.png";
        const int c_Width = 16;
        const int c_Height = 16;
        SDL_Texture *m_SpriteTexture;
        SDL_Rect src = {.x = 0, .y = 0, .w = 16, .h = 16 };
```

```
        Uint32 m_CurrentFrame = 0;
        int m_NextFrameTime;
        const float c_Velocity = 300.0;
        const float c_AliveTime = 2000;
        float m_TTL;

        Projectile();
        void Move();
        void Render();
        void Launch(Vector2D &position, Vector2D &direction);
};
```

The last class we must change is our `Star` class. The `Star` class is now going to be able to attract the spaceships in our game gravitationally. To do this, we will be adding a constant attribute that defines the maximum range of our gravitational force. In reality, gravity extends on forever, but for our game, we do not want the gravity to affect our spaceships when the star is off-screen (or at least very far off-screen). Because of this, we are going to limit the distance of the gravitational effect to 500 pixels. We will also add a new function to our class called `ShipGravity`. We will be passing a `Ship` object into this function, and the function will modify the velocity of the ship based on the squared distance to the `Star` object. This is what the new version of the `Star` class definition will look like:

```
class Star : public Collider {
    public:
        const float c_MaxGravityDistSQ = 250000.0; // 300 squared

        SDL_Texture *m_SpriteTexture;
        SDL_Rect m_src = {.x = 0, .y = 0, .w = 64, .h = 64 };
        SDL_Rect m_dest = {.x = 0, .y = 0, .w = 64, .h = 64 };

        std::vector<Emitter*> m_FlareList;

        Uint32 m_CurrentFrame = 0;
        int m_NextFrameTime;

        Star();

        void Move();
        void Render();

        void ShipGravity( Ship* s );
};
```

Changing collider.cpp

The next file we will change is the `collider.cpp` file, which holds the functions we declared in our `Collider` class definition. The only change will be the addition of a single function, `ElasticCollision`. This function modifies the position and velocity of our two colliders based on the mass and the starting velocities of those objects. This is what the `ElasticCollision` function looks like:

```cpp
void Collider::ElasticCollision( Collider* collider ) {
    if( collider->m_Mass == STAR_MASS || m_Mass == STAR_MASS ) {
        return;
    }

    Vector2D separation_vec = collider->m_Position - m_Position;

    separation_vec.Normalize();
    separation_vec *= collider->m_Radius + m_Radius;

    collider->m_Position = m_Position + separation_vec;

    Vector2D old_v1 = m_Velocity;
    Vector2D old_v2 = collider->m_Velocity;

    m_Velocity = old_v1 * ((m_Mass - collider->m_Mass)/(m_Mass +
    collider->m_Mass)) +
    old_v2 * ((2 * collider->m_Mass) / (m_Mass + collider->m_Mass));

    collider->m_Velocity = old_v1 * ((2 * collider->m_Mass)/(m_Mass +
    collider->m_Mass)) +
    old_v2 * ((collider->m_Mass - m_Mass)/(m_Mass + collider->m_Mass));
}
```

The first thing the function does is check to see whether either collider has the mass of a star. If either is a star, we do not change their velocities. The star's velocity does not change, because it is too massive to move, and the object colliding with the star does not change its mass because it is destroyed in the collision:

```cpp
if( collider->m_Mass == STAR_MASS || m_Mass == STAR_MASS ) {
    return;
}
```

After the mass check, we need to adjust the position of the colliders so that they are not overlapping. Overlap can happen because the position of our objects changes every frame and is not continuous. Because of this, we need to move the position of one of our objects so that it is barely touching the other object. A more accurate way to do this would have been to modify the position of both objects by half the amount we modify the one object, but in different directions. For simplicity, we will only be changing the position of one of the colliders:

```
separation_vec.Normalize();
separation_vec *= collider->m_Radius + m_Radius;

collider->m_Position = m_Position + separation_vec;
```

After that, we will modify the velocities of the two collider objects using the masses and the starting velocities of those two objects:

```
Vector2D old_v1 = m_Velocity;
Vector2D old_v2 = collider->m_Velocity;

m_Velocity = old_v1 * ((m_Mass - collider->m_Mass)/(m_Mass +
collider->m_Mass)) +
old_v2 * ((2 * collider->m_Mass) / (m_Mass + collider->m_Mass));

collider->m_Velocity = old_v1 * ((2 * collider->m_Mass)/(m_Mass +
collider->m_Mass)) +
old_v2 * ((collider->m_Mass - m_Mass)/(m_Mass + collider->m_Mass));
```

If you want to learn more about the formula we used to calculate the new velocities, check out the Wikipedia article regarding elastic collisions at `https://en.wikipedia.org/wiki/Elastic_collision`.

Changes to star.cpp

In our `star.cpp` file, we will need to modify our `Star` class's constructor function, as well as its `Move` function. We will also need to add a new function called `ShipGravity`. The first thing we will do is add the following line somewhere in our `Star` class constructor:

```
m_Mass = STAR_MASS;
```

After that, we will need to define our `ShipGravity` function. The following code defines that function:

```
void Star::ShipGravity( Ship* s ) {
    Vector2D dist_vec = m_Position - s->m_Position;
    float dist_sq = dist_vec.MagSQ();

    if( dist_sq < c_MaxGravityDistSQ ) {
        float force = (c_MaxGravityDistSQ / dist_sq) * delta_time;
        dist_vec.Normalize();
        dist_vec *= force;
        s->m_Velocity += dist_vec;
    }
}
```

The first line creates a `dist_vec` vector, which is a vector representing the distance between the star's position and the ship's position. The second line gets the squared distance between the star and the ship. After that, we have an `if` block that looks like this:

```
if( dist_sq < c_MaxGravityDistSQ ) {
    float force = (c_MaxGravityDistSQ / dist_sq) * delta_time;
    dist_vec.Normalize();
    dist_vec *= force;
    s->m_Velocity += dist_vec;
}
```

This `if` block is checking the square distance against the maximum distance where gravity affects the ship, which we defined in the `c_MaxGravityDistSQ` constant. Because gravity decreases with the square of the distance between the star and our ship, we compute the scalar force by dividing the maximum gravitation distance by 50 times the distance squared to our spaceship. The value of 50 was picked rather arbitrarily and was the result of me playing around with the numbers until the force of gravity felt right to me. You may choose a different value if you would prefer your gravitational force to be different. You may also choose to modify the maximum gravitational distance by changing the value of `c_MaxGravityDistSQ` that we defined in `game.hpp`. The following lines are used to turn our scalar force value into a vector force value that is pointing from our ship to our star:

```
dist_vec.Normalize();
dist_vec *= force;
```

Now that we have converted `dist_vec` into a force vector that points in the direction of our star, we can add that force vector to our ship's velocity to create the gravitational effect on our ship:

```
s->m_Velocity += dist_vec;
```

The final change we need to make is to the `Move` function. We will need to add two calls to the `ShipGravity` function; one call to create the gravitational effect on the player, and a second call to create the gravitational effect on the enemy spaceship. Here is the new version of the `Move` function:

```
void Star::Move() {
    m_NextFrameTime -= diff_time;

    if( m_NextFrameTime <= 0 ) {
        ++m_CurrentFrame;
        m_NextFrameTime = ms_per_frame;
        if( m_CurrentFrame >= 8 ) {
            m_CurrentFrame = 0;
        }
    }

    ShipGravity( player );
    ShipGravity( enemy );
}
```

The last two lines are new. Make sure you add these two lines to the `Move` function:

```
ShipGravity( player );
ShipGravity( enemy );
```

Changing the main.cpp file

After updating our `star.cpp` file, we need to change the `main.cpp` file to incorporate our elastic collisions. We need to make all of these changes to the `collisions()` function. Here is the new version of `collisions` in its entirety:

```
void collisions() {
 Asteroid* asteroid;
 std::vector<Asteroid*>::iterator ita;
    if( player->m_CurrentFrame == 0 && player->CompoundHitTest( star ) ) {
        player->m_CurrentFrame = 1;
        player->m_NextFrameTime = ms_per_frame;
        player->m_Explode->Run();
        large_explosion_snd->Play();
    }
    if( enemy->m_CurrentFrame == 0 && enemy->CompoundHitTest( star ) ) {
        enemy->m_CurrentFrame = 1;
        enemy->m_NextFrameTime = ms_per_frame;
        enemy->m_Explode->Run();
        large_explosion_snd->Play();
```

```
        }
    Projectile* projectile;
    std::vector<Projectile*>::iterator it;
    for(it=projectile_pool->m_ProjectileList.begin();
    it!=projectile_pool->m_ProjectileList.end();
    it++) {
        projectile = *it;
        if( projectile->m_CurrentFrame == 0 && projectile->m_Active ) {
            for( ita = asteroid_list.begin(); ita != asteroid_list.end();
                ita++
            ) {
                asteroid = *ita;
                if( asteroid->m_Active ) {
                    if( asteroid->HitTest( projectile ) ) {
                        asteroid->ElasticCollision( projectile );
                        projectile->m_CurrentFrame = 1;
                        projectile->m_NextFrameTime = ms_per_frame;
                        small_explosion_snd->Play();
                    }
                }
            }
            if( projectile->HitTest( star ) ){
                projectile->m_CurrentFrame = 1;
                projectile->m_NextFrameTime = ms_per_frame;
                small_explosion_snd->Play();
            }
            else if( player->m_CurrentFrame == 0 && ( projectile->HitTest(
            player ) ||
                    player->CompoundHitTest( projectile ) ) ) {
                if( player->m_Shield->m_Active == false ) {
                    player->m_CurrentFrame = 1;
                    player->m_NextFrameTime = ms_per_frame;
                    player->m_Explode->Run();
                    large_explosion_snd->Play();
                }
                else {
                    hit_snd->Play();
                    player->ElasticCollision( projectile );
                }
                projectile->m_CurrentFrame = 1;
                projectile->m_NextFrameTime = ms_per_frame;
            }
            else if( enemy->m_CurrentFrame == 0 && ( projectile-
            >HitTest( enemy ) || enemy->CompoundHitTest( projectile ) )
            ) {
                if( enemy->m_Shield->m_Active == false ) {
                    enemy->m_CurrentFrame = 1;
                    enemy->m_NextFrameTime = ms_per_frame;
```

```
                enemy->m_Explode->Run();
                large_explosion_snd->Play();
            }
            else {
                enemy->ElasticCollision( projectile );
                hit_snd->Play();
            }
            projectile->m_CurrentFrame = 1;
            projectile->m_NextFrameTime = ms_per_frame;
        }
    }
}
for( ita = asteroid_list.begin(); ita != asteroid_list.end(); ita++ ) {
    asteroid = *ita;
    if( asteroid->m_Active ) {
        if( asteroid->HitTest( star ) ) {
            asteroid->Explode();
            small_explosion_snd->Play();
        }
    }
    else { continue; }
    if( player->m_CurrentFrame == 0 && asteroid->m_Active &&
        ( asteroid->HitTest( player ) || player->CompoundHitTest(
        asteroid ) ) ) {
        if( player->m_Shield->m_Active == false ) {
            player->m_CurrentFrame = 1;
            player->m_NextFrameTime = ms_per_frame;
            player->m_Explode->Run();
            large_explosion_snd->Play();
        }
        else {
            player->ElasticCollision( asteroid );
            small_explosion_snd->Play();
        }
    }
    if( enemy->m_CurrentFrame == 0 && asteroid->m_Active &&
        ( asteroid->HitTest( enemy ) || enemy->CompoundHitTest(
        asteroid ) ) ) {
        if( enemy->m_Shield->m_Active == false ) {
            enemy->m_CurrentFrame = 1;
            enemy->m_NextFrameTime = ms_per_frame;
            enemy->m_Explode->Run();
            large_explosion_snd->Play();
        }
        else {
            enemy->ElasticCollision( asteroid );
            small_explosion_snd->Play();
        }
```

```
        }
    }
    Asteroid* asteroid_1;
    Asteroid* asteroid_2;
    std::vector<Asteroid*>::iterator ita_1;
    std::vector<Asteroid*>::iterator ita_2;
    for( ita_1 = asteroid_list.begin(); ita_1 != asteroid_list.end();
         ita_1++ ) {
        asteroid_1 = *ita_1;
        if( !asteroid_1->m_Active ) { continue; }
        for( ita_2 = ita_1+1; ita_2 != asteroid_list.end(); ita_2++ ) {
            asteroid_2 = *ita_2;
            if( !asteroid_2->m_Active ) { continue; }
            if( asteroid_1->HitTest( asteroid_2 ) ) {
                asteroid_1->ElasticCollision( asteroid_2 );
            }
        }
    }
}
```

In the first part of this function, we loop over the projectiles and check to see whether they hit an asteroid or a ship. If the projectile hits an asteroid or a ship when that ship has its shields up, we want to create an elastic collision with the projectile. The projectile will still be destroyed, but the ship or asteroid will have a modified velocity based on the collision. Here is the code for the projectile loop:

```
for( it = projectile_pool->m_ProjectileList.begin(); it !=
projectile_pool->m_ProjectileList.end(); it++ ) {
    projectile = *it;
    if( projectile->m_CurrentFrame == 0 && projectile->m_Active ) {
        for( ita = asteroid_list.begin(); ita != asteroid_list.end();
        ita++ ) {
            asteroid = *ita;
            if( asteroid->m_Active ) {
                if( asteroid->HitTest( projectile ) ) {
                    asteroid->ElasticCollision( projectile );
                    projectile->m_CurrentFrame = 1;
                    projectile->m_NextFrameTime = ms_per_frame;
                    small_explosion_snd->Play();
                }
            }
        }
        if( projectile->HitTest( star ) ){
            projectile->m_CurrentFrame = 1;
            projectile->m_NextFrameTime = ms_per_frame;
            small_explosion_snd->Play();
        }
```

```
            else if( player->m_CurrentFrame == 0 &&
                    ( projectile->HitTest( player ) ||
                      player->CompoundHitTest( projectile ) ) ) {
                if( player->m_Shield->m_Active == false ) {
                    player->m_CurrentFrame = 1;
                    player->m_NextFrameTime = ms_per_frame;

                    player->m_Explode->Run();
                    large_explosion_snd->Play();
                }
                else {
                    hit_snd->Play();
                    player->ElasticCollision( projectile );
                }
                projectile->m_CurrentFrame = 1;
                projectile->m_NextFrameTime = ms_per_frame;
            }
            else if( enemy->m_CurrentFrame == 0 &&
                    ( projectile->HitTest( enemy ) ||
                      enemy->CompoundHitTest( projectile ) ) ) {
                if( enemy->m_Shield->m_Active == false ) {
                    enemy->m_CurrentFrame = 1;
                    enemy->m_NextFrameTime = ms_per_frame;
                    enemy->m_Explode->Run();
                    large_explosion_snd->Play();
                }
                else {
                    enemy->ElasticCollision( projectile );
                    hit_snd->Play();
                }
                projectile->m_CurrentFrame = 1;
                projectile->m_NextFrameTime = ms_per_frame;
            }
        }
    }
}
```

The first series of checks this loop performs is against every asteroid. It looks for an active asteroid with which it currently collides. If those conditions are true, the first thing it does is call the `ElasticCollision` function on the asteroid, passing in the projectile:

```
for( ita = asteroid_list.begin(); ita != asteroid_list.end(); ita++ ) {
    asteroid = *ita;
    if( asteroid->m_Active ) {
        if( asteroid->HitTest( projectile ) ) {
            asteroid->ElasticCollision( projectile );
            projectile->m_CurrentFrame = 1;
            projectile->m_NextFrameTime = ms_per_frame;
            small_explosion_snd->Play();
```

```
          }
      }
```

This code is the same as the earlier version, but with the addition of this call to
`ElasticCollision`:

```
    asteroid->ElasticCollision( projectile );
```

Later in our loop through each active projectile, we will add a call to the
`ElasticCollision` function if a projectile strikes your player's spaceship while its shields
are up:

```
    else if( player->m_CurrentFrame == 0 &&
            ( projectile->HitTest( player ) ||
              player->CompoundHitTest( projectile ) ) ) {
        if( player->m_Shield->m_Active == false ) {
            player->m_CurrentFrame = 1;
            player->m_NextFrameTime = ms_per_frame;
            player->m_Explode->Run();
            large_explosion_snd->Play();
        }
        else {
            hit_snd->Play();
            player->ElasticCollision( projectile );
        }
        projectile->m_CurrentFrame = 1;
        projectile->m_NextFrameTime = ms_per_frame;
    }
```

We will do the same for an enemy spaceship struck by a projectile while its shields are up:

```
    else if( enemy->m_CurrentFrame == 0 &&
            ( projectile->HitTest( enemy ) ||
              enemy->CompoundHitTest( projectile ) ) ) {
        if( enemy->m_Shield->m_Active == false ) {
            enemy->m_CurrentFrame = 1;
            enemy->m_NextFrameTime = ms_per_frame;
            enemy->m_Explode->Run();
            large_explosion_snd->Play();
        }
        else {
            enemy->ElasticCollision( projectile );
            hit_snd->Play();
        }
        projectile->m_CurrentFrame = 1;
        projectile->m_NextFrameTime = ms_per_frame;
    }
}
```

After looping over all of the active projectiles, the `collisions` function loops over all of the asteroids looking for a collision between an asteroid and one of the ships. If the ship does not have its shields activated, the ship is destroyed. We do not make any modifications to this part of the code. In previous versions of our code, if the ship did have its shields up, we destroyed the asteroid. Now, we will have an elastic collision, which will cause the spaceship and the asteroid to bounce off one another. This is what this `asteroid` loop looks like:

```
for( ita = asteroid_list.begin(); ita != asteroid_list.end(); ita++ ) {
    asteroid = *ita;
    if( asteroid->m_Active ) {
        if( asteroid->HitTest( star ) ) {
            asteroid->Explode();
            small_explosion_snd->Play();
        }
    }
    else {
        continue;
    }

    if( player->m_CurrentFrame == 0 &&
        asteroid->m_Active &&
        ( asteroid->HitTest( player ) ||
          player->CompoundHitTest( asteroid ) ) ) {
        if( player->m_Shield->m_Active == false ) {
            player->m_CurrentFrame = 1;
            player->m_NextFrameTime = ms_per_frame;

            player->m_Explode->Run();
            large_explosion_snd->Play();
        }
        else {
            player->ElasticCollision( asteroid );
            small_explosion_snd->Play();
        }
    }
    if( enemy->m_CurrentFrame == 0 &&
        asteroid->m_Active &&
        ( asteroid->HitTest( enemy ) ||
          enemy->CompoundHitTest( asteroid ) ) ) {
        if( enemy->m_Shield->m_Active == false ) {
            enemy->m_CurrentFrame = 1;
            enemy->m_NextFrameTime = ms_per_frame;

            enemy->m_Explode->Run();
            large_explosion_snd->Play();
        }
```

```
        else {
            enemy->ElasticCollision( asteroid );
            small_explosion_snd->Play();
        }
    }
}
```

There are now two calls to `ElasticCollision`. One of the calls occurs when the player ship collides with an asteroid and the player ship has its shields up. The other occurs when the enemy ship collides with an asteroid, and the enemy ship has its shields up.

The last change we must make to our `collisions()` function is the addition of a new double `asteroid` loop that will loop through all our asteroids looking for collisions between two of them. That creates a fun effect where asteroids bounce off one another like billiard balls. If there is a collision detected between two of the asteroids, we call `ElasticCollision`:

```
Asteroid* asteroid_1;
Asteroid* asteroid_2;

std::vector<Asteroid*>::iterator ita_1;
std::vector<Asteroid*>::iterator ita_2;

for( ita_1 = asteroid_list.begin(); ita_1 != asteroid_list.end(); ita_1++ )
{
    asteroid_1 = *ita_1;
    if( !asteroid_1->m_Active ) {
        continue;
    }

    for( ita_2 = ita_1+1; ita_2 != asteroid_list.end(); ita_2++ ) {
        asteroid_2 = *ita_2;
        if( !asteroid_2->m_Active ) {
            continue;
        }

        if( asteroid_1->HitTest( asteroid_2 ) ) {
            asteroid_1->ElasticCollision( asteroid_2 );
        }
    }
}
```

Changes to asteroid.cpp and projectile.cpp

We have to make a small addition to both `asteroid.cpp` and `projectile.cpp`. We have added a new attribute called `m_Mass` to the `Collider` class, so all classes derived from `Collider` inherit this attribute. The `m_Mass` attribute is used by our `ElasticCollision` function to determine how these objects will move after an elastic collision. The ratio between the mass of a spaceship and the mass of a projectile will be used to calculate the amount of recoil that occurs when the spaceship shoots a projectile. The first modification is to the `Projectile` class constructor. Here is the new version of that constructor:

```
Projectile::Projectile(): Collider(4.0) {
    m_Active = false;

    SDL_Surface *temp_surface = IMG_Load( c_SpriteFile );

    if( !temp_surface ) {
        printf("failed to load image: %s\n", IMG_GetError() );
        return;
    }
    m_SpriteTexture = SDL_CreateTextureFromSurface( renderer, temp_surface
    );

    if( !m_SpriteTexture ) {
        printf("failed to create texture: %s\n", IMG_GetError() );
        return;
    }

    SDL_FreeSurface( temp_surface );

    m_Mass = 1.0;
}
```

The only modification is the final line, where we set `m_Mass` to `1.0`:

```
m_Mass = 1.0;
```

The next constructor that needs to be modified is in the `asteroid.cpp` file. We need to modify the `Asteroid` class constructor. Here is the new version of the `Asteroid` constructor:

```
Asteroid::Asteroid( float x, float y, float velocity, float rotation ):
Collider(8.0) {
    SDL_Surface *temp_surface = IMG_Load( ADSTEROID_SPRITE_FILE );
    if( !temp_surface ) {
        printf("failed to load image: %s\n", IMG_GetError() );
        return;
```

```
    }
    else { printf("success creating asteroid surface\n"); }
    m_SpriteTexture = SDL_CreateTextureFromSurface( renderer, temp_surface
    );
    if( !m_SpriteTexture ) {
        printf("failed to create texture: %s\n", IMG_GetError() );
        return;
    }
    else { printf("success creating asteroid texture\n"); }
    SDL_FreeSurface( temp_surface );
    m_Explode = new Emitter((char*)"/sprites/Explode.png", 100, 0, 360,
    1000, 0.3, false, 20.0, 40.0, 10, 0, 0, 5, 1.0, 2.0, 1.0, 2.0,
    0xffffff, 0xffffff, 0.01, 10, false, false, 800, 8 );
    m_Explode->m_parent_rotation_ptr = &m_Rotation;
    m_Explode->m_parent_x_ptr = &(m_Position.x);
    m_Explode->m_parent_y_ptr = &(m_Position.y);
    m_Explode->m_Active = false;
    m_Chunks = new Emitter((char*)"/sprites/small-asteroid.png",40,0,360,
    1000, 0.05, false, 80.0, 150.0, 5,0,0,10,2.0,2.0,0.25, 0.5, 0xffffff,
    0xffffff, 0.1, 10, false, true, 1000, 8 );
    m_Chunks->m_parent_rotation_ptr = &m_Rotation;
    m_Chunks->m_parent_x_ptr = &m_Position.x;
    m_Chunks->m_parent_y_ptr = &m_Position.y;
    m_Chunks->m_Active = false;
    m_Position.x = x;
    m_Position.y = y;
    Vector2D direction;
    direction.x = 1;
    direction.Rotate( rotation );
    m_Direction = direction;
    m_Velocity = m_Direction * velocity;
    m_dest.h = m_src.h = m_dest.w = m_src.w = 16;
    m_Rotation = rotation;
    m_Active = true;
    m_CurrentFrame = 0;
    m_NextFrameTime = ms_per_frame;

    m_Mass = 100.0;
}
```

Once again, the only line we will add is the final line where we set m_Mass to 100.0:

```
m_Mass = 100.0;
```

Changes to the ship.cpp file

The first change to the ship.cpp file will be to the Ship constructor. This is a simple change that we need to make to the end of the constructor function, where we will be setting the mass of the ship to 50.0. Here is the new version of the Ship class constructor:

```
Ship::Ship() : Collider(8.0) {
    m_Rotation = PI;

    m_LastLaunchTime = current_time;

    m_Accelerating = false;

    m_Exhaust = new Emitter((char*)"/sprites/ProjectileExpOrange.png", 200,
                        -10, 10,
                        400, 1.0, true,
                        0.1, 0.1,
                        30, 0, 12, 0.5,
                        0.5, 1.0,
                        0.5, 1.0,
                        0xffffff, 0xffffff,
                        0.7, 10,
                        true, true,
                        1000, 6 );

    m_Exhaust->m_parent_rotation_ptr = &m_Rotation;
    m_Exhaust->m_parent_x_ptr = &(m_Position.x);
    m_Exhaust->m_parent_y_ptr = &(m_Position.y);
    m_Exhaust->m_x_adjustment = 10;
    m_Exhaust->m_y_adjustment = 10;
    m_Exhaust->m_Active = false;

    m_Explode = new Emitter((char*)"/sprites/Explode.png", 100,
                        0, 360,
                        1000, 0.3, false,
                        20.0, 40.0,
                        10, 0, 0, 5,
                        1.0, 2.0,
                        1.0, 2.0,
                        0xffffff, 0xffffff,
                        0.0, 10,
                        false, false,
                        800, 8 );

    m_Explode->m_parent_rotation_ptr = &m_Rotation;
    m_Explode->m_parent_x_ptr = &(m_Position.x);
    m_Explode->m_parent_y_ptr = &(m_Position.y);
```

```
        m_Explode->m_Active = false;

        m_Direction.y = 1.0;

        m_Active = true;
        m_Mass = 50.0;
    }
```

The only line that was changed was the very last line:

```
m_Mass = 50.0;
```

We will also need to change the Shoot function to add a recoil. A few lines will be added to modify the velocity of the ship by adding a vector that is in the opposite direction to where the ship is facing, and has a magnitude based on the velocity and relative mass of the projectile fired. Here is the new Shoot function:

```
void Ship::Shoot() {
    Projectile* projectile;
    if( current_time - m_LastLaunchTime >= c_MinLaunchTime ) {
        m_LastLaunchTime = current_time;
        projectile = projectile_pool->GetFreeProjectile();
        if( projectile != NULL ) {
            projectile->Launch( m_Position, m_Direction );
            player_laser_snd->Play();
            m_Velocity -= m_Direction * (projectile->c_Velocity *
projectile->m_Mass /
m_Mass);
            CapVelocity();
        }
    }
}
```

These are the two lines that we are adding to the function:

```
m_Velocity -= m_Direction * (projectile->c_Velocity * projectile->m_Mass /
m_Mass);
CapVelocity();
```

Compiling the physics.html file

Now that we have added physics, it is time to compile our code. We can build the physics.html file with the following em++ command:

```
em++ asteroid.cpp audio.cpp camera.cpp collider.cpp emitter.cpp
enemy_ship.cpp finite_state_machine.cpp locator.cpp main.cpp particle.cpp
```

```
player_ship.cpp projectile_pool.cpp projectile.cpp range.cpp
render_manager.cpp shield.cpp ship.cpp star.cpp vector.cpp -o physics.html
--preload-file audio --preload-file sprites -std=c++17 -s USE_WEBGL2=1 -s
USE_SDL=2 -s USE_SDL_IMAGE=2 -s SDL2_IMAGE_FORMATS=["png"] -s
USE_SDL_IMAGE=2 -s SDL2_IMAGE_FORMATS=["png"]
```

The following screenshot may look similar to earlier versions, but when you fire your projectiles, the ship will accelerate backward. If you collide with an asteroid when your shields are on, you will bounce off them like a billiard ball. Get too close to the sun, and the gravity will begin to attract your ship:

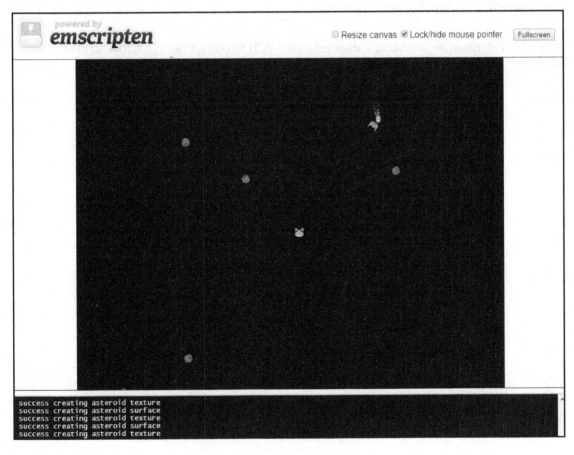

Figure 13.1: physics.html screenshot

Summary

In this chapter, we discussed the history of physics in computer games, and how that history dates back to the very first computer game, *SpaceWar!*. We talked about the physics that we already have in our game, which includes the conservation of momentum. We briefly discussed Newton's third law and how it applies to games, and we then added more Newtonian physics to our game by using the third law. We added a gravitational field to our star and had it attract the spaceships in our game with a force that decreases with the square of the distance between the two objects. Finally, we added elastic collisions between our spaceships, projectiles, and asteroids.

In the next chapter, we will add a **user interface** (**UI**) to our game. We will also break the game up into multiple screens and add a mouse interface.

14
UI and Mouse Input

A **user interface (UI)** defines the interaction between a computer program and the user. In our game, our interaction so far has been limited to a keyboard interface that controls our player's spaceship. When we wrote our particle system configuration apps, we used HTML to define a more robust user interface, which allowed us to input values to configure our particle system. From that user interface, our code had to interact with the WebAssembly code indirectly. That is a technique you could continue to use for games if you wanted to leverage HTML to define your user interface, but it has a few disadvantages. First of all, we may want user interface elements that overlay the content of our game. Going through the DOM for this kind of effect is not very efficient. It is also easier to have interactions between our UI and objects from within the game if the UI elements are rendered inside of the game engine. In addition, you may be developing your C/C++ code to be used for a platform as well as a web release. If this is the case, you may not want HTML to have much of a role in your user interface.

In this chapter, we will be implementing a few UI features inside our game. We will need to implement a `Button` class, which is one of the simplest and most common UI elements. We will also need to implement a separate screen and game state so that we can have a starting and an ending game screen.

 You will need to include several images and audio files in your build to make this project work. Make sure that you include the `/Chapter14/sprites/` and `/Chapter14/audio/` folders from this project's GitHub repository. If you haven't downloaded the GitHub project yet, you can get it online here: `https://github.com/PacktPublishing/Hands-On-Game-Development`.

In this chapter, we will be covering the following topics:

- UI requirements
- Getting mouse input
- Creating a button
- The start game screen
- The game over screen

UI requirements

The first thing we will need to do when implementing our UI is to decide on some requirements. What exactly do we need for our user interface? The first part of that is deciding what game screens we need for our game. This is usually the kind of thing you do early in the game design process, but because I am writing a book about WebAssembly, I have saved this step for a later chapter. Deciding what screens your game needs usually involves a storyboard and a process by which you either talk through (if more than one person is working on the game) or think through the way a user will interact with your web page, as well as the game that is on that page:

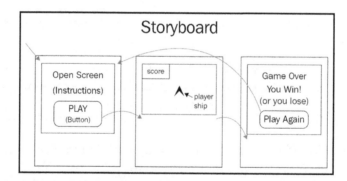

Figure 14.1: Storyboard example for our user interface

You don't have to draw a storyboard, but I find it useful when thinking through what I need for a game's UI. It is even more useful when you need to relay that information to another team member or an artist. When thinking through what we need in this game for the preceding storyboard, I came up with the following list of requirements:

- Opening screen
- Instructions

- Play button
- Game play screen
- Score text
- Game over screen
- You win message
- You lose message
- Play again button

Opening screen

Our game needs an opening screen for a few reasons. First of all, we don't want the game to start as soon as the user loads up the web page. There are a lot of reasons the user may load up the web page and not start playing the instant the web page has completely loaded. If they are on a slow connection, they may turn away from the computer while the game is loading up and may not notice the second it loads. If they reached this page by clicking a link, they might not be prepared to start playing the instant the game loads. It is also good practice in general to have something the player must do to acknowledge they are ready before throwing them into gameplay. The opening screen should also include some instructions for basic gameplay. Arcade games have a long history of putting simple instructions on the cabinet to tell the player what they must do to play the game. Famously, the game Pong came with the instructions *Avoid missing ball for high score* printed on the cabinet. Unfortunately, we do not have an arcade cabinet to print our instructions on, so using the opening game screen is the next best thing. We will also need a button that will allow the user to begin playing the game when they click it, as follows:

Figure 14.2: Opening screen image

Play screen

The play screen is the screen we have always had. It is the screen where the player moves their spaceship around, trying to destroy the enemy spaceship. We may not need to change how this screen works, but we will need to add transitions to and from this screen based on the game state. The game will need to transition to our play screen from the opening screen when the player clicks a button. The player will also need to transition from the screen to the game over screen if either of the ships are destroyed. This is shown here:

Figure 14.3: The original screen is now the play screen

Game over screen

If one of the spaceships is destroyed, the game is over. If the player's ship is destroyed, then the player loses the game. If the enemy ship is destroyed, then the player wins the game. The *game over screen* lets us know that the game is over and tells us if the player has won or lost. It also needs to provide a button that allows our player to play the game again if they would like to. The game over screen is shown here:

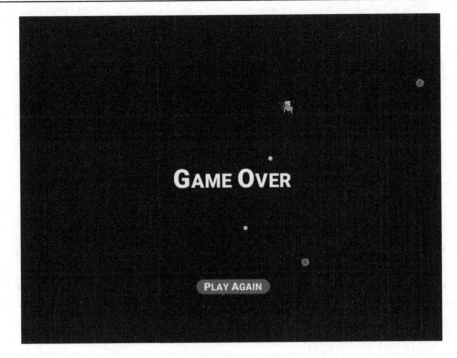

Figure 14.4: Game over screen

Mouse input

Before we can implement a button, we need to learn how to use mouse input in SDL. The code we used to get the keyboard input is in our `main.cpp` file. Inside the `input` function, you will find a call to `SDL_PollEvent`, followed by a few different switch statements. The first switch statements check the `event.type` for `SDL_KEYDOWN`. The second switch checks `event.key.keysym.sym` to see which key we pressed:

```
if( SDL_PollEvent( &event ) ){
    switch( event.type ){
        case SDL_KEYDOWN:
            switch( event.key.keysym.sym ){
                case SDLK_LEFT:
                    left_key_down = true;
                    break;
                case SDLK_RIGHT:
                    right_key_down = true;
                    break;
                case SDLK_UP:
```

```
            up_key_down = true;
            break;
        case SDLK_DOWN:
            down_key_down = true;
            break;
        case SDLK_f:
            f_key_down = true;
            break;
        case SDLK_SPACE:
            space_key_down = true;
            break;
        default:
            break;
    }
    break;
```

When we are looking for mouse input, we need to use the same `SDL_PollEvent` function to retrieve our mouse events. The three mouse events we are concerned with are `SDL_MOUSEMOTION`, `SDL_MOUSEBUTTONDOWN`, and `SDL_MOUSEBUTTONUP`. Once we know the kind of mouse event we are dealing with, we can use `SDL_GetMouseState` to find the x and y coordinates of our mouse when the event occurs:

```
if(SDL_PollEvent( &event ) )
{
    switch (event.type)
    {
        case SDL_MOUSEMOTION:
        {
            int x_val = 0;
            int y_val = 0;
            SDL_GetMouseState( &x_val, &y_val );
            printf("mouse move x=%d y=%d\n", x_val, y_val);
        }
        case SDL_MOUSEBUTTONDOWN:
        {
            switch (event.button.button)
            {
                case SDL_BUTTON_LEFT:
                {
                    int x_val = 0;
                    int y_val = 0;
                    SDL_GetMouseState( &x_val, &y_val );
                    printf("mouse down x=%d y=%d\n", x_val, y_val);
                    break;
                }
                default:
                {
```

```
                    break;
            }
        }
        break;
    }
    case SDL_MOUSEBUTTONUP:
    {
        switch (event.button.button)
        {
            case SDL_BUTTON_LEFT:
            {
                int x_val = 0;
                int y_val = 0;
                SDL_GetMouseState( &x_val, &y_val );
                printf("mouse up x=%d y=%d\n", x_val, y_val);
                break;
            }
            default:
            {
                break;
            }
        }
        break;
    }
}
```

Now that we can receive mouse input, let's create a simple user interface button.

Creating a button

Now that we know how to capture mouse input in WebAssembly using SDL, we can use this knowledge to create a button that can be clicked by a mouse. The first thing we will need to do is create a `UIButton` class definition inside of the `game.hpp` file. Our button will have more than one sprite texture associated with it. Buttons usually have a hover state and a clicked state, so we will want to display an alternative version of our sprite if the user is hovering the mouse cursor over the button, or has clicked the button:

Figure 14.5: Button states

To capture these events, we will need functions to detect whether the mouse has clicked on our button or hovered over it. Here is what our class definition looks like:

```
class UIButton {
    public:
        bool m_Hover;
        bool m_Click;
        bool m_Active;
        void (*m_Callback)();

        SDL_Rect m_dest = {.x = 0, .y = 0, .w = 128, .h = 32 };
        SDL_Texture *m_SpriteTexture;
        SDL_Texture *m_ClickTexture;
        SDL_Texture *m_HoverTexture;

        UIButton( int x, int y,
        char* file_name, char* hover_file_name, char* click_file_name,
        void (*callback)() );

        void MouseClick(int x, int y);
        void MouseUp(int x, int y);
        void MouseMove( int x, int y );
        void KeyDown( SDL_Keycode key );
        void RenderUI();
};
```

The first three attributes are button state attributes that tell our render function what sprite to draw, or if the button is inactive, not to draw anything. The m_Hover attribute will cause our renderer to draw m_HoverTexture if it is true. The m_Click attribute will cause our renderer to draw m_ClickTexture if it is true. Finally, m_Active, if set to false, will cause our renderer not to draw anything.

The following line is a function pointer to our callback:

```
void (*m_Callback)();
```

This function pointer is set in our constructor and is the function that we call whenever someone clicks on the button. After the function pointer, we have our destination rectangle, which will have the location, width, and height of the button image file after the constructor runs:

```
SDL_Rect m_dest = {.x = 0, .y = 0, .w = 128, .h = 32 };
```

Then, we have three textures. These textures are used to draw an image to our canvas and chosen during the render, based on the state flags we discussed earlier:

```
SDL_Texture *m_SpriteTexture;
SDL_Texture *m_ClickTexture;
SDL_Texture *m_HoverTexture;
```

Next, we have the constructor function. This function takes in the x and y screen coordinates of our button. After that, there are three strings, which are the locations of the three PNG files we will use to load our textures. The last parameter is a pointer to the callback function:

```
UIButton( int x, int y,
          char* file_name, char* hover_file_name, char* click_file_name,
          void (*callback)() );
```

Then, there are the three functions we will need to call after we call `SDL_PollEvent`, based on the current state of the mouse:

```
void MouseClick(int x, int y);
void MouseUp(int x, int y);
void MouseMove( int x, int y );
```

The `KeyDown` function will take a key code if a key is pressed, and if the key code matches our hotkey, we would like to use it as an alternative to clicking the button with the mouse:

```
void KeyDown( SDL_Keycode key );
```

The `RenderUI` function is similar to the `Render` functions we've created for other objects. The difference between `RenderUI` and `Render` is that the `Render` function will take the camera position into account when rendering a sprite to the screen. The `RenderUI` function will always render in canvas space:

```
void RenderUI();
```

In the next section, we will create user interface state information to track the current screen.

Screen states

Before we begin adding new screens to our game, we will need to create some screen states. We will do most of the management of these states from within the main.cpp file. Different screen states will require different input, will run different logic, and different render functions. We will manage all of this at the highest level of our code as functions called by our game loop. We will define a list of possible states from within the game.hpp file as an enumeration:

```
enum SCREEN_STATE {
    START_SCREEN = 0,
    PLAY_SCREEN = 1,
    PLAY_TRANSITION = 2,
    GAME_OVER_SCREEN = 3,
    YOU_WIN_SCREEN = 4
};
```

You may notice that even though there will only be three different screens, we have a total of five different screen states. START_SCREEN and PLAY_SCREEN are the start screen and play screen respectively. The PLAY_TRANSITION state transitions the screens between START_SCREEN and PLAY_SCREEN by fading in the gameplay instead of having an abrupt switch to play. We will use two different states for our game over screen. These states are GAME_OVER_SCREEN and YOU_WIN_SCREEN. The only difference between these two states is the message that's displayed when the game is over.

Changes to games.hpp

There are a few additional changes we will need to make to our game.hpp file. In addition to our UIButton class, we will need to add a UISprite class definition file. The UISprite is just a plain, ordinary image drawn in canvas space. It will not have any functionality on top of just being a sprite rendered as a UI element. Here is what the definition looks like:

```
class UISprite {
    public:
        bool m_Active;
        SDL_Texture *m_SpriteTexture;
        SDL_Rect m_dest = { .x = 0, .y = 0, .w = 128, .h = 32 };
        UISprite( int x, int y, char* file_name );
        void RenderUI();
};
```

Like the button, it has an active state that's represented by the `m_Active` attribute. If this value is false, the sprite will not render. It also has a sprite texture and a destination attribute that tells the renderer what to draw and where to draw it:

```
SDL_Texture *m_SpriteTexture;
SDL_Rect m_dest = {.x = 0, .y = 0, .w = 128, .h = 32 };
```

It has a simple constructor that takes in the x and y coordinates where we will render the sprite on the canvas, and the file name of the image in the virtual filesystem from which we will load the sprite:

```
UISprite( int x, int y, char* file_name );
```

Finally, it has a render function called `RenderUI` that will render the sprite to the canvas:

```
void RenderUI();
```

Modifying the RenderManager class

The `RenderManager` class will need a new attribute and a new function. In previous versions of our game, we had one type of background that we could render, and that was our scrolling starfield. When we render our start screen, I would like to use a new custom background that includes some instructions for how to play the game.

Here is the new version of the `RenderManager` class definition:

```
class RenderManager {
    public:
        const int c_BackgroundWidth = 800;
        const int c_BackgroundHeight = 600;
        SDL_Texture *m_BackgroundTexture;
        SDL_Rect m_BackgroundDest = {.x = 0, .y = 0, .w =
        c_BackgroundWidth, .h = c_BackgroundHeight };
        SDL_Texture *m_StartBackgroundTexture;

        RenderManager();
        void RenderBackground();
        void RenderStartBackground(int alpha = 255);
        void Render( SDL_Texture *tex, SDL_Rect *src, SDL_Rect *dest,
        float rad_rotation = 0.0,
                    int alpha = 255, int red = 255, int green = 255,
                    int blue = 255 );
        void RenderUI( SDL_Texture *tex, SDL_Rect *src, SDL_Rect *dest,
        float rad_rotation = 0.0,
                    int alpha = 255, int red = 255, int green = 255,
```

```
                           int blue = 255 );
    };
```

We have added a new `SDL_Texture`, which we will use to render the background image in the start screen:

```
    SDL_Texture *m_StartBackgroundTexture;
```

In addition to the new attribute, we have added a new function to render that image when the start screen is active:

```
    void RenderStartBackground(int alpha = 255);
```

The alpha value that's passed into this function will be used to fade out the start screen during the `PLAY_TRANSITION` screen state. That transition state will begin when the player clicks the "Play" button and will last for about a second.

New external variables

We need to add three new `extern` variable definitions that will reference variables we declare in the `main.cpp` file. Two of these variables are pointers to `UISprite` objects, and one of these variables is a pointer to a `UIButton`. Here are the three `extern` definitions:

```
    extern UISprite *you_win_sprite;
    extern UISprite *game_over_sprite;
    extern UIButton* play_btn;
```

We use these two `UISprite` pointers in the game over screen. The first, `you_win_sprite`, is the sprite that will be displayed when the player wins the game. The second sprite, `game_over_sprite`, is the sprite that will be displayed when the player loses. The final variable, `play_btn`, is the play button that will be displayed on the start screen.

Changes to main.cpp

We manage the new screen states from within our game loop. Because of this, we will make most of the changes in the `main.cpp` file. We will need to break the `input` function up into three new functions, one for each of our game screens. We will need to break our `render` function into `start_render` and `play_render` functions. We don't need an `end_render` function because we will continue to use the `play_render` function when the end screen is displayed.

We will also need a function to display the transition between the start screen and the play screen. Inside of the game loop, we will need to add logic to perform different loop logic based on the current screen.

Adding global variables

The first change we need to make to our `main.cpp` file is to add new global variables. We will need new global variables for our user interface sprites and buttons. We will need a new global variable to represent the current screen state, the transition time between states, and a flag telling us if the player has won the game. Here are the new global variables we need in the `main.cpp` file:

```
UIButton* play_btn;
UIButton* play_again_btn;
UISprite *you_win_sprite;
UISprite *game_over_sprite;
SCREEN_STATE current_screen = START_SCREEN;
int transition_time = 0;
bool you_win = false;
```

The first two variables are `UIButton` object pointers. The first is `play_btn`, which is the start screen button that the user will click to begin playing the game. The second is `play_again_btn`, which is a button on the end game screen the player can click to restart the game. After the UIButtons, we have two `UISprite` objects:

```
UISprite *you_win_sprite;
UISprite *game_over_sprite;
```

These are the sprites that are displayed on the end game screen. Which sprite is displayed depends on whether or not the player destroyed the enemy ship or vice versa. After those sprites, we have a `SCREEN_STATE` variable, which is used to track the current screen state:

```
SCREEN_STATE current_screen = START_SCREEN;
```

The `transition_time` variable is used to keep track of the amount of time left in the transition state between the start screen and the play screen. The `you_win` flag is set when the game is over and is used to keep track of who won the game.

Input functions

The previous version of our game had a single `input` function that used `SDL_PollEvent` to poll for key presses. In this version, we want an input function for each of the three screen states. The first thing we should do is rename the original `input` function `play_input`. This will no longer be a universal input function, – it will only perform the input functionality for the play screen. Now that we have renamed our original input function, let's define the input function for our start screen and call it `start_input`:

```
void start_input() {
    if(SDL_PollEvent ( &event ) )
    {
        switch (event.type)
        {
            case SDL_MOUSEMOTION:
            {
                int x_val = 0;
                int y_val = 0;
                SDL_GetMouseState( &x_val, &y_val );
                play_btn->MouseMove(x_val, y_val);
            }
            case SDL_MOUSEBUTTONDOWN:
            {
                switch (event.button.button)
                {
                    case SDL_BUTTON_LEFT:
                    {
                        int x_val = 0;
                        int y_val = 0;
                        SDL_GetMouseState( &x_val, &y_val );
                        play_btn->MouseClick(x_val, y_val);
                        break;
                    }
                    default:
                    {
                        break;
                    }
                }
                break;
            }
            case SDL_MOUSEBUTTONUP:
            {
                switch (event.button.button)
                {
                    case SDL_BUTTON_LEFT:
                    {
                        int x_val = 0;
```

```
                                int y_val = 0;
                                SDL_GetMouseState( &x_val, &y_val );
                                play_btn->MouseUp(x_val, y_val);
                                break;
                        }
                        default:
                        {
                                break;
                        }
                    }
                    break;
                }
                case SDL_KEYDOWN:
                {
                        play_btn->KeyDown( event.key.keysym.sym );
                }
            }
        }
    }
}
```

Like our `play_input` function, the `start_input` function will be making a call to
`SDL_PollEvent`. In addition to checking `SDL_KEYDOWN` to determine whether a key was
pressed, we will also be checking three mouse events: `SDL_MOUSEMOTION`,
`SDL_MOUSEBUTTONDOWN`, and `SDL_MOUSEBUTTONUP`. When checking for those mouse
events, we will call the `play_btn` functions based on the `SDL_GetMouseState` values we
retrieve. A mouse event will trigger the following code:

```
case SDL_MOUSEMOTION:
{
    int x_val = 0;
    int y_val = 0;
    SDL_GetMouseState( &x_val, &y_val );
    play_btn->MouseMove(x_val, y_val);
}
```

If `event.type` was `SDL_MOUSEMOTION`, we create `x_val` and `y_val` integer variables and
use a call to `SDL_GetMouseState` to retrieve the x and y coordinates of our mouse cursor.
We then call `play_btn->MouseMove(x_val, y_val)`. This passes the mouse x and y
coordinates to the play button, which uses those values to determine whether the button is
in a hover state. We do something similar if `event.type` is `SDL_MOUSEBUTTONDOWN`:

```
case SDL_MOUSEBUTTONDOWN:
{
    switch (event.button.button)
    {
        case SDL_BUTTON_LEFT:
```

```
        {
            int x_val = 0;
            int y_val = 0;

            SDL_GetMouseState( &x_val, &y_val );
            play_btn->MouseClick(x_val, y_val);
            break;
        }
        default:
        {
            break;
        }
    }
    break;
}
```

If the mouse button is pressed, we look inside of `event.button.button` to see if the button that was clicked was the left mouse button. If it is, we use `x_val` and `y_val` in combination with `SDL_GetMouseState` to find the mouse cursor position. We use those values to call `play_btn->MouseClick(x_val, y_val)`. The `MouseClick` function will determine whether the button click fell within the button and if so, it will call the button's callback function.

The code that executes when the event is `SDL_MOUSEBUTTONUP` is very similar to `SDL_MOUSEBUTTONDOWN`, with the exception that it calls `play_btn->MouseUp` instead of `play_btn->MouseClick`:

```
case SDL_MOUSEBUTTONUP:
{
    switch (event.button.button)
    {
        case SDL_BUTTON_LEFT:
        {
            int x_val = 0;
            int y_val = 0;

            SDL_GetMouseState( &x_val, &y_val );
            play_btn->MouseUp(x_val, y_val);
            break;
        }
        default:
        {
            break;
        }
    }
    break;
}
```

In addition to the mouse events, we will be passing keyboard events to our button. This is done so that we can create a hotkey that will trigger the callback:

```
case SDL_KEYDOWN:
{
    play_btn->KeyDown( event.key.keysym.sym );
}
```

The end_input function

After the `start_input` function, we will define the `end_input` function. The `end_input` function is very similar to the `start_input` function. The only significant difference is that the `play_btn` object is replaced by the `play_again_btn` object, which will have a different callback and SDL texture associated with it:

```
void end_input() {
    if(SDL_PollEvent( &event ) )
    {
        switch(event.type)
        {
            case SDL_MOUSEMOTION:
            {
                int x_val = 0;
                int y_val = 0;
                SDL_GetMouseState( &x_val, &y_val );
                play_again_btn->MouseMove(x_val, y_val);
            }
            case SDL_MOUSEBUTTONDOWN:
            {
                switch(event.button.button)
                {
                    case SDL_BUTTON_LEFT:
                    {
                        int x_val = 0;
                        int y_val = 0;
                        SDL_GetMouseState( &x_val, &y_val );
                        play_again_btn->MouseClick(x_val, y_val);
                        break;
                    }
                    default:
                    {
                        break;
                    }
                }
                break;
            }
```

```
                    case SDL_MOUSEBUTTONUP:
                    {
                        switch(event.button.button)
                        {
                            case SDL_BUTTON_LEFT:
                            {
                                int x_val = 0;
                                int y_val = 0;
                                SDL_GetMouseState( &x_val, &y_val );
                                play_again_btn->MouseUp(x_val, y_val);
                                break;
                            }
                            default:
                            {
                                break;
                            }
                        }
                        break;
                    }
                    case SDL_KEYDOWN:
                    {
                        printf("SDL_KEYDOWN\n");
                        play_again_btn->KeyDown( event.key.keysym.sym );
                    }
                }
            }
        }
    }
```

The render functions

In previous versions of our game, we had a single render function. Now, we must have a render function for both our start screen and our play screen. The existing renderer will become our new play screen renderer, so we must rename the `render` function `play_render`. We also need to add a rendering function for our start screen called `start_render`. This function will render our new background and `play_btn`. Here is the code for `start_render`:

```
void start_render() {
    render_manager->RenderStartBackground();
    play_btn->RenderUI();
}
```

The collisions function

There will need to be some minor modifications to the `collisions()` function. When a player ship or an enemy ship gets destroyed, we will need to change the current screen to the game over screen. Depending on which ship gets destroyed, we will either need to change it to the win screen or the lose screen. Here is the new version of our collisions function:

```
void collisions() {
 Asteroid* asteroid;
 std::vector<Asteroid*>::iterator ita;
    if( player->m_CurrentFrame == 0 && player->CompoundHitTest( star ) ) {
        player->m_CurrentFrame = 1;
        player->m_NextFrameTime = ms_per_frame;
        player->m_Explode->Run();
        current_screen = GAME_OVER_SCREEN;
        large_explosion_snd->Play();
    }
    if( enemy->m_CurrentFrame == 0 && enemy->CompoundHitTest( star ) ) {
        enemy->m_CurrentFrame = 1;
        enemy->m_NextFrameTime = ms_per_frame;
        current_screen = YOU_WIN_SCREEN;
        enemy->m_Explode->Run();
        large_explosion_snd->Play();
    }
    Projectile* projectile;
    std::vector<Projectile*>::iterator it;
    for(it=projectile_pool->m_ProjectileList.begin();
    it!=projectile_pool->m_ProjectileList.end();it++){
        projectile = *it;
        if( projectile->m_CurrentFrame == 0 && projectile->m_Active ) {
            for( ita = asteroid_list.begin(); ita!=asteroid_list.end();
            ita++ ) {
                asteroid = *ita;
                if( asteroid->m_Active ) {
                    if( asteroid->HitTest( projectile ) ) {
                        asteroid->ElasticCollision( projectile );
                        projectile->m_CurrentFrame = 1;
                        projectile->m_NextFrameTime = ms_per_frame;
                        small_explosion_snd->Play();
                    }
                }
            }
        }
        if( projectile->HitTest( star ) ){
            projectile->m_CurrentFrame = 1;
            projectile->m_NextFrameTime = ms_per_frame;
            small_explosion_snd->Play();
```

```
            }
            else if( player->m_CurrentFrame == 0 &&
                ( projectile->HitTest( player ) || player->CompoundHitTest(
                  projectile ) ) ) {
                if( player->m_Shield->m_Active == false ) {
                    player->m_CurrentFrame = 1;
                    player->m_NextFrameTime = ms_per_frame;
                    current_screen = GAME_OVER_SCREEN;
                    player->m_Explode->Run();
                    large_explosion_snd->Play();
                }
                else {
                    hit_snd->Play();
                    player->ElasticCollision( projectile );
                }
                projectile->m_CurrentFrame = 1;
                projectile->m_NextFrameTime = ms_per_frame;
            }
            else if( enemy->m_CurrentFrame == 0 &&
                ( projectile->HitTest( enemy ) || enemy->CompoundHitTest(
                  projectile ) ) ) {
                if( enemy->m_Shield->m_Active == false ) {
                    enemy->m_CurrentFrame = 1;
                    enemy->m_NextFrameTime = ms_per_frame;
                    current_screen = YOU_WIN_SCREEN;
                    enemy->m_Explode->Run();
                    large_explosion_snd->Play();
                    enemy->m_Shield->m_ttl -= 1000;
                }
                else {
                    enemy->ElasticCollision( projectile );
                    hit_snd->Play();
                }
                projectile->m_CurrentFrame = 1;
                projectile->m_NextFrameTime = ms_per_frame;
            }
        }
    }
    for( ita = asteroid_list.begin(); ita != asteroid_list.end(); ita++ ) {
        asteroid = *ita;
        if( asteroid->m_Active ) {
            if( asteroid->HitTest( star ) ) {
                asteroid->Explode();
                small_explosion_snd->Play();
            }
        }
        else { continue; }
        if( player->m_CurrentFrame == 0 && asteroid->m_Active &&
```

```
        ( asteroid->HitTest( player ) || player->CompoundHitTest(
         asteroid ) ) ) {
          if( player->m_Shield->m_Active == false ) {
              player->m_CurrentFrame = 1;
              player->m_NextFrameTime = ms_per_frame;

              player->m_Explode->Run();
              current_screen = GAME_OVER_SCREEN;
              large_explosion_snd->Play();
          }
          else {
              player->ElasticCollision( asteroid );
              small_explosion_snd->Play();
          }
      }
      if( enemy->m_CurrentFrame == 0 && asteroid->m_Active &&
        ( asteroid->HitTest( enemy ) || enemy->CompoundHitTest( asteroid
          ) ) ) {
          if( enemy->m_Shield->m_Active == false ) {
              enemy->m_CurrentFrame = 1;
              enemy->m_NextFrameTime = ms_per_frame;

              enemy->m_Explode->Run();
              current_screen = YOU_WIN_SCREEN;
              large_explosion_snd->Play();
          }
          else {
              enemy->ElasticCollision( asteroid );
              small_explosion_snd->Play();
          }
      }
  }
}
Asteroid* asteroid_1;
Asteroid* asteroid_2;
std::vector<Asteroid*>::iterator ita_1;
std::vector<Asteroid*>::iterator ita_2;
for( ita_1 = asteroid_list.begin(); ita_1 != asteroid_list.end();
ita_1++ ) {
    asteroid_1 = *ita_1;
    if( !asteroid_1->m_Active ) { continue; }
    for( ita_2 = ita_1+1; ita_2 != asteroid_list.end(); ita_2++ ) {
        asteroid_2 = *ita_2;
        if( !asteroid_2->m_Active ) { continue; }
        if(asteroid_1->HitTest(asteroid_2)) {
        asteroid_1->ElasticCollision( asteroid_2 ); }
    }
  }
}
```

You will notice that every line where the player is destroyed, there is a call to `player->m_Explode->Run()`. We now follow that line with a call to `current_screen = GAME_OVER_SCREEN` to set the screen to the player lose screen. Another way we could have done this is by adding a function to the `Ship` class, which runs both the explosion animation and sets the game screen, but I chose to modify fewer files by making the change inside of the `main` function. If we were using this project for more than demonstration purposes, I probably would have done it the other way.

The other changes we have made to collisions are similar. Whenever an enemy was destroyed by running the `enemy->m_Explode->Run()` function, we followed it with a line that set the current screen to the "you win" screen, like this:

```
current_screen = YOU_WIN_SCREEN;
```

The transition state

A sudden transition from the start screen into gameplay can be a little jarring. To make the transition smoother, we will create a transition function called `draw_play_transition`, which will use an alpha fade to transition our screen from the start screen to the gameplay screen. Here is what that function looks like:

```
void draw_play_transition() {
    transition_time -= diff_time;
    if( transition_time <= 0 ) {
        current_screen = PLAY_SCREEN;
        return;
    }
    render_manager->RenderStartBackground(transition_time/4);
}
```

This function uses the `transition_time` global variable we created earlier and subtracts the time in milliseconds since the last frame. It uses that value divided by 4 as the alpha value when drawing the start screen background to fade it out as it transitions to the gameplay. When the transition time drops below 0, we set the current screen to the play screen. When the transition begins, we set `transition_time` to 1,020 milliseconds, which is a bit more than a second. Dividing that value by 4 gives us a value that transitions from 255 (full opacity) to 0 (full transparency).

The game loop

The game_loop function will need to be modified to perform different logic for each screen. Here is what the new version of the game loop will look like:

```
void game_loop() {
    current_time = SDL_GetTicks();
    diff_time = current_time - last_time;
    delta_time = diff_time / 1000.0;
    last_time = current_time;
    if( current_screen == START_SCREEN ) {
        start_input();
        start_render();
    }
    else if( current_screen == PLAY_SCREEN || current_screen ==
            PLAY_TRANSITION ) {
        play_input();
        move();
        collisions();
        play_render();
        if( current_screen == PLAY_TRANSITION ) {
            draw_play_transition();
        }
    }
    else if( current_screen == YOU_WIN_SCREEN || current_screen ==
            GAME_OVER_SCREEN ) {
        end_input();
        move();
        collisions();
        play_render();
        play_again_btn->RenderUI();
        if( current_screen == YOU_WIN_SCREEN ) {
            you_win_sprite->RenderUI();
        }
        else {
            game_over_sprite->RenderUI();
        }
    }
}
```

We have new branching logic that branches based on the current screen. The first `if` block runs if the current screen is the start screen. It runs the `start_input` and `start_render` functions:

```
if( current_screen == START_SCREEN ) {
    start_input();
    start_render();
}
```

The play screen and the play transition have the same logic as the original game loop, except for the `if` block around `PLAY_TRANSITION` at the end of this block of code. This draws the play transition by calling the `draw_play_transition()` function that we defined earlier:

```
else if( current_screen == PLAY_SCREEN || current_screen == PLAY_TRANSITION
) {
    play_input();
    move();
    collisions();
    play_render();
    if( current_screen == PLAY_TRANSITION ) {
        draw_play_transition();
    }
}
```

The final block of code in the function is for the game over screen. It will render `you_win_sprite` if the current screen is `YOU_WIN_SCREEN` and will render `game_over_sprite` if the current screen is `GAME_OVER_SCREEN`:

```
else if( current_screen == YOU_WIN_SCREEN || current_screen ==
        GAME_OVER_SCREEN ) {
    end_input();
    move();
    collisions();
    play_render();
    play_again_btn->RenderUI();
    if( current_screen == YOU_WIN_SCREEN ) {
        you_win_sprite->RenderUI();
    }
    else {
        game_over_sprite->RenderUI();
    }
}
```

Play and play again callbacks

After our changes to the game loop, we need to add some callback functions for our buttons. The first of these functions is the `play_click` function. This is the callback that runs when the player clicks the play button on the start screen. This function will set the current screen to the play transition and set the transition time to 1,020 milliseconds:

```
void play_click() {
    current_screen = PLAY_TRANSITION;
    transition_time = 1020;
}
```

After that, we will define the `play_again_click` callback. This function runs when the player clicks the **play again** button on the game over screen. Because this is a web game, we will use a little trick to simplify this logic. In a game written for almost any other platform, you would need to create some reinitialization logic that would have to go back through your game and reset the state of everything. We are going to *cheat* by simply reloading the web page using JavaScript:

```
void play_again_click() {
    EM_ASM(
        location.reload();
    );
}
```

This cheat won't work for all games. Reloading some games would cause unacceptable delays. For some games, there may be too much state information that we need to keep. However, for this game, reloading the page is a quick and easy way to get the job done.

Changes to the main function

We use the `main` function in our application to perform all of the game initialization. This is where we will need to add some code to initialize the sprites we will use on our game over screen and our new buttons.

In the following code snippet, we have our new sprite initialization lines:

```
game_over_sprite = new UISprite( 400, 300, (char*)"/sprites/GameOver.png"
);
game_over_sprite->m_Active = true;
you_win_sprite = new UISprite( 400, 300, (char*)"/sprites/YouWin.png" );
you_win_sprite->m_Active = true;
```

You can see that we are setting the game_over_sprite coordinates and the you_win_sprite coordinates to 400, 300. That will place these sprites in the center of the screen. We are setting both sprites to be active because they will only be rendered on the end game screen anyway. Later in the code, we will call the constructors for our UIButton objects:

```
play_btn = new UIButton(400, 500,
                    (char*)"/sprites/play_button.png",
                    (char*)"/sprites/play_button_hover.png",
                    (char*)"/sprites/play_button_click.png",
                    play_click );

play_again_btn = new UIButton(400, 500,
                    (char*)"/sprites/play_again_button.png",
                    (char*)"/sprites/play_again_button_hover.png",
                    (char*)"/sprites/play_again_button_click.png",
                    play_again_click );
```

This places both of these buttons at 400, 500, centered on the x-axis, but near the bottom of the game screen on the y-axis. The callbacks are set to play_click and play_again_click, which we defined earlier. Here is what the entire main function looks like:

```
int main() {
    SDL_Init( SDL_INIT_VIDEO | SDL_INIT_AUDIO );
    int return_val = SDL_CreateWindowAndRenderer( CANVAS_WIDTH,
    CANVAS_HEIGHT, 0, &window, &renderer );
    if( return_val != 0 ) {
        printf("Error creating renderer %d: %s\n", return_val,
        IMG_GetError() );
        return 0;
    }
    SDL_SetRenderDrawColor( renderer, 0, 0, 0, 255 );
    SDL_RenderClear( renderer );
    game_over_sprite = new UISprite( 400, 300,
    (char*)"/sprites/GameOver.png" );
    game_over_sprite->m_Active = true;
    you_win_sprite = new UISprite( 400, 300,
    (char*)"/sprites/YouWin.png" );
    you_win_sprite->m_Active = true;
    last_frame_time = last_time = SDL_GetTicks();
    player = new PlayerShip();
    enemy = new EnemyShip();
    star = new Star();
    camera = new Camera(CANVAS_WIDTH, CANVAS_HEIGHT);
    render_manager = new RenderManager();
    locator = new Locator();
```

```
enemy_laser_snd = new Audio(ENEMY_LASER, false);
player_laser_snd = new Audio(PLAYER_LASER, false);
small_explosion_snd = new Audio(SMALL_EXPLOSION, true);
large_explosion_snd = new Audio(LARGE_EXPLOSION, true);
hit_snd = new Audio(HIT, false);
device_id = SDL_OpenAudioDevice(NULL, 0, &(enemy_laser_snd->spec),
NULL, 0);
if (device_id == 0) {
    printf("Failed to open audio: %s\n", SDL_GetError());
}
SDL_PauseAudioDevice(device_id, 0);
int asteroid_x = 0;
int asteroid_y = 0;
int angle = 0;
// SCREEN 1
for( int i_y = 0; i_y < 8; i_y++ ) {
    asteroid_y += 100;
    asteroid_y += rand() % 400;
    asteroid_x = 0;
    for( int i_x = 0; i_x < 12; i_x++ ) {
        asteroid_x += 66;
        asteroid_x += rand() % 400;
        int y_save = asteroid_y;
        asteroid_y += rand() % 400 - 200;
        angle = rand() % 359;
        asteroid_list.push_back(
        new Asteroid( asteroid_x, asteroid_y,
                    get_random_float(0.5, 1.0),
                    DEG_TO_RAD(angle) ) );
        asteroid_y = y_save;
    }
}
projectile_pool = new ProjectilePool();
play_btn = new UIButton(400, 500,
                (char*)"/sprites/play_button.png",
                (char*)"/sprites/play_button_hover.png",
                (char*)"/sprites/play_button_click.png",
                play_click );
play_again_btn = new UIButton(400, 500,
                (char*)"/sprites/play_again_button.png",
                (char*)"/sprites/play_again_button_hover.png",
                (char*)"/sprites/play_again_button_click.png",
                play_again_click );
emscripten_set_main_loop(game_loop, 0, 0);
return 1;
}
```

In the next section, we will define functions in our `ui_button.cpp` file.

ui_button.cpp

The UIButton object has several functions that must be defined. We have created a new ui_button.cpp file that will hold all of these new functions. We will need to define a constructor, as well as MouseMove, MouseClick, MouseUp, KeyDown, and RenderUI.

First, we will include our game.hpp file:

```
#include "game.hpp"
```

Now, we will define our constructor function:

```
UIButton::UIButton( int x, int y, char* file_name, char*
hover_file_name, char* click_file_name, void (*callback)() ) {
    m_Callback = callback;
    m_dest.x = x;
    m_dest.y = y;
    SDL_Surface *temp_surface = IMG_Load( file_name );

    if( !temp_surface ) {
        printf("failed to load image: %s\n", IMG_GetError() );
        return;
    }
    else {
        printf("success creating ui button surface\n");
    }
    m_SpriteTexture = SDL_CreateTextureFromSurface( renderer,
    temp_surface );
    if( !m_SpriteTexture ) {
        return;
    }
    SDL_QueryTexture( m_SpriteTexture,
                      NULL, NULL,
                      &m_dest.w, &m_dest.h );
    SDL_FreeSurface( temp_surface );

     temp_surface = IMG_Load( click_file_name );
    if( !temp_surface ) {
        printf("failed to load image: %s\n", IMG_GetError() );
        return;
    }
    else {
        printf("success creating ui button click surface\n");
    }
    m_ClickTexture = SDL_CreateTextureFromSurface( renderer,
    temp_surface );
```

```
    if( !m_ClickTexture ) {
        return;
    }
    SDL_FreeSurface( temp_surface );

    temp_surface = IMG_Load( hover_file_name );
    if( !temp_surface ) {
        printf("failed to load image: %s\n", IMG_GetError() );
        return;
    }
    else {
        printf("success creating ui button hover surface\n");
    }
    m_HoverTexture = SDL_CreateTextureFromSurface( renderer,
    temp_surface );

    if( !m_HoverTexture ) {
        return;
    }
    SDL_FreeSurface( temp_surface );

    m_dest.x -= m_dest.w / 2;
    m_dest.y -= m_dest.h / 2;

    m_Hover = false;
    m_Click = false;
    m_Active = true;
}
```

The constructor function starts by setting the callback function from the passed in parameter:

```
    m_Callback = callback;
```

Then, it sets the m_dest rectangle's x and y coordinates from the parameters we passed in:

```
    m_dest.x = x;
    m_dest.y = y;
```

After that, it loads three different image files into three different textures for the button, the button's hover state, and the button's clicked state:

```
    SDL_Surface *temp_surface = IMG_Load( file_name );

    if( !temp_surface ) {
        printf("failed to load image: %s\n", IMG_GetError() );
        return;
    }
```

```
    else {
        printf("success creating ui button surface\n");
    }
    m_SpriteTexture = SDL_CreateTextureFromSurface( renderer, temp_surface
    );

    if( !m_SpriteTexture ) {
        return;
    }
    SDL_QueryTexture( m_SpriteTexture,
                      NULL, NULL,
                      &m_dest.w, &m_dest.h );
    SDL_FreeSurface( temp_surface );

    temp_surface = IMG_Load( click_file_name );

    if( !temp_surface ) {
        printf("failed to load image: %s\n", IMG_GetError() );
        return;
    }
    else {
        printf("success creating ui button click surface\n");
    }
    m_ClickTexture = SDL_CreateTextureFromSurface( renderer, temp_surface
    );

    if( !m_ClickTexture ) {
        return;
    }
    SDL_FreeSurface( temp_surface );

    temp_surface = IMG_Load( hover_file_name );
    if( !temp_surface ) {
        printf("failed to load image: %s\n", IMG_GetError() );
        return;
    }
    else {
        printf("success creating ui button hover surface\n");
    }
    m_HoverTexture = SDL_CreateTextureFromSurface( renderer, temp_surface
    );

    if( !m_HoverTexture ) {
        return;
    }
    SDL_FreeSurface( temp_surface );
```

The preceding code should look pretty familiar because loading an image file into an `SDL_Texture` object is something we have done a lot at this point. After that, we use the width and height values we queried earlier to center the destination rectangle:

```
m_dest.x -= m_dest.w / 2;
m_dest.y -= m_dest.h / 2;
```

Then, we set our hover, click, and active state flags:

```
m_Hover = false;
m_Click = false;
m_Active = true;
```

The MouseMove function

We need a function to determine whether the mouse cursor has been moved to hover over our button. We call the `MouseMove` function from our input function, and we pass in the current mouse cursor x and y coordinates. We check these coordinates against our `m_dest` rectangle to see if they overlap. If so, we set our hover flag to `true`. If not, we set the hover flag to `false`:

```
void UIButton::MouseMove(int x, int y) {
    if( x >= m_dest.x && x <= m_dest.x + m_dest.w &&
        y >= m_dest.y && y <= m_dest.y + m_dest.h ) {
        m_Hover = true;
    }
    else {
        m_Hover = false;
    }
}
```

The MouseClick function

The `MouseClick` function is very similar to the `MouseMove` function. It is also called from our input function when the user presses the left mouse button. The x and y coordinates of the mouse cursor are passed in, and the function uses the `m_dest` rectangle to see if the mouse cursor was over the button when it was clicked. If it was, we set the click flag to `true`. If not, we set the click flag to `false`:

```
void UIButton::MouseClick(int x, int y) {
    if( x >= m_dest.x && x <= m_dest.x + m_dest.w &&
        y >= m_dest.y && y <= m_dest.y + m_dest.h ) {
        m_Click = true;
```

```
    }
    else {
        m_Click = false;
    }
}
```

The MouseUp function

When the left mouse button is released, we call this function. No matter what the mouse cursor coordinates are, we want to set the click flag to `false`. If the mouse was over the button at the time the button was released, and the button is clicked, we need to make a call to our callback function:

```
void UIButton::MouseUp(int x, int y) {
    if( m_Click == true &&
        x >= m_dest.x && x <= m_dest.x + m_dest.w &&
        y >= m_dest.y && y <= m_dest.y + m_dest.h ) {
        if( m_Callback != NULL ) {
            m_Callback();
        }
    }
    m_Click = false;
}
```

The KeyDown function

I could have made the key down function a little more flexible. It would have been better to have the hotkey set to a value that's set in the object. That would have supported more than a single button on a screen. As it is, if someone hits the *Enter* key, all the buttons on the screen will be clicked. This is not a problem for our game because we aren't going to have more than one button on a screen, but if you want to improve the hotkey functionality, this shouldn't be too difficult. As the function is, it hard codes the key it is checking against to `SDLK_RETURN`. Here is the version of the function we have:

```
void UIButton::KeyDown( SDL_Keycode key ) {
    if( key == SDLK_RETURN) {
        if( m_Callback != NULL ) {
            m_Callback();
        }
    }
}
```

The RenderUI function

The `RenderUI` function checks the various state flags in the button and renders the correct sprite based on those values. If the `m_Active` flag is `false`, the function doesn't render anything. Here is the function:

```
void UIButton::RenderUI() {
    if( m_Active == false ) {
        return;
    }
    if( m_Click == true ) {
        render_manager->RenderUI( m_ClickTexture, NULL, &m_dest, 0.0,
                                  0xff, 0xff, 0xff, 0xff );
    }
    else if( m_Hover == true ) {
        render_manager->RenderUI( m_HoverTexture, NULL, &m_dest, 0.0,
                                  0xff, 0xff, 0xff, 0xff );
    }
    else {
        render_manager->RenderUI( m_SpriteTexture, NULL, &m_dest, 0.0,
                                  0xff, 0xff, 0xff, 0xff );
    }
}
```

In the next section, we will define functions in our `ui_sprite.cpp` file.

ui_sprite.cpp

The `UISprite` class is pretty simple. It has only two functions: a constructor and a rendering function. Like with every other CPP file in our project, the first thing we must do is include the `game.hpp` file:

```
#include "game.hpp"
```

Defining the constructor

The constructor is very familiar. It sets the `m_dest` rectangle's `x` and `y` values to the values that were passed into the constructor. It loads the texture from the virtual filesystem using the `file_name` variable that we passed in as a parameter. Finally, it centers the `m_dest` rectangle using the width and height values that were retrieved using the `SDL_QueryTexture` function. Here is the code for the constructor:

```
UISprite::UISprite( int x, int y, char* file_name ) {
    m_dest.x = x;
    m_dest.y = y;
    SDL_Surface *temp_surface = IMG_Load( file_name );

    if( !temp_surface ) {
        printf("failed to load image: %s\n", IMG_GetError() );
        return;
    }
    else {
        printf("success creating ui button surface\n");
    }

    m_SpriteTexture = SDL_CreateTextureFromSurface( renderer,
    temp_surface );

    if( !m_SpriteTexture ) {
        return;
    }
    SDL_QueryTexture( m_SpriteTexture,
                      NULL, NULL,
                      &m_dest.w, &m_dest.h );
    SDL_FreeSurface( temp_surface );
    m_dest.x -= m_dest.w / 2;
    m_dest.y -= m_dest.h / 2;
}
```

The RenderUI function

The RenderUI function for our sprite is also straightforward. It checks to see if the sprite is active, and if it is, calls the render manager's RenderUI function. Here is the code:

```
void UISprite::RenderUI() {
    if( m_Active == false ) {
        return;
    }
    render_manager->RenderUI( m_SpriteTexture, NULL, &m_dest, 0.0,
                              0xff, 0xff, 0xff, 0xff );
}
```

Compile ui.html

Now that we have added a user interface to our game, let's compile it, serve it from our web server or emrun, and open it up in a web browser. Here is the em++ command we need to compile our ui.html file:

```
em++ asteroid.cpp audio.cpp camera.cpp collider.cpp emitter.cpp
enemy_ship.cpp finite_state_machine.cpp locator.cpp main.cpp particle.cpp
player_ship.cpp projectile_pool.cpp projectile.cpp range.cpp
render_manager.cpp shield.cpp ship.cpp star.cpp ui_button.cpp ui_sprite.cpp
vector.cpp -o ui.html --preload-file audio --preload-file sprites -
std=c++17 -s USE_WEBGL2=1 -s USE_SDL=2 -s USE_SDL_IMAGE=2 -s
SDL2_IMAGE_FORMATS=["png"] -s USE_SDL_IMAGE=2 -s SDL2_IMAGE_FORMATS=["png"]
```

The new version will open to our start screen. If you want to play the game, you will now need to click the *Play* button. Here is a screenshot:

Figure 14.6: Opening screen

You will notice that the *opening screen* has instructions on how to play the game. It is usually good to have an opening screen in an action-oriented web game because the player isn't always ready to play when the page loads. Not all web games need an opening screen. My website, `classicsolitaire.com`, doesn't have a single one. This is because solitaire is a turn-based game where the player isn't thrown into the action right away. The user interface needs of your game are likely to be different than the game we are writing for this book. So, sketch up a storyboard and take the time to gather requirements. You'll be glad you did.

Summary

In this chapter, we spent some time gathering requirements for our user interface. We created a storyboard to help us think through what screens we require for our game and how they might look. We discussed the layout for our opening screen, and why we need it. We then broke out the screen that had been our entire game into the play screen. Then, we discussed the layout of the game over screen and what UI elements we required for it and learned how to use SDL to retrieve mouse input. We also created a button class as a part of our user interface, as well as an enumeration for our screen states and discussed transitions between those states. We then added a sprite user interface object, before modifying our render manager to allow us to render our start screen's background image. Finally, we made changes to our code to support multiple game screens.

In the next chapter, we will learn how to write new shaders and implement them using WebAssembly's OpenGL API.

Shaders and 2D Lighting 15

We have already touched on shaders in Chapter 3, *Introduction to WebGL*. SDL, unfortunately, doesn't allow the user to customize its shaders without digging into the source code of the library and modifying them there. Those kinds of modifications are beyond the

scope of this book. It is not uncommon to use SDL in combination with OpenGL. SDL can be used to render the user interface for the game while OpenGL renders the game objects. This chapter will deviate from many of the earlier chapters in that we will not be mixing SDL and OpenGL directly in the game we have been writing. Updating the game to support an OpenGL 2D rendering engine would require a complete redesign of the game up to this point. However, I would like to provide a chapter for those interested in creating a more advanced 2D rendering engine to get their feet wet with combining OpenGL and SDL and writing shaders for that engine.

 You will need to include several images in your build to make this project work. Make sure that you include the /Chapter15/sprites/ folder from this project's GitHub repository. If you haven't downloaded the GitHub project yet, you can get it online here: https://github.com/ PacktPublishing/Hands-On-Game-Development-with-WebAssembly.

In this chapter, we will do the following:

- Recreate the app we made in Chapter 3, *Introduction to WebGL*, using a combination of SDL and OpenGL for WebAssembly
- Learn how to create a new shader that loads and renders multiple textures to a quad
- Learn about normal maps and how they can be used to create the illusion of depth on a 2D game object
- Learn how to approximate the Phong lighting model in 2D using normal maps in OpenGL and WebAssembly

Using OpenGL with WebAssembly

Emscripten is capable of compiling C/C++ code that uses either OpenGL ES 2.0 or OpenGL ES 3.0 by mapping those calls to WebGL or WebGL 2 calls, respectively. Because of this, Emscripten only supports a subset of the OpenGL ES commands that correspond to the commands available inside of the WebGL library you use. For instance, if you would like to use OpenGL ES 3.0, you will need to include WebGL 2 when compiling by passing the `-s USE_WEBGL2=1` parameter to the Emscripten compiler. In this chapter, we will be using OpenGL ES 2.0 in combination with SDL to render sprites using shaders, and later we will be using SDL to render an icon that represents the location of a light source in our application. SDL provides many features that are absent from OpenGL, such as an audio library, an image loading library, and mouse and keyboard input libraries. In many ways, SDL is better suited to rendering the game's user interface as it renders objects to screen coordinates instead of to the OpenGL clip space. Behind the scenes, the WebAssembly version of SDL is also using the Emscripten OpenGL ES implementation, which relies on WebGL. So, having a better understanding of WebAssembly's OpenGL implementation can help us to take our game development skills to the next level, even if we will not be using those skills in the game we have developed for this book.

More about shaders

We briefly introduced the concept of shaders back in `Chapter 2`, *HTML5 and WebAssembly*. Shaders are a critical part of modern 3D graphics rendering. Back in the early days of computer and video games, graphics were all 2D, and how fast graphics could render was a function of how fast the system could move pixels from one data buffer to another. This process is called *blitting*. One significant advance in these early days came when Nintendo added a **Picture Processing Unit (PPU)** to their Nintendo Entertainment System. This was an early piece of hardware that was designed to speed up graphics processing by moving pixels without using the game system's CPU. The Commodore Amiga was also a pioneer in these early 2D graphics coprocessors, and by the mid-1990s, hardware for blitting became a standard in the computer industry. In 1996, games such as Quake began to create a demand for consumer 3D graphics processing, and early graphics cards began to provide GPUs that had fixed function pipelines. This allowed applications to load geometry data and execute non-programmable texturing and lighting functions on that geometry. In the early 2000s, Nvidia introduced the GeForce 3. This was the first GPU that supported a programmable pipeline. Eventually, these programmable pipeline GPUs began to standardize around a *unified shader model*, which allows programmers to write in a shading language such as GLSL for all graphics cards that support that language.

GLSL ES 1.0 and 3.0

The language we will be using to write our shaders is a subset of the GLSL shader language called GLSL ES. This shader language happens to work with WebGL and so is supported by the version of OpenGL ES that has been ported to WebAssembly. The code we are writing will run on both GLSL ES 1.0 and 3.0, which are the two versions of GLSL ES supported by WebAssembly.

If you are wondering why there is no support for GLSL ES 2.0, it's because it doesn't exist. OpenGL ES 1.0 used a fixed function pipeline and so it had no shader language associated with it. When the Khronos Group created OpenGL ES 2.0, they created GLSL ES 1.0 as the shader language to go with it. When they released OpenGL ES 3.0, they decided that they wanted the version number of the shader language to be the same number as the API. Therefore, all the new versions of OpenGL ES will come with a version of GLSL that bears the same version number.

GLSL is a language that is very similar to C. Each shader has a `main` function that is its entry point. GLSL ES 2.0 only supports two shader types: *vertex shaders* and *fragment shaders*. The execution of these shaders is highly parallel. If you are used to thinking along single—threaded lines, you will need to reorder your brain. Shaders are frequently processing thousands of vertices and pixels at the same time.

I briefly discussed the definition of a vertex and a fragment in Chapter 3, *Introduction to WebGL*. A vertex is a point in space, and a collection of vertices define the geometry that our graphics card uses to render to the screen. A fragment is a pixel candidate. Multiple fragments usually go into determining the pixel output.

Each vertex of the geometry that's passed to a vertex shader is processed by that shader. Values are then passed using a *varying variable* to a large number of threads that are processing individual pixels through a fragment shader. The fragment shader receives a value that is interpolated between the output of more than one of the vertex shaders. A fragment shader's output is a *fragment*, which is a pixel candidate. Not all fragments become pixels. Some fragments are dropped, which means they won't render at all. Other fragments are blended to form a completely different pixel color. We created one vertex and one fragment shader in Chapter 3, *Introduction to WebGL*, for our WebGL application. Let's walk through converting that application into an OpenGL/WebAssembly app. Once we have a working application, we can further discuss shaders and new ways we can write those shaders to improve our 2D WebAssembly game.

WebGL app redux

We will now walk through what it takes to rewrite the WebGL app we made in Chapter 3, *Introduction to WebGL*, using SDL and OpenGL. If you don't remember, this was a very simple app that drew a spaceship to our canvas and moved it 2 pixels to the left and one pixel up every frame. The reason we made this app was that it was about the simplest thing I could think to do in WebGL that was more interesting than drawing a triangle. For this same reason, it will be the first thing we will do with OpenGL for WebAssembly. Go ahead and create a new file called `webgl-redux.c` and open it up. Now, let's go ahead and start adding some code. The first chunk of code we need is our `#include` commands to pull in all of the libraries we will need for this app:

```
#include <SDL2/SDL.h>
#include <SDL2/SDL_image.h>
#include <SDL_opengl.h>
#include <GLES2/gl2.h>
#include <stdlib.h>
#include <emscripten.h>
```

The first line includes the standard SDL2 library. The second library, `SDL_image.h`, is the library we are using to load our image files. The third line in this file that includes `SDL_opengl.h`, and is the library that will allow us to mix our SDL and OpenGL calls. Including `GLES2/gl2.h` gives us access to all of the OpenGL commands that we can use with OpenGL ES 2.0. As always, we include `stdlib.h` to let us use the `printf` command, and `emscripten.h` provides us with the functions we need for compiling to target WebAssembly using the Emscripten compiler.

After our `#include` commands, we have a series of `#define` macros that define the constants we need for our game:

```
#define CANVAS_WIDTH 800
#define CANVAS_HEIGHT 600
#define FLOAT32_BYTE_SIZE 4
#define STRIDE FLOAT32_BYTE_SIZE*4
```

The first two define our canvas width and canvas height. The remaining `#define` calls are used to set up values we will be using when we define our vertex buffers. After these `#define` macros, we define the code for our shaders.

Shader code

The following few blocks of code I am about to show you will define the shaders we need to create our 2D lighting effect. Here is the vertex shader code:

```
const GLchar* vertex_shader_code[] = {
    "precision mediump float; \n"
    "attribute vec4 a_position; \n"
    "attribute vec2 a_texcoord; \n"

    "uniform vec4 u_translate; \n"

    "varying vec2 v_texcoord; \n"

    "void main() { \n"
        "gl_Position = u_translate + a_position; \n"
        "v_texcoord = a_texcoord; \n"
    "} \n"
};
```

This is the same shader code that we used when we created the WebGL version of this app. It looks a little different in C because JavaScript can use a multiline string that makes reading the code a little more clear. Like in the WebGL version, we use the precision call to set the floating-point precision to medium. We set up attributes to receive the position and UV texture coordinate data as vectors. We will pass in these vectors using a vertex buffer object. We define a uniform translate variable that will be the same value used for all vertices, which in general is not the way we would do this for a game, but will work just fine for this app. Finally, we define a varying v_texcoord variable. This variable will represent the texture coordinate value we pass from the vertex shader into the fragment shader. The main() function in this vertex shader is very simple. It adds the u_translate uniform variable translation value that's passed into the vertex shader to the attribute position of the vertex passed in via a_position, to get the final vertex position we set using the gl_Position variable. After that, we pass the texture coordinate of the vertex to the fragment shader by setting the v_texcoord varying variable to a_texcoord.

After defining our vertex shader, we create the string that defines our fragment shader. The fragment shader receives an interpolated version of v_texcoord, which is the varying variable that's passed out of our vertex shader. You will need to put on your parallel processing hat for a moment to understand how this works. When the GPU is processing our vertex shader and fragment shader, it is not doing this one at a time, but is likely processing thousands of vertices and fragments at once. The fragment shader is also not receiving the output from a single one of these threads, but a value that is mixed from more than one of the vertices that are currently being processed.

For example, if your vertex shader has a varying variable as output called X, and your fragment is halfway between a vertex where X is 0 and a vertex where X is 10, then the value in the varying variable coming into your fragment will be 5. This is because 5 is halfway between the two vertex values of 0 and 10. Likewise, if the fragment is 30% of the way between your two points, the value in X will be 3.

Here is the definition of our fragment shader code:

```
const GLchar* fragment_shader_code[] = {
    "precision mediump float; \n"
    "varying vec2 v_texcoord; \n"

    "uniform sampler2D u_texture; \n"

    "void main() { \n"
        "gl_FragColor = texture2D(u_texture, v_texcoord); \n"
    "} \n"
};
```

As with our vertex shader, we start out by setting the precision. After that, we have a varying variable, which is an interpolated value for our texture coordinate. This value is stored in `v_texcoord` and will be used to map our texture to a pixel color. The last variable is a uniform variable of type `sampler2D`. This is a block of memory where we have loaded our texture. The only thing that the main function of this fragment shader does is use the built-in `texture2D` function to grab a pixel color out of our texture using the texture coordinates we passed into the fragment shader.

OpenGL global variables

After defining our shaders, we need to define several variables in C that we will use to interact with them:

```
GLuint program = 0;
GLuint texture;

GLint a_texcoord_location = -1;
GLint a_position_location = -1;

GLint u_texture_location = -1;
GLint u_translate_location = -1;

GLuint vertex_texture_buffer;
```

OpenGL uses reference variables to interact with the GPU. The first two of these variables are of type GLuint. A GLuint is an unsigned integer, and using the GLuint type is just an OpenGL type. Seeing GLuint instead of unsigned int is a nice way to give someone reading your code a hint that you are using this variable to interact with OpenGL. The program variable will eventually hold a reference to a program that will be defined by your shaders, and the texture variable will hold a reference to a texture that's been loaded into the GPU. After the references to program and texture, we have two variables that will be used to reference shader program attributes. The a_texcoord_location variable will be a reference to the a_texcoord shader attribute, and the a_position_location variable will be a reference to the a_position shader attribute value. The attribute references are followed up by two uniform variable references. If you are wondering what the difference between a uniform and attribute variable is, a uniform variable remains the same value for all vertices, whereas an attribute variable is vertex-specific. Finally, we have a reference to our vertex texture buffer in the vertex_texture_buffer variable.

After we define these values, we need to define our quad. As you may remember, our quad is made up of six vertices. This is because it is made up of two triangles. I talked about why we set the vertex data this way in Chapter 3, *Introduction to WebGL*. If you find this confusing, you may want to go back to that chapter for a little review. Here is the definition of the vertex_texture_data array:

```
float vertex_texture_data[] = {
    // x,      y,         u,     v
    0.167,    0.213,     1.0,  1.0,
   -0.167,    0.213,     0.0,  1.0,
    0.167,   -0.213,     1.0,  0.0,
   -0.167,   -0.213,     0.0,  0.0,
   -0.167,    0.213,     0.0,  1.0,
    0.167,   -0.213,     1.0,  0.0
};
```

SDL global variables

We are still going to be using SDL to initialize our canvas for OpenGL rendering. We will also be using SDL to load our image data from the virtual filesystem. Because of this, we have the following SDL related global variables we need to define:

```
SDL_Window *window;
SDL_Renderer *renderer;
SDL_Texture* sprite_texture;
SDL_Surface* sprite_surface;
```

After that, we need variables to hold our sprite width and height values when we load an image using SDL:

```
int sprite_width;
int sprite_height;
```

When we draw the ship to the canvas, we will need x and y coordinates for that ship, so we will create a few global variables to hold those values:

```
float ship_x = 0.0;
float ship_y = 0.0;
```

Finally, we are going to create a function prototype for our game loop. I want to define our game loop after we define our main function because I would like to step through our initialization first. Here is the function prototype for our game loop:

```
void game_loop();
```

The main function

Now, we have come to our `main` function. There is quite a bit of initialization that we will need to do. We are not only initializing SDL, like we did when we were creating our game. We will also need to do several initialization steps for OpenGL. Here is the `main` function in its entirety:

```
int main() {
 SDL_Init( SDL_INIT_VIDEO );
 SDL_CreateWindowAndRenderer( CANVAS_WIDTH, CANVAS_HEIGHT, 0, &window,
&renderer );
    SDL_SetRenderDrawColor( renderer, 0, 0, 0, 255 );
    SDL_RenderClear( renderer );
    GLuint vertex_shader = glCreateShader(GL_VERTEX_SHADER);
    glShaderSource( vertex_shader,1,vertex_shader_code,0);
    glCompileShader(vertex_shader);
    GLint compile_success = 0;
    glGetShaderiv(vertex_shader, GL_COMPILE_STATUS, &compile_success);
    if(compile_success == GL_FALSE)
    {
        printf("failed to compile vertex shader\n");
        glDeleteShader(vertex_shader);
        return 0;
    }
    GLuint fragment_shader = glCreateShader(GL_FRAGMENT_SHADER);
    glShaderSource( fragment_shader,1,fragment_shader_code,0);
    glCompileShader(fragment_shader);
```

```
glGetShaderiv(fragment_shader, GL_COMPILE_STATUS,&compile_success);
if(compile_success == GL_FALSE)
{
    printf("failed to compile fragment shader\n");
    glDeleteShader(fragment_shader);
    return 0;
}
program = glCreateProgram();
glAttachShader( program,vertex_shader);
glAttachShader( program,fragment_shader);
glLinkProgram(program);
GLint link_success = 0;
glGetProgramiv(program, GL_LINK_STATUS, &link_success);
if (link_success == GL_FALSE)
{
    printf("failed to link program\n");
    glDeleteProgram(program);
    return 0;
}
glUseProgram(program);
u_texture_location = glGetUniformLocation(program, "u_texture");
u_translate_location = glGetUniformLocation(program,"u_translate");
a_position_location = glGetAttribLocation(program, "a_position");
a_texcoord_location = glGetAttribLocation(program, "a_texcoord");
glGenBuffers(1, &vertex_texture_buffer);
glBindBuffer( GL_ARRAY_BUFFER, vertex_texture_buffer );
glBufferData(GL_ARRAY_BUFFER,
sizeof(vertex_texture_data),vertex_texture_data, GL_STATIC_DRAW);
sprite_surface = IMG_Load( "/sprites/spaceship.png" );
if( !sprite_surface ) {
    printf("failed to load image: %s\n", IMG_GetError() );
    return 0;
}
sprite_texture = SDL_CreateTextureFromSurface( renderer,
sprite_surface );
if( !sprite_texture ) {
    printf("failed to create texture: %s\n", IMG_GetError() );
    return 0;
}
SDL_QueryTexture( sprite_texture,NULL, NULL,&sprite_width,
&sprite_height );
glTexImage2D( GL_TEXTURE_2D,0,GL_RGBA,sprite_width,sprite_height,
                0,GL_RGBA,GL_UNSIGNED_BYTE,sprite_surface );
SDL_FreeSurface( sprite_surface );
glBlendFunc(GL_SRC_ALPHA, GL_ONE_MINUS_SRC_ALPHA);
glEnable(GL_BLEND);
glEnableVertexAttribArray(a_position_location);
glEnableVertexAttribArray(a_texcoord_location);
```

```
    glVertexAttribPointer(a_position_location,2,GL_FLOAT,GL_FALSE,4 *
    sizeof(float),(void*)0 );
    glVertexAttribPointer(a_texcoord_location,2,GL_FLOAT,GL_FALSE,
                     4 * sizeof(float),(void*)(2 * sizeof(float)));
    emscripten_set_main_loop(game_loop, 0, 0);
}
```

Let me break this into some more digestible pieces. The first thing we need to do in our main function is the standard SDL initialization stuff. We need to initialize the video module, create a renderer, and set the draw and clear colors. By now, this code should look pretty familiar to you:

```
SDL_Init( SDL_INIT_VIDEO );
SDL_CreateWindowAndRenderer( CANVAS_WIDTH, CANVAS_HEIGHT, 0, &window,
&renderer );
SDL_SetRenderDrawColor( renderer, 0, 0, 0, 255 );
SDL_RenderClear( renderer );
```

Next, we need to create and compile our vertex shader. This requires several steps. We need to create our shader, load the source code into the shader, compile the shader, then check to make sure there weren't any errors when compiling. Basically, these steps take your code, compile it, and then load the compiled code into the video card to execute it later. Here are all the steps you need to perform to compile your vertex shader:

```
GLuint vertex_shader = glCreateShader(GL_VERTEX_SHADER);
glShaderSource( vertex_shader,
                1,
                vertex_shader_code,
                0);

glCompileShader(vertex_shader);

GLint compile_success = 0;1
glGetShaderiv(vertex_shader, GL_COMPILE_STATUS, &compile_success);
if(compile_success == GL_FALSE)
{
    printf("failed to compile vertex shader\n");
    glDeleteShader(vertex_shader);
    return 0;
}
```

After compiling the vertex shader, we need to compile the fragment shader. This is the same process. We start by calling `glCreateShader` to create a fragment shader. We then load our fragment shader source code using `glShaderSource`. After that, we call `glCompileShader` to compile our fragment shader. Finally, we call `glGetShaderiv` to see whether a compiler error occurred when we attempted to compile our fragment shader:

```
GLuint fragment_shader = glCreateShader(GL_FRAGMENT_SHADER);
glShaderSource( fragment_shader,
                1,
                fragment_shader_code,
                0);

glCompileShader(fragment_shader);
glGetShaderiv(fragment_shader, GL_COMPILE_STATUS, &compile_success);

if(compile_success == GL_FALSE)
{
    printf("failed to compile fragment shader\n");
    glDeleteShader(fragment_shader);
    return 0;
}
```

For simplicity, I kept the error message vague for when of the shaders failed to compile. It only tells you which shader failed to compile. Later in this chapter, I will show you how to get a more detailed error message from the shader compiler.

Now that we have our shaders compiled, we need to link our shaders into a program, and then tell OpenGL that this is the program we want to use. If you are writing a game using OpenGL, there is a good chance you will be using more than one program. For example, you may want to have lighting effects on some objects in your game, but not others. Some game objects may require rotation and scaling, while others may not.

 As you will learn in the next chapter, using multiple programs with WebGL has a significantly higher CPU hit than it does in a native OpenGL app. This has to do with the web browser's security checks.

For this application, we will be using a single program, and we will use the following code to attach our shaders and link them to the program:

```
program = glCreateProgram();
glAttachShader( program,
                vertex_shader);

glAttachShader( program,
                fragment_shader);
```

```
glLinkProgram(program);

GLint link_success = 0;

glGetProgramiv(program, GL_LINK_STATUS, &link_success);

if (link_success == GL_FALSE)
{
    printf("failed to link program\n");
    glDeleteProgram(program);
    return 0;
}
glUseProgram(program);
```

The glCreateProgram function creates a new program and returns a reference ID for it. We will store that reference ID in our program variable. We make two calls to glAttachShader that will attach our vertex and fragment shader to the program we just created. We then call glLinkProgram to link the program shaders together. We call glGetProgramiv to verify that the program linked successfully. Finally, we call glUseProgram to tell OpenGL that this is the program we would like to use.

Now that we are using a specific program, we can retrieve the references to the attribute and uniform variables inside of that program with the following lines of code:

```
u_texture_location = glGetUniformLocation(program, "u_texture");
u_translate_location = glGetUniformLocation(program, "u_translate");

a_position_location = glGetAttribLocation(program, "a_position");
a_texcoord_location = glGetAttribLocation(program, "a_texcoord");
```

The first line retrieves a reference to the u_texture uniform variable, and the second line retrieves a reference to the u_translate uniform variable. We can use these references later to set these values inside of our shader. The two lines after that are used to retrieve references to the a_position position attribute and the a_texcoord texture coordinate attribute inside of our shaders. Like the uniform variables, we will be using these references to set the values in our shaders later on.

Now, we will need to create and load data into a vertex buffer. The vertex buffer holds all of the attribute data for each vertex we will render. If we were rendering a 3D model, we would need to load it with model data that we retrieved externally. Luckily for us, all we need to render are some two-dimensional quads. Quads are simple enough that we were able to define them in an array earlier.

Before we can load that data into a buffer, we will need to generate that buffer with a call to `glGenBuffers`. We will then need to *bind* the buffer using `glBindBuffer`. Binding a buffer is just the way you tell OpenGL which buffers you are currently working on. Here is the code to generate and then bind our vertex buffer:

```
glGenBuffers(1, &vertex_texture_buffer);
glBindBuffer( GL_ARRAY_BUFFER, vertex_texture_buffer );
```

Now that we have a buffer selected, we can put data into that buffer using a call to `glBufferData`. We will pass in `vertex_texture_data` that we defined earlier. It defines both the x and y coordinates of our quad's vertices and the UV mapping data for those vertices:

```
glBufferData(GL_ARRAY_BUFFER, sizeof(vertex_texture_data),
             vertex_texture_data, GL_STATIC_DRAW);
```

After buffering our data, we will use SDL to load a sprite surface. Then, we will create a texture from that surface, which we can use to find the width and height of the image we just loaded. After that, we call `glTexImage2D` to create an OpenGL texture from that SDL surface. Here is the code:

```
sprite_surface = IMG_Load( "/sprites/spaceship.png" );

if( !sprite_surface ) {
    printf("failed to load image: %s\n", IMG_GetError() );
    return 0;
}

sprite_texture = SDL_CreateTextureFromSurface( renderer, sprite_surface );

if( !sprite_texture ) {
    printf("failed to create texture: %s\n", IMG_GetError() );
    return 0;
}

SDL_QueryTexture( sprite_texture,
                  NULL, NULL,
                  &sprite_width, &sprite_height );

glTexImage2D( GL_TEXTURE_2D,
              0,
              GL_RGBA,
              sprite_width,
              sprite_height,
              0,
              GL_RGBA,
              GL_UNSIGNED_BYTE,
```

```
                    sprite_surface );

    SDL_FreeSurface( sprite_surface );
```

Most of the previous code should have looked pretty familiar. We have been
using IMG_Load to load an SDL surface from the virtual filesystem for a while now. We
then used SDL_CreateTextureFromSurface to create an SDL texture. Once we had the
texture, we used SDL_QueryTexture to figure out what the image width and height are,
and we stored those values in sprite_width and sprite_height. The next function call
is new. The GlTexImage2D function is used to create a new OpenGL texture image. We
pass in sprite_surface as our image data, which we had loaded a few lines earlier. The
last line frees the surface using SDL_FreeSurface.

We then add two lines that enable alpha blending in our game:

```
glBlendFunc(GL_SRC_ALPHA, GL_ONE_MINUS_SRC_ALPHA);
glEnable(GL_BLEND);
```

After enabling alpha blending, we have several lines that set up the attributes in our
shaders:

```
glEnableVertexAttribArray(a_position_location);
glEnableVertexAttribArray(a_texcoord_location);

glVertexAttribPointer(
        a_position_location,      // set up the a_position attribute
        2,                        // how many attributes in the position
        GL_FLOAT,                 // data type of float
        GL_FALSE,                 // the data is not normalized
        4 * sizeof(float),        // stride (how many array items until
                                  //the next position)
        (void*)0                  // starting point for attribute
);

glVertexAttribPointer(
        a_texcoord_location,      // set up the a_texcoord attribute
        2,                        // how many attributes in the
                                  //texture coordinates
        GL_FLOAT,                 // data type of float
        GL_FALSE,                 // the data is not normalized
        4 * sizeof(float),        // stride (how many array items
                                  //until the next position)
        (void*)(2 * sizeof(float)) // starting point for attribute
);
```

The first two lines enable the `a_position` and `a_texcoord` attributes in our shaders. After that, we have two calls to `glVertexAttribPointer`. The calls to `glVertexAttribPointer` are used to tell our shader where the data that's assigned to each specific attribute is located in our vertex buffer. We filled our vertex buffer with 32-bit floating point variables. The first call to `glVertexAttribPointer` sets the location of the values assigned to the `a_position` attribute using the reference variable we created in `a_position_location`. We then pass in the number of values we use for this attribute. In the case of position, we pass in an x and a y coordinate, so this value is 2. We pass in the data type for our buffer array, which is a floating-point data type. We tell the function we are not normalizing the data. The `stride` value is the second to last parameter. This is the number of bytes that are used for a vertex in this buffer. Because each vertex in the buffer is using four floating-point values, we pass in `4 * sizeof( float )` for our stride. Finally, the last value we pass in is the offset in bytes to the data we are using to populate this attribute. For the `a_position` attribute, this value is 0 because the position comes at the beginning. For the `a_texcoord` attribute, this value is `2 * sizeof(float)` because there are two floating-point values that we used for `a_position` that precede our `a_texcoord` data.

The final line in the `main` function sets the game loop callback:

```
emscripten_set_main_loop(game_loop, 0, 0);
```

The game loop

Our game loop is pretty simple. In our game loop, we will use OpenGL to clear the canvas, move our ship, and render our ship to the canvas. Here is the code:

```
void game_loop() {
    glClearColor( 0, 0, 0, 1 );
    glClear( GL_COLOR_BUFFER_BIT|GL_DEPTH_BUFFER_BIT );

    ship_x += 0.002;
    ship_y += 0.001;

    if( ship_x >= 1.16 ) {
        ship_x = -1.16;
    }

    if( ship_y >= 1.21 ) {
        ship_y = -1.21;
    }

    glUniform4f(u_translate_location,
```

```
            ship_x, ship_y, 0, 0 );

    glDrawArrays(GL_TRIANGLES, 0, 6);
}
```

The first two lines of the game loop clear the canvas:

```
glClearColor( 0, 0, 0, 1 );
glClear( GL_COLOR_BUFFER_BIT|GL_DEPTH_BUFFER_BIT );
```

After that, we have several lines that update the ship's x and y coordinates, and then set the new coordinates in the shader:

```
ship_x += 0.002;
ship_y += 0.001;

if( ship_x >= 1.16 ) {
    ship_x = -1.16;
}

if( ship_y >= 1.21 ) {
    ship_y = -1.21;
}

glUniform4f(u_translate_location,
            ship_x, ship_y, 0 );
```

Finally, the game loop uses glDrawArrays to draw our spaceship to the canvas:

```
glDrawArrays(GL_TRIANGLES, 0, 6);
```

Compiling and running our code

You will want to download the sprites folder from the GitHub project so that you can include the image files that we need to compile and run this project. Once you have those images and have saved the code we just wrote into the webgl-redux.c file, we can compile and test this new application. If it is successful, it should look just like the Chapter 3, *Introduction to WebGL*, WebGL version. Run the following emcc command to compile the app:

```
emcc webgl-redux.c -o redux.html --preload-file sprites -s USE_WEBGL2=1 -s
USE_SDL=2 -s USE_SDL_IMAGE=2 -s SDL2_IMAGE_FORMATS=["png"]
```

If the app runs successfully, you should have a spaceship that is moving from left to right and up the HTML canvas. Here is a screenshot of a working version of the app:

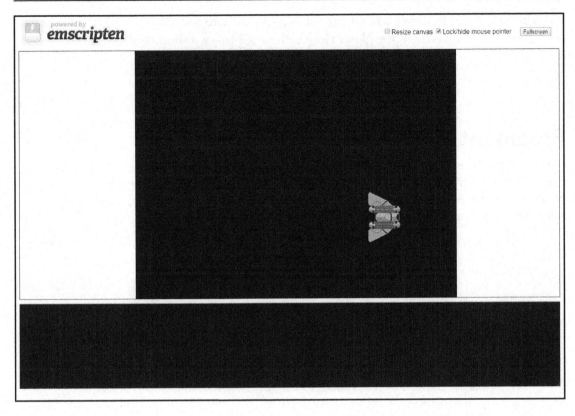

Figure 15.1: Screenshot of the OpenGL and SDL app

In the next section, we will learn how to blend textures from within a shader.

Mixing textures for a glow effect

Now, we will spend some time learning how to load more than one texture into our program. We will add the colors of those two textures to create a pulsing glow effect. To do this, we will need to modify our fragment shader to receive a second texture and a time uniform variable. We will pass that variable into a sine wave function, which will use it to calculate the strength of our glowing engines. We will need to add some code to keep track of the time that has passed, as well as some new initialization code to load the second texture. We can begin by copying `webgl-redux.c` to a new file called `glow.c`. Now that we have the new `glow.c` file, we can walk through the changes we will need to make our glowing engine effect. The first code change is the addition of a new `#define` macro to define a value for 2π.

We will use a value that cycles from 0 to 2π and feeds it into a sine wave function to create the pulsing effect on our engine glow. Here is the `#define` we should add near the beginning of our `glow.c` file:

```
#define TWOPI 6.2831853 // 2π
```

Fragment shader changes

After that new macro, we will need to make some changes to our fragment shader code. Our vertex shader code will remain the same because the process of determining the position of our vertex will not be any different than it was in the previous version of the app. Here is the updated version of the fragment shader:

```
const GLchar* fragment_shader_code[] = {
    "precision mediump float; \n"
    "varying vec2 v_texcoord; \n"

    "uniform float u_time; \n"
    "uniform sampler2D u_texture; \n"
    "uniform sampler2D u_glow; \n"

    "void main() { \n"
        "float cycle = (sin(u_time) + 1.0) / 2.0; \n"
        "vec4 tex = texture2D(u_texture, v_texcoord); \n"
        "vec4 glow = texture2D(u_glow, v_texcoord); \n"
        "glow.rgb *= glow.aaa; \n"
        "glow *= cycle; \n"
        "gl_FragColor = tex + glow; \n"
    "} \n"
};
```

We have added a new uniform variable called `u_time` that will be used to pass in a time-based variable that will cycle between 0 and 2π. We have also added a second `sampler2D` uniform variable called `u_glow` that will hold our new glow texture. The first line of our `main` function calculates a value between `0.0` and `1.0` based on the value in `u_time`. We retrieve the sampled values out of `u_texture` and `u_glow` using the built-in `texture2D` function. This time, instead of storing a value from the texture directly into `gl_FragColor`, we save those two values into `vec4` variables called `tex` and `glow`. We are going to be adding those two values together, so to keep things from getting too bright everywhere, we multiply the `rgb` (red green and blue) values in our `glow` sample color by the alpha channel. After that, we multiply all the values in our `glow` color by the `cycle` value we computed earlier.

The value in `cycle` will follow a sine wave oscillating between the values 0.0 and 1.0. That will cause our `glow` value to cycle up and down over time. We then compute our fragment color by adding the `tex` color to the `glow` color. Then, we store the output value in `gl_FragColor`.

OpenGL global variable changes

Next, we will need to update our OpenGL-related variables so that we can add three new global variables. We will need a new variable called `glow_tex`, which we will use to store a reference to the glow texture. We also need two new reference variables for our two new uniform variables in our shader, called `u_time_location` and `u_glow_location`. Here is what the new block of OpenGL variables will look like once we have added those three new lines:

```
GLuint program = 0;
GLuint texture;
GLuint glow_tex;

GLint a_texcoord_location = -1;
GLint a_position_location = -1;
GLint u_texture_location = -1;
GLint u_glow_location = -1;
GLint u_time_location = -1;

GLint u_translate_location = -1;
GLuint vertex_texture_buffer;
```

Other global variable changes

After our OpenGL global variables, we will need to add a new block of time-related global variables. We need them to have our shader cycle through values for our engine glow. These time-related variables should look pretty familiar. We have used techniques similar to the one we are about to use in the game we have been developing. Here are those global time variables:

```
float time_cycle = 0;
float delta_time = 0.0;
int diff_time = 0;

Uint32 last_time;
Uint32 last_frame_time;
Uint32 current_time;
```

We need to add one more SDL-related global surface variable, which we will use to load our glow texture. Add the following line near the block of global variables that precedes the `main` function:

```
SDL_Surface* glow_surface;
```

Changes to main()

We will be making some significant modifications to the initialization we are doing in our `main` function. Let me start by showing you the entire function. Then, we will walk through all of the changes, one at a time:

```
int main() {
    last_frame_time = last_time = SDL_GetTicks();

    SDL_Init( SDL_INIT_VIDEO );

    SDL_CreateWindowAndRenderer( CANVAS_WIDTH, CANVAS_HEIGHT, 0,
    &window, &renderer );

    SDL_SetRenderDrawColor( renderer, 0, 0, 0, 255 );
    SDL_RenderClear( renderer );

    GLuint vertex_shader = glCreateShader(GL_VERTEX_SHADER);

    glShaderSource( vertex_shader,
                    1,
                    vertex_shader_code,
                    0);

    glCompileShader(vertex_shader);

    GLint compile_success = 0;
    glGetShaderiv(vertex_shader, GL_COMPILE_STATUS, &compile_success);

    if(compile_success == GL_FALSE)
    {
        printf("failed to compile vertex shader\n");
        glDeleteShader(vertex_shader);
        return 0;
    }

    GLuint fragment_shader = glCreateShader(GL_FRAGMENT_SHADER);

    glShaderSource( fragment_shader,
                    1,
```

```
                    fragment_shader_code,
                    0);

glCompileShader(fragment_shader);
glGetShaderiv(fragment_shader, GL_COMPILE_STATUS,
&compile_success);

if(compile_success == GL_FALSE)
{
    printf("failed to compile fragment shader\n");
    glDeleteShader(fragment_shader);
    return 0;
}

program = glCreateProgram();
glAttachShader( program,
                vertex_shader);

glAttachShader( program,
                fragment_shader);

glLinkProgram(program);

GLint link_success = 0;

glGetProgramiv(program, GL_LINK_STATUS, &link_success);

if (link_success == GL_FALSE)
{
    printf("failed to link program\n");
    glDeleteProgram(program);
    return 0;
}

glUseProgram(program);

u_glow_location = glGetUniformLocation(program, "u_glow");
u_time_location = glGetUniformLocation(program, "u_time");

u_texture_location = glGetUniformLocation(program, "u_texture");
u_translate_location = glGetUniformLocation(program,
"u_translate");

a_position_location = glGetAttribLocation(program, "a_position");
a_texcoord_location = glGetAttribLocation(program, "a_texcoord");

glGenBuffers(1, &vertex_texture_buffer);
```

```
glBindBuffer( GL_ARRAY_BUFFER, vertex_texture_buffer );
 glBufferData(GL_ARRAY_BUFFER, sizeof(vertex_texture_data),
 vertex_texture_data, GL_STATIC_DRAW);

sprite_surface = IMG_Load( "/sprites/spaceship.png" );

    if( !sprite_surface ) {
        printf("failed to load image: %s\n", IMG_GetError() );
        return 0;
    }

    sprite_texture = SDL_CreateTextureFromSurface( renderer,
    sprite_surface );

    if( !sprite_texture ) {
        printf("failed to create texture: %s\n", IMG_GetError() );
        return 0;
    }

    SDL_QueryTexture( sprite_texture,
                      NULL, NULL,
                      &sprite_width, &sprite_height );

    glTexImage2D( GL_TEXTURE_2D,
                  0,
                  GL_RGBA,
                  sprite_width,
                  sprite_height,
                  0,
                  GL_RGBA,
                  GL_UNSIGNED_BYTE,
                  sprite_surface );

    SDL_FreeSurface( sprite_surface );

    glGenTextures( 1,
                   &glow_tex);

    glActiveTexture(GL_TEXTURE1);
    glEnable(GL_TEXTURE_2D);
    glBindTexture(GL_TEXTURE_2D, glow_tex);

    glow_surface = IMG_Load( "/sprites/glow.png" );

    if( !glow_surface ) {
        printf("failed to load image: %s\n", IMG_GetError() );
        return 0;
    }
```

```
glTexImage2D( GL_TEXTURE_2D,
                0,
                GL_RGBA,
                sprite_width,
                sprite_height,
                0,
                GL_RGBA,
                GL_UNSIGNED_BYTE,
                glow_surface );

glGenerateMipmap(GL_TEXTURE_2D);

SDL_FreeSurface( glow_surface );

glUniform1i(u_texture_location, 0);
glUniform1i(u_glow_location, 1);

glBlendFunc(GL_SRC_ALPHA, GL_ONE_MINUS_SRC_ALPHA);
glEnable(GL_BLEND);

glEnableVertexAttribArray(a_position_location);
glEnableVertexAttribArray(a_texcoord_location);

glVertexAttribPointer(
    a_position_location,        // set up the a_position attribute
    2,                          // how many attributes in the position
    GL_FLOAT,                   // data type of float
    GL_FALSE,                   // the data is not normalized
    4 * sizeof(float),          // stride (how many array items until
                                //the next position)
    (void*)0                    // starting point for attribute
);

glVertexAttribPointer(
    a_texcoord_location,        // set up the a_texcoord attribute
    2,                          // how many attributes in the
                                //texture coordinates
    GL_FLOAT,                   // data type of float
    GL_FALSE,                   // the data is not normalized
    4 * sizeof(float),          // stride (how many array items
                                //until the next position)
    (void*)(2 * sizeof(float)) // starting point for attribute
);

emscripten_set_main_loop(game_loop, 0, 0);
}
```

The first line in our `main` function is new. We use that line to set `last_frame_time` and `last_time` to the system time, which we retrieve using `SDL_GetTicks()`:

```
last_frame_time = last_time = SDL_GetTicks();
```

After that, we will not make any changes until we get to the section of code where we retrieve our uniform locations. We will need to retrieve two more uniform locations from our program, so right under our call to `glUseProgram`, we should make the following calls to get the uniform locations for `u_glow` and `u_time`:

```
u_glow_location = glGetUniformLocation(program, "u_glow");
u_time_location = glGetUniformLocation(program, "u_time");
```

The following block of code must come after we call `SDL_FreeSurface` to free the `sprite_surface` variable. This code block will generate a new texture, activate it, bind it, and load the `glow.png` image into that texture. It will then free the SDL surface and generate mipmaps for our texture. Finally, we set the uniform locations for our textures using `glUniform1i`. Here is the code we use to load our new texture:

```
glGenTextures( 1,
               &glow_tex);

glActiveTexture(GL_TEXTURE1);
glEnable(GL_TEXTURE_2D);
glBindTexture(GL_TEXTURE_2D, glow_tex);

glow_surface = IMG_Load( "/sprites/glow.png" );

if( !glow_surface ) {
    printf("failed to load image: %s\n", IMG_GetError() );
    return 0;
}

glTexImage2D( GL_TEXTURE_2D,
              0,
              GL_RGBA,
              sprite_width,
              sprite_height,
              0,
              GL_RGBA,
              GL_UNSIGNED_BYTE,
              glow_surface );

SDL_FreeSurface( glow_surface );

glGenerateMipmap(GL_TEXTURE_2D);
```

```
glUniform1i(u_texture_location, 0);
glUniform1i(u_glow_location, 1);
```

 If you are not familiar with Mipmaps, you may be wondering what the `glGenerateMipmap(GL_TEXTURE_2D);` line does. When you scale textures using OpenGL, those textures take time to generate. Mipmaps are a way to speed up scaling by performing some power of two scaled versions of your images while the game is initializing. This will reduce the amount of time it will take to scale these images at runtime.

Updating game_loop()

To cycle the glow effect on our spaceship's engines, we will need to add some code to our game loop that will cycle from 0.0 through 2π. We will then pass this value into the shader as the u_time uniform variable. We need to add this new block of code to the beginning of the game loop function:

```
current_time = SDL_GetTicks();

diff_time = current_time - last_time;

delta_time = diff_time / 1000.0;
last_time = current_time;

time_cycle += delta_time * 4;

if( time_cycle >= TWOPI ) {
    time_cycle -= TWOPI;
}

glUniform1f( u_time_location, time_cycle );
```

The first line uses `SDL_GetTicks()` to retrieve the current clock time. We then subtract the last time from the current time to get a value for the `diff_time` variable. This will tell us the number of milliseconds between this frame and the previous frame generated. After that, we calculate `delta_time`, which will be the fraction of a second between this frame and the previous frame. After we have calculated `diff_time` and `delta_time`, we set the `last_time` variable to `current_time`.

We do this so that the next time we go through the game loop, we will have the time this frame ran. All of those lines have been in previous iterations of our code. Now, let's get a value for `time_cycle`, which we will pass into the `u_time` uniform variable in our fragment shader. First, add `delta-time * 4` to time cycle with the following line:

```
time_cycle += delta_time * 4;
```

You may be wondering why I multiply it by 4. Initially, I hadn't added a multiple, which meant the engine glow cycled roughly every 6 seconds. This felt like the cycle was taking too long. Playing with the number, a multiple of 4 just felt right to me, but there is no reason you need to stick with this specific multiple if you would prefer your engines to cycle either faster or slower.

Because we are using a sine function to cycle our glow level, we need to make sure that when our time cycle hits `TWOPI`, we subtract `TWOPI` from our `time_cycle` variable:

```
if( time_cycle >= TWOPI ) {
    time_cycle -= TWOPI;
}
```

Now that we have calculated the value for our cycle, we set that value using the `u_time_location` reference variable using a call to `glUniform1f`:

```
glUniform1f( u_time_location, time_cycle );
```

Compiling and running our code

Now that we have made all of the code changes we need, we can go ahead and compile and run the new version of our app. Compile the `glow.c` file by running the following `emcc` command:

```
emcc glow.c -o glow.html --preload-file sprites -s USE_WEBGL2=1 -s
USE_SDL=2 -s USE_SDL_IMAGE=2 -s SDL2_IMAGE_FORMATS=["png"]
```

If the build is successful, running `glow.html` in your web browser should show the spaceship moving as it was before. However, now, there will be a glow effect on the engines. This glow will cycle up and down and look as follows when the engine is at maximum glow:

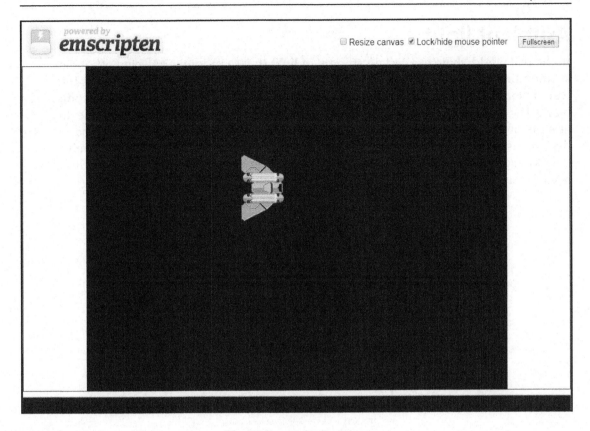

Figure 15.2: Screenshot of the glow shader app

In the next section, we will discuss the Phong 3D lighting model.

3D lighting

I would like to briefly discuss 3D lighting because we will be approximating it with 2D lighting effects. The Phong lighting model is the standard for three-dimensional lighting models in computer graphics. It was a model for lighting created by Bui Tuong Phong at the University of Utah in 1975, but it was not until the late 1990s that desktop computers became fast enough to implement the model in games. Since then, the lighting model has become the standard for 3D game development. It combines ambient, diffuse, and specular lighting to render geometry. We won't be able to implement a proper version of the lighting model because we aren't writing a 3D game. However, we can implement an approximation of the model by using 2D sprites and normal maps to go along with those sprites.

Ambient light

In the real world, there is a certain amount of light that's randomly reflected off of the surrounding surfaces. This creates lighting that will illuminate everything evenly. If it weren't for ambient lighting, an object in the shadow of another object would be completely black. The amount of ambient lighting varies based on the environment. In a game, the amount of ambient lighting is usually decided based on the mood and look a game designer is attempting to achieve. For 2D games, ambient lighting may be effectively the only kind of lighting we have. In 3D games, relying entirely on ambient light produces models that look flat:

Figure 15.3: A sphere with only ambient lighting

Diffuse light

Diffuse lighting is light that comes from a specific direction. If you look at a three-dimensional object in the real world, the side facing a light source will look brighter than the side facing away from that light source. This gives objects in a 3D environment an actual 3D appearance. In many 2D games, diffuse lighting is not created with a shader, but is included in the sprite by the artist that created it. In a platformer game, for instance, the artist may assume that there is a light source that comes from above the game objects. The artist would design the game objects to have a kind of diffuse lighting by changing the colors of the pixels in the artwork. For many 2D games, this will work perfectly fine. If you would, however, like to have a torch in your game that changes the look of the game objects as they move by, you need to design shaders that are capable of doing that work:

Figure 15.4: Sphere with diffuse lighting

Specular light

Some objects are shiny and have reflective patches that create bright highlights. When light hits a surface, it has a reflective vector based on the angle that the light hits the surface, relative to the normal of the surface it is hitting. The intensity of specular highlights is based on the reflectivity of the surface, combined with the angle of view, relative to the reflected light angle. A specular highlight on a game object can make it appear smooth or polished. Not all game objects require this kind of lighting, but it looks great on objects you want to shine:

Figure 15.5: Sphere with specular lighting

In the next section, we will discuss normal maps and how they are used in modern games.

Normal maps

Normal mapping is a method that's used for creating very detailed models using relatively low polygon counts in 3D games. The idea is that rather than creating a surface with a huge number of polygons, a game engine could use a low polygon model that had a normal map where each pixel in the normal map would contain the x, y, and z values of a normal using the red, green, and blue colors of the image. Inside of a shader, we could then sample the normal map texture in the same way we sample other texture maps. However, we could use the normal data to help us calculate the lighting effects on our sprites. If, in our game, we wanted our spaceships to always be lit relative to the star in the center of the gameplay area, we could create a normal map for our spaceships and create a light source in the center of our game. We will now create an app to demonstrate the use of normal maps for 2D lighting.

Creating a 2D lighting demo app

We can start our lighting app by creating a new C file called `lighting.c`. The macros at the beginning of `lighting.c` are the same macros we used in `glow.c`, but we can remove the `#define TWOPI` macro because it is no longer needed. Here are the macros we will have in our `lighting.c` file:

```
#include <SDL2/SDL.h>
#include <SDL2/SDL_image.h>
#include <SDL_opengl.h>

#include <GLES3/gl3.h>
#include <stdlib.h>
#include <emscripten.h>

#define CANVAS_WIDTH 800
#define CANVAS_HEIGHT 600
#define FLOAT32_BYTE_SIZE 4
#define STRIDE FLOAT32_BYTE_SIZE*4
```

The vertex shader code in this file will be very similar to the vertex shader code we had in our `glow.c` file. The one change we will make is done by removing the `u_translate` uniform variable. We are doing this because we will be centering our shaded sprite image, and we will allow the user to move the light around the canvas. Here is the new version of the vertex shader:

```
const GLchar* vertex_shader_code[] = {
    "precision mediump float; \n"
```

```
    "attribute vec4 a_position; \n"
    "attribute vec2 a_texcoord; \n"
    "varying vec2 v_texcoord; \n"

    "void main() { \n"
        "gl_Position = a_position; \n"
        "v_texcoord = a_texcoord; \n"
    "} \n"
};
```

Fragment shader updates

Now, we will need to create a new version of our fragment shader. This shader will load a normal map in addition to the original texture loaded. This normal map will be used to calculate lighting normals on our game object. This version of the shader will use a 2D form of the Phong lighting model, in that we will be calculating ambient, diffuse, and normal lighting for the sprite we are rendering. Here is the code for our new fragment shader:

```
const GLchar* fragment_shader_code[] = {
    "precision mediump float; \n"

    "varying vec2 v_texcoord; \n"

    "uniform sampler2D u_texture; \n"
    "uniform sampler2D u_normal; \n"
    "uniform vec3 u_light_pos; \n"

    "const float ambient = 0.6; \n"
    "const float specular = 32.0; \n"
    "const vec3 view_pos = vec3(400, 300,-100); \n"
    "const vec4 light_color = vec4( 0.6, 0.6, 0.6, 0.0); \n"

    "void main() { \n"
        "vec4 tex = texture2D(u_texture, v_texcoord); \n"

        "vec4 ambient_frag = tex * ambient; \n"
        "ambient_frag.rgb *= light_color.rgb; \n"

        "vec3 norm = vec3(texture2D(u_normal, v_texcoord)); \n"
        "norm.xyz *= 2.0; \n"
        "norm.xyz -= 1.0; \n"

        "vec3 light_dir = normalize(gl_FragCoord.xyz - u_light_pos); \n"

        "vec3 view_dir = normalize(view_pos - gl_FragCoord.xyz); \n"
        "vec3 reflect_dir = reflect(light_dir, norm); \n"
```

```
         "float reflect_dot = max( dot(view_dir, reflect_dir), 0.0 ); \n"
         "float spec = pow(reflect_dot, specular); \n"
         "vec4 specular_frag = spec * light_color; \n"

         "float diffuse = max(dot(norm, light_dir), 0.0); \n"
         "vec4 diffuse_frag = vec4( diffuse*light_color.r,
          diffuse*light_color.g, "
                                   "diffuse*light_color.b,  0.0);     \n"
         "gl_FragColor = ambient_frag + diffuse_frag + specular_frag; \n"
     "} \n"
};
```

Let's break down what is going on inside of the new version of the fragment shader. The first thing you will notice is that we have two `sampler2D` uniform variables; the second one is called `u_normal` and is used to sample the normal map for our image:

```
"uniform sampler2D u_texture; \n"
"uniform sampler2D u_normal; \n"
```

After our samplers, we need a `uniform vec3` variable that holds the position of our light. We we call this `u_light_pos`:

```
"uniform vec3 u_light_pos; \n"
```

We will be using several constants in our new fragment shader. We will need factors for ambient and specular lighting, as well as the view position and the light color. We will be defining those constants in the following four lines of code:

```
"const float ambient = 0.6; \n"
"const float specular = 0.8; \n"
"const vec3 view_pos = vec3(400, 300,-100); \n"
"const vec4 light_color = vec4( 0.6, 0.6, 0.6, 0.0); \n"
```

Inside of our `main` function, the first thing we will need to do is get the ambient fragment color. Determining the ambient color is pretty easy. All you need to do is multiply the texture color by the ambient factor, then multiply it again by the light color. Here is the code that computes the value for the ambient component of the fragment:

```
"vec4 tex = texture2D(u_texture, v_texcoord); \n"
"vec4 ambient_frag = tex * ambient; \n"

"ambient_frag.rgb *= light_color.rgb; \n"
```

After calculating our ambient color component, we need to calculate the normal of our fragment from the normal map texture that we passed into the shader. The texture uses the red color to represent the normal's x value. The green represents the y value. Finally, blue represents the z value. The colors are all floating points that go from 0.0 to 1.0, so we will need to modify the normal's x, y, and z components to go from −1.0 to +1.0. Here is the code we use to define the normals:

```
"vec3 norm = vec3(texture2D(u_normal, v_texcoord)); \n"
"norm.xyz *= 2.0; \n"
"norm.xyz -= 1.0; \n"
```

To convert the values in the norm vector from 0.0 into 1.0, −1.0, and +1.0, we need to multiply the values in the normal vector by 2, and then subtract one. After calculating the value of the normal, we need to find the direction of our light source:

```
"vec3 light_dir = normalize(gl_FragCoord.xyz - u_light_pos); \n"
```

We are normalizing the value with the normalize GLSL function because we won't have any light falloff in this app. If you had a game with a torch, you might want a sharp falloff based on the square of the distance from the light source. For this app, we are assuming that the light source has an infinite range. For our specular lighting, we will need to calculate our view direction:

```
"vec3 view_dir = normalize(view_pos - gl_FragCoord.xyz); \n"
```

We set the view_pos vector to the center of our canvas, so our specular lighting should be the greatest when our light source is in the center of our canvas as well. You will be able to test this out when you compile the app. After calculating the view direction, we will need to calculate the reflection vector, which we will also use in our specular lighting calculation:

```
"vec3 reflect_dir = reflect(light_dir, norm); \n"
```

We can then calculate the dot product of these two vectors, and raise them to the power of our specular factor (defined as 32 earlier) to calculate the amount of specular lighting we will need for this fragment:

```
"float reflect_dot = max( dot(view_dir, reflect_dir), 0.0 ); \n"
"float spec = pow(reflect_dot, specular); \n"
"vec4 specular_frag = spec * light_color; \n"
```

After that, we calculate the diffuse component for the fragment using the dot product of the normal and the light direction. We combine that with the light color to get our diffuse component value:

```
"float diffuse = max(dot(norm, light_dir), 0.0); \n"
"vec4 diffuse_frag = vec4(diffuse*light_color.r, diffuse*light_color.g,
diffuse*light_color.b, 0.0); \n"
```

Finally, we add all of those values together to find our fragment value:

```
"gl_FragColor = ambient_frag + diffuse_frag + specular_frag; \n"
```

OpenGL global variables

After defining our fragment shader, we need to define a series of OpenGL-related global variables. These variables should be familiar to you from the previous two versions of this app. There are a few new variables that we should take note of. We will no longer have just one program ID. SDL uses its own program, and we will need an ID for that program as well. We will call this variable `sdl_program`. We will also need new references for our textures. In addition, we will need new references for the uniform variables that we pass into our shader. Here is the new version of our OpenGL global variable code:

```
GLuint program = 0;
GLint sdl_program = 0;
GLuint circle_tex, normal_tex, light_tex;
GLuint normal_map;

GLint a_texcoord_location = -1;
GLint a_position_location = -1;
GLint u_texture_location = -1;
GLint u_normal_location = -1;
GLint u_light_pos_location = -1;

GLint u_translate_location = -1;
GLuint vertex_texture_buffer;

float vertex_texture_data[] = {
    // x,      y,       u,    v
     0.167,   0.213,    1.0,  1.0,
    -0.167,   0.213,    0.0,  1.0,
     0.167,  -0.213,    1.0,  0.0,
    -0.167,  -0.213,    0.0,  0.0,
    -0.167,   0.213,    0.0,  1.0,
     0.167,  -0.213,    1.0,  0.0
};
```

SDL global variables

Some of the SDL variables were the same as the ones we used in the previous apps we created for this chapter. The other variables for lighting and normals are new to this section. Here are the SDL-related global variables we will need for this app:

```
SDL_Window *window;
SDL_Renderer *renderer;

SDL_Texture* light_texture;

SDL_Surface* surface;

int light_width;
int light_height;

int light_x = 600;
int light_y = 200;
int light_z = -300;
```

We need to declare an SDL_Texture variable called light_texture, which we will use to hold the SDL texture for our light icon. We will be using SDL to draw our light icon instead of drawing it using OpenGL. We will use one surface pointer variable to load all of our textures, freeing that surface immediately after we create the texture. We need the width and height value to keep track of the width and height of our light icon. We will also need values to keep track of the x, y, and z coordinates of our light source.

Function prototypes

Because I would like to put the code for the main function before the code for our other functions, we will need a few function prototypes. In this app, we will have a game loop function, a function to retrieve mouse input through SDL, and a function to draw our light icon using SDL. Here is what those function prototypes look like:

```
void game_loop();
void input();
void draw_light_icon();
```

The main function

Like in the other apps we have created in this chapter, our `main` function will need to initialize both SDL and OpenGL variables. The beginning of the `main` function is the same as it was at the beginning of our glow app. It initializes SDL, then compiles and links the OpenGL shaders and creates a new OpenGL program:

```
int main() {
    SDL_Init( SDL_INIT_VIDEO );
    SDL_CreateWindowAndRenderer( CANVAS_WIDTH, CANVAS_HEIGHT, 0,
    &window, &renderer );
    SDL_SetRenderDrawColor( renderer, 0, 0, 0, 255 );
    SDL_RenderClear( renderer );

    GLuint vertex_shader = glCreateShader(GL_VERTEX_SHADER);

    glShaderSource( vertex_shader,
                    1,
                    vertex_shader_code,
                    0);

    glCompileShader(vertex_shader);

    GLint compile_success = 0;
    glGetShaderiv(vertex_shader, GL_COMPILE_STATUS, &compile_success);

    if(compile_success == GL_FALSE)
    {
        printf("failed to compile vertex shader\n");
        glDeleteShader(vertex_shader);
        return 0;
    }

    GLuint fragment_shader = glCreateShader(GL_FRAGMENT_SHADER);

    glShaderSource( fragment_shader,
                    1,
                    fragment_shader_code,
                    0);

    glCompileShader(fragment_shader);
    glGetShaderiv(fragment_shader, GL_COMPILE_STATUS,
    &compile_success);

    if(compile_success == GL_FALSE)
    {
        printf("failed to compile fragment shader\n");
```

```
            GLint maxLength = 0;
            glGetShaderiv(fragment_shader, GL_INFO_LOG_LENGTH, &maxLength);

            GLchar* errorLog = malloc(maxLength);
            glGetShaderInfoLog(fragment_shader, maxLength, &maxLength,
            &errorLog[0]);
            printf("error: %s\n", errorLog);

            glDeleteShader(fragment_shader);
            return 0;
        }

    program = glCreateProgram();
    glAttachShader( program,
                    vertex_shader);

    glAttachShader( program,
                    fragment_shader);

    glLinkProgram(program);

    GLint link_success = 0;

    glGetProgramiv(program, GL_LINK_STATUS, &link_success);

    if (link_success == GL_FALSE)
    {
        printf("failed to link program\n");
        glDeleteProgram(program);
        return 0;
    }

    glDeleteShader(vertex_shader);
    glDeleteShader(fragment_shader);
    glUseProgram(program);
```

After initializing SDL and creating the OpenGL shader program, we need to get uniform variable references for our OpenGL shader program. Two of these references are new to this version of the program. The u_normal_location variable will be a reference to the u_normal sampler uniform variable, and the u_light_pos_location variable will be a reference to the u_light_pos uniform variable. Here is the new version of our references:

```
u_texture_location = glGetUniformLocation(program, "u_texture");
u_normal_location = glGetUniformLocation(program, "u_normal");
u_light_pos_location = glGetUniformLocation(program, "u_light_pos");
u_translate_location = glGetUniformLocation(program, "u_translate");
```

After grabbing the references to our uniform variables, we need to do the same for our attributes:

```
a_position_location = glGetAttribLocation(program, "a_position");
a_texcoord_location = glGetAttribLocation(program, "a_texcoord");
```

We then need to generate the vertex buffer, bind it, and buffer the data from the array we created earlier. This should be the same code that we had in the glow.c file:

```
glGenBuffers(1, &vertex_texture_buffer);

glBindBuffer( GL_ARRAY_BUFFER, vertex_texture_buffer );
glBufferData( GL_ARRAY_BUFFER, sizeof(vertex_texture_data),
              vertex_texture_data, GL_STATIC_DRAW);
```

Next, we will need to set up all of our textures. Two of them will be rendered using OpenGL, while the other will be rendered using SDL. Here is the initialization code for all three of the textures:

```
glGenTextures( 1,
               &circle_tex);

glActiveTexture(GL_TEXTURE0);
glBindTexture(GL_TEXTURE_2D, circle_tex);

surface = IMG_Load( "/sprites/circle.png" );
if( !surface ) {
    printf("failed to load image: %s\n", IMG_GetError() );
    return 0;
}

glTexImage2D( GL_TEXTURE_2D,
              0,
              GL_RGBA,
              128, // sprite width
              128, // sprite height
              0,
              GL_RGBA,
              GL_UNSIGNED_BYTE,
              surface );

glUniform1i(u_texture_location, 1);
glGenerateMipmap(GL_TEXTURE_2D);

SDL_FreeSurface( surface );

glGenTextures( 1,
               &normal_tex);
```

```
glActiveTexture(GL_TEXTURE1);
glBindTexture(GL_TEXTURE_2D, normal_tex);

surface = IMG_Load( "/sprites/ball-normal.png" );

if( !surface ) {
    printf("failed to load image: %s\n", IMG_GetError() );
    return 0;
}

glTexImage2D( GL_TEXTURE_2D,
              0,
              GL_RGBA,
              128, // sprite width
              128, // sprite height
              0,
              GL_RGBA,
              GL_UNSIGNED_BYTE,
              surface );

glUniform1i(u_normal_location, 1);
glGenerateMipmap(GL_TEXTURE_2D);

SDL_FreeSurface( surface );

surface = IMG_Load( "/sprites/light.png" );

if( !surface ) {
    printf("failed to load image: %s\n", IMG_GetError() );
    return 0;
}

light_texture = SDL_CreateTextureFromSurface( renderer, surface );

if( !light_texture ) {
    printf("failed to create light texture: %s\n", IMG_GetError() );
    return 0;
}

SDL_QueryTexture( light_texture,
                  NULL, NULL,
                  &light_width, &light_height );

SDL_FreeSurface( surface );
```

This is a fairly large block of code, so let me walk through it a piece at a time. The first three lines generate, activate, and bind the circle texture so that we can begin to update it:

```
glGenTextures( 1,
               &circle_tex);

glActiveTexture(GL_TEXTURE0);
glBindTexture(GL_TEXTURE_2D, circle_tex);
```

Now that we have the circle texture ready to update, we can load the image file using SDL:

```
surface = IMG_Load( "/sprites/circle.png" );

if( !surface ) {
    printf("failed to load image: %s\n", IMG_GetError() );
    return 0;
}
```

Next, we need to load that data into our bound texture:

```
glTexImage2D( GL_TEXTURE_2D,
              0,
              GL_RGBA,
              128, // sprite width
              128, // sprite height
              0,
              GL_RGBA,
              GL_UNSIGNED_BYTE,
              surface );
```

Then, we can activate that texture, generate mipmaps, and free the surface:

```
glUniform1i(u_texture_location, 1);
glGenerateMipmap(GL_TEXTURE_2D);

SDL_FreeSurface( surface );
```

After doing this for our circle texture, we need to do the same series of steps for our normal map:

```
glGenTextures( 1,
               &normal_tex);

glActiveTexture(GL_TEXTURE1);
glBindTexture(GL_TEXTURE_2D, normal_tex);
surface = IMG_Load( "/sprites/ball-normal.png" );

if( !surface ) {
```

```
        printf("failed to load image: %s\n", IMG_GetError() );
        return 0;
}

glTexImage2D( GL_TEXTURE_2D,
        0,
        GL_RGBA,
        128, // sprite width
        128, // sprite height
        0,
        GL_RGBA,
        GL_UNSIGNED_BYTE,
        surface );

glUniform1i(u_normal_location, 1);
glGenerateMipmap(GL_TEXTURE_2D);

SDL_FreeSurface( surface );
```

We will handle the final texture differently because it will only be rendered using SDL. This should be pretty familiar to you by now. We need to load the surface from the image file, create a texture from the surface, query the size of that texture, and then free the original surface:

```
surface = IMG_Load( "/sprites/light.png" );

if( !surface ) {
    printf("failed to load image: %s\n", IMG_GetError() );
    return 0;
}

light_texture = SDL_CreateTextureFromSurface( renderer, surface );

if( !light_texture ) {
    printf("failed to create light texture: %s\n", IMG_GetError() );
    return 0;
}

SDL_QueryTexture( light_texture,
                NULL, NULL,
                &light_width, &light_height );

SDL_FreeSurface( surface );
```

Now that we have created our textures, we should set up our alpha blending:

```
glBlendFunc(GL_SRC_ALPHA, GL_ONE_MINUS_SRC_ALPHA);
glEnable(GL_BLEND);
```

The last line of our `main` function uses Emscripten to call the game loop:

```
emscripten_set_main_loop(game_loop, 0, 0);
```

The game_loop function

Now that we have our `main` function defined, we need to define our `game_loop`. Because the `game_loop` function is rendering using both SDL and OpenGL, we need to set our vertex attribute pointers each time through the loop before we render in OpenGL. We will also need to switch between more than one OpenGL program because SDL uses a different program for shading than the one we are using for OpenGL. Let me begin by showing you the entire function, and then we can walk through it one piece at a time:

```
void game_loop() {
    input();

    glGetIntegerv(GL_CURRENT_PROGRAM, &sdl_program);
    glUseProgram(program);

    glClearColor( 0, 0, 0, 1 );
    glClear( GL_COLOR_BUFFER_BIT|GL_DEPTH_BUFFER_BIT );

    glBindBuffer(GL_ARRAY_BUFFER, vertex_texture_buffer);
    glVertexAttribPointer(
        a_position_location,       // set up the a_position attribute
        2,                         // how many attributes in the
                                   //position
        GL_FLOAT,                  // data type of float
        GL_FALSE,                  // the data is not normalized
        4 * sizeof(float),         // stride (how many array items
                                   //until the next position)
        (void*)0                   // starting point for attribute
    );

    glEnableVertexAttribArray(a_texcoord_location);
    glBindBuffer(GL_ARRAY_BUFFER, vertex_texture_buffer);
    glVertexAttribPointer(
        a_texcoord_location,       // set up the a_texcoord attribute
        2,                         // how many attributes in the texture
                                   //coordinates
        GL_FLOAT,                  // data type of float
        GL_FALSE,                  // the data is not normalized
        4 * sizeof(float),         // stride (how many array items until
                                   //the next position)
        (void*)(2 * sizeof(float)) // starting point for attribute
```

```
);

glUniform3f( u_light_pos_location,
             (float)(light_x), (float)(600-light_y), (float)(light_z) );

glDrawArrays(GL_TRIANGLES, 0, 6);

glUseProgram(sdl_program);
draw_light_icon();
}
```

The first line of the game loop calls the `input` function. This function will use input from the mouse to set the light position. The second and third lines retrieve the SDL shader program and save it to the `sdl_program` variable. Then, it switches to the custom OpenGL shaders with a call to `glUseProgram`. Here are the two lines of code we call to save the current program and set a new one:

```
glGetIntegerv(GL_CURRENT_PROGRAM, &sdl_program);
glUseProgram(program);
```

After that, we call OpenGL to clear the canvas:

```
glClearColor( 0, 0, 0, 1 );
glClear( GL_COLOR_BUFFER_BIT|GL_DEPTH_BUFFER_BIT );
```

Next, we need to set our geometry:

```
glBindBuffer(GL_ARRAY_BUFFER, vertex_texture_buffer);
glVertexAttribPointer(
          a_position_location,    // set up the a_position attribute
          2,                      // how many attributes in the
                                  //position
          GL_FLOAT,               // data type of float
          GL_FALSE,               // the data is not normalized
          4 * sizeof(float),      // stride (how many array items
                                  //until the next position)
          (void*)0                // starting point for attribute
);

glEnableVertexAttribArray(a_texcoord_location);
glBindBuffer(GL_ARRAY_BUFFER, vertex_texture_buffer);
glVertexAttribPointer(
    a_texcoord_location,          // set up the a_texcoord attribute
    2,                            // how many attributes in the texture
                                  //coordinates
    GL_FLOAT,                     // data type of float
    GL_FALSE,                     // the data is not normalized
    4 * sizeof(float),            // stride (how many array items until
```

```
                                        //the next position)
         (void*)(2 * sizeof(float))     // starting point for attribute
    );
```

We then use a call to `glUniform3f` to set the `vec3 uniform u_light_pos` variable to the `light_x`, `light_y`, and `light_z` global variables we defined earlier. These light positions can be moved using the mouse. The code that allows the user to move the light will be defined later when we write the `input` function. After we set the values for our light positions, we can draw our triangles using OpenGL:

```
    glDrawArrays(GL_TRIANGLES, 0, 6);
```

Finally, we need to switch back to our SDL program and call the `draw_light_icon` function, which will draw our light icon using SDL:

```
    glUseProgram(sdl_program);
    draw_light_icon();
```

The input function

Now that we have defined our game loop, we will need to write a function to capture our mouse input. I want to be able to click our canvas and have the light icon and light source move to the location I just clicked. I would also like to be able to hold the mouse button down and drag the light icon around the canvas to see how the shading works when the light is in different locations on the canvas. Most of this code will look very familiar. We use `SDL_PollEvent` to retrieve an event and look to see if the left mouse button is down, or if the user has moved the scroll wheel. If the user has turned the scroll wheel, the `light_z` variable is changed, which will, in turn, change the z position of our light source. We use the `static int mouse_down` variable to track whether or not the user pressed the mouse button. If the user pressed the mouse button, we would call `SDL_GetMouseState` to retrieve the `light_x` and `light_y` variables, which will modify the x and y positions of our light source. Here is the code for the input function in its entirety:

```
void input() {
    SDL_Event event;
    static int mouse_down = 0;

    if(SDL_PollEvent( &event ) )
    {
        if(event.type == SDL_MOUSEWHEEL )
        {
            if( event.wheel.y > 0 ) {
```

```
                light_z+= 100;
        }
        else {
            light_z-=100;
        }

        if( light_z > 10000 ) {
            light_z = 10000;
        }
        else if( light_z < -10000 ) {
            light_z = -10000;
        }
    }
    else if(event.type == SDL_MOUSEMOTION )
    {
        if( mouse_down == 1 ) {
            SDL_GetMouseState( &light_x, &light_y );
        }
    }
    else if(event.type == SDL_MOUSEBUTTONDOWN )
    {
        if(event.button.button == SDL_BUTTON_LEFT)
        {
            SDL_GetMouseState( &light_x, &light_y );
            mouse_down = 1;
        }
    }
    else if(event.type == SDL_MOUSEBUTTONUP )
    {
        if(event.button.button == SDL_BUTTON_LEFT)
        {
            mouse_down = 0;
        }
    }
  }
}
```

The draw_light_icon function

The last function we need to define in our `lighting.c` file is
the `draw_light_icon` function. This function will use SDL to draw our light icon based on
the values in the `light_x` and `light_y` variables. We create an `SDL_Rect` variable called
`dest` and set the x, y, w, and h attributes of that structure. We then call `SDL_RenderCopy` to
render our light icon in the proper location. Here is the code for that function:

```
void draw_light_icon() {
    SDL_Rect dest;
    dest.x = light_x - light_width / 2 - 32;
    dest.y = light_y - light_height / 2;
    dest.w = light_width;
    dest.h = light_height;

    SDL_RenderCopy( renderer, light_texture, NULL, &dest );
}
```

Compiling and running our lighting app

When we compile and run our lighting app, we should be able to click and drag our light
around the canvas. We have a small circle that is associated with a normal map. Together
with our shading and lighting, it should make that circle look more like a shiny button.
Execute the following command on the command line to compile the `lighting.html` file:

```
emcc lighting.c -o lighting.html --preload-file sprites -s USE_SDL=2 -s
USE_SDL_IMAGE=2 -s SDL2_IMAGE_FORMATS=["png"]
```

Now, you should be able to serve the `lighting.html` file from a web server, or emrun. Here is what the app should look like if everything went well:

Figure 15.6: Screenshot of the 2D lighting app

Summary

In this chapter, we took a closer look at shaders after introducing the concept back in Chapter 3, *Introduction to WebGL*, when we built a WebGL app. It is helpful to have an understanding of WebGL when you are using OpenGL for WebAssembly because each call to OpenGL from WebAssembly is internally calling the corresponding WebGL functions. We started by rebuilding that WebGL app using a combination of OpenGL ES and SDL in C++ and compiled it to WebAssembly. We then learned how we could use OpenGL and shaders to mix different textures in interesting ways. We used this knowledge to create a pulsing glow around the spaceship's engines. Finally, we discussed 3D lighting and normal maps, and then developed a 2D lighting model and created an app that allows us to light a simple circle with that lighting model. This app demonstrates the possibilities in 2D lighting by allowing us to move our light around a 2D circle with a normal map, which is used to give that 2D surface the appearance of depth.

In the next chapter, we will discuss debugging our WebAssembly application and the tools we can use for performance testing.

Debugging and Optimization
16

In this final chapter, we are going to discuss two topics that will be helpful as you go on to create games using Emscripten and build in WebAssembly. We are going to discuss the topics of debugging and optimization. We will debug before optimizing, because building your code to output more debuging information prevents optimization. We will start by using some basic debugging techniques, such as printing a stack trace and defining debug macros that we can remove by changing a compile flag. We will then move on to some more advanced debugging techniques, such as compiling with Emscripten flags, which allow us to trace through our code in Firefox and Chrome. We will also discuss some of the differences between debugging using the Firefox and Chrome developer tools.

 You will need to include several images in your build to make this project work. Make sure that you include the /Chapter16/sprites/ folder from this project's GitHub repository. If you haven't downloaded the GitHub project yet, you can get it online here: https://github.com/ PacktPublishing/Hands-On-Game-Development-with-WebAssembly.

After we have finished discussing debugging, we will move on to optimization. We will discuss the optimization flags you can use with Emscripten, as well as the use of profilers to determine where your game or app may be having performance issues. We will discuss general techniques for optimizing your code for WebAssembly deployment. Finally, we will discuss optimizations related to web games and WebGL calls made by the WebAssembly module.

Debug macro and stack trace

One way you can start debugging your code is by using `#define` to create a debugging macro, which we can activate by passing a flag into the Emscripten compiler. However, this will resolve to nothing if we don't pass that flag. Macros are easy to add, and we can create a call that prints a line if we are running with our debug flag, but will not slow down performance if we aren't. If you are not familiar with preprocessor commands, they are commands that are issued to the compiler that evaluate while the code is compiled instead of at runtime. For instance, if I used a `#ifdef PRINT_ME` command, the line of code would only be compiled into our source code if the `PRINT_ME` macro is defined either with a `#define PRINT_ME` macro on a line earlier in the code, or if we compiled the source with the `-DPRINT_ME` flag passed into the compiler when we ran the compiler. Let's say we had the following block of code in our `main` function:

```
#ifdef PRINT_ME
    printf("PRINT_ME was defined\n");
#else
    printf("nothing was defined\n");
#endif
```

If we did, we would have compiled and ran that code. The web browser's console prints the following:

"nothing was defined"

If we compiled it with the `-DPRINT_ME` flag and then ran the code at the command line, we would see the following printed:

"PRINT_ME was defined"

If you disassembled the code into WebAssembly text, then you wouldn't see any hint of the original `printf` statement that printed "nothing was defined". At compile time, the code is removed. This makes preprocessor macros very useful when creating code that we want to include during the development phase.

If you are using the `-D` flag to include debug macros in your code, make sure that you don't include that flag when you are compiling for release, as that will continue to include all of your debug macros when you don't want them. You may want to consider having a `-DRELEASE` flag that overrides your `-DDEBUG` flag when you compile your code for general release.

Keeping all of your `printf` calls confined to a macro is a good way to make sure you removed all the calls to `printf` that will slow down your app when you publish it. Let's try this out by starting with the `webgl-redux.c` file as a baseline. From the code we created in the previous chapter, copy and paste `webgl-redux.c` into a file called `debug.cpp`. We will add our debug macro at the beginning of this file. Immediately after the line that includes `emscripten.h`, but before the line of code that defines the canvas width, add the following block of code:

```
#ifdef DEBUG
    void run_debug(const char* str) {
        EM_ASM (
            console.log(new Error().stack);
        );
        printf("%s\n", str);
    }

    #define DBG(str) run_debug(str)
#else
    #define DBG(str)
#endif
```

This code will only compile the `run_debug` function if we pass the `-DDEBUG` flag to the compiler. The user shouldn't run the `run_debug` function directly, because it will not exist if we don't use the `-DDEBUG` flag. Instead, we should use the `DBG` macro function. This macro exists regardless of whether we use the `-DDEBUG` flag. If we use this flag, the function calls the `run_debug` function. If we don't use this flag, the calls to `DBG` magically disappear. The `run_debug` function not only uses `printf` to print out a string, but also uses `EM_ASM` to dump a stack trace to the JavaScript console. A stack trace logs out every function that is currently on the JavaScript stack. Let's add a few function calls that will eventually call our `DBG` macro. These should be added immediately before the `main` function:

```
extern "C" {
    void inner_call_1() {
        DBG("check console log for stack trace");
    }
    void inner_call_2() {
        inner_call_1();
    }
    void inner_call_3() {
        inner_call_2();
    }
}
```

Inside our `main` function, we should add a call to `inner_call_3()`, as follows:

```
int main() {
    inner_call_3();
```

Now, let's compile our `debug.cpp` file with the following command:

```
emcc debug.cpp -o index.html -DDEBUG --preload-file sprites -s USE_SDL=2 -s
USE_SDL_IMAGE=2 -s SDL2_IMAGE_FORMATS=["png"]
```

This compiles the `debug.cpp` file into an `index.html` file. If we serve that file from a web server and open it in a browser, we will see the following in our JavaScript console:

```
Error
  at Array.ASM_CONSTS (index.js:1901)
  at _emscripten_asm_const_i (index.js:1920)
  at :8080/wasm-function[737]:36
  at :8080/wasm-function[738]:11
  at :8080/wasm-function[739]:7
  at :8080/wasm-function[740]:7
  at :8080/wasm-function[741]:102
  at Object.Module._main (index.js:11708)
  at Object.callMain (index.js:12096)
  at doRun (index.js:12154)

(index):1237 check console log for stack trace
```

You will notice that we have a stack trace, followed by our message, `check console log for stack trace`, which was the string we passed into the `DBG` macro. One thing you may notice if you look carefully is that this stack trace is not very helpful. Most of the functions in the stack trace are labeled `wasm-function`, which, from a debugging perspective, is kind of useless. This is because we lose the function names in the compilation process. To keep these names, we will need to pass the `-g4` flag to Emscripten when we compile. The `-g` flag, followed by a number, tells the compiler how much debugging information to preserve in the compilation process, with `-g0` being the least amount of information and `-g4` being the most. If we want to create source maps that map our WebAssembly to the C/C++ source code it was created from, we will need to pass in the `-g4` command, and if we want to know the functions called by our stack trace, we are going to need `-g4` for that as well. Let's try recompiling with our `-g4` flag. Here is the new version of the `emcc` command:

```
emcc debug.cpp -o index.html -g4 -DDEBUG --preload-file sprites -s
USE_SDL=2 -s USE_SDL_IMAGE=2 -s SDL2_IMAGE_FORMATS=["png"]
```

Now, reload the page and check the console. In the following snippet, we have the new stack trace:

```
Error
  at Array.ASM_CONSTS (index.js:1901)
  at _emscripten_asm_const_i (index.js:1920)
  at __Z9run_debugPKc (:8080/wasm-function[737]:36)
  at _inner_call_1 (:8080/wasm-function[738]:11)
  at _inner_call_2 (:8080/wasm-function[739]:7)
  at _inner_call_3 (:8080/wasm-function[740]:7)
  at _main (:8080/wasm-function[741]:102)
  at Object.Module._main (index.js:11708)
  at Object.callMain (index.js:12096)
  at doRun (index.js:12154)
  (index):1237 check console log for stack trace
```

This is much more readable. You can see all of the inner call functions we defined, as well as the `main` function. But what happened to `run_debug`? It came out looking like this:

```
__Z9run_debugPKc
```

What's happening here is called C++ name mangling, and we discussed it briefly in earlier chapters. Because C++ allows for function overloading, the compiler *mangles* the names of functions so that each version of the function has a different name. We were able to prevent this in our calls to `inner_call_1`, `inner_call_2`, and `inner_call_3` by placing them in a block labeled `extern "C"`. This tells the compiler not to mangle the names of these functions. It isn't strictly necessary for debugging, but I wanted to demonstrate how adding functions to this block can allow for easier recognition of our functions inside a stack trace. Here is what that same stack trace looks like if I remove the `extern "C"` block:

```
Error
  at Array.ASM_CONSTS (index.js:1901)
  at _emscripten_asm_const_i (index.js:1920)
  at __Z9run_debugPKc (:8080/wasm-function[737]:36)
  at __Z12inner_call_1v (:8080/wasm-function[738]:11)
  at __Z12inner_call_2v (:8080/wasm-function[739]:7)
  at __Z12inner_call_3v (:8080/wasm-function[740]:7)
  at _main (:8080/wasm-function[741]:102)
  at Object.Module._main (index.js:11708)
  at Object.callMain (index.js:12096)
  at doRun (index.js:12154)
  (index):1237 check console log for stack trace
```

As you can see, all of our inner call functions are mangled. In the next section, we will be discussing source maps.

Source maps

Now, let's briefly discuss source maps. Back in the early days of the web, it was decided that users should be able to view all of the source code on every web page. Early on, this was always HTML, but later, JavaScript was added and became something a user could view in an attempt to understand the workings of a given web page. Today, this is not possible in most cases. Some code today, such as TypeScript, is transpiled into JavaScript from another language. If you are writing JavaScript, you may use Babel to convert the latest JavaScript to run on older web browsers. Uglify or Minify may be used to remove white space and shorten variable names. If you need to debug the original source code, a source map is a tool you can use to map the JavaScript running in your browser back to the original source.

A source map is a JSON file that contains data mapping for the machine-generated JavaScript output code and points it back to either the handwritten JavaScript or in an alternative language, such as TypeScript or CoffeeScript. There are two ways that an application can tell the web browser that there is a source map file associated with a given piece of code. We can include a comment with the `sourceMappingURL` directive in the code, or we could include a `SourceMap` inside the HTTP header for that file. If we are using the `sourceMappingURL` comment method, add the following line to the end of the output JavaScript file:

```
//# sourceMappingURL=http://localhost:8080/debug.wasm.map
```

This is usually done programmatically during the build process. The alternative method would add the following line to the HTTP header:

```
SourceMap: http://localhost:8080/debug.wasm.map
```

In the next section, we will discuss browser-based WebAssembly debugging tools.

Browser debugging

Debugging WebAssembly in a web browser is still pretty crude. For example, at the time of writing, it is still not possible to directly *watch* a variable using the debugger. In both Firefox and Chrome, you must occasionally refresh your browser to see the CPP source file. Unlike debugging JavaScript, the WebAssembly debuggers feel (ironically) buggy. In Chrome, you frequently have to click the **step over** button several times to advance the line of code. In both browsers, breakpoints sometimes fail to work.

I frequently have to remove and then re-add a break point to get them to work again. It is still early days for WebAssembly source maps and in-browser debugging, so the hope is that the situation will improve soon. Until it does, try combining debugging in the browser with the addition debug statements, as I advised earlier.

Compiling your code for debugging

As I mentioned earlier, we will need to compile our app to support source maps that we can use for in-browser debugging in Firefox and Chrome. Currently, the only browsers that support in-browser debugging are Firefox, Chrome, and Safari. I will only be covering Firefox and Chrome in this book. You can compile the debug.cpp file for use with the WebAssembly debugger using the following emcc command:

```
emcc -g4 debug.cpp -o debug.html --source-map-base http://localhost:8080/ --preload-file sprites -s USE_SDL=2 -s USE_SDL_IMAGE=2 -s SDL2_IMAGE_FORMATS=["png"] -s MAIN_MODULE=1 -s WASM=1
```

The first new flag is -g4, which instructs the compiler to have the highest amount of debugging data and create source map files for our WebAssembly. After that comes the --source-map-base http://localhost:8080/ flag, which tells the compiler to add the sourceMappingURL$http://localhost:8080/debug.wasm.map string to the end of the debug.wasm file. This allows the browser to find the source map file that is associated with the debug.wasm file. The last two new flags are -s MAIN_MODULE=1 and -s WASM=1. I'm not sure why either of these flags are required to make the source mapping work. Both of these flags are explicitly telling the compiler to run the default behavior. However, at the time of writing, if you don't include these flags, browser debugging will not work. This feels like a bug to me, so it is possible that by the time you are reading this, emcc will not require those final two flags. Compiling with the preceding command will allow you to test using the WebAssembly debugger on Chrome and Firefox. If you really want to debug on Opera, Edge, or some other debugger that doesn't support WebAssembly debugging yet, you do have an alternative.

Using asm.js as an alternative for debugging

For whatever reason, you may feel that debugging using Edge or Opera may be necessary. If you feel that you must debug in a browser that doesn't have a WebAssembly debugger, you could compile for asm.js as an alternative. If so, change the -s WASM=1 flag to -s WASM=0, and you will be set. This will create a JavaScript file instead of a WASM file, but the two files (in theory) should behave the same.

Debugging using Chrome

Chrome has some great tools for debugging JavaScript, but is still pretty raw when it comes to debugging WebAssembly. After you have built the app, open it up in Chrome, and then open up Chrome Developer Tools:

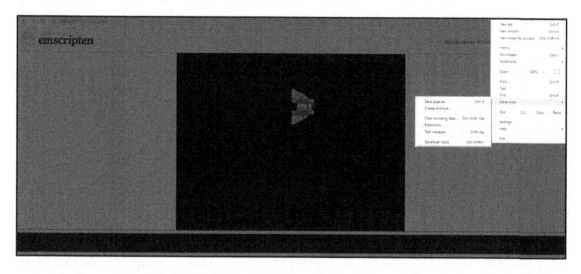

Figure 16.1: Screenshot of opening Chrome Developer Tools using the menu

You can open it up using the menu in the top left of the browser, as seen in the preceding screenshot, or you can open the developer tools by pressing *Ctrl + Shift + I* on your keyboard. When you load up your `debug.html` file in Chrome, you need to click on the **Sources** tab in the developer window. This is what this should look like if you are on the **Sources** tab:

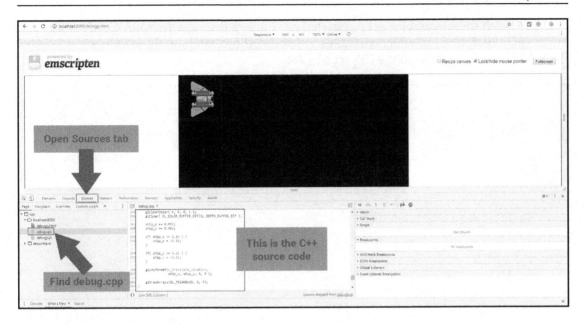

Figure 16.2: Screenshot using the sources tab in Chrome Developer Tools

If you don't see `debug.cpp` in the **Sources** tab, you may need to click the browser's reload button next to the URL at the top to reload the page. As I stated earlier, the interface feels a little buggy, and sometimes the CPP file doesn't load on the first try. Hopefully, this will have changed by the time you read this. Once you select the CPP file, you should be able to see the C++ code from our `debug.cpp` file in the code window in the center of the Developer Tools window. You can set breakpoints in the C++ code by clicking on the line number next to the line of code where you would like a breakpoint. You can then step through the code using the buttons above the `Watch` variables. Although the watch variables don't work at the time of writing, you may want to try it anyway. WebAssembly is improving on an almost daily basis, and bug fixes are constantly happening, so by the time you read this, things may have changed. If not, you may use the `Local` variables to get some idea of what values are changing.

You can watch these variables get populated as you step through the source code, and you can frequently determine which variables are updated by watching these values change. Take a look at the following screenshot:

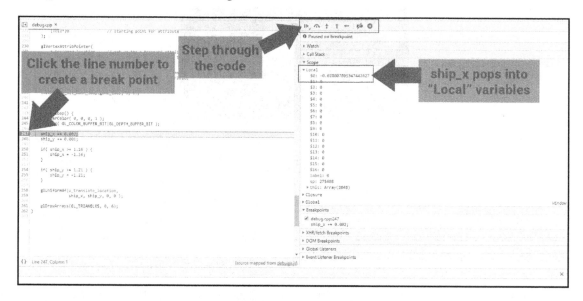

Figure 16.3: Screenshot of the debug tools in the Chrome browser

At the time of writing, you need to click the **step over** button more than once to get the line to advance in the C++ code window. In Chrome, the **step over** button is advancing one WebAssembly instruction per click instead of one C++ instruction. This may have changed by the time you read this, but don't be surprised if you need to click **step over** more than once to advance through the code.

Debugging using Firefox

Firefox has a number of advantages and disadvantages compared to Chrome. On the plus side, you can click the **step over** button once in Firefox per line in your C++ code. On the minus side, this makes knowing which local variables are changing in response to the line you are executing more difficult to track. These Local variables are a little like registers in a register-based assembly language so that the same variable may get moved in and out of a few of them. It can be a little easier to follow along with the values if you have to click the button once per assembly instruction. However, if you are more interested in tracing through the flow of your code than knowing what values change for each WebAssembly instruction, Firefox is much better for that.

To open up your Firefox **Developer Tools**, click the menu button in the top right corner of the browser window and select **Web Developer**:

Figure 16.4: Web Developer tools in the Firefox browser

Once on the Web Developer menu, click the **Debugger** menu item to open up the Debugger window:

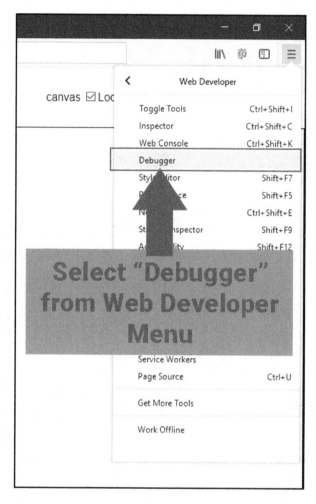

Figure 16.5: Screenshot of opening Debugger in Firefox

Instead of selecting the debugger through the menu system, you can use the shortcut keys *Ctrl + Shift + C* to open up the Inspector, and then select the **Debugger** tab from the **Web Developer** window. Here is what this looks like when you are in the Firefox Debugger:

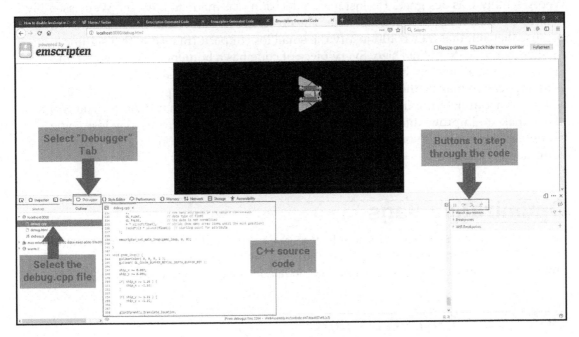

Figure 16.6: Screenshot of using Debugger in the Firefox browser

Right now, debugging will need to combine the use of debugging macros, as discussed in the previous section, with the ability of the browser to fully understand what is going on.

Firefox Developer Edition

I am briefly going to mention the Firefox Developer Edition. If you prefer to use Firefox as your primary WebAssembly development browser, you may want to consider using Firefox Developer Edition. The Developer Edition pushes forward updates to the web developer tools faster than the standard version of Firefox. Because WebAssembly is so new, updates that improve the development experience are likely to show up in the Developer Edition weeks or months earlier than they will become available in the standard version. At the time of writing, there is no significant difference between the two versions, but if you are interested in trying it out, it is available at the following web address: `https://www.mozilla.org/en-US/firefox/developer/`.

Optimizing for WebAssembly

Optimizing your WebAssembly code is partially about decision making and experimenting. It is about discovering what works for your particular game or app. When WebAssembly was designed, for instance, a decision was made to have the WebAssembly bytecode run on a virtual stack machine. The designers of WebAssembly made this choice because they felt that they could justify the small loss of performance with a significantly smaller bytecode download size. Every piece of code has a bottleneck somewhere. In OpenGL applications that bottleneck will be interfacing with the GPU. The bottleneck for your application may be the memory, or it may be CPU-bound. Optimizing code, in general, is about determining what the holdup is and deciding what trade-off you would like to make to improve things. If you optimize for download size, you may lose some runtime performance. If you optimize for runtime performance, you may have to increase your memory footprint.

Optimization flags

Emscripten provides us with a large selection of flags to optimize for different potential bottlenecks. All of the optimization flags will result in varying degrees of longer compile times, so using any of these flags should come late in the development cycle.

Optimizing for performance

We can use the $-O$ flags for general optimization. $-O0$, $-O1$, $-O2$, and $-O3$ provide different levels of trade-off between compile time and code performance. The $-O0$ and $-O1$ flags provide minimal optimization. The $-O2$ flag offers most of the optimization you get from the $-O3$ flag, but with significantly shorter compile times. Finally, $-O3$ provides the highest level of optimization, but takes substantially longer than any other flag to compile, so it is a good idea to wait until you are nearing the end of development to begin using it. In addition to the $-O$ flags, `-s AGGRESSIVE_VARIABLE_ELIMINATION=1` can be used to increase performance, but may result in larger bytecode download sizes.

Optimizing for size

There are two other -O flags that I didn't mention in the preceding section. Those flags are used to optimize for bytecode download size instead of purely optimizing for performance. The -Os flag takes about as long as -O3, and provides as much performance optimization as it can, but sacrifices some of the -O3 optimizations in favor of smaller download sizes. -Oz is like -Os, but prioritizes smaller download sizes even further by sacrificing even more performance optimization, which results in smaller bytecode. Another way to optimize for size is to include the -s ENVIRONMENT='web' flag. You should only use this flag if you are compiling for the web. It removes any source code that is used to support other environments, such as Node.js.

Unsafe flags

In addition to the safe optimization flags we have been using up until this point, Emscripten also allows for two *unsafe* flags that can improve performance, but come at the risk of potentially breaking your code. These flags are high risk/high reward optimizations that you should only use before the bulk of testing is complete. Using the --closure 1 flag runs the Closure JavaScript compiler, which performs very aggressive optimization on the JavaScript in our app. However, you shouldn't use the --closure 1 flag unless you are already familiar with using the closure compiler and the effects that compiler could have on JavaScript. The second *unsafe* flag is the --llvm-lto 1 flag, which enables *Link Time Optimization* during the LLVM compile step. This process can break your code, so take extreme care when using this flag.

Profiling

Profiling is the best way to determine what bottlenecks exist in your source code. When you are profiling WebAssembly modules, I recommend that you use the --profiling flag when compiling. You can profile without it, but all of the module functions you call will be labeled wasm-function, which can make your life more difficult than it needs to be. After compiling your code with the --profile flag, open up a new *Incognito* window in Chrome.

You can do this by either pressing the *CTRL + SHIFT + N* keys, or through the menu in the top right corner of the browser:

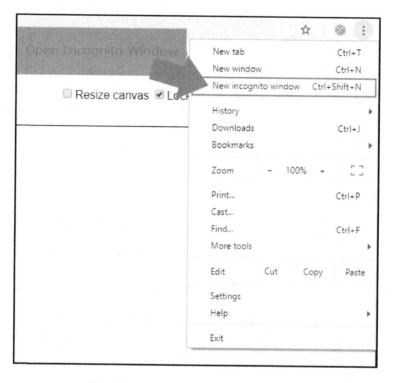

Figure 16.7: Opening an Incognito window in the Chrome browser

Opening an Incognito window will prevent any Chrome extensions from running when profiling your app. This will prevent you from having to wade through the code in those extensions to get to the code in your app. Once you have opened an Incognito window, press *Ctrl + Shift + I* to inspect the page. This will open up Chrome Developer Tools at the bottom of the browser window. Inside Chrome Developer Tools, select the **Performance** tab, as you can see in the following screenshot:

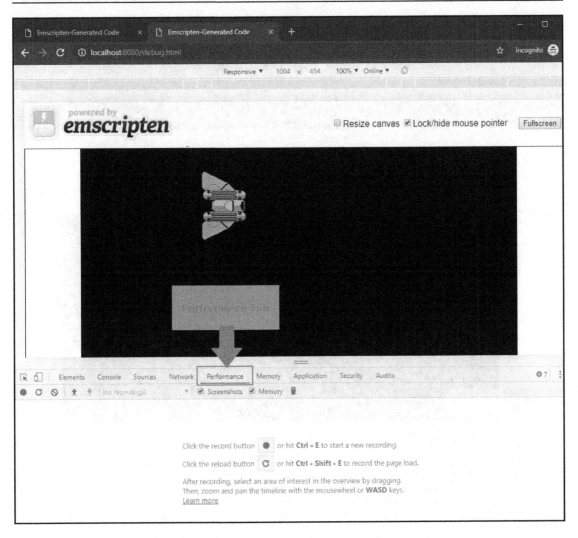

Figure 16.8: The Performance tab in the Chrome browser

Now, click the **Record** button and let it run for a few seconds. After you have recorded for five or six seconds, click the **Stop** button to stop profiling:

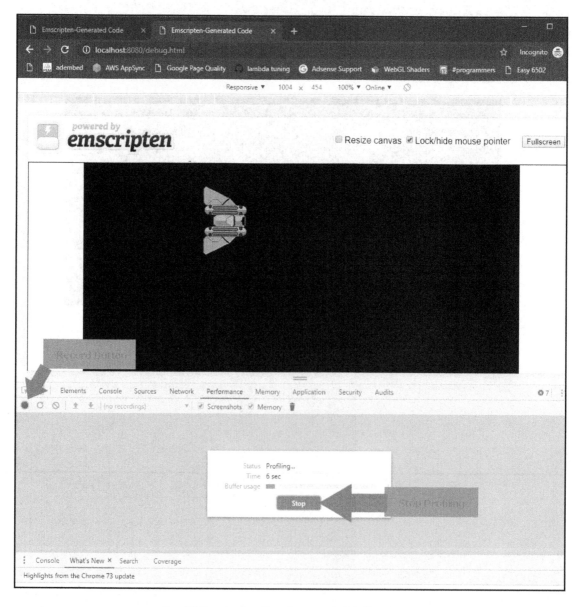

Figure 16.9: Screenshot of recording performance metrics in the Chrome browser

After you stop profiling, you will see data within the performance window. This is called the **Summary** tab, and displays data in the form of a pie chart that breaks down the number of milliseconds your app is spending on various tasks.

As you can see, the vast majority of the time, our app is idle:

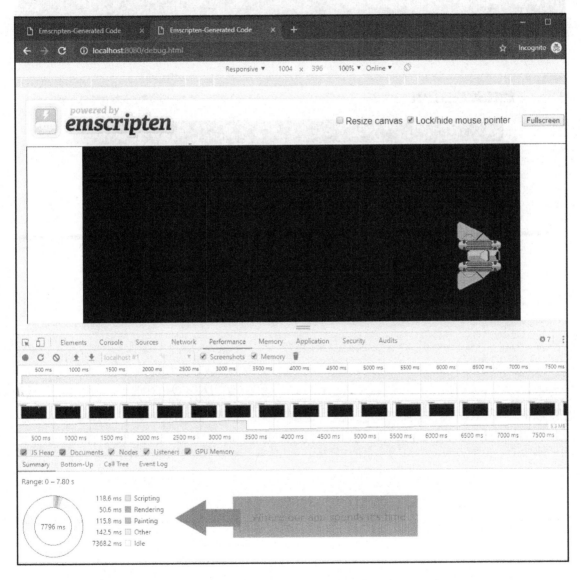

Figure 16.10: Performance overview in the Chrome browser

The summary is interesting. It can tell you where your bottleneck is on a very high level, but to evaluate our WebAssembly, we will need to look in the **Call Tree** tab. Click on the **Call Tree** tab, and you will see the following window:

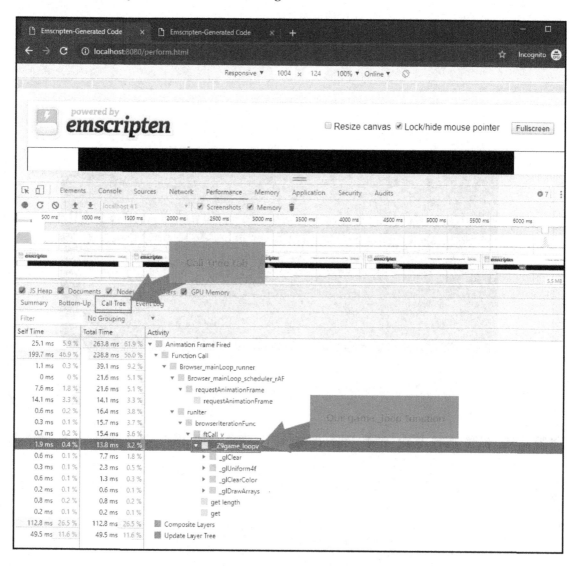

Figure 16.11: Screenshot of the Call Tree in the Chrome browser

Because our `game_loop` function is being called every frame, we can find the call inside the `Animation Frame Fired` tree. Drill down, looking for `game_loop`. When we find the function, it is mangled because it is a C++ function. So, instead of seeing `_game_loop`, we see `_Z9game_loopv`, although you may see something mangled differently. If you would like to prevent this mangling, you can wrap this function in an `extern "C"` block.

You can see that the execution of this function took a total of 3.2% of the browser's CPU time. You can also look at each of the OpenGL calls from within this function. If you take a look at our game loop, more than half of the CPU time is spent in `_glClear`. This is not a problem for this application, because the vast majority of the browser CPU time is spent idle. If, however, our game loop function was taking up a large percentage of the CPU time, we would need to see where in that function we were spending it.

Problems with try/catch blocks

At the time of writing, try/catch blocks are known to cause significant performance issues in WebAssembly modules, so only use them if they're absolutely necessary. You may want to use them during the development phase, and remove them when building for release. Some of the `-O` optimization flags will remove try/catch blocks, which you need to be aware of if you plan on using them in production. If you want to use try/catch blocks in your production build, you will need to compile using the `-s DISABLE_EXCEPTION_CATCHING=0` flag. This will tell the compiler not to remove the try/catch blocks from the optimized version of your bytecode. If you would like to remove your try/catch blocks from unoptimized development code, you can do so by using the `-s DISABLE_EXCEPTION_CATCHING=1` flag.

Optimizing OpenGL for WebAssembly

It is important to remember that any calls to OpenGL from WebAssembly are calling WebGL using a function table. Part of the reason this is important is because any time you use OpenGL ES and OpenGL functionality that is not available in WebGL, Emscripten must perform some very slow software emulation on those functions. It is also important to remember that WebGL calls are more expensive than OpenGL calls on a native platform because WebGL is sandboxed, and various security checks are performed by the browser when it calls WebGL. Emscripten provides you with several flags that allow you to emulate OpenGL and OpenGL ES calls that are not available in WebGL. For performance reasons, however do not use these functions unless you absolutely have to.

Using WebGL 2.0 if possible

WebGL 2.0 is faster than WebGL 1.0, but, at the time of writing, it is supported on far fewer browsers. Just compiling your WebGL 1.0 code to WebGL 2.0 will give you about a 7% performance improvement. However, before you choose to do this, you may want to consult `https://caniuse.com/#search=webgl2` to see whether the browsers you are targeting support WebGL 2.0.

Minimizing the number of OpenGL calls

Calls to OpenGL from WebAssembly are not as fast as those same calls from a natively compiled application. A call to OpenGL from WebAssembly is making a call to a WebGL analog. WebGL was built to execute inside a web browser and performs some security checks to verify that we are not asking WebGL to do anything malicious. This means that we must account for that additional overhead when writing OpenGL that's targeting WebAssembly. There are cases where two or three calls to OpenGL for a native application would be faster than combining those calls into a single OpenGL call. However, that same code in WebAssembly might run faster if you condensed it into a single call to OpenGL. When optimizing for WebAssembly, try doing what you can to minimize the number of OpenGL calls, and use your profiler to verify that the new code is faster.

Emscripten OpenGL flags

Several Emscripten linker flags can have a significant effect on performance. Some of the flags were created to ease porting of code to WebAssembly, but have the potential to create performance problems. Others can improve performance under the right conditions.

The `-s FULL_ES2=1` and `-s FULL_ES3=1` linker flags emulate the entire OpenGL ES 2.0/3.0 API. As I mentioned earlier, by default, the OpenGL ES 2/3 implementations in WebAssembly only support subsets of OpenGL ES 2/3 that are compatible with WebGL. This is because WebGL is doing the rendering in WebAssembly. There may be a reason why you absolutely need a feature of OpenGL ES 2/3 that is not available by default. If so, you can use the `-s FULL_ES2=1` or `-s FULL_ES3=1` flags to emulate that feature in the software. This will come at a price when it comes to performance, so take that into consideration if you decide to use it.

The `-s LEGACY_GL_EMULATION=1` flag is used to emulate old versions of OpenGL that use the fixed function pipeline. It is also not recommended that you use this flag because of the poor performance that will result. This flag exists for people who are looking to port old code to WebAssembly.

If you want to use WebGL 2 to gain the performance increase associated with it, use the `-s USE_WEBGL2=1` linker flag. If you have code that was written for WebGL 1.0, but would like the performance gains of WebGL 2.0, you can try compiling to WebGL 2.0 to see whether you used any code that was not backward compatible in WebGL 2.0. If it doesn't compile with this flag, you can try the `-s WEBGL2_BACKWARDS_COMPATIBILITY_EMULATION=1` linker flag, which will allow you to compile your WebGL 1.0 code so that you can use it in WebGL 2.0.

Summary

In this chapter, we talked about different strategies we can use to debug and optimize our WebAssembly code. We discussed writing C macros, which allow us to easily remove calls to print to the console when we move from development into production. We talked about source maps, what they are, and how they can help us to debug our WebAssembly code from within a browser. We discussed using the debugger in both Chrome and Firefox to step through WebAssembly's source code. Finally, we discussed optimization in WebAssembly, what compiler options are available in Emscripten, and how we can go about improving our WebGL performance.

This is the end

Congratulations! You should be well on your way to developing your own games or apps in WebAssembly. I hope that you enjoyed learning how we can use WebGL to build games for the web. If you have any questions, comments, or would just like to say hi, you can find me on the following platforms:

- **Twitter**: https://twitter.com/battagline
- **LinkedIn**: https://www.linkedin.com/in/battagline/
- **YouTube**: https://www.youtube.com/channel/UCaJYTBKp0vM1rLT82PcXwKQ

Other Books You May Enjoy

If you enjoyed this book, you may be interested in these other books by Packt:

Hands-On Deep Learning for Games
Micheal Lanham

ISBN: 978-1-78899-407-1

- Learn the foundations of neural networks and deep learning.
- Use advanced neural network architectures in applications to create music, textures, self driving cars and chatbots.
- Understand the basics of reinforcement and DRL and how to apply it to solve a variety of problems.
- Working with Unity ML-Agents toolkit and how to install, setup and run the kit.
- Understand core concepts of DRL and the differences between discrete and continuous action environments.
- Use several advanced forms of learning in various scenarios from developing agents to testing games.

Hands-On Game Development Patterns with Unity 2019
David Baron

ISBN: 978-1-78934-933-7

- Discover the core architectural pillars of the Unity game engine.
- Learn about software design patterns while building gameplay systems.
- Acquire the skills to recognize anti-patterns and how to avoid their adverse effect in your codebase.
- Enrich your design vocabulary so you can better articulate your ideas on how to better your game's architecture.
- Gain some mastery over Unity's API by writing well-designed code.
- Get some game industry insider tips and tricks that will help you in your career.

Leave a review - let other readers know what you think

Please share your thoughts on this book with others by leaving a review on the site that you bought it from. If you purchased the book from Amazon, please leave us an honest review on this book's Amazon page. This is vital so that other potential readers can see and use your unbiased opinion to make purchasing decisions, we can understand what our customers think about our products, and our authors can see your feedback on the title that they have worked with Packt to create. It will only take a few minutes of your time, but is valuable to other potential customers, our authors, and Packt. Thank you!

Index

Made in the USA
Monee, IL
26 July 2020